MEDIEVAL AND MODERN HISTORY

STUBBS

SEVENTEEN LECTURES

ON THE STUDY OF

MEDIEVAL AND MODERN HISTORY

AND KINDRED SUBJECTS

DELIVERED AT OXFORD, UNDER STATUTORY OBLIGATION

IN THE YEARS 1867—1884

BY

WILLIAM STUBBS

NEW YORK

Howard Fertig

1967

never once, in the course of my seventeen years of office, did I think that there would come a time when I could look back on this part of my work with pleasure or grateful regret. And I fear that this will be only too obvious to any one who tries to read this book. But I have said more than enough about it; and I will content myself with adding that the following are only a selection from a larger number of exercises delivered under the same conditions. Most of the omitted lectures have seen the light in other places. The second lecture of 1867 was made part of the Introduction to the second volume of Roger Hoveden, in the Rolls Series. The lectures of 1868 and 1874, on Anglo-Saxon literature and monastic history, formed part of a plan which I finally discarded after the restoration of Professor Earle to the Anglo-Saxon Chair, and, by themselves, do not seem to justify publication. Those for 1869 on Comparative Constitutional History, and for 1871 on Scottish Constitutional History, would have required a larger apparatus of notes, and more labour of revision, than I could at present afford, to qualify them for a permanent form, and are as a matter of necessity excluded. The lectures for 1870 form the Introduction to my *Select Charters*; those for 1873 were utilized as the seventh chapter of the *Constitutional History*; those for 1875 as the fourteenth chapter; and those for 1872 in the preface to the second volume of the Memoriale of Walter of Coventry.

W. CESTR.

Dee Side, Chester:
May 17, 1886.

P.S.—The last line on page 114 seems obscure. The reference is to the division taken in the House of Commons, during the debate on the Universities Bill, April 30, 1877, on the amendment 'to omit the word *and*.'

CONTENTS.

I.

INAUGURAL.

(Feb. 7, 1867.)

T HE giving of an Inaugural Lecture is an occasion which compels and may well excuse a little trepidation. The speaker, although he is wisely restrained by academic decorum from courting or fearing the thunder, propitious or otherwise, of right or left, cannot divest himself of the feeling that he is really about to take the omens of his future success, and cannot but be anxious to make, if he possibly can, a promising beginning. This is especially the case when he is called upon, as I am now, for the first time in his life, to address an academic, I may even say an educated, audience. He has not learned the tone of authority which befits the professorial character: it is no mere matter of form for him to deprecate adverse criticism; he feels that he must introduce himself, in a way that is of necessity painful both to his self-respect and to his modesty, to an audience from whom he has at least as much to learn as he can ever hope to teach them. I can indeed hardly use the word teach without reservation. I am so sensible of the greatness of the field, the variety of the instruments, the infinite multitude of the workers employed on the subject to which my labours in this place are to be devoted, that I am afraid even to advertise myself as a teacher, and would rather be looked on as a helper and trainer in a school in which every man has to learn his own lessons.

For I am thoroughly convinced that the purpose which is answered by the study of Modern and Medieval History is twofold; it is at once the process of acquisition of a stock of facts, an ignorance of which unfits a man from playing the very humblest part as a citizen, or even watching the politics of his own age with an intelligent apprehension ; and it is an educational discipline directed to the cultivation of powers for whose development, as it seems to me, no other training is equally efficacious. It is but natural that I should speak thus of a study which has been to me the pleasure, rest, and comfort of a somewhat busy and anxious life, to whose teachings I feel myself indebted for whatever power of judgment, critical experience, or speculative equity, if I may be allowed to use such a form of words, I am conscious of possessing. I wish to undervalue no other system of training, no other field of inquiry, but I speak of this as I love it, and as, if a sound purpose of doing with my might what my hand has found to do can be any pledge of honest and effectual work, I trust those who will apply themselves to it with my assistance will come to love it and profit by it as well. But as I shall have, no doubt, to say more than enough about myself before I finish this lecture, I will proceed now, in that desultory way which the nature of an inaugural lecture necessitates, to say something about my founder and my predecessors ; and, having done that, to enlarge somewhat on the place which our study has among the pursuits of this University, the method of training, and the end which I propose to myself in the work that lies before me. I have pleaded guilty to a natural trepidation, I have acknowledged that what I have to say will be desultory. I think that the circumstances account for both, and trust to you for an equitable consideration.

The Professorship of Modern History was founded in the year 1724 by King George I ; a prince of whom those who would say the worst must allow that he was an honest and harmless sovereign, whilst a professed panegyrist would most wisely content himself with saying that his reign is the commencement of an era during which the happiness of the kingdoms he ruled, their progress in knowledge, political intelligence, wealth, domestic and social comfort, have increased in a ratio unprecedented and unparalleled : during which the exertion of English influence in the councils and contests of the world has been effective beyond precedent and parallel, and has been used, if not always in the most enlightened way, always for the end and for the cause that seemed to be just and right. The process of events, and the action of various systems of politics, have in a great measure served to alter the views which at the time were taken of the wars of the last century and of the early years of the present. We have learned some of us to approve, and more perhaps to acquiesce in, proceedings which our fathers looked on as in the last degree unrighteous and intolerable. The days in which men go to war for an idea, and accept subjugation because they cannot afford to be sentimental, can safely smile at the errors of statesmen and the short-sightedness of kings, to whom justice and honesty were still justice and honesty, although disguised in the mock solemnities of dynastic shadows. But we will not deny either to kings or to peoples the credit of zeal for what they believed to be right, and the glory they had, so far as it was real, of counting no cost too great to be incurred for what they saw to be the cause of order and of society. They fought, as they believed, for their own existence and ours.

George I, whatever may have been his personal faults, and, however little adapted he may have seemed in his own days, or may seem now, to fulfil the ideal character of kingship in a free and enlightened people, comes on the stage of English History as the representative of a principle which has been found to answer, and as the inaugurator of a period of national prosperity. So far at least we have no cause to blush for our founder. But as our founder, I think we may look at him more closely. The house of Brunswick has always had the reputation for the good sense to patronise literature, and especially historical literature. Not to seek for precedents so far back as Henry the Lion, who superintended the writing of the annals of his country in the twelfth century, it will perhaps suffice to give a general reference to the enormous number of historical books which, during the sixteenth, seventeenth, and eighteenth centuries, issued under ducal patronage from the presses of Helmstadt, Hanover, and Göttingen. George himself had been the patron of Leibnitz, of Jo. George Eccard, Burckhard Gotthilf Struve, and Johann Lorenz von Mosheim, whom I name rather as familiar to English ears

Kennett, of Atterbury, Wake, and Gibson, although in these days they are chiefly known, if known at all, as antiquaries or controversialists, mark a period of historical exertion second to none either in the importance of its researches or in the value of their results.   Cambridge began the modern study of English History with Parker, Oxford followed up briskly with Savile and Camden, Selden, Gale, Fulman, and Fell; men, who, if they did not pretend to shine as Historians, are entitled to the eternal gratitude of all students, and appreciated at least that true and fundamental canon of composition that the materials for History must be provided before History can be written.   From Oxford, or from the studies of Oxford men, proceeded nearly all the great collections of English Historians; and the old school of students was now well represented by Thomas Hearne.   But at the time when this professorship was founded this class of men were either withdrawn, like Tanner and Kennett, to other work, or relegated by their own political sympathies and Whig liberality, like Hearne and Baker, to the comparative uselessness of literary retirement. Nor, I think, were the ministers of the crown very careful as to the hands in which they placed the engine of education, from which so much might have been hoped.   To speak with the utmost respect of my early predecessors, I do not find that they were men to whom the study of History, either English or foreign, is in any way indebted, until we come down to Dr. Nares at the beginning of the present century.   They probably owed their position to their political connexions or to literary eminence of other kinds.   It is no wonder that under the circumstances the place of History among the studies of the University became worse rather than better, or, like that of Moral Philosophy, was lost altogether.

Passing on from Dr. Nares, of whom I speak with all gratitude, remembering well, as many of the elders amongst my hearers can doubtless remember likewise, the days when his weighty volumes were almost the only available sources of information for later history: we come to the great name, never to be pronounced without reverence even by his opponents, of the man whose sincerity, energy, and power of training, made him the prime mover of this generation. What Arnold might have done for the study of History in this place, had his time been given to it or been prolonged sufficiently to produce any appreciable effect on it, may be estimated by the effect of his work on other branches and in other places of education. I say it with diffidence, rather because I fear your criticism than because I have any doubt of the truth of the assertion, I believe that the one thing which Arnold wanted to perfect the balance of his admirable judgment, and to direct the current of his overflowing sympathies, was that experience of critical difficulties and moral incompatibilities which becomes practically, to the devoted student of History, a training in itself. Of Dr. Cramer I can say little. He was well furnished as a scholar and a most accomplished man : his contributions to literary history are exceedingly valuable : but his time here was short; he was not a young man when he undertook the office : he had other cares which took him away from Oxford. Most of all perhaps during the time of his holding this office all the thinking men of the University were engrossed in controversies on matters interesting, most interesting to all, in which, however much a historical training might have profited them, it was too late to forge their weapons when they were in the midst of battle. Of the two professors who preceded me, I must not, need not, say much : you are far better able than I am to appreciate their work here : but I may say that none of you can more sincerely than I do admire the learning, acuteness, earnestness, and eloquence of Professor Goldwin Smith : learning, acuteness, earnestness, and eloquence never more signally admirable than when employed, as we have so often rejoiced to see them employed, on the behalf of Christian Truth against philosophic sciolism.

The circumstances under which I return to Oxford and begin my work here are, for many reasons, most encouraging; so encouraging as to afford, I think, some grounds of apprehension that the responsibility is heavier than I ought to have undertaken. In no respect does the Oxford I find on my return contrast more favourably with the Oxford I left sixteen years ago. At that time the professorship of Church History had been founded, and was filled by one [Robert Hussey] who was undoubtedly the founder of the modern study of that subject in Oxford. I mean the study of the history of the Church as a whole, not from points of controversy to supply weapons for the discomfiture of opposing theologians, but as the life of the Christian Church itself, the whole history of the body of which the modern nations claim in their spiritual character to be members. But the theological exigencies of the time had so far narrowed the field of inquiry that it was practically restricted to the first three centuries, or at the outside to the period embraced under the topics of the general councils. The attempt which he made to extend the range by introducing the study of the Venerable Bede as a text-book was, as you are aware, foiled by the impossibility of getting together a lecture on a matter that was neither connected with the controversies of the day, nor required to be known by candidates for holy orders. The College libraries then as now afforded abundant resources for any student who would take up the subject for himself, but my grateful recollection of the first acquaintance made with Hearne, Dugdale, and Prynn, in Christ Church Library, is inseparably connected with the reminiscence of the amused, and I am glad to remember approving, surprise, with which Dean Gaisford took me unawares at my note-book. It is possible that the rooms of the Architectural Society in Holywell were the school in which a taste for medieval history, at least, was insensibly acquired.

The introduction of new studies into the course of University training was viewed with apprehension by many: some perhaps of us who are now here were inclined to waver between a mistrust of innovations which seemed likely to break down the traditionary character of our education and the desire of welcoming a study of all others the most germane to the true and perpetual genius of Oxford. I may now, I suppose, say it without offence, I think that the distrust of the new studies, at all events of the study of Modern History, was owing quite as much to the management of their advocates as to the conservative habits of the opponents. I am not sure that either party would have admitted, or indeed would now admit, what, to adopt a proper professorial tone, I may say is certain, that whilst of all studies in the whole range of knowledge, the study of law affords the most conservative training, so the study of Modern History is, next to Theology itself, and only next in so far as Theology rests on a divine revelation, the most thoroughly religious training that the mind can receive. It is no paradox to say that Modern History, including Medieval History in the term, is co-extensive in its field of view, in its habits of criticism, in the persons of its most famous students, with Ecclesiastical History. We may call them sister studies, but, if they are not really one and the same, they are twin sisters, so much alike that there is no distinguishing between them. Men who are bent on seeing only differences and ignoring points of agreement refused to see that in 1850, and I dare say refuse to see it still.

So much, however, has changed and changed rapidly in sixteen years ; so many old friends have sought new fields of work, so great changes have passed over the moral and intellectual atmosphere of Oxford, that one is prone to forget that in truth the precedent era from 1830 to 1850 was itself only a transient phase, and not to be looked on as stamping for ever the character of the University. I for one can rejoice in looking back on those days, and I can look forward with hope and sympathy to what is before us in these respects. If I regret the absence of some things that were pleasant in the old life, at least I can appreciate much of that which promises to be the charm of the new. Happily removed for all these years from Oxford controversies, and I am glad to say that in the humblest way I have not had a finger in them, I can still clothe the old life with that gladness which for most men gilds the recollection of undergraduate days. But the world did not stop with me when I left Oxford, and I trust, if God shall spare me, to work with a good heart as long as it is called to-day.

I rejoice then to find on my return the School of Law and Modern History occupying a well-defined and still improving position, and bestowing honours which the men most honoured in the other contests of the academic arena are glad not only to win but to work for. The Modern History School has thriven with very little nursing ; and it needs but a glance at the class lists to show that there has been and continues to be, I will not say abundant promise, but actual work done in the cause of historical study by those who have distinguished themselves in our examinations. It is not invidious to mention the names of some who have challenged public criticism by their books, and have not merely shown in them the usefulness of historical training, but conferred lasting benefits on the students that follow them. The Law and Modern History School helped at least to train my excellent colleague, the Chichele Professor, for his labours ; and it has helped to give us from Mr. Kington an English life of Frederick II, from Mr. Bryce a monograph on the Western Empire, which have already taken their place as standard books on our shelves. But far more than this has been done by the direction into the same channel of a considerable part of the more industrious teaching power of the Colleges, so that there is now a strong and, I hope, an increasing, staff of College tutors, whose time and mind are devoted primarily to the cultivation of this study. With these my occasional visits here as examiner have put me into communication, and the association with them in their work is to my mind one of the happiest incidents of my present position. I would, indeed, that this thought had been without the drawback that, at the very moment of my return, I in common with the whole of the rest of the University should have to lament the loss of one [Dr. Shirley], noble, good, and wise far beyond his years, who had watched and worked for the development of this study from the day of its introduction to Oxford, whose labours and influence were ever used for good and for every thing that was good, whose early promotion and effective character had marked him out as the man who was to do great things for the University and the Church of God in this age. Seldom has so much promise, seldom have so great earnests of great work been so sadly or so fatally blighted : we cannot look that his place can ever in all respects be so filled that there will not still be much, very much, to desiderate ; for it

is not Oxford alone that laments him, nor the cause of
Historical study only with which he had identified himself
both here and throughout the literary world. But I will
not touch on questions beyond the scope of my present consideration.

Besides the very advantageous position which, without
nursing, I repeat, our study has attained here, in men, books,
and honours, the immense treasures of historical lore which
are now being poured liberally from the great storehouses of
record throughout Europe, but most especially in England,
form a feature of the present time that promises to renew the
youth of the Historic Muse. The great Continental collections
of Historians are growing slowly but substantially ; the German
collection, begun in 1826, nearly rivals the French one a
century its senior ; the Sardinian Government had one of its
own, which we may hope will not be smothered for the sake
of more ambitious plans ; the Vatican itself, under the kindly
influence of a German Oratorian, has begun to thaw from its
old reserve. Last and greatest, our own national work under
the direction of Lord Romilly has in eight years proved itself
more than a worthy rival both in bulk and workmanship of
the older repositories. And not to speak of the collection of
Historians, of which from my own connexion with it I am
obliged to speak with modesty and reserve, the extracts and
abstracts of public and private documents found in our Record
offices and in those of Spain and Venice are rapidly filling our
libraries with cases of stout green volumes from which the
history of the most eventful of our years is being rewritten,
and which will soon involve the necessity of a new Macaulay
as they have already brought into being a new Burnet and
a new Robertson.

From this sudden breaking up of the fountains of historical
refreshment I dare not augur what results may follow, or what
new worlds may be opening for other generations to exercise
their logical acuteness and their historical perspicacity upon.
We have our work set, in a literary point of view, in arranging,
and bringing into bearing on one another, the masses of information that are threatening to overwhelm us. Happily, there is

no lack of helpers; the great German hive of historical workers
is busy as we are on our archives: such and so close are the
ties which now, owing to the facilities of travelling and communication, the abundance of libraries and the accessibility of
records, the extension of literary and investigative sympathies,
and, I am happy to think, the extinction of literary jealousies,
are now binding the historical scholars of Europe, that I think
and hope that the day is coming when, although we may not
cease to quarrel with and criticise one another, there will be a
great republic of workers able and willing to assist one another;
not working for party purposes, unfettered by political prejudices, and although as strong partizans and politicians as ever,
anxious above all to find the truth, and to purify the cause
that each loves best from every taint of falsehood, every inclination to calumny or concealment. I confess that it is towards
this consummation that my dearest wishes as a student of
History are directed; and that I anticipate with the greatest
pleasure the prospect of being instrumental and able to assist
in the founding of an historical school in England, which
shall join with the other workers of Europe in a common
task; which shall build, not upon Hallam and Palgrave and
Kemble and Froude and Macaulay, but on the abundant
collected and arranged materials on which those writers tried
to build whilst they were scanty and scattered and in disorder.
The time cannot be far off when all the records of the medieval
world which are in existence will be in print either in full or
in such abundant abstracts as will be thoroughly trustworthy
representations of their contents; when every great Library will
contain copies of them all, and when every town will contain
a great Library. The seed sown by the old Record Commission,
by presenting copies of their publications to the municipal
corporations and principal provincial libraries, marks an era,
as antiquaries well know, in the development of antiquarian
study and the preservation of archæological treasures. We
may hope to see the same principle extended now, and although the chief labours of the historian must continue to find
their place in his own study, as no library can supersede the
need of books at home, still no man may be obliged to keep

all his ideas in chronic effervescence and all his hopeful dis-, coveries in a state of tantalising suspension, in the hope that once a year he can visit the Bodleian or the British Museum. For that day of many students, many books, many libraries, and many readers, I look with confidence; in the meantime I do hope and trust that my work here, although this may not be its primary aim or its most successful use, may help in a humble way to educate workers for the good time coming.

For I desire to introduce myself to you, not as a philosopher nor as a politician, but as a worker at history. Not that I have not strong views on politics, nor short and concise opinions on philosophy, but because this is my work, and I have taken it up in all sincerity and desire of truth, and wish to keep to my work and to the sort of truth that I can help on in the inquiry; because you have plenty of politicians and plenty of scholars to whom, if they wish to have it, I certainly will not begrudge the name of philosophers. I suppose that it is truth we are all seeking, and that though the sorts of truth are distinct and the ways that we work in are very different, when we have found what we seek for we shall find all our discoveries combine in harmony; and I trust and believe that the more sincerely, the more single-heartedly we work each of us, the nearer we consciously come to the state where we shall see the oneness and glory and beauty of the truth itself. So that the theologian, the naturalist, the historian, the philosopher, if he work honestly, is gaining each for his brother, and being worked for each by his brother, in the pursuit of the great end, the great consummation of all. We may all speak humbly, the theologian because of the excellence of his subject, the rest because of the vastness of our field of work, the length of our art and the shortness of our life; but we cannot afford to speak contemptuously of any sort of knowledge, and God forbid that we should speak contemptuously or hyper-critically of any honest worker.

The subject-matter of Modern Historical inquiry has peculiar advantages for the training of the powers most constantly in exercise in a practical generation. Compared with the study of Ancient History it is like the study of life compared with

that of death, the view of the living body compared with that of the skeleton. The student of Ancient History has his advantages ; he can speculate on his skeleton, he can penetrate more deeply into the framework of ancient society, so far as his materials allow him ; he can handle the different parts and form his political hypotheses as it pleases him, according to the various ways in which his skeleton can be put together ; he is little troubled by the fear of new facts, or new developments making their appearance suddenly to put to flight his calculations ; he has all the existing materials for his investigation before him, or within easy reach ; he has for the geographical area of his work a portion of the earth and its peoples that has had, since the roll of its own historians was closed, little to do with the active work of the world. He can work out principles at his will ; he can educate his taste and analyse and experiment to the very ne plus ultra of critical subtilty. But the principles he works out and the results of his criticism are alike things that give the world no new knowledge, or exercise no direct influence on the interests of real life. And in this is one of the great incidental uses of classical training as an engine of education. You have in its languages and histories and philosophies, the most elegant, the most compact, the most ingenious systems on which the mind of man can be exercised ; and you have them in such isolation, so set apart altogether from personal or party or national or scholastic propensions, that the lessons to be drawn from them are for the most part as safe, as unexciting, as far removed from the heart and interests of life, as any proposition in mathematics.

In Modern History, on the contrary, you are dealing with the living subject : your field of examination is the living, working, thinking, growing world of to-day ; as distinguished from the dead world of Greece and Rome, by the life that is in it, as it is in geographical area and in the embarrassing abundance of the data from which only in their full integrity it is safe, or ever will be safe, to attempt to philosophise. England, France, Germany, the East, regions that have but a shadowy existence in the background of the pictures in

which living Egypt, Rome, and Asia stand before us, after thousands of years of death, in the bright colouring and life-like grouping of yesterday ; these are the area in which the modern historian seeks and finds the interests of his pursuit. Italy, the common ground of the sister studies, the strange borderland between light and darkness, in which alone the past seems to live and the present for the most part to be a living death, has a double existence that fits and unfits her for the free handling of either.

And in this new and modern and living world there has been since the era began, such a continuity of life and development that hardly one point in its earliest life can be touched without the awakening some chord in the present. Scarcely a single movement now visible in the current of modern affairs but can be traced back with some distinct-ness to its origin in the early middle ages ; scarcely a move-ment that has disturbed the world since the invasion of our barbarian ancestors but has its representative in the chart of law or thoughts or territory to this day. Not a dynasty that is trembling out its little span of days now, but re-presents in its shattered tottering throne some great hero, some great heroic movement, that has won the gratitude of the medieval world. Not a country revolutionised and levelled until it hardly knew itself, until it scarcely remem-bered the names of its rivers and mountains, has been able utterly to obliterate the boundaries, or the customs, or the affinities of its old divisions. The dynastic traditions of Europe are rooted and grounded in the distant past : the principle of nationalities, new in its fashion of announcement and most unlucky in its prophet, is rooted and grounded in a past more distant still ; the principle of freedom, in their effect on which only the dynastic and national ideas have their true political value, rests on a yet more ancient foundation, but on one that is peculiar to the modern field of study, for it was brought into the world and proclaimed and made possible by the Church.

It is Christianity that gives to the modern world its living unity and at the same time cuts it off from the death of the past.

The Church in its spiritual work, the Church in its intellectual
work, the Church in its work with the sword, or with the
plough, or with the axe; the soul and spirit of all true civilisation, of all true liberty, of all true knowledge ; the Church in its
work of evil, in the abasement of its divine energies, in the
vile fetters of priest-craft, in the blind paroxysms of popular
fanaticism, in the strange varying fortunes that allies Ireland
with Rome, Scotland with Geneva, setting father against son,
and husband against wife, the herald of peace with a sword ;
such an influence so wide in its extension, so deep in its pene-
tration, so ancient in the past, and in the future eternal, could
by itself account for the unity, the life of modern history : the
life, the soul of a body which thrills at every touch.   The
student cannot handle his subject-matter as he can a skeleton ;
if he is a true student he knows himself to be at work among
living influences, some active, some slumbering, but all of
which are so vital and so entangled that he cannot move
without making someone feel, or without being himself affected
in his process and in his judgment by the system of which he
is himself a part.   Modern History is the history of ourselves,
of the way in which we came to be what we are, of the education of our nation, of the development of our government, of
the fortunes of our fathers, that caused us to be taught and
governed and placed as we are, and formed our minds and
habits by that teaching, government, and position ; and as for
the soul, that other portion of us,—unchanged by education,
government or fortune, unchanged and untrained in the development and education of the world, unchanged except by
the Spirit of God beginning at the beginning in every one
that is new born of Him,—that gift in which almost alone we
trace the unity of our nature with that of the ancient world,
in its waywardness, and short-sightedness, and self-will, what
can all history tell us other or more than this, how God sent
light into the world and men loved darkness rather than light,
how they have perverted, but not closed the way of eternal life?

But if the student of Modern History finding himself at
work among such subjects misses the facility with which
Ancient History may be handled, he has the advantage to

begin with, that the interest of his own department is un-flagging and inexhaustible : every day adds a new develop-ment of the old elements, he feels that he is living in his subject, it is living all around him. And this being so, he is conscious that he is working with a different set of mental powers from those which he works with on the old world ; I speak under correction, for I do not pretend to look at the subject as a question of psychology, simply for the moment as one of education. It is in a manner analogous to a training for association with men in the world ; the student must look for Truth, and work for Justice, but he must work for such truth and justice as is attainable. He must not, as in Ancient History, amuse himself with principles however valuable or however generally applicable, because he has to deal with rights : his inquiry is more into laws than into principles, more into facts than into laws. He must act as a judge not as a philosopher, all the better judge for being somewhat of a philosopher, but never in the philosopher forgetting that he is a judge. And as in practical matters we, ordinary men that is, are seldom called upon to act as judges except in ques-tions where their own sympathies or interests are concerned ; the faculty to be trained is the judgment, the practical judgment at work among matters in which its possessor is deeply interested, not from the desire of Truth only, but from his own involution in the matters of which he is to judge.

I think that there are few lessons more necessary for men to learn, not merely who are going to take to public life, but who are going to live and move as men among their fellows, than these :—that there are few questions on which as much may not be said on one side as on the other : that there are none at all on which all the good are on one side, all the bad on the other, or all the wise on one and all the fools on the other ; that the amount of dead weight in human affairs, call it stupidity or what you will, is pretty equally divided between the advocates of order and the advocates of change, giving to the one party much of its stability and to the other much of its momentum : that intolerance is no prerogative of heterodoxy, nor tolerance the inseparable accompaniment of the conscious possession of truth, a condition which might of all others the best afford to be tolerant, the most merciful and pitiful of error: that all generalisations, however sound in logic, are in morals and practical matters ipso facto false; that there is no room for sweeping denunciations, or trenchant criticisms in the dealings of a world whose falsehoods and veracities are separated by so very thin a barrier: to learn that simple assertion however reiterated can never make proof: that a multitude of half believers can never make faith: that argument never convinces any man against his will: that silence is not acquiescence: that the course of this world is anything but even and uniform: that such by-words as reaction and progress are but the political slang which each side uses to express their aversions and their propensions; above all, that no material success, no energy of development, no eventual progress or consolidation, can atone for the mischief done by one act of falsehood, treachery or cruelty. Most of these lessons are truisms. Yes, but there are no truisms in facts: there are no truths which may not be stated as truisms, but there are no truths which a sound judgment can be warranted in despising.

When the student comes to apply these lessons to the judgment of the characters and events of the history that he is studying, and to carry his experience of the past into the present, he finds, if his study has taught him facts as well as maxims, that the great necessity of practical judgment is patience and tolerance, and that the highest justice must rest content for a time to see many things continue wrong that cannot be righted without a greater wrong.

The stock of information from which the student draws these practical lessons is itself the matter on which in the further stages of present history he is called upon to exercise them. He has a part to play in the politics of his own age: he must have made himself acquainted with the national identity of nations, the rights and claims, the sins and punishments and probations of dynasties ; the origins and accretions of parties ; the growth of the influences to which their owners give the name of principles. The stock of information accumulated is only secondary in importance to the habits of judgment formed by the study of it. For we want to train not merely students but citizens ; and citizens of the great communities—the church and the civilised world; to be fitted not for criticism or for authority in matters of memory, but for action. And so it is not views of men and states that are to be taught them, but the power of judging that is to be cultivated, and the information on which that power is to be exercised that is to be imparted, and the faculty of accumulation to be directed to good and pure sources. It is not to make proselytes to one system of politics or another that the work of education is to be directed; a university is no political club or propaganda; I desire to use my office as a teacher of facts and of the right habit of using them.

And to do this we must begin at the right end, work from the past forwards, not backwards from the present. Our students ought not to go into the world a prey to newspaper correspondents : they ought not to go into public life ready to be moulded to the political views of the first clique that may catch hold of them. So far as the fundamental principles of politics go, that is indeed impossible, for men are born most certainly with constitutional inclinations, some to order and others to change ; and the power of the earliest education is exerted to direct those inclinations into channels most in accordance with the views of the educators : so by attraction or repulsion, by reaction or by hereditary succession, not by the lessons of books or views of philosophers, young men's sides are taken in life before they know it. But there is still far more in common between the wise and sound of opposing parties than there is between the sound and the corrupt of the same ; between the thinkers of opposite parties and the thinkers and the fools of the same. We should teach both sides to teach themselves.

Am I to be understood as stating the purpose of the study of History to be the production of scepticism in politics? Surely not. Rather I maintain that there is so much of good in both the opposing views that good men are pretty equally divided between the two ; and that there is so much, I will not say evil, but questionable and debateable, that thoughtless and interested men make their capital of, that thoughtless and interested men are equally divided too; and so much that is obvious to the meanest sense, that stupidity and intolerance are in much the same proportion. What we want to see is men applying to history and politics the same spirit in which wise men act in their discipline of themselves: not to cease to be partisans, not to cease to hold and utter strong opinions, but to be as careful in their party behaviour and in their support of their opinions, as they are in their behaviour in social circles, their conversation in social life. The first object of the true politician, as of the true patriot, is to keep himself and his party true, and then to look for success: to keep himself and his party pure, and then to secure victory: to abolish meanness and corruption where he has influence, rather than to make capital by denouncing it where his de-nunciation can only provoke a retort. The sound politician, on whichever side he may be and however thorough he may be, believes that his scheme of politics is the one in which the benefit of his country is most entirely involved, and he wishes the position of his country to be impregnable; to be im-pregnable it must be sound: if his party represents to him his country, his party must be sound, and it concerns him much more closely to purify his own ranks than those of his enemy. Success is certain to the pure and true: success to falsehood and corruption, tyranny and aggression, is only the prelude to a greater and an irremediable fall.

If our students go from us with the certainty of this lesson impressed on them, with information to guide and cultivated power enough to form judgment, we, whatever our private convictions may be, may rest assured both that our own duty has been done, and that the best has been done for the world in which they are to act. Politicians, happily, seldom live to see the final outcome of their aspirations; life is too short to witness a constitutional struggle in all its growth, and, as matters approach the compromise, the minds of the actors modify, or new, more moderate, counsellors see in the process of circumstances grounds for receding somewhat from the rigorous line drawn by the less practical design of their elders. So the world moves on in a line straighter than the rules of either party would have made it ; and it is well that it is so, the education of a political life is long, and the time for active work in it, for the most part, extremely short. A good deal of enthusiasm is worn out before the action begins, or else the difference between the result and the design would be intolerable to a sincere believer in his own system.

We must, I repeat, if we are to qualify ourselves for forming a sound judgment on these matters, begin at the beginning. We must not work back from popular prejudices, or from philosophic ideas, or from the prominent subject of to-day. The history of Poland cannot be truly viewed by one who starts from the Partition ; the history of Turkey cannot be truly read from the standing point of the balance of power ; that of Germany does not begin, as politicians nowadays join in insisting, from the treaties of Vienna. There are rights that are not turned into wrongs, and wrongs that cannot be turned into rights, by any treaties. There are hopes that cannot, ought not to, be dashed into despair by any pacifications. There are sentiments, if you please to call them so, which depend on long ages of deeply implanted sympathies, of long experience of common suffering and common success, on a firm basis of right and popular love, that may be dismissed by an aggressive politician as emptiness and vanity, but which are the only true basis of free government, the only safe support of thrones, the only true tie of nationalities.

With these things and the deep wide range of facts from which they spring, the student of history must make himself acquainted, and being acquainted he learns to sympathise. Unlike the genealogist and the local antiquary, he does not work back from the particular sympathy to the old foundation, but begins with the beginning and works up to the situation, the sentiment, the sympathy, or the antipathy of the day. Need I adduce the parallel from the sacred sister study ? Who ever became a theologian by working back from the doctrinal or ritual questions of yesterday ? Nay, who is qualified to give an opinion above that of a newspaper letter-writer on such subjects, who has not begun from the Upper Chamber at Jerusalem and worked his way from the coming of the day-star, through the gloom and twilight of the ages, towards the bright shining, such shining as it is, of these days, before he ventures to apply the *spectrum analysis* to the doctrinal light of the nineteenth century?

There is a contrary error; the true student has learned that the past is no more a whole without the present than the present without the past; that the past has no claim to infallibility any more than the present, that the past has had no power, no moral right to dispose of the present by a deed in mortmain. To be a slave of old traditions is as great a folly as to be a slave of new quackeries; but the fault is in the slavish use, not in the old traditions nor in the modern nostrums; and the former error is perhaps the less pardonable as it is a sin against greater light.

I am aware that there are great difficulties; if there were not History would be no matter of study, politics would be no ground of controversy. There is the great question, where does fact end and opinion begin? there is the great question, at what point in the study of modern and medieval history does the sympathy of his own day force itself into the judgment of the student? There is the question, can any length of acquiescence turn a wrong thing into a right one; any length of prescription turn an abuse into a right? How far are men bound by the acts of their fathers, or by their own acts when deceived or ill-informed? Then there is the further question, how far is the moralist—righteous, free, unprejudiced as he may be—qualified to answer these questions off-hand? Each application of each question has its own modifying circumstances. I can only say that the man who knows the facts and has formed the habit of judging on them, is better able and more likely to answer them rightly than the man who has not. Some people will call him dogmatic, but he who has read and thought ought to be able to have an opinion, and he who has one of his own will always be deemed dogmatic by the many who take theirs from the newspapers. He is dogmatic if he ventures to express a doubt where the infallible of the time being has laid down a certainty.

To turn for a moment to the general question. I should not like to be thought to be advocating my study on the mere grounds of utility; although I believe that utility, both as regards the training of the study and the information attained in it, to be the highest, humanly speaking, of all utilities; it helps to qualify a man to act in his character of a politician as a Christian man should. But this is not all; beyond the educational purpose, beyond the political purpose, beyond the philosophical use of history and its training, it has something of the preciousness of everything that is clearly true. In common with Natural Philosophy it has its value, I will not say as Science, for that would be to use a term which has now become equivocal, but it has a value analogous to the value of science; a value as something that is worth knowing and retaining in the knowledge for its own and for the truth's sake. And in this consists its especial attraction for its own votaries. It is not the pleasure of knowing something that the world does not know,—that doubtless is a motive that weighs with many minds, a motive to be accepted as a fact, though it may not be worth analysis. It is not the mere pleasure of investigating and finding with every step of investigation new points of view open out, and new fields of labour, new characters of interest ;—that investigating instinct of human nature is not one to be ignored, and the exercise of it on such inexhaustible materials as are before us now is a most healthy exercise, one that cannot but strengthen and develope the whole mind of the man who uses it, urging him on to new studies, new languages, new discoveries in geography and science. But even this is not all. There is, I speak humbly, in common with Natural Science, in the study of living History, a gradual approximation to a consciousness that we are growing into a perception of the workings of the Almighty Ruler of the world; that we are growing able to justify the Eternal Wisdom, and by that justification to approve ourselves His children ; that we are

coming to see, not only in His ruling of His Church in her
spiritual character but in His overruling of the world to
which His act of redemption has given a new and all-interest-
ing character to His own people, a hand of justice and mercy,
a hand of progress and order, a kind and wise disposition ever
leading the world on to the better, but never forcing, and out
of the evil of man's working bringing continually that which
is good. I do not fear to put it before you in this shape ;
I state my own belief, and it is well that you should know it
from the first.

The study of History is in this respect, as Coleridge said
of Poetry, its own great reward, a thing to be loved and
cultivated for its own sake. If there are few who do really
love and care for history, and I remember with sorrow that
such was the remark of Dr. Shirley the last time that I
had any lengthened conversation with him, is it not the
result of a neglect of the principles which I have tried to
express to you as the ideal of the study to my mind? It has
not been well used of late years ; it has been taught as a task
to children ; it has been valued only as an instrument to
strengthen the memory; it has been under-valued in its true
character of mental training ; it has been learned to qualify
men to make effective speeches to ignorant hearers, and to
indite brilliant articles for people who only read periodicals ;
it has been begun from the standing point of popular in-
fatuation ; it has been begun from the advanced ground of
ecclesiastical or political partisanship ; it has been made an
embellishment for wordy eloquence, a source of subjects for
pictorial talent that has evolved grouping, features and circumstances, from its own consciousness ; it has been written
as a poem, but without the inspiration of poetry, as philosophy without the thoughtfulness or humility of the true
philosophic spirit; it has been written for readers already
known, counted and pandered to. What wonder that there
are few who love it for its own sake, when there are so few
who know it as it is !

In this respect, as I have said, I hope and trust that the
better time is coming, when the universality of the training

and the outpouring of the sources of knowledge will make
imposture futile, and adulteration unprofitable.   I hope and
trust that in that good time our training here will be found
to be a part of the true higher training, and the knowledge acquired in it to lead up to the true and highest
Knowledge.

II.

ON THE PRESENT STATE AND PROSPECTS
OF HISTORICAL STUDY.

(May 17, 1876.)

Some things may be said but not printed, some may be printed and not published; many that are published are not, and need not be, read. Many more would be better left unsaid. The following pages contain a good deal that falls within each of these descriptions. They were written with a full determination that they should not be printed. Circumstances which need not be detailed have led me to alter this resolution. Still there is much in them that would have been said otherwise or omitted if they had been meant for publication. Some things too are omitted that ought to have been said. It is obvious that no attempt has been made at completeness or exhaustiveness of detail. By what I have said or left unsaid, I trust that I have wounded no one. Certainly all was meant in gratitude and kindness.

A FEW days ago, in turning over the contents of my old lecture drawer, I came upon two newspaper cuttings, which a vanity, pardonable I hope after the lapse of ten years, had conserved in company with even more perishable matter. The slips contained the reviews, of the *Pall Mall Gazette* and the *Saturday Review*, of my inaugural lecture as Regius Professor of Modern History. The latter of the two critiques was in itself worth preserving, for it was an early effort of a dear friend who has since made himself a great name in the region of historical study. It was an article full of blessing and good omen, with a sufficient amount of dogmatism to prove that the writer believed himself entitled to criticise; and it contained, with all its precious balm, enough of the element of blister to produce a wholesome irritation: for the one or two points in the lecture on which I had bestowed especial pains were described as praiseworthy but illusory. The *Pall Mall* review, the authorship of which I never learned, was a kindly article also, giving a fair *résumé* of what I had said, and ending with the remark that, although it was clear from the tone of my lecture that I should take a somewhat clerical view of history, still that was not to be deplored, as in the interests of truth it was desirable that the clerical view should have its own exponent.

The incident suggested to me that I should once more look at the inaugural lecture, and see for myself how the hopes and anticipations of 1866 looked in 1876. I found myself reading over the record of feelings and impressions of ten years ago with as much freshness as if they had been another man's ; and the happy thought struck me of turning my reflexions to account in the form of public lectures. It would relieve me of the puzzling anxiety over which six weeks of spring are wasted every year—what shall I take as the subject of the two solemn statutable lectures imposed upon the unhappy professor, who, without this annual mortification, might be in danger of thinking more highly of himself than he ought to think ? It might also seem that, after ten years' occupation of this chair, I might have occasion to review the progress of the study in which I have had so great an interest ; and it might also perhaps help me to gauge the amount of interest which the study itself is receiving in Oxford ; for a notice that I have something to say about myself, and about those whom I might fairly expect to be present to hear me, would perhaps attract a larger audience than a much more elaborate vindication of S. Dunstan, or an inquiry into the merits of the customs duties as a part of the budget of King Edward I. It is true, I thought, I shall have to say some things about myself ; I shall have to blush for my confessions of failure and for my assertions of success ; I may, if I am fortunate in my company, have to make some of them blush too. But what is that among friends ? and here I know none but friends. There may be some who have a vested interest in stupidity and false criticism, but I am thankful to say that I do not know even their names ; and all who take a real and genuine interest in my studies, whether I know them or not, I am proud to look upon as friends with whom I need practise no reticence or concealment. So with your good leave I will dismiss myself first.

The thought that ten of the best years of a man's life have been given to work like this is a very serious one. What

have I done? How have I done it? How far have I fulfilled my own hopes? How far have I realised the good
wishes of my friends? How have I justified the good opinion
of those who placed me where I am? Perhaps it would be
more modest if I left it to others to judge and to pass judgment. But I would rather try to report what I have tried to
do, and how I have tried to do it, than leave it unsaid. No
man is so fit to review a book as the author himself, because
he both knows what he meant to say and will be the first to
hear and feel what his kind friends the critics would make the
world believe that he has said. In the first place, let me say
that I have tried to fulfil the promise which I made in my inaugural lecture—'I desire to introduce myself to you not as
a philosopher, not as a politician, but as a worker at history.'
That I have worked at history is, I think, proved by the bulk
of the results: for during the ten years I have completed ten
volumes, and nearly an eleventh volume, of the English Historians published by the Master of the Rolls; I have edited
the whole of the third volume and assisted in the first and
second volumes of the Councils of the English Church; I
have published the volume of Select Charters, which has now
passed into a third edition, and two volumes of the Constitutional History of England, besides other work edited or passed
through the press for practical aid in historical study. I am
aware that it is not the bulk but the character of the work by
which it must ultimately be tried; I can only say that I hope
my work has not been unworthy of Oxford, or of England.
Judging from the reception accorded to it, I think I should
say that it has met with more appreciative and intelligent
reception in Germany than in England; and I may add that
I believe that I owe to this the honour, and a very great
honour I esteem it, of an invitation to take part as a fellow
editor in the great series of German Historical Monuments,
known for the last fifty years under the name of Pertz, which
has now passed into the hands of a commission of which Dr.
Waitz is the chief. I am proud indeed to be an instrument,
in the humblest way, in repaying the debt which English
history owes to German scholarship.

Further than this I shall not speak of my books, except to
point out how, by giving a clerical complexion to my work, I
have fulfilled the auguries of the kindly critic in the *Pall
Mall.* A kindly critic in the New York *Nation*, reviewing
the first volume of the Constitutional History, has described
the writer as entirely free from political bias, and adds that,
' what is more surprising, he appears to be scarcely influenced
by ecclesiastical sentiment or prejudice.' Well, I thought, when
I read that notice, here is at last a man who takes a right view
of the clerical character. Here am I, steeped, as I fondly
believe, in clerical and conservative principles, and yet able to
take such a view of matters as scarcely to betray ecclesiastical
prejudice or political bias. Seriously speaking, that is just
what I wish. I understand the clerical spirit and mind to be
that which regards truth and justice above all things, which
believes what it believes firmly and intelligently, but with a
belief that is fully convinced that truth and justice must in
the end confirm the doctrine that it upholds ; with a belief
that party statement, and highly coloured pictures of friend
and foe, are dangerous enemies of truth and justice, and
damage in the long run the cause that employs them ; that
all sides have everything to gain and nothing to lose by full
and fair knowledge of the truth. And a clerical view of professional responsibility I take to be the knowledge that I am
working in God's sight and for His purposes. If such be a
right view, I rejoice to have evidence of my success in realising it. If it be a mistaken one, well, I will claim credit for
good intentions as well as steady work.

I wish that my conscience were equally clear as to the
other branch of professorial usefulness, oral teaching or lecturing. On this topic I proposed in my inaugural lecture to set
before myself two leading principles : the first was to begin
at the beginning—' We must begin at the right end, work
from the past forwards, not backwards from the present.' I
meant, of course, not merely that I did not intend to read
history backwards, which would be a difficult process in
lecture, but that I should start from the beginning of the
modern period and treat the course of historical progress

generally and in natural order, rather than, by choosing topics which owed their importance to the interests of the day, work in the reverse order. I intended, in fact, to trace the gradual development of the modern world rather than to trace back particular points of development to their original germs. I have on the whole followed out that idea, although from time to time I have varied it with a course of analytical lectures. The result has been that, during these ten years I have never got beyond the year 1648. I have gone over the whole of the political history of Europe generally, and over that of England and Germany, with great minuteness, throughout the greater part of that long series of years ; but beyond the Thirty Years' War I have not gone. I may add that there were two reasons for this ; one, because I found the later history already in very good hands, a favourite subject with my colleague the Chichele Professor, and very well represented by the College Lecturers on History ; the other, that my own separate line of study and work lay in the earlier portion mainly, and it would have been somewhat distracting to be treating widely distant periods of history at the same time. A third reason, I am free to confess, was that I had some misgivings as to the use-fulness of the later period as a topic of historical education, until the foundation of the earlier knowledge had been well and strongly laid. I have often questioned whether it were indeed desirable to exercise the minds of young men, old enough to have strong political feelings, not old enough to exert a calm historical judgment, on periods of history teeming with the very same influences as those which are at work at this moment ; at least before they had had an adequate train-ing in the earlier history and were able to account for the origin and trace the earlier workings of those influences, so as to be able at least to accord an equitable sufferance to those who take a view contrary to their own. My apprehensions have not been shared by other teachers here, and it is well that no misgivings of mine should have acted so as to leave the treatment of modern history in this respect inadequate. I do not decide the matter, but simply state my own reason for holding back.

And this leads me to recur to the other principle upon which
I proposed to act, and which struck the imagination of my reviewer as illusory or useless. My idea was and is, that, as mankind is roughly divided between the advocates of order and the
advocates of change, and as both classes contain about an equal
number of good, bad, and indifferent, of the wise, of the sensible and of the stupid, it was a function of the historical teacher,
not to try to make them all think alike or to set himself up
as a judge, saying to the one side you are all wrong, or to the
other you are all right, but to present to both the facts and
courses of events, which are the stores out of which both sides
must draw their weapons, in such a fair and just view that
they might be safely used by either. Simply, it was not my
work to make men Whigs or Tories, but to do my best, having
Whigs and Tories by nature as the matter I was to work
upon, to make the Whigs good, wise, sensible Whigs, and the
Tories good, wise, sensible Tories; to teach them to choose
their weapons and to use them fairly and honestly. Well, I
still adhere to that view, and every year what I see in public
life around me confirms my belief in the truth and value of
the principle. How far I have been successful in acting upon
it I cannot of course say; but I feel sure that the growth of
sound historical teaching would have spared us such national
humiliation as we have undergone, during the last few years,
in the treatment of the Public Worship Act, the Judicature
Act, and the Royal Titles Act. I am quite sure that both the
speakers and writers on those subjects would have been very
much wiser and more modest men, if they had, I will not say
attended my lectures, but passed a stiff examination in the
History School: if we could not have made them wiser, we
would at all events have made them sadder.

Well, are these statements of principle made merely to
cover the sad fact that I have not been a successful lecturer?
that I have to join in the professorial chorus of complaint
that the professorial and tutorial systems have not yet dove-
tailed into one another with all the completeness that could
be wished? Perhaps it is so. I have sometimes felt a little
hurt that, after preparing and advertising a good course of

lectures,—and I feel no modesty in speaking thus, because I believe that good and thoughtful work will make good lectures,—I have had to deliver them to two or three listless men ; sometimes I have felt hurt that, in the combined lecture list, when it appeared, I found the junior assistant tutor advertising a course on the same subject, or at the very same hours as my own. But I will allow gratefully that such occasions have been few ; I am pleased to remember that my classes, although they have never been very large, have as a rule been very faithful ; that the combination system has brought me far more men than, on the most sanguine computation, it could have taken from me ; and that I believe the real cause why professorial lectures are less useful than they should be, is the perhaps unfortunate fact that nearly all study in Oxford is directed towards the securing of honours in the Class Lists. Tutors, lecturers, and pupils are all working for the Schools ; even the professorial statutes are drawn with a view to usefulness mainly in that direction ; nor could any professor, however eminent, expect to get a considerable class to attend eighteen or even twelve lectures a term on any subject that would not pay—if I may use the current language on so solemn an occasion. The result is that, so far as lectures go, the professor has to take his chance of a class among the general run of college lecturers, without that power of commanding attendance which the college lecturers have. It is scarcely surprising that the weaker goes to the wall, and that the professor has to yield his place to younger men who perhaps may themselves owe some portion of their success to what they have learned from him. In saying this, I am not speaking of myself, for it would not be exactly true of me, but on the general question. For myself I am quite ready to accept the consolation and to declare that it is really much better, both for the growth of historical study, and for the development of the educational instrument, that there should be a dozen or fifteen college lecturers working away with large classes when I have only a few stray men, than that I should be lecturing to large assemblies of men who came to me simply because they had nowhere else to go. And I am quite willing that my character as a professor should stand or fall by my other work.

And now let me cease to speak of myself. It will be best perhaps that I should arrange what I have to say in circles; and, taking Oxford first, proceed to remark next on the position of historical study in England generally, and then outside England in Europe and America. Oxford first. There can, I think, be no doubt that the growth of the study of History at Oxford during the last ten years has been continuous and very rapid. I have no hesitation in saying this, because no one will think that I claim any credit for myself in it. The foundation work was done before I became professor, and the principal teachers who helped in the laying that foundation, are working vigorously now at the superstructure. We have had great losses, I grieve to say, and great gains. I think I will not mention names: your memories will advert at once to the losses; the gains are here to speak for themselves. It is no small ground of congratulation to be able to say that, whilst our losses have not weakened us, our gains have very greatly strengthened us; our position is strong enough not to be shaken by the loss; our study is still in such a growing state as to be able to incorporate and amalgamate or assimilate all new helps. And that result speaks well for us in several ways. In the first place, our corporate strength is much greater. The History teaching in the colleges is not left to the accidental supply of teachers who have an aptitude for the subject in common with all the other subjects of the University course, but every college has its own recognised History Tutor or Lecturer; and these, or most of them, are acting together. Whether in the Board of Studies or in the meetings of combined lecturers, they are able to exert on the study itself a concentrated influence which tells very effectively on the students who are reading for the Schools. The objection that might suggest itself to those who do not know Oxford, that such a corporate union may tend to cramp the freedom of study and, in preventing desultory or straggling reading, may discourage independent research, will not hold here, so long at least as the system of

examinations remains what it is. There is no risk of the
History Lecturers ever forming a clique, or close school of
History, as a single glance at the list of them is sufficient to
prove. But in the second place, the multiplication and association of lecturers enables us to offer a systematic and continuous reading of History to the student. Each lecturer
will, as time advances, find out his own strongest period, or
his friends will find it for him; and then the student, who
chooses to give his time to the work, will be able to obtain a
thorough guidance through the several stages of his subject;
and the historical training will be both continuous and complete. And, in the third place, the opportunity of reading
continuously, under a series of able teachers of different tones
of mind and different schools of thought, will most certainly
be a great advantage to the student who wishes to take History as a real part of his mental training. I hope and trust
that this will always be the case; and that, although we may
be earnest and glad to work together, we may never be in
danger of thinking all alike, on those topics at least upon
which constitutional opinion and controversial criticism must
be content to permit difference of view. In this aspect the
training for the School of History may become a beneficial
training for public life; and although that is not the sole or
the primary object in my eyes of the study of History here, it
is a most important one; we must try to furnish men who will
not be merely good historians, but good citizens, or, as I said
before, good Whigs and good Tories. And there is another
point in which great advantage may be hoped from the increase and combination of teachers, which I can only just
indicate now—I mean the connexion which is to be looked
forward to between the University course and the teaching of
our great schools and local institutions of education.

Next to the strengthening of the historical staff, the
separation of the School of Jurisprudence from the School of
History is the most important point of our Oxford history.
And this change, although it was anxiously desired by many
teachers of both subjects, was not adopted without some
serious apprehensions. Whether the joint School, so young

as it was, was sufficiently strong to bear the shock of division;
whether the supply of teachers would be sufficient; whether
each subject by itself was substantive enough to furnish the
training for a class examination of high character; whether
the separation would not produce a tendency to eliminate
History from the Law teaching and Law from the History
teaching, were questions which might well cause misgiving.
Some of them have been solved in the process of experiment.
Both Schools have increased their numbers and raised their
standard since the division; as to the supply of teachers, what
I have just said as to the increase and co-operation of the
History teachers is a sufficient answer for them; the Law
professors can, I believe, give a like answer. As to the third
point, the substantive value of historical training, opinions
will still differ; I for my part have no desire that, as an
educational instrument, the History training should take the
place of the classical and mathematical training, which must
always form the chief part of the school education, and the
strongest and favourite work of the University career. But
as a further stage of training, I maintain that the reading of
History may claim an equal place with all the other studies
pursued here: I believe that a man who has taken a good
Class in Moderations would, so far as mental training is concerned, do wisely in taking up a fresh subject, especially
Modern History. As a piece of professional training for the
work of a schoolmaster or a clergyman, it may not be so, at
all events during the present state of school education; I
only allege it as a means of mental culture. There is however
a fourth question, which time will have to answer, and for
which time must supply a remedy, if the mischief comes. It
will be a fatal thing for the study of History here, if the study
of Law should ever be quite eliminated from the History
course; and as fatal for the study of Law if it should ever
come to be read on its merely scientific or on its merely empiric sides. With our present Law teachers both of these are
alike impossible. The lectures of Sir Henry Maine, Dr. Bryce,
and Mr. Holland are to a great extent historical lectures, and
are as great an advantage to the History students as they are

to the Law students. I hope that in a humble sort of way
some work of the other School is found useful to the lawyers.
But this may not always be so. I think that it is a point
that will need watching. The great fault of the old combined
School was that there was no unity about the prescribed reading. Much of the Law, that was superadded to the History,
had no more real connexion with it than a similar bulk of
entomological reading might have had; and the really important historical side of Law was not brought in. I am not
sure that, even now, both Schools would not be benefited by
a more distinct method; and, whilst I should be glad to have
a section of legal history more definitely and generally made
a part of the History examination, I should very greatly
regret to see the Law Board proceeding further than they
have done in shutting out History from their scheme. But
this is going beyond my last. It seems to me, however, in
connexion with my own study, that the growth of jurisprudence, the history of foreign codes, ancient and .modern,
and the connexion between legal and constitutional growth,
are, as well as international law, a common ground between
the two studies; and I am not inclined to surrender the
rights of my School in them any more than I should wish the
lawyers to leave them wholly to us. To some extent the
relation of the studies is the same as that which subsists
between Ecclesiastical History and Theology; each is a very
maimed affair without the other. It will not be our fault if
the common ground is altogether lost.

Next, to descend from the higher regions to the lower,
I would say a word about the Historical Prizes. And in what
I have to say, I hope I shall not be understood to cast any
slight on the very meritorious essays which have in the last
few years received the Arnold, Stanhope, and Lothian Prizes.
I have been on each occasion a judge, and have very carefully
and anxiously observed the character of the productions sent
in. The fact that in several instances the Prizes have not
been awarded is a proof that where they have been awarded
they have been, in the opinion of the judges, thoroughly well
merited. But the experience of these years has not, on the

whole, been encouraging. Of the Stanhope I need say little : it is intended to be an undergraduate prize ; the style of writing is scarcely of less importance in the estimation of the judges, as guided by the intention of the donor, than is the matter of the essay. For the Stanhope, too, there have always been plenty of competitors and no lack of creditable, very creditable, essays. But for the Arnold, which is a graduates' prize, and for the Lothian, which is common to both bachelors and undergraduates, I am sorry to say that there has not been lately good competition. I speak primarily of the modern side of the Arnold Prize ; the ancient side has been still more unproductive of good work. This lack of competition is not, I am sure, a sign of flagging interest in these studies. It is to be explained by a very obvious circumstance—namely, that urgent desire which at present prevails among the Honour men to get speedy returns for their accumulation of class knowledge. Quick returns are generally associated with small profits ; and I cannot help thinking that many men, who rush into tutorial work as soon as they have got through the Schools, would do much better, and make ultimately much greater profit, by continuing their reading, or at all events by blending tutorial work with some literary industry such as writing for the Prizes. It looks rather as if they were afraid that the stores of knowledge which have received the brand of the Examination School might loose their freshness and applicability unless they were immediately put to use in one particular way. I am aware that this is no new snare ; and twenty-eight years ago, when I myself was subjected to the temptation, it was hardly less a snare than it is now. But then, as a rule, men went into the Schools younger than they do now ; there were fewer Schools and fewer first class men ; less ardent competition perhaps among private tutors, and on the whole more leisure for continued reading. There may be other reasons for the result that I complain of. The ignorance with which the Lothian Prize, a handsome prize of £40, open to all graduates and undergraduates up to their twenty-seventh term, has been disregarded, is, to say the least, curious. The subjects proposed, for which I am in a measure responsible, have perhaps not carried on their face the recommendations of general or popular interest ; and Foreign History does not of course receive so much attention as English History. But none of these is a satisfactory reason. The view which I have every reason to believe that the founder of the Lothian Prize had before him was not merely to stimulate historical reading but really to help to increase the stores of historical knowledge by the production of valuable monographs on points of foreign history. My own idea of what we should look for is something like the small but most valuable dissertations which are produced in some of the German Universities as exercises for the doctorate. These are the work of men of twenty-three or twenty-four, just the age at which our high-class men graduate ; and they are the result of their private reading, approved and authorised, so to speak, by their professors. Within the last few weeks I have received two such essays on subjects mainly of English interest, in fact upon portions of our history which I myself have treated : a tract on the 'Dialogus de Scaccario,' by Mr. Liebermann, of Göttingen ; and one on the capture of Lisbon by the English crusaders in 1147, by Mr. Cosack, of the University of Halle. I mention these not because I have any credit to claim for them, for I am criticised quite as calmly and unsparingly as any other Englishman may expect to be in German reviews, but because I take them to be a sign of a sort of literary culture which we ought not to be ashamed to imitate. Unlike most of our ordinary historic reviews, they have a permanent value : they are not condemned, as some very good English work of the kind is, to be the padding of popular magazines,—the ever uncut leaves that interpose between the two sensational stories by which the magazine lives,—but they are put together and stored up for the days when either the writers or some who have profited by the reading of them can use them in more continuous, more consolidated, work. Now it is useless to argue that we cannot do this. Mr. Dicey's Essay on the Privy Council, which took the Arnold Prize in 1860, is a proof that our prize system is

not incapable of such success, although it cannot ensure it.
Dr. Bryce's Essay on the Holy Roman Empire, in 1863, is
not exactly a case in point, for it is not a study of some
minute fact or institution, but a brilliant sketch of the whole
course of one of the great influences which make up modern
history; but not to be invidious, there are other essays which
do more or less approach the standard of deep research and
sound criticism which I wish to see adopted. I have sometimes thought that it would be a good plan to give a number
of alternative theses for such a valuable prize; but I will
content myself with a recommendation that, if any new benefactor wishes at once to encourage critical study and reward
research, he should establish a prize for which the competitors
should choose their own subject, to be approved by the judges
a year before the time fixed for sending in the essays. Such
an experiment might fairly be tried. There are, I believe,
quite sufficient inducements of a local and personal kind, connected with History, which would draw the intelligent student
into much more earnest work than any thesis simply imposed
as a test of his powers. Local history, family history, the
possession of important documents such as may be found in
every country house, and almost every parish register or court
roll, open ways of access to historical interest of a varied kind,
in which the extent of research may be almost unbounded,
in which a critical spirit may be trained and disciplined, and
the results of which are sure to be valuable, certainly invaluable to the worker himself. Well, I do not wish to see the
Lothian essays devoted to points of very minute history, and
it is of foreign history that they are, by the injunction of the
founder, to treat; but I think that some latitude in the
choice of subjects for prize dissertations might be conveniently
adopted, say for college prizes; and if any college will try the
experiment, I will gladly serve as a judge for the purpose.

What I have said about the Lothian Prize, its value, and
the really important work which, if it were taken up by
classmen after they have passed through the Schools, it
might be made to ensure, will, I hope, have fallen on some
ears that will attend to it.

The mention of these prizes leads on to the further point, the encouragement given to the study of History at this moment by scholarships, exhibitions and fellowships bestowed after a competitive examination in History. On this a very few words will suffice, and those shall not be dogmatic or even positive. I would not say a word to discourage the idea, or a word that might seem to show that I wished to determine my own way the result of the experiment that is being at present tried. But, until public school education, until school education generally, has much more completely assimilated, and found a more comfortable place for historical teaching, I should deprecate any large increase of historical exhibitions for boys coming up to the University. Holding, as I do, that a sound classical training must be the foundation of successful historical study, and sure as I am that nothing but such training can prepare a man to be a good historical teacher, I should not give a historical exhibition to a boy who does not show some promise of taking good Honours in Moderations. In most instances I think it would be better not to give it until Moderations are over ; of course, however, I am speaking with a view to the study of History, and not to the pecuniary interests of candidates for scholarships. Example has shown us that it is of little use to hope to promote a study like this by over-nursing. One reason, I think, that we have had such success as we have had, is that we have had no such nursing ; that the study itself, and such a modicum of honour as could be gained in the Class Schools, has been the main incentive to historical reading here. We are, I am quite willing to allow,—nay, I am most anxious that we should remember,—but at the beginning of our work ; we have very much to do still before the History School of Oxford can take its stand besides the historical schools of Paris, or Bonn, or Göttingen, or Munich, or Vienna ; but having well begun, we have half won our place already.

What I have said of scholarships is in its way true of competitive examination for fellowships. If a college desires simply to acquire a creditable Fellow, a mere historic ex-

amination may be as good as any other; if a college desires
a good History Tutor, I conceive that the best way to get
him would be to subject the History candidates (selected in
the first instance on the ground of their Honours acquired in
the History Schools) to a sound examination in the work of
the Literæ Humaniores School, in which teaching power is at
present most fully developed. If a college desires to have
what is called a man of research, I am not sure but the best
way to obtain him would be to choose him without examination. There are not, I believe, many men worthy of such
distinction who are not already marked out by work done.

The whole question of research is difficult, the direction as
well as the endowment of it. I confess that I do not like
the idea of giving a man an income which would by itself
be sufficient to make work unnecessary, and telling him to
devote himself to research as he pleases. Not to consider
cases in which the duty of research would, like other duties
heretofore, be eluded,—and idle professorships would take the
place of idle fellowships,—the temptation to desultory research
must in every case be very great, and desultory research,
however it may amuse or benefit the investigator, seldom
adds much to the real stock of human knowledge. We have
had enough spent already on self-culture taken for granted.
If we would provide for research it must, so far as History is
concerned, be done by paying for results. Let me not be
misunderstood. For results I should rather say work done.
There are fields of work in History as well as in Natural
Science in which experiment is to be treated as result. If
a scientific man tries some new and costly combination of
chemicals, if a practical gunfounder or shipbuilder attempts
some grand and novel scheme of artillery or naval architecture,
and, after making careful calculations, fails, his failure is a
result for which he has a right to be paid ; it is an addition
to our knowledge to have learned that such and such combinations do not produce the effect which it was calculated
that they would produce. So in historical study I should
place among the lawful researches and results, the investigation of foreign libraries, the exploration of unsearched

districts for the purpose of collecting inscriptions, the calendaring and cataloguing of manuscripts,—all sorts, in fact, of
investigations on which it was, *a priori*, reasonably probable
that discoveries would be made ; provided such investigations
were carried out systematically, provided the work were well
done, even if, in that sense of result, there were no result but
the discovery that there was nothing to discover. I do not
mean to say that the successful researcher should be placed on
a level with the unsuccessful, although his success would
probably be in itself remunerative, and the element of good
fortune should not be left out of account.

Well, I should like to see us send an occasional envoy to
the Vatican Library, or to the great libraries of the Roman
princes ; or to send a trained scholar, chosen not by competition, but because his peculiar qualifications forced him
upon our notice, to watch the explorations at Olympia or at
Troy. More generally, however, I think that the endowment of research should take the form of payment for actual
results. Find your man of research, and set him to the work
of research ; pay him something by way of retaining fee,
which you may safely do when you have caught him, but let
the liberal remuneration for work actually produced be the
real endowment, be it books written, books edited, coins or
manuscripts collected, as the case may be. The further
point, how to reward men of research when their day of
research is over, scarcely belongs to this subject ; for the rule
must be the same, I conceive, in all departments of knowledge :
it is a question of pensioning those who have deserved well
of us, not of securing any further addition to the sum of
knowledge.

The rule that we should first find the man of research and
then endow him, not found a chair of research and then find
the man to fill it, applies to another important matter which
is very much forced upon our minds at this moment. And
I must request you to take what I have to say upon it not as
any final conclusion, but as the view which at this moment
presents itself to me as most feasible, but which circumstances
may at any time modify. If we are to look on the measures

of change which are at present imminent, as likely to settle
the future of the University for any considerable number of
years, we must look about us and see whether our staff of
historical teachers and searchers is sufficient for present
needs, if it is likely to be sufficient for future needs, how by
careful speculation and economic arrangement we can best
utilise the means which we have a right to expect under
any re-apportionment of academic resources. Now I am
not prepared to allow that our staff of historical teachers is
either sufficient in itself or organised in the best way at the
present moment. I am quite sure that, if our study advances
during the next ten years in anything like the same ratio in
which it has advanced during the last ten years, we shall
need more professors and an organisation of teaching, which,
like the present organisation of Natural Science professors,
may be not so much dependent as we now are on the tutorial
system in the colleges. It is most important to observe that,
if impending changes alter the collegiate system or affect its
available resources, the University will have to supply a large
part of the teaching power, now provided by the colleges, in
the shape of an increased professoriate or sub-professoriate.
I should not like to have to make even an estimate now of
the staff that we may require in ten or twenty years, and
I should very much deprecate any measure which, taking the
present as the standard of our needs, should prevent us from
securing such development as the occasion for it may arise.
At the present moment we want a Professor of Later Ecclesiastical History, to take up the subject at the point at which
the department assigned to the Regius Professor comes to an
end. We want a permanent chair of Indian History. The
labours of our friend the present Indian Reader have shown
us how thoroughly that study, the importance of which can
scarcely be over-rated by Englishmen, falls in with the current of our University work. I say a permanent chair,
because that is a subject of permanent necessity, not a subject
like palæography or numismatology, in which the labours of
one good professor may serve for two or three generations,
and the endowment of the man is of equal importance with

the endowment of the chair or study. It is the belief of a
large class of scholars that we require a professorship of
English History by itself; and it is certainly desirable that
no chance should be allowed of English History being without adequate representation. I think it is unlikely that that
should be the case, or that both the Regius and Chichele
Professors at the same time should devote themselves to
Foreign History; but it might as well be made certain, and
English History is a subject which might well employ the
energies of three or four professors. I am not, however, an
advocate for tying down the History professors to particular
branches of the subject; I am sure that each will work best
if he is left to devote himself to his own specially chosen
department, and that, provided the whole field of teaching
be sufficiently well covered, the more freedom that can be
given, the better for both teacher and learner.

However, whilst with this limitation the permanent chairs
may be expected to represent the whole field of teaching, it
seems to me most important that for our greater extension
we should employ the means which the Board of Historical
Studies were among the first to suggest in their answer to
the questions of the late Vice-Chancellor, and avail ourselves
of the services of professors-extraordinary: that is, as I have
begun by saying, find a man who is making himself a great
authority and teacher in a special department, and bring him
here and make him a professor, not considering whether, when
he is gone, we can find another as good to fill his place, but
simply taking him as a very good godsend and making the
best of him. Of course we should never choose the professor
of a worthless subject, but worthless subjects do not often
attract the men whose services would be otherwise worth
having. Historical teaching, method and criticism, may
however be exemplified in very many sections of the great
subject: and it might be very well indeed, the general balance
being otherwise preserved, to have a professor-extraordinary
who would exemplify them, for instance, in the minute
working out of the lessons of the reign of Edward III, or
of the age of the Reformation, or of the reign of Charles I

or Queen Anne. So research might be combined with teaching, the discipline of research might be itself inculcated, and
the voice of research be made to attune itself to the work of
teaching.

But whether we want a present reinforcement, or content
ourselves with looking forward to a probable development, we
must not let the opportunity escape. We must not ask too
much, but we must ask the University to keep its eyes open
to what we believe to be our certain and noble future, and not
to make the modesty of our present petitions the limit of her
prospective liabilities in our behalf. We must ask her to
secure for us a competence for the moment and ample freedom
for growth and expansion. As to any definite finality, any
perfect and exhaustive division of periods and duties, any
theoretically complete staff of professors of History, I confess
that I am not disposed to be anxious. If the study flourishes
and is not cramped for means, the completeness and the neat-
ness of system will grow as it grows : and we may be content
to let it grow so.

In conclusion, that is, of this part of my subject,—the condition and prospects of historical education, apart from the
general subject of the *bona fide* development of historical
study,—I should say a word or two about teaching in schools.
And this I do with great diffidence, because I have no experience in such work ; at the same time I trust that I shall
not make any impracticable suggestions. For the growth and
development of the study, as an instrument of education, we
must look for much help to the public schools and other great
feeders of University life. If they find it possible to incorporate it permanently with their course of work intro-
ductory to the University career, the men will come up better
prepared for such training as we can give them, and so more
and more ready to assist in the growth of the growing study.
Now although this seems simple enough to say, in reality it
involves a great deal. It means not only that the great
schools should have History masters who can keep themselves
abreast with the rising tide of knowledge, but a constant
revision or provision of improved text-books. It seems to me

that the great schools are awake to the necessity, and that the publishers of school books are vying with one another in the production of manuals which will combine the conclusions of the most advanced students with simplicity of plan, and, we may hope, attractiveness in treatment. Only there is no finality to be looked for. We must not expect manuals that, like the old grammars, will keep their places for two or three centuries. Every few years great discoveries are made ; the use of the comparative method, long ago applied superficially and partially to History, has now become, owing to its employment in other fields of work, far more valuable and remunerative ; and more especially in regard to early periods with respect to which error and misapprehension are the greatest among fairly educated people, and almost ineradicable from otherwise fairly useful text-books. To take the simple instance, which will perhaps have occurred to some of you : the proved discovery of the forgery of Ingulf's History of Crowland Abbey was a fact that necessitated the revision of every standard book on early English History. It is more than forty years since that discovery, long ago suspected, was proved beyond the possibility of doubt. Yet to this day the Ingulfine leaven remains in our elementary books, nay, in more than elementary books, in standard works of History, from which it is almost impossible to eliminate it ; it remains as a warning light—a wandering marsh-fire—to caution the reader not to accept too abjectly the conclusions of his authority. Even the recently published list of landowners of England, called somewhat fantastically by the leaders of public opinion the new Domesday, contains in its introduction a quotation from Ingulf, made apparently without any suspicion of falseness. But it is not only the name of the writer, but the more subtle influence of conclusions drawn from his fabrications that are to be guarded against : and these lie at the very basis of our popular histories. For school books it is absolutely necessary that such primary errors should be corrected at once ; for it is impossible, at least at present, to suppose that the reading of original authorities can be to any great extent introduced into the scholastic course as is done in Germany. And this will necessitate constant revision.

Another point to be watched is the not unnatural desire of teachers to attract the minds of boys to the picturesque and dramatic sides of the subject, to the neglect of the greater lesson, the investigation of causes and effects and the connexion of events. I would almost rather that boys were attracted by the reading of Ivanhoe and the Talisman, books which do not pretend to be true, and are full of strange misrepresentations of manners and thought, than by a serious history composed with a view to the picturesque only or mainly. The ivy may conceal the structure of the building far too much for safety. We cannot safely content ourselves with fanciful grouping or imaginary drawing of character and situation. Let us trust the novelist so far. There are novels that may well be trusted so far; Miss Yonge's Chaplet of Pearls, and Dove in the Eagle's Nest, for instance—beautiful and, I think, perfect pictures of manners and reflexions of ideas. We will attract but not educate by such books. Our real education in History must not be less precise or severe than the discipline of language or of natural science ; it cannot be valuable if it be desultory.

One point more. If the study of periods of History is to become part of a school education, I trust that due care will be taken not to dwell unnecessarily on, or to choose for exaggerated illustration, those periods which are connected most closely with the questions and controversies of to-day. Of all things in the world except a controversial woman, a controversial boy is the most disagreeable, the most pragmatic, the most irrepressible, the most aggressive. Now even in the training of children we want to train the judgment. That training is the great educational or disciplinary object of historic teaching, the formative as distinct from the material acquisition that results or should result from it. The judgment must be trained in cooler air and by milder methods than are found in the battle-field of modern politics. Surely boys and girls should be taught elementary history, should be trained in the exercise of the powers that can trace cause and effect in historical narrative, should be given credit for the germs of a critical faculty and helped to cultivate it, before they are plunged into the details of the struggles of puritanism and absolutism, or the deep religious divisions, that for three centuries have separated Christendom into two camps and do so still. Let them learn the history of early England and early France before they are called to exert their tender judgment on the Great Rebellion or the French Revolution. If the teachers had been so taught the experiment would never have been tried.

III.

ON THE PRESENT STATE AND PROSPECTS
OF HISTORICAL STUDY.

(May 20, 1876.)

IN the remarks which I took upon myself to offer in the last Lecture on the present prospects of Historical study, I think that I managed to touch upon every point of special interest to Oxford and the educational use of my subject : to touch upon every point, I say, because it was neither necessary nor possible to treat exhaustively of any one. I may have to recur in the present Lecture to some of the more general or more prominent topics, but I propose now to take a view of the broader side of the subject, Historic study and its position in England and Europe. as affected by the work of the last ten years ; not with any special view to the educational importance of the work, but generally as a material and substantial branch of human knowledge.

Taking England first ; the first point I shall notice is the great spread of the taste for history which has marked the period. This may be tested in two ways. The great number of new books and reprints of old ones, the large editions and re-issues of standard books, school books, and volumes of essays, and the number of reviews of historical books, or short historical articles in magazines and newspapers, are one branch of proof ; the more lively interest taken in the preservation of historical monuments, whether in the shape of documents or in that of architectural and antiquarian remains, is another. I am not prepared to say that the last ten years have witnessed the introduction of any entirely new elements in either branch, or that we are not yet a long way off from the state of things which we may wish for, when the publication of a great historical discovery may be welcomed with as much ardour as a new poem or a new book of travels, and when the preservation of public and private memorials will become the care of every family and individual that possesses them, as well as of the nation at large. But we have gone on steadily improving ourselves ; not to speak yet of the important works which have met appreciative readers, I would adduce such points as these : the revival and extension of the work of the learned Societies, especially the Camden and Surtees Societies ; the wide-spread interest taken in the work of the Commission for examining Historical Manuscripts in private hands ; and the Parliamentary discussions on the preservation of Historic monuments. Each of these three matters may claim an important bearing on the growth of historic culture. In each we see those private and personal influences combined and utilised for good purposes, which too often have been wasted upon mere pomps and vanities, or mere archæological trifling.

The expansion and extension of genealogical study is a very remarkable feature of our own times. Men are apparently awaking to the fact that there are other families besides those described in the peerage, that those families have their records, played their part in history, furnished the bone and sinew of national action, and left traces behind them which it behoves their descendants to search out and keep in remembrance. There is nothing in this that need be stigmatised as vain and foolish ; it is a very natural instinct, and it appears to me to be one of the ways in which a general interest in national history may be expected to grow. It is an increasing pursuit both in America and in England, and certainly helps, by the promotion of careful investigation and by the publication of recondite memorials, the more complete adjustment of personal and local details. This has no doubt helped largely the work of the Manuscripts Commission ; it has enabled the learned societies to attempt larger and more costly works, and has been the portal by which many, destined and qualified to be valuable historical helpers, have entered the field of historic study.

Local history and minute archæology have been of use in the same way : the Harleian Society has published heraldic visitations; the local societies have printed subsidy rolls and old legal memoranda ; old county histories have been republished ; little popular county histories are found in every farm-house in the country, where the editors or compilers have contrived, by mingling the *utile* of the directory with the *dulce* of historic memoranda, to stimulate the curiosity of every class.

I have called this a revival, and so it is ; these pursuits do not seem to admit of much development, one flourishes and another languishes, as may be traced very clearly in the pages of the Archæologia ; twenty years ago architectural antiquities were the great object of local study, now through a genealogical period we are perhaps working our way to a constitutional one, which I shall be most happy to welcome. I think that just now, when so many of our most ancient institutions, the manorial system and the ecclesiastical and civil judicature of old times, are either falling into desuetude or being ruthlessly abolished, it would be a good work for local zeal to put on record what memory and custom can still supply as to the working of these old institutions. I wish to see a manorial map of England as it exists now or as it existed twenty years ago, reflecting as it must do the condition of territorial power at the time when it became impossible to create new manors, in the reign of Edward I ; reflecting, as it could easily be made to do, the local and dynastic arrangements of parties and families during the fourteenth, fifteenth, and seventeenth centuries, arrangements which still survive but are destined, by the operation of legal changes most of them intended to facilitate the alienation of land and to amend the administration of justice, to speedy extinction.

Well, I only adduce these as feeders, so to speak, of the stream of historic interest. Here and there they add a really precious contribution, but chiefly they are valuable as drawing in students to the higher and nobler study. Without them I doubt not we should have our Macaulays and Froudes, our Maines and our Freemans, but without them those writers would have to dispense with nine-tenths of their intelligent and interested readers; and without their contributions the historians of the grand school would have to content themselves with portrait painting; they would lose all minute details of character, and background and foreground alike of local colouring. The 'Worthies of All Souls' have shown us how even more directly and more personally the dry stores of the College Treasury can bring us into relation with the great men of old days, and the same plan followed out by the Colleges generally would serve to fill up a great gap in our national history.

But considering the magnitude of the subject, I have said enough about local influences. They prove the increasing interest, but they do not yet prove that interest to be of the most refined and educated character. If we test it by the character of the work it welcomes, we shall perhaps be inclined to put a drag on historic zeal. I cannot help thinking that although sound historical books find a hearty welcome for the most part, unsound and sensational books, which pretend to the character of history, are too often welcomed quite as heartily. High patronage as well as large circles of readers seem now and then to waste themselves on trashy books which owe their circulation to advertising skill or to pretentious claptrap. I cannot of course mention names, but I do not doubt that you can supply them. Now, although this is an unfortunate waste of power and strength, it is not wholly to be deplored: a taste for history must exist before it can be educated, and it will, until it is thoroughly educated, be liable to be misled and waste itself on what is unprofitable. But to whom does it belong to educate and refine it? That place is claimed by the reviewers. But I take leave to say that it is with the reviewers that the improvement should begin; and it is a sad truth that the improvement in reviewing has not yet gone far enough. By reviewing I mean what strictly speaking reviewing should be, and I take leave to say it because, having never been a reviewer, having in fact written but one article of the kind in my whole life, I have been for many years a steady reader of reviews. It is easier perhaps to say, with regard to this point, what we do not want than what we want. We do not want sledge-hammer articles, that demolish an unhappy pretender without attempting to tell us what he pretended or attempted to do; or niggling articles, which enumerate the mistakes and misstatements of a book, ignoring the fact that, with much carelessness of detail, the author has shown a great grasp of knowledge of his subject, skill in grouping and colouring, and power in investing the subject with true and real interest; we do not want reviews in the grand style, which seem to be intended to prove that the writer knows or believes himself to know more of the subject than the author whom he is reviewing. All these sorts of reviews are either injurious to knowledge or useful only by way of advertisement. I need scarcely point out to you that the reviewer, as a reviewer, is a man of many books and many subjects, the author is generally a man of one book or one subject. Ten to one the most indifferent author knows more of his book (I speak of *bona fide* authors, not of book-makers) than his reviewer does. In fairness he has a right to demand that his critic should have tried to put himself in his place and looked at the subject from his point; but how very seldom does he find himself so treated. What we want, I take it, in historical reviewing is that the critic should first give a fair account of the work; that he should exhibit, in doing this, just so much superior knowledge as will justify his claim to sit in judgment upon it, and not put in a word for mere display; that he should discuss the subject-matter judicially and as a whole, not confining himself to the portions in which he is presumedly better informed, but gauging the work by the author's standard as well as his own; that he should not dogmatise where the points of difference are matters of opinion—how many a sore heart would have been spared if the critic would have said, 'Here we differ,' instead of saying, 'This is a great mistake;'—and finally that, in recounting blemishes, he should not confuse structural with incidental error. I do not recommend German reviews as models for English ones; too often they seem to me to be written by rival competitors in the same field with the author; but as a rule they give more real information as to the work criticised than ours do ; and they are more moderate in denunciation.

So much of our reviewing is done in newspapers and critical notes in magazines and quarterlies that this sort of criticism nearly engrosses the name ; and the great old reviews are come to be collections of essays, the book supposed to be criticised standing merely in the place of text or thesis to a discourse in which neither book nor author may be mentioned. But the historical value of this sort of essay might be very great ; and, as history is of course only one of the subjects that compete for a limited number of places in such periodicals, it has frequently been suggested that we should have a historical review of our own ; by 'we,' I mean the students of history who are at work here or in London and elsewhere connected with the two Universities. Such a design has much to recommend it. It would be very becoming to the English school of history to have an accredited organ ; it ought not to be beyond our powers and resources to maintain such a journal as is kept alive in many of the smaller universities of Germany ; and it would be very useful indeed to have a record of the incidental discoveries, and of the minor studies which every historical scholar makes in the process of his work, many of which are thrown away as soon as the immediate occasion for their use is over, or, being employed as appendices to works already too bulky, remain practically unread and unknown. But there are objections or rather hindrances to such a scheme which have hitherto been sufficient to prevent us from making the attempt. It is very questionable whether we can as yet appeal to a public sufficiently extended, and sufficiently educated, to make the design remunerative to either publishers or contributors : the writers whose work would be most valuable are all of them busy men to whom the writing of two or three articles a year would, if made a matter of *rigueur*, become exceedingly burdensome ; and the prospects of any new review in England at this moment can hardly be called encouraging. The older quarterlies have long ceased to provide us with such reading as was found in the *Edinburgh* and *Quarterly* of fifty years ago, when Hallam, Allen, and Palgrave

were writing on History. Now and then we have contributions to contemporary history, either from the statesman of
the day or from the industrious collector of the gossip of the
last generation, which have a value, and will hereafter have a
greater. Now and then we have a sound critique on new
matter brought out in foreign countries, and careful, well-
considered judgments on the re-reading of re-written history.
Occasionally, very rarely, when a question of theological or
political interest touches upon the more recondite stores of
history, we have an industrious examination of ancient sources
made subservient to the advocacy of some particular theory.
But so far as reviews go, this age is one not of deep study.;
the articles are read by, and therefore written for, men who
care just enough about such matters to induce them to read
fifty pages of cleverly arranged not too exhausting argument.
They share the ephemeral character of the rest of our popular
literature, and, so long as that ephemeral character is a mark
of such productions, it is only courting failure.if we attempt
to add to the list of competitors one which would find, in the
very points which recommend it to the student, characteristics
which would repel those whom, I think I may say, we ought
to try to attract.

Still I do not despair of the plan; only it will require an
amount of devotion as well as an affluence of means, which
are not, it seems to me, at present forthcoming. The confession is, when we look at what is done in Germany, or even
when we look at what is done by private societies in England,
not a thing to be proud of: but the conditions of publishing
and the estimation of literary labour in Germany are so different from what they are here, that the comparison is hardly
fair, and the best English private and local societies have
always made their publications a labour of love to both writer
and editor, whilst by their subscriptions they are secured from
serious loss. On the whole I think that if we were to make
the effort, it might best be done at first by the agency of
a publishing society. Five hundred subscribers, such as sustain the Camden and the Surtees Societies, would launch and
keep afloat even a larger plan than has yet been contemplated.

If I were called on to furnish an illustration of the increased interest felt in historical matters at this day, I might, I think, allege the curious phenomenon of the republication of the Paston letters. Curious, invaluable, as these relics are, they are really unintelligible to all but the innermost ring of historic students. Their language, their localised details, their minutiæ of family history and illustration of manners, are without any meaning to nine people out of ten. Yet they have just been reprinted with a most admirable apparatus of notes and introductions, in a most useable and convenient form, for the small sum of one guinea; a price at which only a very large circulation can repay the editor for his outlay, to say nothing of his labour and the expenditure of stores of carefully gathered knowledge. So far, you may say, so good; but when we remember that the demand for the republication was not the result of awakened historic interest, or even of curiosity as to what the much-talked-of letters might contain, but sprang directly from an ingenious and paradoxical argument on their authenticity written by a well known scholar, who was not, I believe, specially interested in their contents so much as in their external history; that it was promoted by the rumour that our greatest judge was going to investigate their genuineness, and that in the third place the curiosity so provoked was stimulated and encouraged by the unexpected discovery of new stores of similar matter, when, I say, we remember these things, we are bound to confess that the sensational history of the Paston letters, rather than the really valuable matter contained in them, has been the chief element in the demand for their production. However this may be, we bless the accident and rejoice in the result. However the zeal originated, that result is according to knowledge.

It is time, however, that I should proceed to mention some of the more important additions to our historical stores which have marked the period which I have, desultorily I fear, tried to embrace in the general scope of my remarks. I can but mention a few out of many names, and most of those few are above my unpretending criticism. The last ten years have

seen the production of Mr. Freeman's Norman Conquest, which
I believe is well known to us all, and is a monument of
critical erudition and genius in the recreation of historical
life of which Oxford may well be proud. We have seen too
the conclusion, premature and abrupt, of Mr. Froude's great
work, a book to which even those who differ in principle from
the writer will not refuse the tribute of praise as a work of
great industry, power and importance : the conclusion scarcely
less abrupt, though not premature, of the great work of one of
the best and greatest men that Oxford has ever produced, the
Lives of the archbishops of Canterbury by Dr. Hook. Two
out of the three most valuable contributions of Mr. Samuel
Gardiner to the Jacobean and Caroline period, the earnests as
we hope of still greater contributions yet to be looked for :
the studies of Mr. Brewer on the reign of Henry VIII included in his volumes of Calendars of Public documents, but
rivalling in bulk and more than rivalling in interest the
documents themselves ; Mr. Pocock's labours on the same age
in his edition of Burnet and of the early documentary history of
the Reformation ; Professor Rogers's great work, or beginning
of a great work, on medieval economy, the History of Prices ;
these are but a portion of the history work done for England by
men trained in the old Literæ Humaniores School of Oxford ;
how long will it be before the new school will have something
of the sort to show ? To the facile pen of an Oxford man we
owe the production of the most popular manual of our history
that has ever appeared, the Short History of the English
People. To the Oxford Press and the labours self-denyingly
and generously tendered of hard-worked tutors we owe the
translation of Ranke's History of England.

Of this, as one of the original suggesters and promoters of
the undertaking, I may say a word more; for, curiously enough,
the boon conferred by this translation has not been adequately
recognised. Leopold von Ranke is not only beyond all comparison the greatest historical scholar alive, but one of the very
greatest historians that ever lived. Unrivalled stores of knowledge, depth of research, intimate acquaintance with the most
recondite sources, have been, in his case, supplemented by

everything which could be conferred by a long life, continuous study, close association with the great political actors and thinkers of the greatest part of the most eventful century of the world's history. Scarcely less eminent as the founder of the German School of History than as an historian himself, he has had the singular felicity of living to gather up the results of the labours of the men whom he himself started in the career of study. It seemed to me, and it was the idea in which the work was begun and carried out, that for English-men in their own tongue to have from such a man a reading of the most critical period of English history, would be a boon of incalculable value. Not that we regarded him as infallible, not that we looked for him to have the sympathies of an Englishman, but that we did look to have for a period on which no Englishman can look or speak without prejudice, the evidence of a witness and critic who brought unparalleled qualifications and entire impartiality to bear upon it. The reception of the boon by scholars has been most grateful; that our literary guides have condescended to look on Ranke as one of the ruck of German professors, to treat his work as on the same plane with those of the ephemeral writers whose reputation is so carefully nursed in what is called literary society, does appear to me to be one of the discouraging signs of the times to be set against our more sanguine hopes.

To come down to smaller works of a more distinctly educa-tional character; whilst we may regret perhaps that the good example set by Mr. Kitchin and myself in the Clarendon Press Series has not yet been more widely followed, we cannot but regard the competition among the great publishers in producing manuals of history for schools as a most significant mark of growth. Mr. Longmans' Epochs, Mr. Freeman's Manuals, Mr. Green's Primers, Messrs. Rivington's Hand-books, all have in common the mark of a purpose to secure skilled labour of the best sort; boys are not to be taught any longer by book-makers. May the omen be fully borne out by the result.

So far, however, I have mentioned no book except those

in which we here have a direct and personal interest. We should be ungrateful indeed to leave out of ever so general review Mr. Kinglake's great work on the Crimean War, or Mr. Molesworth's on the History of the Period of Parliamentary Reform ; these stand at the head of a list of laborious and able publications, the interest of which depends on the incidents of our own time : to some extent they are attempts to forestall the opinion of posterity, but they are books which, if such books ever are to be written, if the contemporary knowledge and opinion are to be applied to the record of the events to which they are devoted, should be written now before the actors are dead or the public sympathy chilled. So rapid is the progress of political life and opinion that even these great subjects are becoming quickly extinct or lost influences among the crowds of new ones. The Reform History has come to be regarded no longer as a grand revolution, of which its chief agents could predicate perfection and finality, but merely as a single stage in a progress the present velocity of which would have made the projectors dizzy. What shall we say of the Crimean War itself? begun as it was by the wisest men of the nation with the greatest reluctance, but begun because they believed that they ought to keep national promises and to maintain treaties even at the risk of sustaining weak and wicked governments. Why, for all the good that it did, it might never have been fought at all. The treaties that resulted from it are thrown to the winds; the powers that fought it have resumed that natural attitude which treaties might attempt to modify but cannot alter : the crisis that it tried to avert is approaching more quickly and more certainly, and it is reverted to only because in it an experiment which we thought fit to try was tried in vain. The history of our own times does, whilst the events are in progress, seem more important than any history that has gone before ; greater interests are seen to be involved, greater armaments brought into the field, more critical changes follow, more startling principles are enunciated ; yet after all the proportion of historic incident is scarcely changed. The tide began to roll with greater waves at the Reformation, with higher still during the age of Lewis XIV, deep called unto deep in the upheaval of the French Revolution, and the European wars of 1866 and 1870 have proved that the storms grow wilder as the world grows older. But the results are not, so far as we can see, much more permanent, the rapidity of action keeps pace with the growth of the contending influences, and events which centuries ago would have been regarded as striking the knell of Christendom, form the subject of a hasty telegram which we read and say, It is no more than we expected. But I am not going to philosophise; μὴ γένοιτο. When I say that such books as these are not history, but rather the materials of history, I do not mean to undervalue them, but simply to point by them to the fact that until events have come to be seen in due proportion and in their relative bearing, their full history cannot be written; and the most perfect memoirs will need reduction and review. But at the risk of seeming to pass over even more important matters I must pass on.

It is unfortunate, I think, that English writers confine their attention too much to English and French History; and that the History of farther Europe, that of Italy being a partial exception only, is seldom made the subject of research. Carlyle's Frederick II is really the only great work on German or European History which has appeared in England, for nearly half a century, on its merits as a work of History. It will scarcely be claimed for Sir Archibald Alison's valuable works on the period immediately following that of Frederick, that they owe their importance to their character as works of historical research. They were read and are read as any other very interesting book on a very interesting subject, but they do not reach even to the stature of Von Sybel's French Revolution or Lanfrey's work on Napoleon. Carlyle's Frederick is primarily a work of a different sort; although, in the prophetic sight of the writer, that most remarkable book may, at the moment it was written, have borne a conscious reference to events which were still future, but have since most wonderfully illustrated its great theme, the world in general recognised nothing of the sort in it. The author, if he knew himself to

be a *vox clamantis* at the time, must have been astonished at
the rapidity with which his Gospel of Force triumphed as soon
as it had its chance. Some of us shook our heads over it, one
great man amongst us, whose place I am proud to occupy,
I dare not say to fill, did not hesitate to speak words of
summary condemnation; but the doctrine itself was esoteric,
the words, like much else of Carlyle's, were φωνᾶντα συνέτοισιν
but συνέτοισιν only; to the ears of the many they required
the sacred interpreter. Shall I be thought hard if I say that
the popularity of Carlyle's Frederick was not an intelligent
appreciation; that it was Carlyle's reputation and manner
that made men read it; and that it was for the Carlyle not
for the Frederick that they cared, whilst they wholly missed
the prophet's lesson. Such as it is, however, Carlyle's Frederick
stands alone in recent historic work.

There may be good reasons for this. The accumulation of
new material for German and Italian history is perplexing in
itself; the Germans and Italians have scarcely begun to sort
it. The materials for Spanish history are only a little more
accessible than before, and accessible only to workers who are
capable of great fatigue, as well as, what few can pretend to
be, already well qualified to make the very utmost of scanty
opportunities. But making allowance for everything that
can be allowed for, it is, I think, no credit to us that since the
republication of the old Universal History, a hundred years
ago, we have had nothing like a general book of historic
reference undertaken in England, and that, with the exception
of Carlyle, we have had no first-class work on German history
since Archdeacon Coxe wrote on the House of Austria. We
have had sketches and essays, and lectures, and articles in
encyclopædias,—one of which at least, Lardner's Cyclopædia,
furnishes incidentally some very valuable helps,—but nothing
like a comprehensive, well-considered design, such as for its
day the old Universal History was. This I hope is a *lacuna*
which will not exist much longer. Not that it can be filled
up in a day; but that we have in Heeren and Uckert a model
which it will be no disgrace to us to copy, a great credit to
equal or to surpass.

And this leads me on to that further circle of European historic study towards which I have been looking at several points in both these lectures. We ought to be taking advantage of the great interest with which English history is now being read in Germany, and, more than that, we ought to learn from that interest that German history might be quite as remunerative to us as ours is to the Germans. Such has always been my contention. The study of French and Italian history appeals to our fancy, to our ecclesiastical and political tastes, but the history of Germany is bound up with our national and natural identity. And you may depend upon it, in our comparative history we have to receive as much as we have to give. Consider the number of precious contributions that we have received already. Immeasurably the best edition of the Anglo-Saxon Laws, by Schmid ; the work of Lappenberg and Konrad Maurer on Anglo-Saxon Constitutional Antiquities ; Pauli's exhaustive History of Medieval England ; Ranke's History of England under the Stewarts ; Pauli's History of the Present Century, of which the third volume has just appeared, furnishing by far the most accurate and well-proportioned view of recent history, and anticipating, I do not question it, most of the conclusions of the next generation, as to the great men and great events on which we have looked too closely to see them in their due proportion and relations. There is scarcely a nook of our ancient and medieval history which the Germans are not now exploring. To Jaffé we owe the republication, from original texts, of the writings of Aldhelm and Boniface, the first Englishmen who wrote at all. The letters of Alcuin, the great scholar of York and light of learning in the West, have not only been most elaborately edited by Jaffé, Dümmler and Wattenbach, but are being subjected to a minute historical analysis by Professor Sickel at Vienna, an analysis which brings out, and must bring out more and more as it proceeds, the points of international and inter-ecclesiastical intercourse in the critical century of Anglo-Saxon growth. The Roman and the early Christian inscriptions in Britain have found in Dr. Hübner a critic who not only can collect and record and

arrange them, but bring them into comparison and connexion
with the like remains throughout Europe.   Month after month
brings me essays and dissertations, as I said before, upon
minute points of English law, chronology, even geography
and personal history.   What does this mean ?   Not surely
that those scholars are following an erratic fancy in trying to
perfect their knowledge of English history, or that they are
working without plan or leading idea.   I do not indeed
suppose that the scholars and students of Göttingen and
Vienna are doing as Von Moltke and his agents are said to
have done before the war of 1870, collecting plans, and charts,
and itineraries, and models of fortresses, and raised maps·of
provinces, whilst they were training men and officers both at
work and play for conquest.   I do not believe that they want
to take from us anything, not even the pride of knowing more
of our own history than they do, or that they want to engross
to themselves by conquest the whole domain of historical
knowledge.   But I am sure that they have a great object—to
increase human knowledge in minuteness of accuracy as well
as in breadth and firmness of grasp ; to perfect the instruments of historic study; to make, perhaps subordinately and
subsidiarily, their exploration of our history throw light on
the dark places, the obscure passages and flickering popular
institutions of their own land.   I wish that we should do the
same, that we could and would so study not merely the
works of Waitz, Sohm, Brunner and the Maurers, but the
documentary evidence on which those writers have based their
conclusions.

There is very much both of matter and method to be learned
from them.   A few months ago a young American professor
who called on me told me that he was lecturing in one of the
great universities of the United States on constitutional law ;
he had been in doubt where to begin, and was in fact lecturing
on the capitularies of the Frank emperors.   I could not help
thinking that, if he was not really wasting his powder and shot
upon a class that could not appreciate him, he was doing
something that I should like to see done here.   And, within
a very few weeks after, my aspirations were gratified by finding

the Corpus professor lecturing on the Salian law, going further
back, and taking probably a more remunerative subject than
my American friend.

Well, perhaps I am prejudiced by my own especial line of
study in favour of such speculations, but I will go still further
and say that the devotion with which, since the days of
Grimm, the local and municipal institutions of Germany have
been studied sets us a fine example. The publication of
Grimm's collection of Weisthümer has been followed by a
great and general exploration of local archives. Now in
England we do not possess one single complete and detailed
monograph on town life; Drake's Eboracum, published a
century and a quarter ago, is perhaps the best, but in the
lapse of many years a vast amount of new matter has turned
up, by which Drake could be enlarged and improved. Medieval
London still waits for its constitutional historian. The history
of the Cinque Ports, and of the mercantile communities on
the coast, lie at the root of our naval history, and contain the
germs of our international jurisprudence. On them we have
a few law-books which are the peculiar domain of a few legal
offices in London; but their history has yet to be explored.
Every year perhaps we are drawing nearer, for the discoveries
of the Historical MSS. Commission are richer in this than in
any other region; but for the successful investigation, for the
comparison of materials, and for the systematic use of them,
we must look to the association of such labourers as are now
in Germany employed on the history of the Hanse Towns.
Even the Scottish boroughs are in this particular ahead of us;
there is a society for publishing the records of Scottish burgh
life. All the efforts as yet made in England in that direction
have been the result of local and personal interest excited by
merely antiquarian curiosity.

It is time that this went further. It is time too, as I said
before, not only that we had a feudal map of England before
the manorial boundaries are wiped away, but that we had a
careful collection of manorial customs: such a codification in
fact, as is possible, of the ancient unwritten popular law as it
is preserved in these most ancient shadows and skeletons of

the early life of our fathers. And so I come round to the point where I digressed.

We may take pattern by the Germans in collecting these relics, but when we have done so we shall have to bring them to comparison with the similar German collections before we can extract the whole lesson that they would convey. I would not be too sanguine, but I honestly believe that such a comparison would reveal to us points of contact and divergency as yet unsuspected even by the most careful investigators, and would enable us to reproduce the ancient society of our common ancestry in a way that would speedily set at rest some of the most controverted questions of institutional history. In such an investigation we might rely on the help of the greatest foreign scholars; and it is a task to the performance of which every intelligent country gentleman could contribute an appreciable share without stirring from his own muniment room.

If we turn to France and Belgium, we shall find work of the same kind going on, which is only second, if it be indeed second, to the historical industry of Germany. The re-issue of the Recueil des Historiens de France, of the Gallia Christiana, and the Acta Sanctorum, proves that the revival is begun at the right end, from the ecclesiastical side. The reproduction, in the great Patrologia of Migne, of the early medieval historians, as well as the theologians, is an almost portentous fact; one wonders where the readers and students of such collections are to be found, and fears that, after all, such monuments must find their resting-places chiefly on the shelves of the public libraries rather than on the desks of close students. The intermission or retarded issue of the series of *Documents inédits* is perhaps not to be wondered at, when we consider the uncertain tenure of power and the enormous demands made for other purposes on the resources of the recent governments of France; but private enterprise and scholastic co-operation have done much to supply the void caused in this way. The collection of the historians of the Crusade, published under the direction of the Institute, increases and flourishes. The publications of the 'École des Chartes' and of the officers of the National Library, supply in their fine

criticism and deep research two elements that are somewhat
deficient in the other lines of historical work. Local antiquaries and local societies flourish in France as much as in
Germany, and the same spirit of restoration and conservation,
which is exhibited in the case of historic buildings and other
monuments, is conspicuous in the minute reproduction of
chronicles and cartularies. At last constitutional history has
found a home again in the land of Montesquieu. The history
of États Généraux and Parliaments is critically and impartially investigated by men like M. Picot and M. Boutaric.
Ancient laws and customs also are found to have a value besides their importance to the scientific lawyer. M. Fustel de
Coulanges brings to the study of institutions a philosophic
spirit, critical acuteness, and learning which seems not unlikely to have the effect of inducing some of the German
constitutionalists to revise or modify their conclusions. And
lastly, in the foundation of the *Revue Historique*, the best
scholars, in all of these departments, have stretched out the
right hand of fellowship to the workers in other lands, and
occupied their place in the alliance for international knowledge and help in history. It is perhaps true to say that in
the most essential and characteristic parts of our own national
history we have less interest in France than in Germany; but
throughout many ages French and English history, both external and institutional, are bound together as closely as any
two national histories can be ; and that which illustrates the
one cannot but illustrate the other. English writers have
long ago learned that there are other histories worth studying
besides their own : German writers seem to have been late in
learning that the Fatherland has a united and continuous history. France is at last showing that she recognises the fact
that other lands have histories at all, and that the whole of
medieval history is not a mere preparation for the dramatic
glories of the seventeenth and eighteenth centuries. If she
has somewhat to learn from her neighbours, surely we cannot
afford to say that we have not much to learn from her ; much
to hope for, and much to be grateful for, in the co-operation
of her scholars.

There are signs too of a harvest and promises of co-operation in another field which for several centuries has had little community or sympathy with English students. We have all probably been surprised, pleased,—may I not say amused?— by the consequences of the inaugural lecture of the Professor of International Law; at the chorus of praise and harmony between Italian and English lawyers which followed the note struck by him in the mention of Albericus Gentilis. The very fact that Albericus Gentilis was almost forgotten in England and had scarcely been heard of before in Italy, only proves that there was a latent desire of recognition among the Italian literati with which we had scarcely credited them. Now a very great deal may be hoped for from an awakened spirit of this kind, more especially when we remember the enormous mass of historical material which lies ready in Italy for the researches of competent scholars. It would be a waste of words if I were to attempt even to enumerate the treasures which must exist in Rome itself, in the Papal archives, where are, or should be found, the records of that great court of review and international arbitration which the medieval see of Rome claimed to hold. Much has no doubt perished, but much must remain ; much does remain, as the labours of Theiner have shown, to shed new light on the history of remoter Europe. The Church History of the extreme North, of Norway, Iceland, Sweden, Britain, of the Slavonic lands also, has been already illustrated. What could be more remote or insignificant than the Manx Church ? Yet Dr. Munch succeeded in extracting from the Vatican archives matter which settles the main question of her history, on which we had no record. Throughout the middle ages every great event, nay, every small event, that in the remotest way pretended to public interest, was discussed at Rome ; every great power had a diplomatic agency there; every leading or aspiring statesman had there an agent and probably a paid patron. It is not only in the records of the great public offices of Rome, but in the libraries of the princely families which furnished so long the cardinals and confidential ministers of the Papal See, that new matter will be found. The researches of Dr. Brady, the printed results of which I have not seen, but some part of which I saw in MS., brought out of the note-books and diaries of the cardinals of the Elizabethan period, not merely some most important personal and chronological details relative to the English episcopate, but revealed an almost unsuspected web of papal intrigue underlying the better known public action of the popes. Where Dr. Brady, who was working with a definite purpose and not very impartial judgment, stumbled on so much that was valuable, surely much more would be found by a fully equipped investigator. The prizes of this initial research have not fallen to English scholars. Rome is a long way off; English scholars are looked on with suspicion there ; even Dr. Todd was not left to work freely and alone in the Vatican : English visitors on a holiday have far too much else to do ; the endowment of research has not yet advanced far enough to send searchers thither. So it was left for Cardinal Mai to discover and edit the long-lost and long-lamented *Draco Normannicus*, the poetical biography of the Empress Matilda, which was printed by him apparently without any knowledge of its history, but was not published until seventeen years after his death, and in 1871, owing to a review by Dr. Pauli in the *Academy*, was introduced to English scholars. It was a German that discovered, and it is French scholars who are editing that early French poem on the Crusade of Richard I which is said, I believe with certainty, to be the original upon which the Latin author of the *Itinerarium Regis Ricardi* based his work. Just so it was the labours of Dr. Pertz and his agents that unearthed the *Historia Pontificalis* of John of Salisbury among the MSS. of the Bern Library, as he had espied the long-lost *Encomium Emmae* in the library of the Duke of Hamilton. No doubt luck is an element in these discoveries, but a far more powerful element of success was the educated eye, the larger opportunity, the knowledge how to look, and what sort of things to look for. I should not despair of discovering even the lost *Antiocheis*, the poem of Joseph of Exeter on the first Crusade, when the Vatican has proved a safe refuge for a Latin poem on the prophecies of Merlin and for the fragments of Giraldus Cambrensis.

Let us, it may be said, ascertain our own stores first, catalogue our own collections, ascertain what really is contained in the vast collections of Sir Thomas Phillipps and Lord Ashburnham, ransack the muniment rooms of Belvoir and Ripley, and the records of the cathedrals and church courts, before we go to Rome. It is by no means necessary that either should take precedence of the other; but the opportunities for Italian research are enlarging daily, and it is of great importance to catch the chances whilst they are yet new, and engage the co-operation of willing agents before they weary of the work, or fall back into the jealousies and obstructive ways which have so long debarred English students from their treasures.

Whilst we rejoice in the prospect that Italian scholars and scholarship, libraries and charter rooms, are likely to be open to us more generally, we may, I think, congratulate ourselves on having been able to do something for our Northern neighbours. The Icelandic Dictionary and the new recension of the *Sturlunga Saga*, which we have now in hand at the Press under the editorship of our friend Mr. Vigfusson, is surely an earnest of something yet to come. We are not so entirely disinterested in making these offerings to our Scandinavian kinsfolk: true we do not expect to make great discoveries of MSS. treasures, although there are far more unlikely places than Drontheim and Upsala; but we hope to attract new friends to the study of our own history and theirs, the common points of external and internal development which the English here have with their kinsmen and the neighbours of their ancient home.

And whilst we look with hope and gratitude to these elder kinsfolk, we look with hope and gratitude too to our more modern cousins across the Atlantic. Why American historians like Prescott, Ticknor and Motley have chosen Belgian and Spanish History as their special field of work, it is not for me to decide. Possibly it is for the best, and the conviction that it is for the best for them to work in fields in which they are less liable to be entangled in the political quarrels, and made obnoxious to the political feelings of their own country and time, may have determined their choice. If an Englishman cannot write without prejudice about the Rebellion and the Commonwealth, much less can an American. But it is, I take it, a misfortune that the earlier English History has not received its share of attention in the United States. Very much of English life was ripe when it was transplanted thither, and belongs as much almost to them as to ourselves. Judging from the letters of friends and the American reviews of English books, I conceive that this is being amended, and that we may soon have reason to rejoice that American acuteness and industry are applying themselves to this region in which they will find so much to profit both themselves and us. The wonderful and successful labours of Colonel Chester in the minuter department of genealogical research, which have produced so noble a book as his Register of Westminster Abbey, may be another earnest of co-operation that will produce good fruits both here and there. We know that we are kinsfolk, that we have thirteen centuries of common Christian History and culture, and a remoter past common to a much larger family: we may hope that with a fair acquaintance with one another we may diverge no more widely, and never have to be ashamed of our connexion.

I must ask you to pardon me for making these remarks so desultory and so discursive, on the solemn occasion of a public lecture. I need hardly repeat that such solemn occasions are not the most congenial portion of my work here. But I have had somewhat to say, and you must take it as I could say it. If another ten years should see me here, solemnly lecturing from this desk, I shall have no doubt to look back on some anticipations frustrated, and to welcome fuller new opportunities which will have presented themselves. But neither occasional disappointment, nor distaste for peculiar parts of my work, will, I may venture to say, damp the ardour of my hopes for the future of historical study here, or my faith in the permanence and development of a great historical school in England, which will look to Oxford as an 'Alma Mater' and 'Fons Scientiarum.'

IV.

ON THE PURPOSES AND METHODS OF
HISTORICAL STUDY.

(May 15, 1877.)

L AST year, in fulfilment of my statutable obligation to
deliver two solemn lectures annually on some subject of
modern history or political biography, I took occasion of the
fact that I was just completing my tenth year of service as
Professor, to discuss some of the more obvious phenomena
which had, during the preceding ten years, marked the progress
of Historical Study in Oxford first and in Europe generally. As
is invariably the case when one has written a book or made a
speech, subsequent reflexion, after no long time, brings home
to one the conviction that, besides saying much that were
better unsaid, one has left out very much that ought to have
been said if the intention were to be realised with which the
discussion was attempted. In this particular instance, I
confess, one whole region of my subject was left out of sight:
my object, indeed, was principally to view the extension and
advance of the study, and it was only incidentally that I felt
called upon to say a word here and there on the method and
purposes of it. But, judging from the utterances which have
recently, both before and after the delivery of those two lectures,
fallen from the mouths of some of the most clever and cultivated
men of this generation, it would appear that the method and
purpose of historical reading were points by no means second in
interest to the external development of the study of history.

These utterances are in themselves valuable as the mature
judgments of men who have at all events known how to draw
from history precious lessons on the subjects on which they
desired to be taught; but they have an additional value in

setting plainly before us, teachers of history, the views which popular opinion and the men who lead popular opinion upon educational matters formulate regarding the pursuit to which we have devoted ourselves. To us a great many of the statements as well as of the theories that find enthusiastic echoes in mixed audiences, are apt to appear either truisms, or fallacies, or both. In many of them there is an apologetic tone which reminds us to some extent of what we used to hear in common rooms when our History school was first started, as if the study was one that needed some vindication as a bona fide study, valuable in itself and in its results, before it could be allowed to compete with other older and more organised departments of learning. And, as usual, when that is defended which needs no defence, the theories of the advocate produce an effect diametrically opposite to that which he intended ; he seems to hazard on the strength of some occasional or adventitious argument the claim which on its own merits is indisputable. Now far be it from me to attempt even to gather up or analyse, much less to review, the deliberate and elaborate utterances to which I have referred. I am not going to answer or to refute them where they need refutation, or to use them to strengthen my own theories where I agree with them : it may be enough to say that many of them contain good and sound suggestions which recommend themselves as soon as they are heard ; that others are familiar as lecture-room words to all who have any experience in teaching ; and that the worst that can be justly said of any of them is that they prescribe, for the general pursuit of the whole study of History, directions which are valuable in their way in relation to particular portions of it, or for particular purposes for which it may have been undertaken. Instead of reviewing them, then, I shall simply accept them as furnishing suggestions for a brief discussion on points on which it is my privilege to speak, and yours to judge whether what I have to say is worth saying. For I also will claim it as a professorial right to be allowed to utter truisms, and will claim, moreover, as one advantage accruing from our common heritage of error, that, if I utter fallacies, I may have the sympathy of men who know how easy it is, in matters where head and heart are alike engaged, to disparage truth by exaggeration.

Although I am not going to venture on any philosophical arrangement of my topics, or to lay down anything pretending to be a complete theory of the method of historical study, I will begin by saying that there are, as it seems to me, and as I doubt not it seems to you, three different sorts of object or aim in reading History: it may be read for its own sake, it may be learned as a mental discipline, and it may be acquired as a piece of the furniture or apparatus of cultivated life. I have used the words advisedly, for they imply, with diversity of object, diversity of method also. In the first aspect History assumes the dignity of a science, in the second it is a great engine of education, in the third it is in its higher forms a graceful and useful accomplishment, in its lower an indispensable requisite for every-day existence in a civilised country.

The three aims are not by any means incompatible, and the results are of course coincident so far as they go. He who reads History for its own sake gains the educational result in the process, and possesses in the fullest way the stock of knowledge which enables him to read his newspaper, to give his vote, or to pass his opinion on any new book. The man who has gone through the educational training will likewise be able to do these things, besides benefiting by that disciplinary and formative process that qualifies him to give a sound historical judgment on passing events. And it is no small advantage to be able to give an honest, really intelligent vote and to take an interest in a really interesting book. Only, the man who has only read History for the purpose of education has not entered into the fulness of the blessing of the man who reads it for its own sake, and the man who has learned it as he learns French or German from a travelling conversation book, does not gain either the formative effect on the judgment, or the great inheritance of scientific study. These points need no insisting upon; I merely state them to set us clear at starting, and to point out that the method which may be with advantage adopted for one of these purposes will not be applicable for the other two;

popular lectures may serve admirably to the third object, but
be absolutely useless as regards the second ; careful study of
isolated periods may suffice for the second, but will not satisfy
the instincts that are aroused in the pursuit of the first.   But
I will not anticipate what ought to come later on.

In the distinction that I have drawn you will no doubt
recognise your old friends, the professorial, the tutorial, and the
popular view of history.   I will so far admit the charge as to
arrogate to myself the professorial right to make the first the
largest half of my discussion, and devote this lecture to the
first point, leaving the other two for the second.   But there
is a prior question, prior even to the assumption that History
should be studied for its own sake,—Is it worth studying at all?
As I have said, the apologetic tone of many of its advocates
renders it necessary that I should at once state why it needs
no vindication.   If man is not, as we believe, the greatest
and most wonderful of God's works, he is at least the most
wonderful that comes within our contemplation ; if the human
will, which is the motive cause of all historical events, is not
the freest agent in the universe, it is at least the freest agency
of which we have any knowledge ; if its variations are not
absolutely innumerable and irreducible to classification, on the
generalisations of which we may formulate laws and rules, and
maxims and prophecies, they are far more diversified and less
reducible than any other phenomena in those regions of the
universe that we have power to penetrate.   For one great
insoluble problem of astronomy or geology there are a thousand
insoluble problems in the life, in the character, in the face of
every man that meets you in the street.   Thus, whether we
look at the dignity of the subject-matter, or at the nature of
the mental exercise which it requires, or at the inexhaustible
field over which the pursuit ranges, History, the knowledge
of the adventures, the development, the changeful career, the
varied growths, the ambitions, aspirations, and, if you like,
the approximating destinies of mankind, claims a place second
to none in the roll of sciences.   Arising from one of the first
and most anciently cultivated instincts, the desire to know
how we come to be what we are, and how the world comes to

be what it is, the love of history is certainly second in origin to no other sort of love of knowledge. As a search for truth it tries to investigate matters in which the truth may be more difficult to find than it is in mere matters of observation or deduction, but surely its difficulty is not an argument for its disparagement ; as a hoarding up of knowledge, it collects facts and records, the results of which are less exact than those of strict science, but are not less precious even in the eyes of the man who would regard them as mere engines of power.   It is not true that written history is a mere tradition of falsehoods, assumptions and illogical deductions, of what the writers believed, rather than of what they knew, and of what they wished to have believed rather than what was true ; even if it were, it would be no reason why we should not do our best to unmask the falsehood and detect the fallacies. But we have all heard enough of that sort of thing before ; there is, in the most exact science that has subject-matter at all, a mixture of the phenomenal and the real : even the falsehoods and misrepresentations of the record serve as a guide to the discovery of the truth of fact, and certainly serve to train the mind to distinguish historical truth.

Agreeing, then, that both for the great extent of its field of view, the grandeur of its subject-matter, the difficulty of its problems, and the value of its results, the study of history is worth pursuing ; and that, for its own sake, not merely for its effects as an educational agent, or its usefulness in the business of life,—we may allow that, even for its own sake, it may be studied with some variety of aspect or approach. We may work simply for the love of discovery, that is the exercise of the investigative instinct and the pleasure of over-coming difficulties ; or we may work with the beneficent idea of increasing the sum of human knowledge, or of unravel-ling the string which forms the clue to the history of human progress, or of making such generalisations as may constitute the laws of a new historic science.   All these, and perhaps some other purposes may be arranged under our first head, because, although some of them may seem subsidiary to larger and wider general designs, they all have in common the belief in the real value of history itself. Of these purposes, the mere gratification of curiosity, even in its highest and most dignified form, ranks first and lowest; and yet without some infusion of it the genuine love of history is out of the question; and the usefulness of it, even in the humble office of providing materials for men who work with a higher purpose and idea, cannot be gainsaid. The mere archæologist, the mere genealogist, the mere antiquary, are not the parasites of historical study, as they are too often regarded by men who find it easier to borrow than to estimate the results of their researches; they are working bees in the hive of historic knowledge.

And the curious fact that the contemptuous toleration of archæological research is very often found in the speeches and writings of men who profess to set a high value on the study of original sources, a fact so curious as to lead to the conclusion that the critic is dealing on both hands with unknown quantities, may serve to lead on to the question— What are, and what is the value of the study of, original sources? We hear a great deal about them at the present day; not only are our bookshelves actually broken down with the weight of them, but the exact study of them is becoming a subordinate science with method and rules of its own, and with a great apparatus of material appliances in the shape of palæographical tests; a science of historical palmistry, if that is the word, that attempts to refer, by distinctions of penmanship, parchment, paper, ink, illumination and abbreviation, every manuscript to its own country, district, age, school, and even individual writer. Truly we may say the study of Geschichtsquellen is not to be approached without clean hands and an open mind. And after the initial investigation comes the criticism; first we have to identify, then we have to value our historical inventory. Both these processes are involved in the study of original sources; it means not merely the reading, or the restriction of reading to, the primary authorities, but the weighing and critical analysis of the primary authorities themselves.

Perhaps you think that I am misusing terms when I speak of analysing primary authorities, but I will explain directly what I mean; only a word first on the interest and value of the processes I refer to. If I were drawing a comparison between ancient and medieval and modern history as remunerative studies, this is probably the first point in which I should claim superior interest for the latter. In ancient history we have wonderful models of thoughtful writing, and ingenious record of primitive tradition, tradition at least that is so far primitive that to us no further analysis is possible. There are exceptional departments even here; recent discoveries in Assyriology and Egyptology are opening up regions of interest which appear to me to be absolutely beyond parallel or comparison; new records of most ancient life which not only lie out of the scope within which criticism, up to the last twenty or thirty years, confined itself, but which must, if they be approached with due reverence and delicacy of touch, reveal a strange and hitherto unread age of the world's History, and in it the springs of an older cultivation than we have been used to dwell upon, and the links that bind the great civilisations of the Western world with the earliest, but not perhaps less magnificent, civilisations of the East. In these we may hope one day to read a new and clear page of the fair record of human history, of which we have bright but unconnected glimpses in the incidental notices of Holy Scripture. But outside of these, and the study of them is to most of us only in its beginning, the study of ancient History is mainly the study of classical History; and in classical History, splendid as our materials are, they have been in our hands for ages. Every bone of the great skeleton has long been put into its place : criticism upon it is becoming more and more every year the rearrangement of the critical material collected long ago, or the reconstruction of the History with all the charm which novel treatment, without novel material, can supply. Unluckily we can only, in a very fragmentary way, trace back, in commenting on Herodotus or Livy, the actual line of tradition by which they received what they report to us ; as to Thucydides and Tacitus the chain is less fragmentary, and, of course, in the narrative of contemporary writers we look less for traces of earlier authority than for traces of sympathy and antipathy, personal knowledge and direct authenticity.   But, as a rule, we may say the study of ancient classical History lies within a confined area, every manuscript, every inscription, every coin, and every map of which has long been known, into which rash speculation never ventures without having cause for bitter repentance, and in which anything like a new discovery, such as the recent finds at Troy and Mycenæ, is so very new, that when it does come to pass no one knows what to make of it.   The very definiteness of all connected with this study makes it, for educational purposes, an incomparable discipline.   As a study of knowledge for its own sake, as a field of discovery and profitable speculation, as a department in which the sum of human knowledge is likely to be largely increased, I confess I think that it promises perhaps less than the study of later History.   As a ground for fresh and remunerative exploration, I am sure it is still less promising.

To return, however, to the original sources.   We all know how large a debt modern and medieval History owes to the ecclesiastical writers.   From the very beginning of the middle ages, Annals, Chronicles, and Histories poured in comparative abundance from the religious houses of England and the Continent, records which serve to check and correct one another at almost every turn, and which, for some of the more dramatic incidents of History, enable us to reconstruct a picture of the event, viewed by different minds from different points and in different lights, in a perfection which has no parallel at all in ancient history.   Such, for instance, is the picture of the life and death of Becket ; some great scenes in the life of Simon de Montfort ; some portions of the history of the Norman Conquest.   I mention these, not only because they are well known, but because they lie within the region for our knowledge of which we are altogether indebted to ecclesiastical writers.   Now these ecclesiastical writers have for the most part two great points of interest in the direction of research.   All, or almost all, are members of religious houses, and all are members of a great fraternity in close and direct correspondence.   The annalist is the annalist of his monastery or his cathedral; his monastery or his cathedral has had a history, has records, charters, a library, a scriptorium for multiplying copies of record, perhaps a school of annalists of which the representative man appropriates and assimilates the labours. He is a member of a great fraternity of newsmongers; every visitor to the monastery, every pilgrim, every journey of the abbot or bishop up to parliament, every letter from abroad, contributes something to the multifarious store. Such a chronicle as that of Matthew Paris contains every one of those elements and perhaps more; he was an antiquary, zealous of the history and fame of his own monastery, skilled in charters and in everything bearing on its origin and growth, the position of its estates, and the character of its inmates: he was a compiler who appropriated and digested the work of a whole school of earlier annalists; he was an eye-witness of much that he records of contemporary history, acquainted with the great men of the day; he had travelled and learned much, he had stayed at home and learned more, asking questions of every one who came down that way. Matthew Paris is an original authority; but what a fine subject for analysis; what an admirable corpus for the Kritik der Quellen! Further back you have what is called the Anglo-Saxon Chronicle; one of the first set of books that was subjected to the process of speculative analysis, now fifty years ago, by a gentleman who dissected it out of his own consciousness. Our Professor of Anglo-Saxon has shown us what may be done in a part of the field of criticism on the Chronicle, by study of a small number of MSS. and dialectic differences. But there is still probably, in the region of Cartularies and Acta Sanctorum, and in the more minute study of other MSS., something to be done even for this. I may perhaps be allowed to point to my own edition of the Dunstan Memorials as showing, not any completeness of treatment, for I do not pretend to have effected that, but the singular variety and peculiar interest of the fields of investigation in which new discoveries may be expected.

This sort of study has two great charms, besides the value of the results; in common, to compare small things with great, with the discoveries of natural science—botany, for instance. In one way we take a historical series of events and work out the known items of the series, and range the persons and places of our action, until we know where to look for the missing links, and go to look for them and find them. Such a success, and every student of original sources working with zeal and modesty may hope for such, is in a small way like that of the astronomer who, when from calculating the perturbations and so on of the heavenly bodies he has inferred the existence of a hitherto unknown planet, some bright evening and with a new improved glass discovers the real planet of which he has been thinking, and sees in it, not only a great new fact of science, but a proof of the correctness of his computations, a substantial reward for his efforts. And the other is that in every such search, be it successful or not, the inquirer, who is wide awake, is sure to come upon material that is even more valuable than what he looks for; makes discoveries that are not less delightful because they are accidental.

Of course it may be said that a great deal of useless knowledge is accumulated in this way; what good can be done, it may be said, by analysing Matthew Paris, and determining how much of his narrative is drawn from ancient charters, or foreign letters, lives of saints, or such stribiligines: it is his historic power and authority that gives them value, not they that give authority to him. Not quite so, I think, and even if it were so, there might be a lesson in the mere proof of the fact; the analysis is necessary for the due estimate of his value as a historian; the writer who can pass such an ordeal where it is possible to apply it, may be trusted where it is not possible to apply it. But I take the higher ground and say, how far can any knowledge be said to be useless? there may be much useless learning, I allow; accumulations of other men's thoughts, and crude heaps of second-hand memories that are alike useless to their owner and to the world. But not real knowledge, not a substantiated fact, however remote it may seem from the interests and uses of the day, or the object of the day. It may serve to complete a chain of demonstration, the necessity of which is not as yet apparent; it may furnish,

as an undesigned coincidence, an important element in a discussion yet in its elementary stages.   How great is the debt
that History owes to the ant-like instincts of collectors of
memoranda, the recorders of births, deaths, and marriages, the
savers of old letters and old newspapers, of the very things
that seemed most useless.   If there is any useless knowledge
in History, we may say,—as Dr. Maitland said, when people
talked of the Dark Ages, they meant the ages that were dark
to them,—the uselessness of the knowledge is generally the
fault of those who do not know how to use it.

It would be doing great injustice, however, to my subject if
I were to lead you to suppose that I regard the great benefit
arising from the study of original materials to lie in the
gratification of our natural instinctive desire to get to the
bottom of a thing.   I suppose that such an instinct is given
us for some good end, and that that which lies at the bottom
of the historical well is historical truth : Truth that defies the
all-dissolving processes of criticism, or at least such an approach to truth as may be credited to a record incapable of
further analysis.   The results of such minute study are the
little pebbles of the concrete in which the foundations of the
historic superstructure are laid.   Every great historian
has been his own Dry-as-dust, however much he may, as
Carlyle does, point the moral of the lesson of labour with
small type and inverted commas ; for, I take it, the prophet
does not adopt this plan as a means of disguise, but rather to
show that to a great extent historical genius consists in an
unlimited capacity for taking pains.   The man who has, out
of independent study, produced such results, has made a contribution, small or great as the case may be, to the great stock
of sound material which constitutes real knowledge.

This consciousness may be its own reward ; but, as I said
before, if the love of history for its own sake goes no further, such ambition ranks among the lowest forms of the
historical spirit.   We take a real pleasure not only in cutting
out our sound and perfect stone, but in fitting it into its
place in the building : we wish to increase the sum of human
knowledge not only by the accumulation of facts but by fol-

lowing them up and making them a part of history. The
botanist is charmed when he finds a new plant, and the
astronomer when he discovers a new star, but we scarcely
should call the one a botanist or the other an astronomer if
he did not straightway go and fit in his discovery into
the general system of his science, reunite the missing plant
to its kinsfolk in genus, and species and variety, or find
out the relation of his star to the rest, and assign it to its
group and class in the map of the heavens. And I think that
the somewhat compassionate condescension with which archæological inquiry is now and then spoken of, and the study of
original sources also, is owing to the fact that so many inquirers do stop at some such point: hence it is that people
are constantly discovering things which have often been
discovered before, and trumpeting as new results of research
points of fact that have long been ticketed and set in their
places in books where they could easily have found them. The
study of original sources is thus taken to mean the study of
nothing else; a pursuit accordingly which has no other result
than the gratification, by a laborious process, of a curiosity
that might have been gratified by reference to a cyclopædia,
or the amount of training, not itself to be despised if it be
regarded merely as training, which makes the fact that one
has worked out for himself infinitely more precious than one
that he has simply looked out in the dictionary.

But I am not speaking now of the educational aspect of the
subject. Let it suffice to say, that original sources to be studied
remuneratively must be approached with all the apparatus and
all the appliances that previous inquirers have accumulated for the
illustration of them. If that be not done, we shall share the fate
of the astronomer who searches for a new planet with the naked
eye, and the mathematician who discovers perpetual motion.

And so we may go on to another point. The student of
History, for its own sake, may approach his subject with
the desire of adding to the mass of human knowledge by
the ascertaining of truths hitherto imperfectly apprehended;
the completing of series of developments, or delineations of
character, or the explanations of out-of-the-way regions, or

the rehabilitation and analysis of traditions. In these points
he has a wide field of interest, and a most remunerative sphere
of study in exercise and result.

But here we come upon another primary question, Is all
History equally valuable?   You may say to me, we have
accepted your assertion that no knowledge is useless, except by
the fault of the person who possesses it ; but it does not follow
that all is equally useful or equally valuable in itself.   What
history is the best worth studying for its own sake ?   Now
to answer that question fully would take a long time, and
involve a discussion, not only on the nature of History, but on
its co-ordination with other branches of human knowledge,
such as moral philosophy and theology, carrying us into
regions into which I cannot offer to guide you, and must
refer you to the philosophers.   But if you will be satisfied
with a simple answer, I will say that the true field of Historic
study is the history of those nations and institutions in which
the real growth of humanity is to be traced : in which we can
follow the developments, the retardations and perturbations,
the ebb and flow of human progress, the education of the
world, the leading on by the divine light from the simplicity
of early forms and ideas where good and evil are distinctly
marked, to the complications of modern life, in which light
and darkness are mingled so intimately, and truth and falsehood are so hard to distinguish, but in which we believe and
trust that the victory of light and truth is drawing nearer
every day.   The most precious Histories are those in which we
read the successive stages of God's dispensations with man,
the growth of the highest natures, under the most favourable
circumstances, in the most fully developed institutions, in the
successive contributions which those natures, regions and institutions have furnished to the general welfare of the whole.

But I can hear at least one critic say, Is not this assuming
the truth of a doctrine that you are always practically deny-
ing, that the very designation of your professorship, your very
raison d'être, forces you to deny—the Unity of History, the
Continuity of Historic growth, the Education of the world ?
Well, if the Unity of History means what I have said, I

certainly believe in it: but that is not the meaning which is commonly attached to the term, and it is not the meaning in which I have so often had to do battle with the idea. The false idea, or that which to me seems practically misleading in the term the Unity of History, is the acceptance as a practical rule or maxim that there are no new points of departure in human history; that modern life is a continuation of medieval, of ancient and medieval, history, by a continuity and unity that is at all points equally important, of the same consistency in fact. Now this idea has a truth only in the very highest regions of speculation. Every human soul has an equal value in the eyes of the Christian missionary and religious philosopher, but every human life does not convey lessons of the same practical value to the social investigator; every national history does not contribute equally valuable results towards the general progress of mankind, and so neither does every chronological epoch. That perhaps we all allow. Why then should not cycles of history, two, three, or more cycles of history, be allowed to exist, within which all the really important factors have their origin and development, and, it may be, work out their full destiny; successive great dramas of ages, the interest of which is self-contained, although there is enough of common ground between them and those which precede and follow to give them a simple continuity, and although there is doubtless in the divine mind one great plan of cosmical action in which each drama of the human ages serves as a single act or even a single incident? Let scripture history, classical and ecclesiastical history, medieval history and modern history, be read successively and connectedly, so much the better; but why deny that classical history and medieval and modern can be advantageously studied apart? why confine the thoughts to the points on which they are conterminous, continuous and agreed, to the exclusion of those in which they differ, when it is on the points in which they differ that the great contributions to the real history of man are to be traced? In any other sense than that in which I have attempted to limit it and have accepted it, the Unity of History is either the crotchet of a sciolist, or the dream of a universal philosopher.

For just think how the field of view expands; we can never know one thing perfectly unless we know everything; true, but we can try to learn here and there a thing as perfectly as it can be learned, without knowing everything. In the same sense in which the careful study of ancient history is absolutely necessary to the careful study of modern history, the careful study of the latter is absolutely necessary to that of the former. If you read the second alone, where do you find your causes? If you read the first alone, where do you find your consequences? Just in the same way, it may be said, the external history of man cannot be read without an internal reading of his history; no man can approach History without being a consummate moral philosopher; yet is it so? Then most of the great historians of the world have been great moral philosophers without knowing it. But how can a man pretend to understand the moral conformation of his fellows without knowing their physical conformation? Then the moral philosopher must be an anatomist, and the anatomist a chemist, a botanist and geologist, and the geologist an astronomer; i.e. instead of borrowing, and being content to borrow from the kindred and allied sciences what is necessary for the consistent pursuit of our own study, we must know the principles of all, like the sophists of old, and we all know what that ends in, κακῶς ἠπίστατο πάντα. But my friend says, exaggeration is no argument, an answer which, by-the-by, may tell either way: ancient, and modern and medieval history, as you call them, have the same subject-matter, they are connected by certain visible and tangible lines of recorded fact, and they are, as yourself admit, acts of one great drama. Granted: first then, ancient history has much that is common with modern in the region of political thought; second then, the ancient Roman civilisation and literature constitute by themselves, and they are but one of many, a sufficient line of continuity to prove essential identity; third, but it is enough for you to admit the continuity of the world's progress.

Now, if I were arguing against the reading of ancient history in connexion with modern, such an answer would be complete; but, as I am merely protesting against the idea that it is impossible to read modern history from its own starting-point, I will observe, and content myself with observing, first that there are no doubt political thoughts common to ancient and modern life; nay more, that, as has been said, there is very much that is modern in ancient history and much that is ancient in modern history; and yet that that very element of continuity on which the whole discussion hangs is wanting. There may be, I will not say there is, a certain similarity of thought in a leading article of *The Times* and a chapter in Thucydides : the similarity of the circumstances of two political crises may bring out parallels and coincidences ; Constantinople may be the Athens, Alexander II the Xerxes of the day, and anyhow the Bosphorus must be pretty nearly where it was. But the connexion of the political ideas is one of coincidence and not of continuity ; there is not even the life that germinates in the grains of wheat found in Egyptian mummy-pits. Every factor is new, even the area, the nationality of the actors, the whole idea in its origin and every stage of growth is new. Or let the area be the same; what has modern Greece in continuity with ancient Greece, but the soil and sky and the, to it, unintelligible wreck of ancient magnificence, from which it fails apparently to draw even the ordinary lessons of civilisation : what period and region of the whole history of the world conveys a less important lesson than Greece during the Middle Ages of European History ? It is scarcely less so with Italy, except for the fact that during a great part of those ages Italy was the centre and stage of Ecclesiastical History, in which, as I shall point out directly, and in which alone on any large or broad scale, the unity and continuity are to be found.

The vital interest of Medieval and Modern History lies in England, France and Germany, as certainly as that of the ancient lies in the East, in Greece and Italy ; no small part of that of the future lies in the further Western world. The actors in the medieval and. modern drama are the new nations, nations that were unheard of before the decline of the Roman empire began, and which inherited from the civilisation of that empire only the ecclesiastical culture, not the political system, or even the political map, which that system had laid out. The ideas of medieval and modern life are of medieval and modern growth, or if connected with antiquity, connected by a new birth of culture, a re-discovery, a re-creation, not a continuous impulse of vitality. Save in the one region, that of the History of Religion, Ecclesiastical History ; yet in that also the one great fact of the Christian dispensation, which connects the ancient Hebrew isolation with the great Catholic Church life, is itself as much a break as a link of continuity ; so immensely does the new transcend the old, that, in the apostle's words, old things are passed away and behold all things are become new. The Unity and Continuity of Ancient and Modern History is an idea which is realised on a great and intelligible scale in Ecclesiastical History only; and even there the unity is to some extent a unity of ideas, a coincidence of religious and moral motive influences, and not merely of historic continuity. It is in it that the continuity of the Latin civilisation, of the Holy Roman Empire and of the Latin language, Roman Law and Latin literature, is traceable, and to it that we owe them. To it, or to influences which it nourished or provoked, we owe the renaissance, that revival of ancient culture the very title of which is a denial of the continuity which its influences seem to claim for it. But I am not going to usurp the functions of a Professor of Church History, and I am very sure that Church History is not the ground on which the doctrine of the Unity of History is supposed by its advocates to take its stand.

One word more ; I do not deny this Unity in the high region of religious History or in the scarcely less comprehensive grasp which the political philosopher may take of Universal Human Life ; nor do I deny it in the minute archæological investigations in which all particulars great and small have much the same value ; nor do I deny that the student of modern history may gain lessons of immense value from the old. But I do maintain that it is wrong to say that the one cannot be studied without the other ; for the things, persons, ideas, plot and scenery are different in the two ; and more than that, save in the region of Church History, the

precious lessons of the two are not those in which the approxi-
mate continuity may be traced: the continuity lies in the less important, the great contributions of either to the world's growth
lie in the less continuous influences; in the ancient world in
a perished civilisation, in the modern world in one in which
all the fresh springs are, by God's grace, in the new races.

You will, I hope, acquit me now of any desire to undervalue any kind of culture; but, put upon our defence, we must
maintain the strong point, as it seems to us, of our position;
and it is our duty, as well as our right, to say what we think.
Most successful teachers of Modern History have passed
through the gate of the ancient lore; but if they would look
the truth in the face, they would see that the help which that
ancient lore gave to the study of the modern, was first in the
discipline of the mind, for which it furnishes an incomparable
exercise, and secondly in the wealth of illustration with which
it provides them; but the illustrations are not links in an
historic chain, and the fact that the discipline of the mind has
been beneficial by no means implies that the powers cultivated
in the two studies are the same, or the method of the one
applicable without much modification to the exploration of the
other. And this is a point which is scarcely less important
than the more ostensible and obvious one on which I have
dwelt so long.

The method of historic investigation is different in the
two or three regions which we have been comparing. Of
that I have said something in reference to original sources,
and I may have to say something more in reference to
the educational view of Historic study. I will not therefore dwell upon it now; but rest content to base my argument on what I have said; that is, the Unity and Continuity are only traceable in the high regions which belong to
other sciences and other studies, or in the lower departments
of minute archæology; it is well to abstract, and well to make
our own generalisations in the realms that are common to the
two, but it is a poor result if, after fixing our thoughts on the
things in which they agree and excluding those in which they
differ, we find that we have come to generalisations that might

be discovered by intuition and cast away differences in which all that is new and true and precious was inherent.

But thus I come to the region of abstractions and generalisations, and to the old question, How about the science of History? As I hope I made clear before, I do not intend this lecture to be a systematic exposition of my own views or any one else's; and I certainly do not intend to attempt an analysis of History as the subject-matter of a science or philosophy. I am only trying, if possible, to adjust my own impressions to the maxims of our theoretical instructors, and to say a word or two on subjects which recent discussions suggest. It certainly seems curious that, although the advocates of the Unity and Continuity of History, and the believers in the science and philosophy of History, imagine themselves to be diametrically opposed to one another, the weakness of their respective positions seems to be the same. Both prefer to work out generalisations and collect coincidences, rather than to study the drama in its plot and personnel; both decline to look at the subject, as we might say, all round. It is true that this is a fault of theory rather than of practice: a really good historian may, as we all know, combine an earnest faith in the Unity of History with a power of creating most exact and minute reproductions of periods, scenes and characters; and such an advocate might almost convince us of the truth of his doctrine, because his practice is so completely free from the faults which that doctrine seems to the outside critic to involve. I am perhaps in error too on the other side, in speaking of the Science of History and the Philosophy of History in one breath; for certainly there is a Philosophy of History which is not content with abstractions, but busies itself with following up causes and following out consequences, goes behind the scenes of the drama as well as directs a microscopic vigilance on the stage; and there is a sense in which the Unity of History is itself a Philosophy of History. I will then leave out the Philosophy of History, and finish the lecture with a few words on the theory of a science of History.

Shall I be saying too much if I say at once that one great objection to the very idea of reducing History to the lines and rules of exact science lies in the fact I have already stated, that generalisations become obscurer and more useless as they grow wider, and, as they grow narrower and more special, cease to have any value as generalisations at all. Is not a historical science liable, if it can be elaborated at all, to become on the one hand a mere table of political formulæ and on the other a case-book of political casuistry? And, in either case, is it not as a mere political weapon that it is sought for, not as an increase of knowledge, not as an investigation of truth, nor as a study of History for its own sake? And is not the fact that the idea of a science of History finds acceptance, not among practical historians, but among high-paced theorists, a proof that such a possibility belongs to theory and not to practice ; that it is aimed at as a new grace for the all-accomplished doctrinaire, rather than as an object to be sought by those who seek after wisdom ?

There were days, centuries ago, when the schoolmen fancied that they could bring into class and line all human knowledge, and encroach to some extent upon the divine, by syllogisms and conversions and oppositions. Much precious knowledge those men handed down to us, with much verbiage and false logic ; but even they for the most part left History alone. They ticketed every portion of man's moral anatomy, found a rule for every possible case of choice, a reason and a reward for every virtue, and a punishment for every conceivable crime ; they turned generalisations into laws, and deduced from them as laws the very facts from which they had generalised. They benefited mankind by exercising and training subtle wits, and they reduced dialectics, almost, we might say, logic itself, to absurdity. I do not undervalue them, because the great men among them were so great that even such a method did not destroy them : in reading Thomas Aquinas, for instance, one is constantly provoked to say, What could not such a mind have done if it had not been fettered by such a method ?

Such, I imagine, must be the result of every attempt to substitute abstract reasonings for minute examination of facts in the study of History. History repeats itself we know, parallels and cycles recur, the speculative mind can evaluate the curve in which political progress moves, trace the contortions of the unruly spiral, and eschew a cusp as a historic anomaly. But the dealings of human wills, in countless combinations, and circumstances which no theory can ever exhaustively calculate, are not the field for dogmatic assumption or for speculative classification. Perhaps you may think that I am talking at random, that no people ever were so foolish as to suppose that even an exhaustive knowledge of past history could enable a man to prophesy; for such should be the result of a scientific treatment, even if the subject-matter be akin rather to the subject-matter of meteorology than to that of astronomy. It may be so; but the idea is not strange. Experience of life, it is argued, qualifies us for dealing with men; knowledge of human history must qualify us for calculating on the results of even historical contingencies; the practical politician can arrange the factors of his problem so as to work out the solution beforehand; the theoretic explorer of History may so manipulate his factors as to provide for every conceivable combination. Again, I say, it may be so; but not in the regions of life that are worthy of real study; vague generalisations may form the stock-in-trade of the political empiric, but he is an empiric notwithstanding; readiness of observation and fertility of expedient, political genius, the power that interprets events and realises character and motive, are not the result of abstraction even from universal reading.

I grant that genius may do great things with poor instruments and out of small materials. But the scientific triumphs of genius all imply minute knowledge as well as the power of grasping the idea. Owen, from a single bone, could reproduce an entire archaic animal, the real existence of which later discovery vindicated: in that great exploit of scientific genius, there was not only consummate grasp of the idea but enormous knowledge of mechanical anatomy: he did not elaborate the beast out of his own consciousness, nor make a lucky guess; but he looked at his bone all round, and saw its mechanical capabilities, and realised the idea which only could explain the possession of such capa-

bilities. So, to some extent, the historical genius can reconstruct character. From a very incomplete study of History
Scott could create a Richard, the truth of whose portraiture
careful historical scrutiny seems to assure. Out of an enormous amount of material, Carlyle reconstructs for us Frederick
William I of Prussia, a living, moving, tantalising reality.
In both there is the eye and the hand of genius, different as
is the workmanship, distinct as is the result. But although
genius can reconstruct character, it cannot reconstruct events :
it flashes its lightning into the dark, and for the moment we
see battles and alliances, life and death, growth and decline of
heroes, cities and nations ; but it would require many such
flashes to produce one permanent impression ; and for even an
approach to an understanding of the vision we must go down
and map out the land, photograph the heroes, and classify the
populations of the cities. Patient study may not have much
to do with genius ; it has less to do with generalisations : but
without patient study genius will flash with no productive
efficacy, and generalisations will become mere formulæ, useful
neither to teachers nor to learners, neither to statesmen nor to
scholars ; and even with patient study, what results? Surely
that scientific generalisations are but by-play diversions and
amusements, not real lessons : formulæ that are convenient
for a moment now and then, but quite unsafe as implements
of investigation or even as helps for memory : truisms, or
fallacies, or both : or if containing truth, or aiming at universality, diluting the truth until it is useless; assuming a
universality of rule which, when it comes to be applied, is
met with a universality of exception.

There is a ' One in History ' as a One in Nature, but it is
not shown to the man whose idea of science is confined to
making his inventory or ticketing compartments of his cabinet,
even if the mechanism of his museum be ever so complete,
unless he has studied and learned well the conformation
and individual histories of the specimens which he attempts
to classify. Sometimes men classify the specimens which
other men have collected, and claim the character of philosophers without any direct acquaintance with materials at all.

V.

METHODS OF HISTORICAL STUDY.

(May 18, 1877.)

IN my Lecture delivered the other day, in discharge of a
duty which, in the case of a Professor who is willing to
work, might well be dispensed with, I attempted to arrange
some few thoughts on the subject of Historical study which
had occurred to me, on some sort of a plan, carefully dis-
avowing however any attempt at complete or even systematic
treatment; I used the division of the subject which I then
proposed, simply as furnishing pegs on which to hang divers
desultory observations. The principle of division which I
adopted was merely this; that we should view our subject in
three lights; first looking on the study of history as pursued
for its own sake, secondly regarding it as an instrument of
education or training of the mind, and thirdly regarding it
in reference to the ulterior uses to which the results of such
study could be most advantageously applied; in other
words, the student or professorial view, the educatorial or
tutorial view, and the popular or utilitarian view. Without,
as I said, attempting any systematic treatment, I made the
question of History for its own sake an occasion of saying
a word or two on the current ideas touching the study; the
investigation of original materials, the doctrine of the necessary unity and continuity of History, and the much-debated
possibility of the creation of a science of History, in the sense
of science which involves the discovery of general laws and
the classification of human wills and events out of which the
men of the future may prophesy. I have still the other two
heads of my division to trifle with, and, as it is now too late
to modify my plan, I can only ask for your tolerant attention
and proceed, in the hope that what I may have to say on the

practical work of the subject may be better worth saying than what I said on the theory of it, a speculation on speculations.

The first point to be stated in relation with the second head of discussion has merely to be stated; supposing that the study of History is useful as an educational instrument, that is, not only as providing stores of knowledge or amassing tools for future use, but as having a disciplinary and formative virtue, what part of the mind is it on which the disciplinary process acts, and what power or virtue may it be supposed to develope by training? It is perhaps unnecessary for me to say more than this, that I regard the judicial faculty, 'judgment,' as in vulgar unphilosophical language we call it, as that on which historical study produces the most valuable results; I have so often said this from this desk that I feel shy of repeating it; but it does not appear to me to be less true than it did the first time I said it. The study of the early stages of that history in whose later stages we know ourselves to be personally interested, the study of the modern world of which we are parts, as distinguished from that of the ancient world which, except as a matter of culture, is dead to us, affords room for the development of an equitable as well as an unbiassed judgment, which is a great advantage in itself and may be of great practical use in the world. The exclusive study of the more modern phases of history has a tendency to make men partisans or advocates; but the study of the periods just a generation or two further removed produces far more effect on the judgment; and the study of medieval History, that is, of the ages in which the things that are precious to us were rooted and sprang up, but had not yet entered into the phases in which controversy is most bitter, or in which the political questions of the day are most directly engaged, has always seemed to me to furnish very good training; to enable us to approach questions in which we are ourselves engaged, with moderate and cautious treatment, to allow some of them to wait for solution, to determine others by the evidence of fact rather than by prepossession, and to let others alone altogether. Ancient History exercises the critical faculty in a comparatively narrow and exhausted field, although, as a matter of training, every student has to go over the field and exhaust its interest for himself before he gets the benefit of what he is reading ; mere modern politics, as I have said, furnish training only, and that incomplete training, for the advocate and partisan ; the intermediate region is that in which real personal interest may be strongly engaged without much temptation to passionate controversy, and in which therefore the judgment may be best trained for its own perfect development, and for the uses of practical politics when the time for practical controversy and advocacy comes. We learn patience, tolerance, respect for conflicting views, equitable consideration for conscientious opposition ; we see how very differently the men of the particular time seem to have read the course of events, which seem to us to have only one reasonable bearing ; we see how good and evil mingle in the best of men and in the best of causes ; we learn to see with patience the men whom we like best often in the wrong, and the repulsive men often in the right ; we learn to bear with patience the knowledge that the cause which we love best has suffered, from the awkwardness of its defenders, so great disparagement as in strict equity to justify the men who were assaulting it ; we learn too, and this is not the least of the lessons, that there are many points on which no decision as to right or wrong, good or evil, acquittal or condemnation, is to be looked for ; and on which we may say that, as often the height of courage is to say I dare not, and the height of love is to say I will not, so the height of wisdom is to have learned to say, I do not know. I will however leave this point, as it is one on which I may have to say a word under my third head.

The next point after determining the nature of the disciplinary value ascribed to historical study, especially modern historical study, is the question of method. And as I have already said that it does not follow that the best method of studying History in one aspect is the best way of studying it in the other two, I will, for the sake of simplicity, go directly to our own idea of teaching in this place as exemplified in the Examination Statute. That statute was the result of a good deal of consideration and discussion between men of very different views and extent of experience, and I do not know that I should venture to say that it is incapable of improvement ; but it has worked well, and any improvement that may be made in it must be made on the lines of its own plan, which seem to me complete. I take it, however, as a peg for more general remarks. The main feature of it is, as you are doubtless aware, the threefold division into, first, a continuous reading of our national History, second, an epochal treatment of a portion of general European History, and thirdly, the special study of some character or period in the original authorities. The plan thus aims at realising two of the ideas which I discussed the other day, although of course only by way of introduction to the larger fulfilment of the promise ; it attempts in the continuous reading of one subject to convey the lesson of continuity, and in the special subject to invite the student to see what original sources are like, and what is the pleasurable work of studying them.

Now I am not quite sure that our way of studying the special subject is exactly the best method of beginning work on original authorities, but it may very well be the best that we can incorporate in a plan of gaining, in a year and a half's reading, a mental training, or the beginning of a mental training that may serve a lifetime. I am not sure that it would not be more true to the idea, to require the student to read a single book and explore its mechanism and materials, rather than to set before him a character or institution and bid him look for illustration for it in a particular set of books ; but it must be remembered that the immediate object of the reading is to meet the test of examination, and that it would be almost impossible to examine, on one set of questions, a set of men all of whom had been working from different points ; for essay writing it might be invaluable training, but for collective examination it would be unreasonable. I will, then, content myself with remarking that the special subject in the class schools should be regarded

only as a starting-point in independent research ; a sort of
first step in the study of original sources, which we hope may
lead on to further and deeper investigation, but which, as it
has to serve two purposes, can scarcely be likely to satisfy
both ; it is a specimen of minute study, and it is a specimen
of original reading ; but the object of the minute study is
not the book, but the hero or the plot of it.   It is, however,
most encouraging to those who have the future of our
History school at heart to know that the treatment of the
special subject is always one of the best features of our examination ; that in which the best side of the mind of each
examinee is as a rule most distinctly shown.   Regarded then as
a study of a subject, rather than as a first step into the region
of original authorities, this part of our work exemplifies one
of two diametrically opposed methods of reading.   And,
whether there is or is not a science of History, and I believe
that in the reasonable and intelligible sense of the word there
is such a science, there is, I am sure, an art of writing
History and an art of reading it ; and the educational use
of it is an exemplification of the art.

According to this, the reader or the writer may set before
himself two opposite ideas ; he may either wish to produce a
historical statue or group of statuary, we may say, or he may
wish to produce a historical picture.   In the former case he
has to look out his materials first, then to construct from the
careful view of them an idea or model of the object which he
desires to reproduce, and then to work out his idea.   It is
necessary for him to look at his subject all round, to finish it off
completely at every point, and, while seeking for statuesque
unity and perfection, to make truth and reality the first
object.   Everything that in the remotest way bears upon the
history of the person or institution that he is describing, has
its special value ; original sources, the verdict of other historians, tradition, popular conceptions, poetic idealising ; the
place which his object has occupied in the development of
historical life, the results which historical experience has produced or may have produced upon the object; every species
of illustration derivable from archæology, genealogy, law,

morals, and religious history, will have to be ransacked. The result will then, if the writer has chosen his subject well, and with a due estimate of his own powers, be an artistic unity, a perfect image, true to its author's idea, and, if he has not let his own idea prejudice him in the manipulation of his materials, true to the reality, so far as the reality can be discovered. It is of course in the life-like portraiture of great men that success of this sort is most frequently achieved, for it is in the realising of grand character that the strength of historical genius chiefly displays itself. But the same method may be applied to an institution that has a well ascertained growth, and the result in that case will certainly be not less valuable. Still there are certain unities of time, place, and interest, which are more readily united in biography than in institutional history. As valuable History may be so written, so a good deal of History may be so read, in a way, that is, to produce in the mind a perfect image of the character worth studying ; nay, the method is more applicable to the reading than to the writing of History, because it is easier for the mind to receive successive images or phases of the one character, than it is for the writer to reproduce them without becoming tedious ; the realisation in the mind may easily be a regular and orderly development, whilst in the written record of even the best historian it is liable to become a series of postures and attitudes, attended by tricks and mannerisms of style that are unworthy of the serious student.

The second form of our art is analogous to painting, and its result to a picture ; it aims at reproducing not a character or a life, but a situation ; it requires a background and a foreground, scenery and perspective, as well as unity and symmetry ; it studies the relations and positions, the features and habit of each of the persons or groups that the picture contains, and tries to make them true to the eye, whatever they may be to the life. Thoroughness and complete realisation is not a requisite of this sort of work quite so much as accurate reproduction. The painter is not, like the statuary, obliged to look at his figures all round ; he need not go to the back of his picture, or if he does, he will see nothing : so the historian, who works at a situation, will often satisfy himself if his grouping is true and consistent for the moment which he wishes to seize ; and he will not spend much time in trying to show us how the scene comes to be what it is, satisfied that his reproduction is an adequate representation of what it seemed to be. The result will have its value ; for first, the work need not be a whit less conscientious because it is less deep and searching ; and, secondly, because the good workman will only try to reproduce scenes that are worth describing ; the good painter will not waste his genius on revolting or worthless subjects, and the historian of true genius will choose for the employment of his genius scenes from history that may read good and noble lessons to the world that reads him. Such historical writing is far more brilliant, if it is well done, than that which I mentioned first ; but, like everything that is brilliant, it is liable to be counterfeited. Sensational and picturesque writing satisfies the popular taste, and sensational and picturesque writing, adopted as a historical style, is very apt to corrupt and destroy the more valuable features of painstaking and conscientious truthfulness. Popularity is nowhere a greater snare than it is in this region of work, and magazine articles, and review articles, the romance of history, and historic scenes and characters, are produced with great facility when the principal object is to attract the half-educated to read. But, notwithstanding this, both the writing and the study of history in this way has a great value, if it enables the student to realise the situations more vividly, to put himself in the place, so to speak, of his characters, and to represent to his mind's eye, for the purpose of forming an equitable judgment, the several circumstances of the case on which he is trying to adjudge, in somewhat the same way as that in which his characters themselves might have seen them. I should say, then, read history now and then with a view to the picturesque, but do not read it too much, and do not read it at second-hand ; do not write it, or dwell too much on the pictures which are not drawn by the first masters ; try to reproduce, not to copy.

A third form of the art, which combines and adds to these two, borrows its analogue from the domain of another of the arts, and attempts to read not only character and situation but plot also ; and this, I need hardly say, is in result at least very far in value beyond the other two. It involves the complete identification of persons, and the complete realisation of relations ; of persons identified through long historical careers, and of relations varying from moment to moment during the long periods over which the drama extends. It can perhaps afford better than our second form of the art, to discard circumstances and characters that are not essential to the plot, but it cannot afford to neglect a single circumstance or feature that may be essential to it. The result of such writing is seen in its best form in the history of great institutions, great empires that have had definite periods of growth, duration, and decline ; Church History, or different episodes in it ; the history of the Roman empire, or of Athens. It has all the unity of the statuesque, and all the vividness of the picturesque, but a continuity of life and argument that are its own. I need scarcely say that to write this sort of history requires the very highest mental powers, as well as patient training and incredible labour. For even the writing of episodes, as we call them, the minor plots of a great drama, the writer must combine qualities of mind that are combined in but few ; the clear sight that can apprehend the idea that gives life and truth to the story, and the labour that will apply itself to details as if it were only out of the study of the details that life and truth could come.

But although to write such history may well be beyond the reach of nine hundred and ninety-nine out of each thousand of historians, there is no reason why every man who goes into the schools should not try to read history with a special view to the realising of the dramatic plan ; and I think that in our present scheme we hold out to the student the clue which he has to follow in order to succeed ; for both in the study of the general period, and in that of the continuous history of his own country, he will find the dramatic interest strong and capable of almost infinite illustration. More especially if he

can throw himself personally into the action of it; not merely
regarding it as an image, or a picture, or a piece of biography,
but as part of the growth of his own life, of the laws, history,
circumstances, that have helped to make him what he is;
acts that have taken place in scenes with which he is familiar,
great deeds of war and peace done by the men whose blood
runs in his own veins; high aspirations, sympathies and instincts, that he knows are living in his own heart and brain,
not merely by imitation or engrafted life, but with continuous,
hereditary strength. I would not have him read as a partisan,
with the likes and dislikes, the prejudices, the false and artificial
antipathies of modern political life, but with the sympathies of
an Englishman; I would have my brother Yorkshireman, for
instance, learn to look on Fairfax and on Strafford both as
men of flesh and blood, with beliefs, sincerities and virtues
that bring them very near to us, notwithstanding their antagonism to each other, and the gap that widens daily between
us and both of them. I am sure that the more I know of
both of them, the more I find that is admirable and love-
able in them. But perhaps it is easier to grow enthusiastic
here than to maintain judicial calmness; and I will proceed.

There is yet another way of reading and of writing history
which demands its place in our enumeration, which, however,
can scarcely be regarded as educational, because the historic
faculty, whatever it is, must have been already educated
before it can attempt to approach the task. To read and
write with the single and simple purpose of collecting, testing,
and arranging the facts of history, to discover causes and
work out consequences, to determine the rights and wrongs
of questions as they arise, the growth and decline of institutions as they emerge from and retire into darkness when
their work is done, to build up history as a treasure-house of
knowledge, that may enable the man who attempts the task
to read with like facility the history of the past and present,
to solve the difficulties of conflicting testimony, and hold the
balance of equitable judgment between conflicting systems;
the study, for I must recur to the first of our three heads, the
study of History for its own sake can scarcely be regarded as

a method co-ordinate with the other three.   But it unites the
advantages of all three, and furnishes still more formative and
disciplinary influence of its own.   It is, in relation to its subject, an end in itself, and is not to be classed among means
and methods; if there be a science, this is the science.   And
yet, strange to say, this idea, like the others, is apt to be
lowered and made vulgar by the impatience and intolerance
of utilitarian theory; and of all intolerant things utilitarian
theory, or theoretic utilitarianism, is the most so.   As however
I do not wish to use language unnecessarily strong, I will
leave this, and remark upon two other educational theories
connected with the subject.

History may be read either backwards or forwards.   That
is, the man who has time for it may begin at the beginning
and read on to modern times; noting every influence in
its origin and effects, the growth and decay, as I have just
said, of institutions, the origin, complications, and counter-
changes of rights and wrongs; and, whether he reads on a wide
scale or on a narrow one, he will, if he lives long enough,
arrive at such a knowledge of the situation of things at the
present day, as will give him a right to make his opinion
heard.   This is the way in which members of parliament
ought to read history, and I take leave to say that, if they
would submit to hold their tongues until they have so read it,
it would be all the better for the nation and for themselves.

In working thus through the history of our own country,
we should come, no doubt, upon many lines of inquiry as to
institutions that have long been obsolete, and influences that
have no direct representative among the influences of the
day; we shall trace the pedigrees of extinct families, and the
growth and disuse of worn-out fashions of thought, dress and
manners; but without such reading we cannot trace the
origin of existing institutions and influences with anything
like a true appreciation of their proportion and relation to
national life.   We may, as we proceed, have to discard much
that has seemed historical as now become archæological, but
we cannot dispense with the recollection that without that
obsolete material, that obsolete influence or form, that which

has succeeded, survived and continued to flourish, could not have become what it is. The tree that has stood for centuries bears to the microscopic investigator marks of every winter that has passed over it; it has not cast aside one dead leaf or rotten branch which would not, had it remained, have made the tree something different from what it has become. I do not advise microscopic minuteness in this study to the neglect of other methods, but I do claim for it a place and a function; and further than that, I maintain that this synthetic reading of the subject is the best of all ways for those who have time and patience to follow it up. But here we must be cautious; lest having begun to build we be not able to finish; and having begun to read history at the Norman Conquest, we find ourselves stranded at the battle of Waterloo, or earlier still. Observing a due scale and proportion of study, much educational benefit will accrue by beginning at the beginning; neglecting the due scale and proportion, the student may find that instead of educating himself to take his place in the world, he has disqualified himself for being anything but a student all his life; no bad thing perhaps, but not an educational result.

The second and reverse method has strong recommendations to other minds; to take the interesting subject of the day and work back to its beginning, following every branch of inquiry that may present itself, but following it chiefly with a view to the leading idea with which you have started. Here too there is abundant exercise for the historic instinct, the desire of getting to the bottom of everything and looking at it all round; and, regarded as an analytic process, complementary to that synthetic process which I have first stated, some amount of such reading seems absolutely necessary to the education of the student. Still, I question very much whether it is wise to put this idea forward as the best. As the way in which men of modern ways of thinking, and with little time for study, may be invited, tempted to and interested in History, much may be said in its favour, and much has been said on very high authority. But surely it has, unless it be accompanied by some strong corrective, a tendency to educate men for advocates rather than for judges, it leads them into a habit of looking for all that may be said on one side of a subject, rather than for what may be said on both sides; and it certainly leads a man to give to the point from which his investigation started an exaggerated form and influence amongst the earlier competing influences which, as a matter of fact, it has outgrown, or of which it may itself be in some measure a resultant.

The occasional use of this method as a means of study is one thing, the exclusive use of it is another; the use of it as a means of inviting popular attention to history is a third. And it is perhaps in this its third application that it should be regarded with the most favour, but only as a step towards something deeper and sounder. An audience may be attracted by an able lecturer to listen to him on any subject whatever; he takes the subject of the day and works back; Turkey and Russia, we will say. Of course, if his audience is really a popular audience, they bring sadly little information with them to the lecture; a large proportion probably of the elder hearers can go back as far as the Crimean War, most of the audience will have come into this world of trial since that date. Their ideas of right and wrong will be very much prejudiced by the fact that England took a side in that war, and by the grand principle that whatever England does is right; some may be equally convinced, on equally sound principles, that whatever the Aberdeen ministry, that is supposing them to have heard of an Aberdeen ministry, did must have been wrong: probably some will have imbibed the belief that there is a subtle connexion between Russia and Ritualism, or between Turkey and religious toleration as exemplified in the massacre of orthodox Greek Christians and the protection of Roman Catholics and Protestant Missionaries. Well, furnished with materials, prepossessions, fixed ideas and expectancy, it would be a miracle if they did not come away fully persuaded of their competence to decide on the minutest questions of the last Protocol.

Really it does seem to me that this is beginning at the wrong end, and yet I confess it is extremely difficult to suggest anything that is at once theoretically better and practically possible. If it were only for the fact that these questions of the day are to so large extent as they are, doubtful and party, doubtful or party questions; that matters on which our acutest and most honourable statesmen feel bound to take sides diametrically opposed, are by this process subjected to the rough and ready manipulation of men who know nothing about the premises and care nothing about the logical connexion between them and the conclusions, care nothing about the conclusions except in so far as they are the conclusions of a blue or an orange lecturer; the fact itself seems to me a reductio ad absurdum of historical lecturing. Yet, what is to be done? A little learning is a dangerous thing, but what of total ignorance, what of that ignorance which will not bear to be enlightened unless it is played on by passion or party? How shall we remedy this? Here is a question that extends far beyond the scope of my purpose, for it touches the whole great field of popular education; it is an inviting subject, for we are so distinctly at the beginning of our work in this department that a man of my age may safely propound any nostrum, sure that he will not live to see its absolute uselessness proved by an adult generation of historically trained people.

Let me just say, before I go on to the next and last point of my subject, that popular lecturing on history can be only one, ay, and only a secondary one, of the implements of historical education, if the people of the next generation are to be qualified to use the power which the men of this generation have placed in their hands. The schools, the national schools as well as the public schools, must be made to begin at the beginning; at present the blind are leading the blind; God help us, for we are very near the ditch. Lecturing is of little use, if it does not lead men to read for themselves; in many instances it is worse than useless, if it be made a substitute for self-culture. So too with newspaper education; imagine the state, moral and intellectual, of the man who tries to form his mind by reading the daily journals of England since the beginning of the last Long

Vacation.   What value will truth and justice have in the eyes of a man who has read history through such a medium? But again I forbear : one word ; it has been said, perhaps the story is apocryphal, that one well-known politician of our own day, one too whose judgment would have been well worth having on present events, once said something to the effect that there was more valuable political training in one column of *The Times* than in all the pages of Thucydides ; I will venture to say that there are English journals now, claiming a world-wide circulation and assuming to be the very interpreters of history and political morality, in preference to whose lessons I should recommend the student to seek for lessons of history and political morality among the arrowheaded inscriptions of Assyria or the papyri of the Neapolitan Museum.

But I have already run into the third division of my subject : that is the popular view of historic knowledge ; the aspect of it in which it becomes merely a tool or a stock of tools capable of employment for ulterior purposes ; and the methods of teaching it by which with the least trouble the learner can acquire practically useful information. I call this the popular or utilitarian aspect, because it belongs to the catchpenny theory of human life according to which the value of a thing is just as much as it will bring ; the theory that despises science and research, that regards politics as a game between Blue and Orange, that places the interest of Great Britain at the crown and apex of national ambitions, and regards education in general not as the training of the human mind for God's service, a development of powers to His glory and the welfare of our fellow-men, but as a means for the acquisition of a certain sum in the funds ; the theory that regards human souls as factory hands, and ascribes to parliament the power of making a false statement true. But although it is the vulgar view of education, and in this extreme a very vulgar view, it is founded upon a truth. There are many things which a mere acquaintance with the facts of history, however that acquaintance may have been gained, enables a man to do better than he would do them without it. There is a knowledge of history for ordinary practical purposes which may be acquired without either the love of the subject

or going through the disciplinary study of it by way of culture. And this we must not undervalue, because a very little
may be made to go a great way ; and it is quite possible for a
man to wish to take an independent and right view of public
affairs and political duty, who has not, and never had and
never can have, a proper education for forming a complete
judgment. We respect the man who, when he has to vote on
any public question, goes to his books to get up the question instead of voting as the party whip would wish him ; we
would rather that his education had fitted him to do right at
once, that he had studied public questions to begin with, or
that he had, by the culture of educational reading, exercised
his mind to discern between good and evil; but we do not
despise him even if he votes wrong in the end. Even an indifferent Cyclopædia is better than a paid party agent as a
guide in doubtful questions.

Now how can this sort of information be best provided?
I do not know of any expedient that has not been at one
time or other tried ; tried in vain, you say. Not quite in
vain, if such expedient has, as I said, enabled a man to do
better than he would have done without it. We do not
condemn the use of a Ready Reckoner because we think
that a tradesman ought to do and would do better without
it ; it is much safer for his customers than that convenient
leaden canon, the rule of thumb; but we do not think that
a banker who entirely depends on his Ready Reckoner will
ever become Chancellor of the Exchequer. One has known
people too who have thought the Encyclopædia Londinensis
a useful sort of reading for Sunday afternoons ; no doubt it
would enable you, like one of Dickens's heroines, to pass a
number of remarkable opinions upon a remarkable number of
subjects. But seriously, anything should be welcome that
would save a well-intentioned man from the necessity of
taking his rule of political conduct from the leading articles
of party papers. We have had popular histories and pictorial
histories, political Cyclopædias, and Books for the Million; a
whole historical department of the Society for Diffusing Useful Knowledge. Yet it seems as if even for such work, even

where such work would pay, no one has the spirit to undertake it unless he is stirred by something stronger than the desire of being useful, the desire of ventilating some party view or destroying the character of some partisan opposed to him. Imagine a history of England in which the lying story of Hannah Lightfoot appears as an important clue to the difficulties of the reign of George III, and the triumphs of the Commonwealth are regarded as incomplete unless Henrietta Maria can be shown to have been an adulteress. These are extreme cases, because they are cases in which a coarse and violently prejudiced mind has undertaken the task of writing for party purposes; but the infection is not confined to coarse and vulgar minds: it defiles some of the very noblest works, especially historical works, that have ever been written. How can we recommend the man who wants to get up the rights of a case to a history like Macaulay's? how easy must have been the victory of Macaulay's hero if all his adversaries were the pitiful knaves and fools that they appear to him to have been. I am not calling him a slanderer, I do not believe that he was one; or ignorant or careless, for he was most learned and accurate; nor insincere, for he was most sincere; but for all that he was as much a party writer as Clarendon or Prynne, or Burnet, or Collier. And where such a man with such power of portraiture as would make us believe his pictures, if not true, more lifelike and real than if they were true,— where such a man with such knowledge, such memory, such transparent honesty of belief in his own version of history, cannot be relied upon, what shall we poor mortals do? If all the advance in historical study is to result only in the better presentation of party views and party arguments; if no one will write even cram-books without cramming his own disproportioned and one-sided theories down our children's throats, it seems as if it were time to turn over a new leaf; reconcile ourselves with party government and organisation and cut ourselves off from shams. Let men cease to pretend to exercise or to prepare to exercise conscientious judgment. Divide the world between Blue and Orange, and nail your colours to the mast.

For my own part I do not see why an honest partisan
should not write an honest book if he can persuade himself
to look honestly at his subject, and make allowance for his
own prejudices. I know it is somewhat critical work, and
a man who knows himself in one way, may be quite ignorant
of himself in another. I take Hallam as an illustrious
example ; Hallam knew himself to be a political partisan,
and, wherever he knew that political prejudice might darken
his counsel, he guarded most carefully against it : he did not
claim the judicial character without fitting himself for it ;
and where he knew himself to be sitting as judge he judged
admirably : so admirably that the advanced advocates even of
his own views have long ago thrown him over as too timid
and temporising for their purpose. Yet where he was not
awake to his own prejudice, in matters for instance regarding
religion and the Church, in which he seems to have had no
doubt about his own infallibility of negation, how ludicrously
and transparently unfair he is !

I do not see any necessity for this. I do not see why a man
should not say once for all, I like Charles I better than Oliver
Cromwell : I like the cause for which Charles believed himself
to be contending better than that for which Cromwell strove :
Charles is attractive to me, Oliver is repulsive : Charles is my
friend, Oliver is my foe : but, am I bound to maintain that
my friend is always right and my enemy always wrong ; am I
bound to hold Charles for a saint, Oliver for a monster ; am I
bound never to mention Charles without a sigh or Oliver
without a sneer ; am I bound to conceal the faults of the one
and to believe every calumny against the other ? If you like,
put it the other way, believe in the great Protestant statesman, treat Charles as the overrated fine gentleman, the
narrow-minded advocate of a theory which he did not understand, the pig-headed maintainer of the cause you dislike.
You may be a partisan, but can you not believe that, if you believe your own side of the question, truth when it is explored
will be found on your side ? misrepresentation, exaggeration,
dishonesty of advocacy will only disparage the presentment
which you desire to make of your own convictions and your

own prepossessions. Nay, I would go further, and say I should like Charles better than Oliver even if his cause were less my own than I conceive it to be. I am ready to stick to my friends and vote against my unfriends : but why should I shut my eyes to the false and foolish things that my friends do, or to the noble aspirations, honesty, and good intentions of those whom I think wrong in their means and mistaken in their ends. Yet, as I began by saying, without some infusion of spite it seems as if history could not be written ; that no man's zeal is roused to write unless it is moved by the desire to write down. Of course I seem to be stating extreme cases, but it is extreme cases that make their own advertisements, and that do the great mischief. Here the study of ancient history has its great advantage over modern ; yet battles are fought over the character of Tiberius, and the 'lues rehabilitandi' has given a new reading to the history of Marius and Sylla.

The reason which led me to say that even an indifferent book is better than no book at all, that an encyclopedic history or a popular compendium, or a cram-book, or even a party pamphlet is better than no book at all, because even if it misleads and misrepresents, it deceives a man one degree less than he would be deceived by a mere party agent ; because it makes him think, even if the extent of the thinking be that he thinks that he thinks ; because it either suggests to him that he ought to form a judicial opinion, or keeps before his mind the duty of inquiry and furnishes him with a starting-point ; the same reason that led me to say this of popular books, leads me also to estimate at something more than their intrinsic value the popular lectures, or lecture-system, of which we have recently heard a good deal.

We are told that even a short course of lectures, clearly and interestingly delivered, will be sufficient to put the popular mind in possession of such an elementary knowledge of history, its course, influences and material lessons, as will enable men to approach the great questions of the day with some useful amount of foresight and theoretic experience.

Now, if I have mis-stated this prescription, I am very sorry ; but I think I have not. I am quite willing to admit that a

popular lecture may give information that is better than total
ignorance; I am inclined to value highly the inducement to
begin real study which a popular lecture may put before the
mind of the audience ; I am thankful to the popular lecturer,
although he may get no farther than to rouse the hearers to the
sense of the fact that he is talking about things of which they
have no comprehension at all; at all events he tells them that
there is such a study as history.   But I confess that I do not
see my way to go much further, unless I may be allowed
very much to modify the prescribed idea of a popular lecture.
In the first place, as to lectures at all ;—that such oral teaching is an important part of the discipline of education we are
all bound to believe ; it is part of the system under which we
have all grown up, and in a University course it is that one
part of the system which is capable of the most development ;
an implement which has been growing to perfection by the
labours of many generations of tutors and professors.   Yet of
our best lectures, as well as of our worst, it may be certainly
said that that which a hearer carries away with him will be
in exact and direct proportion to that which he brings : or
that a lecture-system, unless it be added upon and followed up
by independent reading, must be a deceptive and even useless
system.   Of course this is a platitude ; but just consider that,
if this be true of us, and true of us in those very subjects in
which we have been training ourselves ever since we were
seven years old, how much stronger is the point of it when it
is applied to lecture-audiences that have not studied their subject, that have not even the elements of the study made accessible to them before they come, and that have not yet
the means of following up the lessons that are then first propounded to them.

   I fail to see that elementary lectures, short courses of
elementary lectures, can convey anything to the mind of
beginners, besides the most elementary teaching.   Twelve
lectures on the scale and plan of Mr. Freeman's Handbook
of Universal History would no doubt contain the marrow
and spirit of Universal History ; but the working-man who
could understand them at the first reading would be fit to be

Prime Minister after a second course. If, then, elementary lecturing is ever to furnish material lessons to ignorant men, it must, I take it, go on in long and progressive courses, and inculcate both patient hearing and the duty of independent reading. But, secondly, historical lecturing to uneducated people must surely begin by interesting them. And accordingly I would place the plan of lecturing on character and institutions, things in which every Englishman must almost of necessity feel his interest aroused as soon as he hears them, first; before the plan of elementary lectures to the people. Even where they do not see the direct application of the lesson, so offered, to their own circumstances, where there may be no such lesson, and no such application, they may be drawn to further study by a very inadequate exposition of a noble life or of a great battle, or even by a historical survey of some scene with the landmarks of which they are familiar. When they are drawn to history, they will not be likely to wish their elementary lessons to be restricted to twelve or to a single course.

Without then at all disparaging such a plan of elementary lecture, I feel certain that some preparation for it must be otherwise provided; if that is to be by lecture, it must be something more directly addressed to our common humanity than an elementary lesson can be; but I think that it must have begun at school, and that unless it has begun at school it will not do very much good. This is rather a dispiriting view for people who are too old to go to school; but then we are not dependent on lectures altogether; there are books enough and to spare, and the man who wants to learn will find time to read.

The moment however that people have, whether by reading at home or by hearing lectures, got beyond the elementary stage of historical study, my doubts about the expediency of popular lectures cease altogether; and I am glad to say this because, in some of the remarks that I have made, you may have thought me unwisely cynical and inclined rather to discourage effort in this direction. Popular lectures to fairly well-educated people, who have not the time or the opportunity of thorough courses of reading, must be valuable; and the experiments which have been tried in some of our large manufacturing towns have been successful in a remarkable degree. I do not shut my eyes to the fact that in such schemes zeal often outruns discretion, that volunteer lecturers are far more likely to spring from the ranks of the unlearned than from the class that has grown old in convincing itself of its own ignorance, and that, as I have said of writing, it may be true of lecturing, the zeal for informing other people may arise from political feeling quite as often as from the benevolent desire of teaching them what is good for them. It is most unfortunate that such teaching should be one-sided: how one-sided it could be made we learned from the history of Mechanics' Institutes; now we may hope that the exertions of the town clergy in their local societies are doing something to redress the balance; and if I could see my way to an administration on sound principles, apart from party organisation, and in the hands of competent teachers, of such a scheme as that known as the University Extension Scheme, I should be inclined to hope very great things from it. I trust that it will be so shortly.

If by these or any other plans we can induce men in authority to make the real teaching of History a part of the training of elementary schools, the first, and by no means the least, step will be taken towards furnishing the next generation of Englishmen with the means of exercising conscientiously, honestly, and judicially, the great political power which is now lodged in their hands. They will learn how to vote, and how to guard against imposture, exaggeration, and unfairness in their leaders as well as in their opponents. And with real political awakening I shall trust that moral and religious progress will do more than keep pace. I go further; if the study of History can really be made an educational implement in schools, it will raise up a generation who not only will know how to vote, but will bring a judgment, prepared, trained, and in its own sphere exercised and developed, to help them in all the great affairs of life. Therefore let us have lectures many and good, books few and good ; but above all school teaching fair, honest, and thorough.

Further I do not think we need look. I do not anticipate Englishmen ever becoming a nation of researchers. We may come, more of us, to love investigation for its own sake, and to love the study of History for the very exercise that it furnishes to our powers, and for the new regions of interest which expand before us as we proceed. Such study must however continue to be the portion of comparatively few, the few who have leisure, or who have the love in such strength as to enable them to overcome all obstacles. On them I trust the coming age will look more kindly than the present; which has much praise for the mere material lesson, and worships the statuesque, the picturesque, and the dramatic, but certainly honours the inquirers, the researchers, with a scanty meed. It is an old, old story. Some of you may remember the passage in Saint Augustine's Confessions, the story he tells of one who was asked how the Deity, being from everlasting, was employed before the heavens and the earth were made ; the reply was ' joculariter,' the great doctor tells us, a very pretty repartee, ' Alta, inquit, scrutantibus gehennas parabat.' He was preparing, to put it gently, a limbo for the advocates of research. ' Haec non respondeo,' says Augustine ; but there are people at all events in one house of parliament who seem to hold the same views : one is glad to see that their number is now reduced to twelve.

VI.

LEARNING AND LITERATURE AT THE COURT OF HENRY II.

(June 11, 1878.)

WE are at present suffering, and may for some little time to come continue to suffer, from a reaction against medievalism. I call it a reaction, for I think it is only caused by a recoil from modes of thought, art, and action, which have been pressed beyond reality, or have been pressed too rigorously. There are not wanting signs that even in architecture, in which the greatest and most permanent traces of medieval genius are found, the world is growing a little impatient of Gothic buildings, whether as imitative creations or as the claimants of exclusive orthodoxy in their art; in poetry it can scarcely be denied that the Arthurian legend has begun somewhat to pall upon most ears; in ritual or ceremonial worship we see much of which we are tempted to ask whether it has any meaning whatever for nine out of every ten of those who profess to value it. The dear delightful middle ages are unfortunately growing into something like a by-word. We are perhaps witnessing the turn of the tide of fashion which set in with Sir Walter Scott, and found its great triumphs under Sir Gilbert; of which, however, all that is real and natural and free will live, whilst that which is forced, unspontaneous and merely imitative, will not long continue to encumber the ground.

If this be indeed the case, it will explain some things that touch the study of history. Three or four years ago I was startled by the remark, which occurred in a review of Mr. Kitchin's History of France in the *Athenæum*, to the effect that all study of the early periods was thrown away, and that the true interest of history begins only where that history has begun to be illustrated by the genius of Mr. Carlyle. But I was scarcely prepared for the recommendation of my friend Professor Pearson, in his recent report on the subject of education to the government of Victoria, that the teaching of history in the Australian High Schools should begin with the year 1700. And why? because the ages that precede are so entirely unlike our own ; there were no railways, no large manufacturing towns, no newspapers to speak of, no such relations as now exist between Lords and Commons, no property tax, no taxation by excise, and a good deal of living religion, which religion exercised over the daily lives and political views of men an influence that is scarcely comprehensible at the present day.

Such a theory, it seems to me, would go a long way towards dispensing with education altogether ; but the expression of such a theory, if it be the result of anything else than a clever man's crotchets, is a mark of a reaction ; and such a reaction as is even painful to one who has spent the best years of his life in attempting to connect the several stages of his country's life and growth ; who believes that the age of railways, and excise and newspapers, would never have been had it not been for the free institutions and high ambitions that were nursed through the preceding ages, and that the present condition of the strength of the world is the direct and continuous result of historical growth and historical training.

It is no wonder, I say, that to me, and those who have pursued the same line of study, this tendency should seem very much to be deprecated. I do not for a moment suppose that it is dangerous ; all experience, all belief in progress and true culture, encourage me to believe that it is adventitious. If Australia can content itself with the history of England since the reign of Queen Anne, America has found out long ago the mistake of crippling the historic instinct with any such limitation ; and American scholars, lawyers, and constitutionalists are working as zealously at the medieval forms as are the students of England, France, and Germany. And not only experience of the past and faith in the future, but sympathy with the historical world both past and future, if

I may use such an expression, inclines me to a protest. Like
the man in Terence, I say 'Humani nil a me alienum puto;'
I have a sympathy with the struggles of the struggling ages,
with the weariness of the weary ages, with the faith of the
ages of faith, with the controversies of the ages of controversy,
with the changes of the ages of change, with the light of the
ages of illumination, with the darkness of the dark ages
themselves. Nay, I am not sure that I may not some day
have to profess myself a convert to the Unity of History and
the Education of the World. For after all, human life is not
essentially changed by railways or excise, or newspapers, or
even by the property tax: the people before the flood ate and
drank, married and were given in marriage, planted and
builded ; still Jacob finds his Rachel at the well, and David
and Jonathan make their covenant together, and David
mourns for Absalom. Natural selection, and the survival of
the fittest, have not done away with sin and sorrow, and,
whatever evolution may have done in the producing of new
types, those new types have not swept away the old. To go
beyond and behind the ancients, what else do we find in Egypt,
Babylon and Nineveh, in Japan, and in the China of imme-
morial sameness? And as there is no history in which we
do not find a sympathy, there is none in which we may not
find a lesson.

But to put aside generalities; the two or three truisms
which I have uttered, and the subject which I have chosen
for these two lectures, are alike suggested by the discussion
which we have seen recently carried on by Mr. Freeman
and Mr. Froude on the subject of Thomas Becket. I am
not going to interfere in a struggle between two such combatants, nor shall I again refer to either of them, but the
opposite lights in which those two champions approach the
common subject, shed some rays on the fashion of thought
which marks not only the two writers, or the two schools of
which they may be supposed to be the disciples, but the two
ways of looking at the middle ages which divide cultivated
men of the present day. And I have thought that I might,
in attempting to sketch the literary life of an age, on which

so many lights from various sides are now brought to bear, contribute somewhat, not perhaps to the true estimation of that age, but to a realisation of, and sympathy with, the life of it, without which no estimation or even understanding of it can be thought possible.

But the men of whom I am going to speak lived 700 years ago — 700 years; as long a time as separated them from Hengist and Horsa, or Hengist and Horsa from Alexander the Great, or Herodotus from the Trojan war ; or us ourselves perhaps from the New Zealander, who, on London Bridge, is to draw the conclusion that Thucydides ascribes to the τοῖς ἔπειτα and to recognise the disproportion between our ruins and our glory. It is true ; but the only thought that this suggests to me is that, if the New Zealander finds in the ruins of the British Museum half as many of the literary productions of our time, as we now possess of the reign of Henry II, the shades of the Victorian literati may, in the Elysian fields of the period, feel a thrill of satisfaction, and say that a great part of their life has escaped Libitina.

In truth, I would call your attention to a point which I have never seen fully set out; the fact that the same age that originated the forms in which our national and constitutional life began to mould itself, was also an age of great literary activity; of very learned and acute men, and of.culture enough to appreciate and conserve the fruits of their labours.

We all know the debt that England owes to the great men of the thirteenth century, to its political, religious, and scholastic life : Simon de Montfort, Grosseteste, Edward I, and the rest ; but I do not remember ever to have seen an estimate of the debt that the thirteenth owed to the twelfth, save and except in the recognition of Henry II's constitutional work. I can now only attempt an outline of any such view as is needed for the purpose, but I think that, when I have briefly reviewed the period, you will allow that in other matters besides constitutional, the glories of the latter age were the result of, and not much in themselves superior to, the glories of the former.

I will begin with the king himself, for, as the medieval

writers were never tired of quoting, 'vulgi turba movetur regis ad exemplar.' Henry II was by his very descent a champion of literary culture. Not to speak of his grandfather, Henry Beauclerc, whose clerkship was very probably of a very elementary sort, he was the lineal descendant of that Fulk the Good who had told King Lothar that ' Rex illiteratus ' was ' asinus coronatus.' He shared too those hereditary characteristics which so strongly marked his two uncles, Baldwin III and Amalric I, Kings of Jerusalem. Both of these princes were, according to William of Tyre, good scholars, and both extremely fond of history. Baldwin was the better professor ; Amalric the better examiner ; Baldwin the more serious and orthodox, Amalric the more superficial ; but both were students of history, and given to reading and discussion—discussion which threatened now and then to go beyond the bounds of orthodoxy.

Peter of Blois gives a similar character of Henry, and in words so nearly resembling those of William of Tyre that the two writers notably confirm one another's probability. And in Peter's sketch this feature comes in quite by the way, for he is describing Henry as a great huntsman. ' He has always in his hands bows and arrows, swords and hunting spears, save when he is busy in council or over his books. For as often as he can get breathing time amid his business cares, he occupies himself with private reading, or takes pains in working out some knotty question among his clerks. Your king,' he is writing to the Archbishop of Palermo, ' is a good scholar, but ours is far better ; I know the abilities and accomplishments of both. You know that the King of Sicily was my pupil for a year ; you yourself taught him the elements of verse-making and literary composition ; from me he had further and deeper lessons, but as soon as I left the kingdom he threw away his books and took to the easy-going ways of the court. But with the King of England there is school every day, constant conversation of the best scholars and discussion of questions.'

He had indeed been well taught ; notwithstanding the troubled times in which his youth had been trained, he had

learned literature at Bristol Castle in the household of his
uncle, Robert of Gloucester; his tutor Matthew, who was some
time his chancellor, and who probably was identical with the
Bishop of Angers, Matthew of London, took him in charge
when he was nine and kept him close at work for four years;
there doubtless he had the acquaintance of Gilbert Foliot,
then Abbot of Gloucester, certainly one of the ablest politicians as well as of the best scholars of the time; whilst,
when political affairs allowed it, he might learn somewhat
more under the eye of Archbishop Theobald of Canterbury,
the patron of Vacarius the lawyer and John of Salisbury the
philosopher.

The hereditary taste for history may perhaps, to some
extent, account for the considerable number of independent
historians who flourished under him; such chroniclers as those
known by the name of Benedict of Peterborough, and Roger
of Hoveden, bear intrinsic marks of having been royal his-
toriographers; one distinguished officer of the Exchequer,
Master Thomas Brown, kept a Roll on which were entered all
the doings of the king: Richard Fitzneal, the High Treasurer
of the Exchequer, composed a similar book, the Tricolumnis,
in which he kept a regular register of Henry's acts and of
the public documents of the time. There was, as we shall
see presently, a fashion for writing history.

But not only so; Henry was also a lawyer. Very early in
his reign we find him, in the Chronicle of Battle, dictating a
new form of writ; he heard and decided law suits, he took an
active part in devising budgets, he took an independent line
on religious toleration, and refused to persecute. All these are
signs of general enlightenment, but the man is even better
known by his friends. Becket indeed was no great scholar
in the early days when the king treated him as an equal
and confidential friend, but later in life, when we find Henry
choosing for companions such men as Hugh of Lincoln and
Baldwin of Canterbury, both of them as remarkable for
learning and eloquence as for piety, or even Giraldus Cambrensis, who had a fund of humour and cleverness that is
as noteworthy as his extensive reading; or Peter of Blois,

who acted for some time as the king's secretary, and, with all his time-serving and self-seeking, was a distinctly learned man in both history and theology, we feel sure that Henry was neither the mere voluptuary that his enemies represented him, nor merely the man of business that his more lasting works prove him to have been.

It has been the fashion to suppose that some literary influences were brought into England from Southern France by Queen Eleanor, and that it was from her that Richard, and perhaps John also, inherited some instincts of the kind. But I confess that, as against the claims of her husband, Eleanor's title to our gratitude depends very much on conjecture, and partly on a confusion between Aquitanian and Provençal civilisation. That Eleanor was a clever and cultivated companion for her husband we may accept as a matter of course, and she probably would have some share in the early education of her sons; but they were very soon removed from her influence, and after the year 1173 she probably saw very little of either them or her husband: whilst in England, court or country, her direct influence could never have been comparable with that of the king. As for her judgments in the Courts of Love, I suppose, we may safely relegate them to the regions of romance, and if they were authentic they would not prove much as to her literary culture. But we may, I think, confidently assume that she was a well-educated woman for those days, and that in her long captivity she had something else to amuse herself with besides needlework. A woman who, after twelve years of seclusion, could come out of prison not only fit to take the reins of government during a short interregnum, but able to exercise great influence in European politics until she was nearly eighty years old, must have possessed not merely vitality and ability, but mental resources also of no ordinary character.

However this may have been, some of her children, if not all, were educated with care, and appear as either possessed of learning themselves or as the patrons of learned men. Henry, the eldest son, was, as we are told, devoted to arms;

if he was not equally accomplished in letters it was not because such accomplishments were undervalued by the people whom he was expected to rule. There is among the letters of Peter of Blois an epistle written in the name of Rotrou, archbishop of Rouen, and at the express wish of the Norman bishops, urging in strong terms, and by cogent examples, the importance of a literary training for a young prince. Julius Cæsar, Alexander the Great, King David, Constantine, Theodosius, Justinian, and Leo are pressed into the service. No doubt the advice was taken ; but the stormy career of the younger Henry does not afford many indications of its results. One book we know, a book unfortunately lost, was especially written for his amusement. Gervase of Tilbury, who, many years after Henry's death, wrote for his grandson, the Emperor Otto, the Otia Imperialia, tells us that he wrote a *Liber Facetiarum* for the young king, in which no doubt he collected the amusing stories of the popes and emperors that were current at the time, some of which are probably preserved for us in the pages of Ralph de Diceto. It is possible that the Otia Imperialia were originally drawn up for the instruction of the same prince. It is curious, however, that in none of the panegyrics of this unfortunate boy is any special stress laid on his knowledge of letters, and it is even possible that the epistle of Archbishop Rotrou was intended as a remonstrance against the exclusively military training of the heir to the crown ; certainly Thomas Becket, to whose care he is said to have been committed in his youth, would, at that period of his career, have been better qualified to instruct him in arms than in letters.

With Richard it was otherwise. In his case we must certainly allow some amount of literary knowledge and skill. We may not perhaps credit him with the quotations from the classical poets which the historians of the third crusade put in his mouth, but we cannot refuse to believe those writers when they tell us of the lampoons of the king's own composition which were sung in the camp in contempt of the Duke of Burgundy ; and the stream of time, in which so many more precious things have been submerged, has brought down to us some few sir-

ventes or satiric lays that entitle Richard to the name of a trou-
vere. His education in the south of France no doubt qualified
him for such compositions; but his father's foreign dominions
may also have furnished him with more valuable instruction.
At the schools of Tours his half-brother Geoffrey was educated,
and there Richard himself may have obtained the elements
of that 'scientia' which is markedly ascribed to him in
contrast with his brothers. Of Geoffrey of Brittany we know
no more than that he was an accomplished knight. John's
reputation for scholarship seems to rest on the fact that he
once borrowed a book of the Abbot of S. Alban's. But the
real interest of such inquiries does not lie in the question
whether such and such kings could read or write, but in the
general character of the court which was kept about them;
the king might be illiterate, but if the court around him was
full of learned men we may safely infer that the central
figure was no contemner of learning. Of the king's daughters
we know little more than that they were all married to
princes who took a conspicuous place among the pioneers of
medieval culture. Matilda, the eldest, was the wife of Henry
of Saxony, who was not only a great conqueror but a great
traveller and collector of chronicles; Eleanor, the second,
married King Alfonso of Castile, the founder of the University
of Palencia; and Johanna, the youngest, William, the good
king of Sicily, who was not only, as we have seen, both an
educated man himself, but also the patron of many learned
Englishmen.

There was something, however, besides the literary wide-
awakeness of Henry and his family that made England and its
Court at the time a centre of literary activity. Henry was
the most powerful king of the West, and his hand was in the
affairs of all the Western kingdoms: and this at the time
when international acquaintance was carried on upon the very
largest scale. There can hardly have been a period of our
history in which the intercourse between England and France
was freer or more frequent. The enormous number of letters
which passed between England and Rome, every letter,
remember, carried by a separate messenger; the stream of

pilgrims to the East, and the prominence given in the
histories of the time to the adventures of the few that
returned ; the cosmopolitan character of the clergy, the frequent promotions of English and Normans in foreign churches,
and their continued intercourse with their friends at home ;
the recourse to foreign Universities, and the honours won by
English scholars at those Universities, were a constant inducement to others to follow them ; the welcome given at the
English Court to foreign scholars, and finally, the fact that the
English Court was open to all exiles from East or West,
North or South ; all these served to arouse and keep awake
that curiosity about foreign matters which will not be satisfied without the acquisition of learning : so that learning is
not sought for itself only, but as a part of the equipment of a
man of the world. A little may go a long way under such
circumstances, but yet every little helps to make a mickle, and
there were many men about, as I shall hope to show you, who
were bent on picking up all they could, and to whom nothing
came amiss.

To run rapidly over the more prominent examples under
each of the heads I have enumerated : in 1155, the first year
of Henry II, there was an embassy from the kings of Norway.
Henry received the envoys, and sent them back with ambassadors of his own and large presents ; and the next year there
was a similar transaction with Sweden. Here at once opens
up a field of interesting investigation. Norway and Sweden
were about as far from England as they are now, but they
seem to have been even more neighbourly. The Norse
settlements in the islands had not forgotten their origin.
The Bishop of Sodor and Man was expected to seek consecration at Drontheim. Just before Henry's accession, the
Bishop of Bergen had visited Fountains Abbey and obtained
a colony of Cistercians for a cell in Norway itself, called,
after that beautiful custom of the order, the House of Light.
Again, in 1164, another Norwegian prelate appears in the
royal accounts as receiving a gift of £3 6s. 8d. ; and again,
in 1182, the Archbishop Eystein, of Nidros, was maintained
for 17 weeks at the expense of the English Court. These

two dates synchronise with the Norwegian revolutions under
Magnus Herlingson and Swerre Birkbain, and we thus learn
how the detailed accounts of those revolutions came into
the English Chronicles of Benedict and Roger of Hoveden,
and William of Newburgh : it was at St. Edmund's that
Archbishop Eystein was entertained at the king's expense from
August 1181 to February 1182. And this leads us on to the
recollection that it was the Englishman Nicolas Breakspere
who had been legate of the Roman see for the settlement of the
Scandinavian churches, before he became pope as Adrian IV,
and so liberally bestowed the realm of Ireland on the king of
the English.

The intercourse with Germany under Frederick Barbarossa
was steady and probably continuous ; for although there was
little love lost between England and the empire, and the Hohenstaufen were always somewhat drawn to France, the quarrel
of Henry with Becket and that of Frederick with Alexander III
so nearly coincided, that there was always a prospect that the
two great sovereigns might make common cause against Lewis
VII. Hence in 1165 there was a German embassy under
the Archbishop of Cologne in London, and the English lords
showed their orthodoxy by refusing to meet the schismatic
prelate at dinner, although Henry's own envoys at Würtzburg
were credibly reported to have given in the national adhesion
to the antipope. The marriage of Matilda with duke Henry,
his subsequent quarrel with the emperor, Henry's negotiations
for the support and restoration of his son-in-law, the long
exile of Henry the Lion and his stay in England, gave English
society much interest in German politics ; so much so, that it
is from the English Chroniclers of this period that much of
the German history of the time has to be written ; and
English writers took sides in the Welf and Hohenstaufen
quarrel, describing both events and characters with partisan
colouring that is rare even in their pictures of home politics.
Thus, too, copies of important documents came to be preserved
in the English Annals, and we are so led to infer that the
relations of the Court, to whose hands primarily these documents must have come, with the recording annalists, were of

the closest description; and we understand how the great Longchamp or Walter of Coutances could send down important dispatches to be copied into the historical collections of Ralph de Diceto. For when we talk of the public and of the court of Henry II, we are not talking of such a vague and abstract idealism as the court and public of the reign of Victoria, made up of society at large at one end and the press and newspaper correspondents at the other, with all that lies between ; the Court is a small body of well-known men, and the public is the aggregate of the clergy and knights who know foreign lands, can speak foreign tongues and take an intelligent interest in European politics. Not to dwell, however, on these points ; in 1176 there were at the English Court at Westminster, on the 12th of November, embassies from Constantinople, and from Frederick I, the Eastern and Western Cæsars, from France, both Rheims and Flanders, and from Henry the Lion ; the same year the Sicilian envoys came to demand Johanna in marriage for their king, and the kings of Navarre and Castile applied to Henry to arbitrate on a great international dispute in Spain. It is true that on this last occasion there were some difficulties of interpretation ; the English could not understand the Spanish envoys, a fact which seems to indicate that thus early Spanish Latin had become somewhat rusty, for of course it must have been in Latin that the negotiations would be conducted ; but the difficulty was surmounted and the arbitration settled ; the documents concerning it, which are totally without interest to the English mind except in so far as they contained a full pedigree of the Spanish dynasties, being circulated among the chroniclers of the time, and so preserved in several authorities.

With Italy and Sicily, owing first to the constant recourse to Rome during the Becket and other Canterbury quarrels, and secondly to the sustained connexion with the Sicilian Normans, which came to its climax in the marriage of Johanna, the offer of the Sicilian crown to Henry himself, and the contract of marriage between Arthur of Brittany and king Tancred's daughter, the relations of the English were very close.

But in fact the diplomatic activity of Henry II throughout

his reign was enormous; all nations of Europe came by
envoys to his court, and his ministers, especially Richard
of Ilchester and John of Oxford, ran about from one end of
Europe to another.   Spain, the most distant in interest of all,
became familiar by the pilgrimages to Compostella and by
the substitution of service against the Moorish infidels for
service against the Turks.   Both Henry and his eldest son,
purposed, or said they purposed, pilgrimages to Compostella,
and it is well known how great was the debt of the infant
kingdom of Portugal to English pilgrims.   We see, too, how
the elaborate surveys of the Spanish coasts found their way
into several of our chronicles, so that Spanish geography,
scarcely less than German political history, owes something to
the English of this period.

To go, however, one step further; the diplomatic intercourse
is illustrated not merely by the occasional visits of ambassadors, but by the constant interchange of letters between
Englishmen abroad and at home, or between Englishmen and
foreigners.   Now the subject of medieval letter-writing is one
on which a very great deal of entertaining discussion might
be taken, but I can now only note a few points in this particular connexion.

At first sight, medieval letters are disappointing; the
amount of sentiment, and especially of religious generalities,
seems altogether out of proportion to the amount of news.
That arises from two causes: firstly, many of our collections of
letters are edited collections, made by the writers, who prided
themselves upon their correct Latinity, and published their
correspondence rather as literary exercises than as historical
memorials; thus, so far from setting special value on the
spontaneous unartificial morsels, which are to us the bonnes
bouches of letter-writing, these men actually cut them out of
their codified letters.   This may be seen in almost every case
in which copies of the original letters can be compared with
the revised editions put out by the writers; especially is it the
case with Alcuin's letters.   Many of the letters of Peter of
Blois look as if they had received the same treatment, and in
the Becket correspondence the reader is often nonplussed by

finding a provoking *etcetera*, which marks the point at which the gossip, or even the serious news, was expunged by the editor.

The other reason is that in very many cases the letters were little more than credentials. The real news was carried by the bearer of the letter, and the real force of the communication was not in the postscript, we may say, but in the postman. Still, we often come upon letters and letter-writers of real interest, and a good man may certainly be known by good letters, although many good men wrote very weak ones. John of Salisbury, among Becket's correspondents, wrote real letters, and those of Richard of Ilchester, preserved among Foliot's, are the writing of a business-like man. Even amidst the wearisome sameness of the Canterbury letters we now and then get a glimpse of life, such as in the letter of Master John from Lombardy, when he explains why he could not write from the Great S. Bernard. ' Pardon me for not writing. I have been on the Mount of Jove ; on the one hand looking up to the heavens of the mountains, on the other shuddering at the hell of the valleys ; feeling myself so much nearer to heaven that I was more sure that my prayer would be heard. " Lord," I said, " restore me to my brethren, that I may tell them, that they come not into this place of torment." Place of torment, indeed, where the marble pavement of the stony ground is ice alone, and you cannot set down a foot safely; where, strange to say, although it is so slippery that you cannot stand, the death, into which there is every facility for a fall, is certain death. I put my hand in my scrip, that I might scratch out a syllable or two to your sincerity ; lo, I found my ink-bottle filled with a dry mass of ice : my fingers, too, refused to write : my beard was stiff with frost, and my breath congealed into a long icicle. I could not write the news I wished.' But this is a digression, and such scraps are not common.

Well, the mass of twelfth century letters is so large that, notwithstanding the drawbacks, they furnish a large contribution to the materials for national, literary, and social history. John of Salisbury, Peter of Blois, Arnulf of Lisieux, Thomas Becket, Gilbert Foliot, the monks of Canterbury,

furnish a series of thick volumes, the many-sided interest
of which is not easily exhausted. These collections contain
news from every part of Christendom ; some of them, although
only a few, are really news letters, containing all that the
writers could pick up, like the news letters of later times.
All, however, contain evidence by which the literary culture,
as well as the political interest felt at the time, may be tested.
The citations of the Latin poets which occur so very frequently
are amusing, and often amusingly inappropriate. There is
something touchingly comic in the monk of Canterbury who
will bring in Ovid's Art of Love as a treasury of stock quotations. Lucan's Pharsalia, Claudian, Statius, even Silius
Italicus, but Ovid most of all, notably more than Virgil and
Horace, seem to have been the storehouse of proverbs. Shall
we be so cruel as to say that the frequency with which particular passages are quoted suggests that the writers betook
themselves to a Margarita Poetica, a dictionary of quotations, rather than to the authors themselves? No, it is only
true in the very penny-a-lining letters of inferior men.
Certainly the best writers, like John of Salisbury, could both
read and criticise the originals. But again I am straying from
the point.

The next head which I mentioned as illustrating the process by which international intercourse worked in a direction favourable to literary progress, was the otherwise curious
and interesting point, the number of Englishmen promoted in
foreign churches ; and, by interchange of good offices, the
cases in which foreigners of note were promoted in the English
Church. I say, in both cases, men of note, because no doubt
many Frenchmen, and even Italians, of whom nothing else is
known, were enriched with English preferment, and, probably,
the few names of Englishmen promoted abroad, which history
has recorded, might be supplemented with large additions if
the records of foreign churches had been kept as carefully as
those of our own. And I am not careful to distinguish here
between Norman and native Englishmen, because, from the
very accession of Henry II, I regard the two elements as
forming one people, and indeed, except in the very highest

ranks of the baronage, it is impossible now to distinguish whether the English or the Norman strain was the strongest in any given Englishman. And for a similar reason, it is not necessary to include the Norman and Angevin provinces in our calculation. Many of the great families from which Norman bishops were taken, such as the Beaumonts and the Bohuns, were equally powerful on both sides of the channel, and, it may be added, in the Norman kingdom of Sicily also. Such men as Rotrou of Beaumont, Archbishop of Rouen, and Henry of Beaumont, Bishop of Bayeux, not only were members of a kinship which counted the English Earls of Warwick and Leicester, and the Norman Counts of Meulan as cousins, but were near relations of the Sicilian kings, and knew how to push in the southern regions the fortunes of their servants : the broken up condition of France left potentates like the Counts of Champagne and Flanders able to treat on an equal footing with the royalties around them, and to govern their own churches quite as freely as the King of France or the Emperor could govern theirs. Hence there was a good deal of international promotion as a matter of course. I shall, however, name only the greatest names: and first take the Englishmen who were promoted abroad.

The two most eminent instances in France and the French speaking countries are the two Johns, John of Poictiers and John of Salisbury; the latter a name that is so intimately bound up with our literary history that it may be adduced to illustrate almost every sort of distinction. John of Poictiers was a native of Kent, probably of Canterbury itself; he was one of the fellow-scholars with Becket and Roger of Pont l'Evêque in the household of Archbishop Theobald, which, as I shall have to note presently, was at that time a substitute in England for the as yet undeveloped Universities ; he ran neck and neck with those great candidates for promotion, and managed, by the adroitness and moderation of his conduct, to steer clear of the difficulties in which they were constantly embroiled with either one another or some third party. Promoted early in the reign of Henry to the rich stall of treasurer at York, John became in 1162

Bishop of Poictiers, and in 1181 Archbishop of Lyons ; that great and semi-independent see he held until 1193, when he resigned and fell back on his minor preferments and the company of the Cistercians of Clairvaux ; but to the day of his death he retained the living of Eynesford in Kent, and kept up a close correspondence with the Canterbury clergy and with the learned men of England, especially Ralph de Diceto, Dean of S. Paul's, with whom he had in his youth competed for the archdeaconry of Middlesex. The letters of John of Poictiers are among the less important contributions to the Becket literature, but they are worth reading as the composition of a man of mark, of sound learning and prudent character, and an eminent canonist. The career of John of Salisbury I shall recur to more particularly further on ; he also was a son of the Church of Canterbury, and retained the closest relations with his Alma Mater as long as he lived.

Another Canterbury man was Ralph de Serris, or Ralph of Sarr in Thanet, who was Dean of Rheims from 1176 to 1194 ; who was a most dutiful son of the church to which he owed his education, and no doubt a faithful agent of the monastic interest, which found at Rheims such powerful protection in the Archbishop William of Champagne and the great family to which he belonged. Of Ralph of Sarr as a literary man I only know that he wrote fairly good Latin. These three men, you will observe, although sons of the Convent of Canterbury, were not monks ; they were pupils of the great school of the monastery and, as clerks of the primate, affiliated to that Church. When they received foreign promotion they had to be released by a formal document from their allegiance to the Mother Church. John of Poictiers was one of the clerks whom Archbishop Baldwin, and Hubert after him, would have made canons of that college at Lambeth which they intended to set up as a centre of ecclesiastical learning and dignity, emancipated from monastic restrictions ; a scheme which, if it had succeeded, might have possibly fixed the University life of England, and its ecclesiastical centre, in London itself.

Not to waste time upon minor names, we go on to Italy: there the greatest name of course is that of Nicolas Breakespere, the pupil of the Monastery of S. Alban's; the great legate of the north, the confidential friend of John of Salisbury, the one English pope, and the bestower of Ireland on Henry II. His life and career lie only on the very edge of the period which we are considering; and I can say no more of him than that he is one of those figures of medieval history of which what little we know is suggestive of a great deal more that we should desire to know. He was unquestionably a great pope; that is, a great constructive pope, not a controversial one, like those who preceded and followed; a man of organising power and missionary zeal; a reformer, and, although he did not take a wise way of showing it, a true Englishman. Next in dignity to him would come, if we were quite sure of anything respecting him, the great Robertus Pullus, who is said to have been made Chancellor of the Apostolic See under Lucius II and Eugenius III, and who likewise lies a little outside our limits. His history has yet to be worked out; but as he is, like John of Salisbury, a historical link of some importance, I must say a word or two about him. We know from a letter of S. Bernard addressed to Ascelin, Bishop of Rochester, between the years 1142 and 1148, that Robertus Pullus was at that time studying with great success in the University of Paris; he was then, it would appear from the Rochester Fasti, Archdeacon of Rochester; and S. Bernard's petition to the Bishop, that he might be allowed to pursue his studies at Paris, is thus quite in character with the usual practice for an archdeacon to go and study for some time in a foreign university before he began the formal exercise of archidiaconal functions. In 1146, or thereabouts, Robert was still at Paris teaching theology, and there John of Salisbury attended his lectures during the last two of the twelve years, dating from 1136, that his education was in progress. If these dates are accurate, it is a little difficult to identify him with the person who appears as Chancellor of the Apostolic See in 1145 and 1146. It is not impossible that he was then for a short time transferred to Rome; this, however, will leave no time for his teaching divinity, as he is said to have done, at Exeter and Oxford. He is mentioned as Chancellor of the Apostolic See by the contemporary writer John of Hexham, who dates him in 1146. Anyhow, he was a man of great mark; that we know from S. Bernard and John of Salisbury, and from his extant works, Sentences, and Sermons. But there was another Robert, also connected with Rochester, also an Italian Chancellor, and mentioned as a distinct person by the same historian of Hexham. He was a native of 'Salesby,' whether Selby or Salisbury I shall not decide, who tried his fortunes in Sicily and became chancellor to King Roger about the same year 1146. Is it possible or probable that he has somehow become confounded with Robertus Pullus? Certain it is that Paris, Archdeacon of Rochester in Henry II's reign, was the nephew of Robertus Pullus; certain it is also that Paris had relations in Sicily, and was chosen as an envoy in 1176 to that court because of his connexions there: it is needless to add that archdeaconries went in those days very frequently from uncle to nephew, and not uncommonly from father to son. Whether, however, we have here two Roberts, or two Roberti Pulli, for the sojourn in Apulia might entitle the second Robert to the name of Pullanus, or only one, we have the starting-point of the usage according to which English ministers were domiciled at the Sicilian Court. Robert may have been the first; he was not the last.

Master Thomas Brown, with whose name the readers of Mr. Freeman's books must have become by this time familiar, was another Englishman, a great financial authority, who enjoyed the confidence of King Roger until the death of that king in 1154. Thomas Brown is the first modern Englishman, if not the first Englishman of any sort, whose name was written in Greek. In that language, as Thomas Brounos, it appears among the attestations of Greek Charters of King Roger. After Roger's death, when a new king arose, who, according to the Dialogus de Scaccario, knew not Thomas, he returned to his native land, and was immediately summoned by Henry II to his restored exchequer; he became the king's almoner, and kept at the exchequer a separate roll of the king's doings.

He had a handsome pension, too, £36 a year, if not more, and an allowance for his nephew Ralph. Madox goes so far as to conjecture that the special duties which were assigned to him were the basis of the later office of Chancellor of the Exchequer.

Another Englishman in Sicily was Herbert, a man of Middlesex, who was Archbishop of Compsa between the years 1169 and 1180; another, more famous, was Richard, surnamed Palmer, Bishop of Syracuse from 1165 to 1183, and Archbishop of Messina from 1183 onwards; a kindly man who entertained the relations of Becket when they were driven into exile. He had the credit of first proposing a matrimonial alliance between the two royal houses, and seems to have been detached from Becket's interests by the hope of obtaining the Bishopric of Lincoln. Walter, Archbishop of Palermo 1169–1187, and Bartholomew his brother, Bishop of Agrigentum, who succeeded him at Palermo, are likewise called Englishmen. So close and continuous was the connexion maintained by these men with the kindred realm that we can quite understand the influences which prevailed on William the Good to propose Henry II as his successor, and Richard I meditating the translation of the Archbishop of Monreale to Canterbury. More apposite, however, to our present subject is the fact that owing to these men and their connexions at home, there was a constant flow of epistolary intercourse between England and Italy, independent of that which moved to and fro between Rome and the English Church. Henry II doubtless availed himself of both currents for his diplomatic intrigues. The King of Sicily and the Bishop of Syracuse, as well as the men of Milan and Bologna, were sub-agents in the great game which he was playing. And the Italians, Italian as they were, learned to feel some interest in England besides a pecuniary one. The books of later Italian heraldry recognise, I fear somewhat apocryphally, the exiled kinsfolk of Becket as the progenitors of the family of Becchetti of Fabriano. Now and then they repaid the loan of Robert Pullus and Thomas Brown with a scholar or clerk of half English birth, as Robert and Thomas had in their turn repaid part of the debt incurred by

England from Lanfranc of Pavia and Anselm of Aosta. But here I must stop; in the other lecture I shall hope to get into the more purely literary half of the subject, and trace some of the results that accrued from these multiplied relations of courts and councils. The subject, superficially as it must be treated in lectures like this, persistently grows upon our hands.

VII.

LEARNING AND LITERATURE AT THE
COURT OF HENRY II.

(June 13, 1878.)

IN following out the inquiry which I began in the last Lecture, in order to complete the outline of our subject and take into account all the influences that conduced to a full literary intercourse between England and the Continent during the period of Henry II, the next point that I should take would be the enumeration of those foreign scholars and literary ecclesiastics who were favoured or promoted in England. This point, however, need not detain us long, for there were very few. England itself had no love for foreigners; whether as captains of mercenaries, or as papal nominees to ecclesiastical preferment, they impartially detested them; and the detestation was very frequently justified by the view which the foreigners took of England and the English; a country out of which as much revenue as could be wrung should be wrung, and a people at whom, when they had plundered them, it was their delight to laugh. Nor were the Angevin kings much inclined to a policy which they knew to be most odious to their subjects; Henry II avoided either ruling or controlling England by foreign ministers, and did very little to encourage an influx of foreign ecclesiastics. Excepting such persons as, like Hugh de Puiset, Bishop of Durham, and two or three others, were closely connected by blood with the royal house, few foreigners were made bishops, and when Becket, according to his biographer, wished to restore learning at the court, he urged the king to recall home the English scholars who were studying abroad. Of the few, who would be all that could be named, the most prominent are Peter of Blois and Master Vacarius.

Peter of Blois seems to have made his home in England,

after he had tried his chances in Sicily, where he had been tutor to William the Good. He settled here about the year 1173, after the Becket troubles were over, and made himself useful to both the king and the archbishops. Like John of Salisbury he made his pen serviceable to his masters, and many of the letters of his composition which are preserved were written in their names. As chancellor or secretary to the Archbishop, as Archdeacon first of Bath and afterwards of London, and Dean of Wolverhampton, Peter seems to have led a scrambling sort of literary existence; being used by the kings and primates on services both diplomatic and ecclesiastical, for which his versatility and command of language qualified him, but not being much trusted or highly promoted. Master Vacarius, on the other hand, was a very obscure, or rather indistinct, person; indeed so little is known of him that it is almost hazardous to commit oneself to the theory that the earlier and later Vacarius were the same person. He is of course known to lawyers as the Lombard scholar, who, in 1149, attempted to introduce the study of the civil law into England and to teach it at Oxford. He is said to have been silenced by King Stephen, and as a teacher he disappears, but from two or three passages in the Becket letters it seems that he remained in England; in the list of the canons of Southwell his name occurs later on in the century, and as late even as 1198 Pope Innocent III commissioned Vacarius, with another ecclesiastic of the northern province, to carry into execution certain letters touching the crusade. If the name is indeed rightly read, and belongs to the Magister Vacarius of 1149, he must have been very old and of little use. The history, however, both of Peter of Blois and of Vacarius, has been carefully worked out by independent writers of authority, and I use them here only as examples. Mere ecclesiastics, such as Simon of Apulia, who was made Bishop of Exeter by King John after having been Dean of York for many years; and ministers of state, such as Walter of Coutances, William of S. Mere l'Eglise, and perhaps William Longchamp, call for no notice in this connexion; and I pass on to the much more important point—the literary intercourse and activity promoted by University life.

I have already mentioned the two or three foreign schools
which were most frequented by English scholars. Paris was the
centre of theological learning and general culture, Bologna was
the school for lawyers, especially the canon lawyers ; for the civil
law, although equally well taught there, did not obtain much
favour with Englishmen ; and besides these, the pupils who
either could not afford to go to Paris, or could afford to exhaust
all the teaching that the neighbour lands afforded, went to the
schools of Tours. Tours had the advantage of being locally
situated within the dominions of the king of England, and
although it did not aspire to the character of a University, as
later understood, it had a very ancient and very eminent
succession of teachers.

John of Salisbury, in the second book of the Metalogicus,
sketches the twelve years of his University career; in 1136
he went to Paris and studied at S. Genevieve's under the
clarus doctor identified with Abelard, who taught him dialectic, as did also Master Alberic, who succeeded, and Robert
of Melun, the English doctor who, after the accession of
Henry II, was invited home again and made Bishop of
Hereford. He then read for three years, with William of
Conches, grammar ; then, with Richard l'Evêque, he attacked
the quadrivium, and, under Peter de Helie, rhetoric : after
that he took to Aristotle again under Adam of Petitpont, an
English scholar who was afterwards made Bishop of S. Asaph ;
his next teacher was William of Soissons, who was attempting
to upset the old logic. At this point of his career, after ten
years of study, he began to take pupils, his poverty com-
pelling. From William of Soissons he went on to Gilbert of
la Porrée and Robert Pullus. He had now reached the study
of divinity and wound up with Simon of Poissy, a faithful
lecturer but somewhat obtuse debater ' fidus lector sed obtusior
disputator ;' if he had gone through the discipline that John
had passed through, it was no wonder. After these twelve
years of study John went to Celles as chaplain or secretary to
the Abbot Peter ; and about 1150 returned to England, where
S. Bernard recommended him to Archbishop Theobald. His
career of usefulness in England thus began just at the time

when Vacarius was teaching law, and Theobald was maintaining the school of literature in his own palace from which so
many conspicuous men afterwards sprang. For thirty years
John continued to live, the central figure of English learning ;
suffering indeed many troubles with Becket, whose companion
he was in his exile, but restored to his home in 1170 ; in
1176 he was made Bishop of Chartres, and he died in 1180.
His career is conspicuous, and he had both ability and opportunity that were given to few.

I can only mention now the names of the other students at
Paris who to some extent trod in his footsteps : Ralph de
Diceto the historian, Archdeacon of Middlesex and Dean of S.
Paul's, studied at S. Genevieve shortly after John of Salisbury;
he lived to the end of the century : Robert of Melun and
Robert Pullus had not only been pupils but teachers at Paris,
and Adam of Petitpont the same ; these have been already
mentioned.   Walter Map, the poet and satirist, afterwards
Archdeacon of Oxford, was another Parisian student ; so was
Giraldus Cambrensis ; so probably were Roger of Hoveden
and most of those ecclesiastics of the time to whom the title
magister is given in formal documents, of whom it would be
useless labour to give a catalogue.   The scholars of Tours were
of the same class.   Bologna was the special university for
young archdeacons ; and, as most archdeacons were appointed
when very young and by family interest, there was a tolerably
rapid succession of them, and I fear it must be added that
they fell into a great many temptations.   We all know of the
question discussed at this period, ' An possit archidiaconus
salvus esse ; ' whatever were the peculiar temptations of his
official career, he was lucky if he passed without debt or
difficulty through his university course.   In 1200 Henry de
Jacea, Archdeacon of Liege, and not only archdeacon but
bishop-elect, was killed in a scuffle with the townsmen of
Paris.   At Bologna debt seems to have been the greater
snare.   Gilbert Foliot, when Bishop of London, had sometimes
two archdeacons at once studying there ; and at the same
time there was resident there a Canon of S. Paul's, Master
David, whose letters have been recently published in the

Spicilegium Liberianum. David was an Englishman who had studied at Clermont and at Paris, and had gone on to Bologna in the idea of qualifying himself for an archdeaconry, of which the bishop had perhaps given him a half promise. At Bologna he had got into debt, and set up as tutor to the young archdeacons; he then went on to Rome, where, by the use of the names of his great patrons, he nearly succeeded in getting a recommendation for the Deanery of S. Paul's. Very ungrateful conduct this was, for the deanery was one of the best things that could be got in London, and Master Ralph de Diceto, who was to be the next dean, was actually being made to allow Mr. David an exhibition of ten pounds a year from his own archdeaconry towards his expenses. It is satisfactory to know that David did not get the deanery, although we know no more about him. The two young archdeacons fulfilled their term of study and one of them became a bishop. All the three had, by the provisions of the cathedral statutes, dispensation from residence whilst they were away at the schools. The statute of S. Paul's, drawn by Ralph de Diceto himself, allowed not only non-residence but a pension of 40s. per annum from the communa or dividend of the canons; the student must go for not less than a year; he might go for two or three. This permission was freely used: the great churches, which had thirty or forty canons, at all stages of the ecclesiastical career, could well afford to dispense with the services of the younger ones, and they, notwithstanding the temptations of University life, could scarcely fail to bring back with them at the end of the time some experience, some culture and knowledge of the world, that fitted them for the occupations of their later life, whether their destiny was to serve the king in his court and embassies, or to make themselves useful in the educational work which was still carried on largely in all the cathedral establishments.

And so by a natural transition we pass to another point of interest, the attempts made by the bishops and clergy to furnish to Englishmen in their own land some of the appliances of learning which they found at the foreign Universities. And this had a particular importance at this

particular time; for there is no doubt that the reign of Henry
II is a period which saw a great development of University
life, if not the very origin of University life itself, at Oxford.
Before this time we hear of Vacarius lecturing in law, and, by
somewhat questionable authority, of Robert Pullus lecturing
on theology here; but both, or either, may have been mere
teachers in the royal court, or private tutors under the Canons
of S. Frideswide.   But before the end of the reign there
was a University with doctors and masters.   Yes, and public
lectures; for did not Giraldus Cambrensis, in 1187, come to
Oxford and read his Expugnatio Hiberniae in public lectures?
and did he not secure himself an audience by entertaining, on
the first day, all the poor of the town at his lodgings, and on
the second all the doctors of the diverse faculties and the
more distinguished scholars; and on the third day the rest
of the scholars, the passmen as we should put it, with the
county people, the townsmen, and the citizens?   Ah! he tells
us, it was a sumptuous and noble affair, a renewal of the old
and authentic days of the poets; 'nor has the present age,
or any antiquity, remembered in England any such gaudy
day.'   It is a lesson for all time.   Beyond, however, the
fact that thus comes full upon us, that in 1187 there was
at Oxford a great school with diverse faculties of doctors,
ergo, a constituted University, we know little or nothing of
University life here so early.   Only we know that those who
in later times might have been able to tell us something true
about this, chose to tell us what was false; and, by hunting
up and forging evidences of greater antiquity, lost their hold,
and prevented us from ever obtaining a hold on the materials
which might have furnished authentic history.   There can be
no doubt that, when the idea of the University had once
impressed itself on the minds of Englishmen, it would rapidly
work a change.   It centralised teaching and it promoted
competition.   Not that the idea had to work itself out on
English ground; our English Universities, however far in
the historic distance we may throw back their origin, must
have been framed on the model of the Continental Universities.   I do not mean that they had not their rise in in-

dependent and special circumstances, or that they were not the successors of more ancient schools of study, many of which continued to exist for some time around the greater cathedrals; but that their University organisation, their degrees and faculties, were borrowed from the established institutions on the Continent. They centralised however, and to a great extent superseded, the earlier schools; they afforded more room for speculation, gave greater scope for competition and greater chances of independence.

But as this was the age of transition from the local to the centralised system, our business now is rather with the earlier than with the later form. I have already said that the household of Archbishop Theobald, in the reign of Stephen, to some extent satisfied the want which was afterwards met by the University system. He provided learned teachers, and his clerks, after learning what they could at Canterbury, went over to Paris and Bologna to take their degrees after sufficient and more advanced study. It was not however only in the palace of the Archbishop of Canterbury that such a school existed. Every great man had a great house and household, with his chapel or collegiate church at his capital house, and his school of clerks as well as pages. Many of these large establishments lasted, with diverse modifications, into comparatively modern times, and one of the traces of survival still subsists in the privilege of noblemen to qualify so many domestic chaplains, although the particular privileges of the chaplains are mostly things of the past. But, of course, as the castles of the Earls were rather schools of knightly than of clerkly accomplishments, the best illustrations of the scholarly life are found in the houses of the prelates.

The king's palace was not less a centre of learned talk and training, although, as the king was seldom at home more than two or three days together, it is not absolutely certain that he would take a strong interest in the matter; the fact of Oxford having been a convenient royal residence may account perhaps for one of the influences that fixed the University here, just as the school of S. Frideswide's priory may account for another. It is in the proof that there existed a general fashion of literary association and conversation that these clusters of scholars, settled in the great houses, are so interesting.

Peter of Blois gives a sketch of one such cluster in the house of the Archbishop. ' Good master,' he writes, ' you blame me for spending my days at court, when I might fructify in the scholastic camps. But this court in which I live is, I assure you, a camp of God, none other than the house of God and the gate of heaven. In the house of my lord the Archbishop are most scholarly men, with whom is found all the uprightness of justice, all the caution of providence, every form of learning. They, after prayers, and before meals (mark the connexion, and think of Giraldus's public lecture), in reading, in disputing, in the decision of causes, constantly exercise themselves. All the knotty questions of the realm are referred to us, and, when they are discussed in the common hearing, each of us, without strife or objectation, sharpens his wits to speak well upon them, and produces, from a more subtile vein, what he thinks the most prudent and sensible advice.' This is in contrast with the turbulent, and sometimes stormy, discussions in the rising Universities.

Herbert of Bosham, one of the biographers of S. Thomas and himself one of the Archbishop's clerks, affords us some glimpses into the working of this institution ; and gives us long discussions between Becket and the learned staff that accompanied him in most of his tribulations. Some of these are very curious ; they show that the Archbishop had amongst his chaplains a staff of professors on a small scale ; this one skilled in canon law, that in historic precedent ; one to whom they looked when an apposite quotation from the poets was wanted, and another who had pretensions to be a philosopher. In one of the supplementary chapters Herbert gives a list of these, the *eruditi Sancti Thomae* ; the catalogue includes, of course, many of the names that I have already mentioned, John of Salisbury, Archdeacon Robert Foliot, and Ralph of Sarr ; besides these there were, Lombardus of Piacenza, afterwards Archbishop of Benevento, Reginald the Lombard, son of Bishop Jocelin of Salisbury, afterwards Bishop of Bath and Archbishop, Gerard la Pucelle, Hugh of Nonant and Gilbert

Glanville, afterwards bishops, and several others; of whom the most famous was Uberto of Milan, afterwards Pope Urban III, who had attached himself to Becket in his exile.

I think that a generation further back, in the household of Theobald or of Henry of Blois, we might perhaps find, if record had remained, a more illustrious list; Theobald certainly contributed the traditions of Bec Abbey, which had gathered round Lanfranc and Anselm, whilst Henry concentrated about him all that remained of the enlightenment and refinement of English and Norman society.

Whilst Theobald, however, collected learned men and Henry collected statuary from Italy, whilst the great Bishop Roger built his miracles of castles, England was a prey to conflicting factions, and every great man was bound above all things to be a politician. Hence the academic and political elements were thus early found in closest union : if Henry, Baldwin and Amalric, discussed deep questions of theology with their councillors, the knotty questions of the realm were laid before Peter of Blois and Giraldus Cambrensis ; and the minds of the *curiales* were, notwithstanding the sneers of the satirists, occupied on the same matters as those of the *scholares*.

To this community of subject it is that we owe some of the most significant anecdotes of the great men of the time : the scraps of conversation of Ranulf Glanville, the great justiciar, who discussed, as he was riding out, the decay of valour among the French ; the amusing exaggerations of Giraldus when he criticises the colloquial Latin of Hubert Walter ; the most interesting details of the friendship between S. Hugh of Lincoln and Henry II ; and very much that enlivens such books as the Polycraticus of John of Salisbury, the de Nugis Curialium of Walter Map, the de Institutione Principum and other discursive productions of Giraldus, the Otia Imperialia of Gervase, and the Satires of Nigel of Canterbury. It is true indeed that men professedly literary would most naturally, I am afraid I cannot say necessarily or invariably, preserve such scraps as might be supposed to have a literary or historical interest ; and therefore that such anecdotes may not be a fair specimen of the ordinary conversations of the educated classes of the time.   Granting that, it is at least pleasant to find that amidst the great and varied mass of literary remains there is so very little, hardly anything, that would show the prevailing tone to have been coarse or base.   There is some profanity, not a little hardness and narrowness, but very little indeed of the foolish and inconvenient jesting which later on becomes the mark of all courtly literature.

If now we were to imagine a foreign scholar visiting England at the period of which we were speaking, either, like Mabillon or Pertz, making an Iter Anglicum to collect materials for history, or like Solon simply, θεωρίης είνεκεν, to see what the world was like, or like the admirable Crichton to air his own erudition and try the mettle of English scholars in literary tournaments, or like John of Salisbury to gather all the knowledge that he could, how would he fare?   He would land, we suppose, at Dover and be lodged in the Benedictine Priory there, where he would find that his visit was recorded among the visits of kings and ambassadors in a precious chronicle that embodied the annals of all public events and copies of public documents ; then he would go on to Canterbury, where he would find himself at once in a great literary centre, with teachers and libraries and all appliances that stand to the population and society of the day in much the same proportion as the literary life of Oxford or Cambridge would at this moment.   He would find Gervase, the sacrist, busy over the chronicles of the kings and the history of his own time ; Nigel writing his verses, polishing the great medieval satire Burnellus, or inditing the prose letter in which he castigates the faults of the secular clergy ; a monk in a strictish convent, but corresponding with the ministers of a powerful and politic court : there too he would find Odo the prior, a great theologian, William the sub-prior and Edward Grim, biographers of S. Thomas ; if he came after 1186 he would find the whole convent busily writing Latin letters, letters in very fair grammatical Latin, garnished with quotations from Ovid and Lucan and the laws canon and civil.   If he went on to Rochester, there he would be entertained by Archdeacon Paris, the nephew of Robert Pullus, possibly a near kinsman of the great chronicler of the next age ; there he might find Bishop Glanville, the preacher of the Third Crusade, one of the learned pupils of S. Thomas, and close kinsman of the great lawyer ; or if he went on to Chichester, he would fall in with the Dean Matthew, or Jordan, or Gervase, all of them members of the same company, and Herbert of Bosham in the close neighbourhood, the squire parson of the time, also a careful and admiring biographer. Going on to Winchester, he would be entertained either by the venerable Bishop Henry, whose memory was a very storehouse of history ; the grandson of the Conqueror and depository of all the great traditions of the generation, the king-maker of the twelfth century, who also had his learned men around him ; or by Richard of Ilchester, the confidential minister of the king, himself no mean adept in the writing of historical dispatches ; Richard of Devizes is there too writing the history of his time ; further on, at Salisbury, another of the eminent ministers is the dean, John of Oxford, a traveller, and lawyer and divine, a man whose very name suggests that he might have been one of the first magistri of his own University : possibly John of Salisbury might be there too, or Reginald, the bishop's son, as archdeacon or bishop, a most intelligent and travelled diplomatist. At Exeter, early in the reign, he would find Bishop Bartholomew, the famous preacher and canonist, Baldwin, the archdeacon and scholasticus, afterwards archbishop and crusader, with his brother Joseph, the poet, who attempted in an Hexameter Epic to rival the glories of Virgil, and in his lost Antiocheis to build up a poetic memorial of the First Crusade ; no mean poet, although ambitious, but considered worthy to rank with the classics edited, in usum serenissimi Delphini, with Dictys of Crete and Dares of Phrygia.

But if our friend was bent northwards, we might take him at once to London and introduce him to the Dean and Chapter of S. Paul's or the great Bishop Foliot and the king's court. At S. Paul's he would meet, ten to one, not only the lord mayor, aldermen, and justices, whom the canon in residence was specially bound to entertain, but any distinguished strangers who happened to be in town : the venerable old dean, Ralph de Diceto, would show him the beautiful MS. of his Imaginationes ; from the canon Richard, the high treasurer, he might learn the history of the Exchequer, or even borrow the precious Tricolumnis before it was lost ; Peter of Blois would be grumbling at the small profits of his archdeaconry, but wisely putting his pen to good interest ; Roger Niger perhaps just flying from the wrath of the king, whom he has exasperated by savage invective ; and the great Foliot himself, the able statesman who pitted all his skill, experience, and learning against the zeal of Becket and lost the game, at least in the opinion of his contemporaries.

At the court would be Ranulf Glanville, the father of the study of English common law, and the astute band of justices who shared with him the confidence of the most sagacious and business-like of kings. Our friend would find the historical mind fairly well awake to the importance of the era in which it found itself: the author of the Gesta Regis Henrici may not yet have chosen to be anonymous, but have been keeping a busy account from day to day of the king's doings ; Thomas Brown would be there with his roll, and Peter of Blois moralising 'de Praestigiis fortunae,' on the magic tricks of Fortune exemplified in the career of his royal patron ; and the author perhaps of the Draco Normannicus awaiting a reward for panegyrising the old Empress Maud ; not to speak again of Ralph de Diceto and Gervase of Tilbury. At Westminster he would fall in with the Abbot Laurence, a theologian of some note in those days when almost every learned man was a theologian. In London indeed, or at Westminster, all the men whom I have mentioned might at any stirring time be found together : William Fitz Stephen, the biographer of Becket, possibly becoming a judge after he had tried his fortune as a scholar, but known to us by the lively picture which he has drawn of London in his own days ; Giraldus Cambrensis, the erratic Norman-Welshman, who, as he would be looked for everywhere, might safely be caught near the king ; even Roger of Hoveden, the learned Rector of Howden and chronicler of the north, but a king's chaplain and occasional justice of the forest. Time would fail him to learn even the names of all the subordinate scholars of London: he goes on northwards by S. Alban's and Peterborough.

Nothing is more curious than the lively historic activity going on in the monasteries: MSS. are copied, luxurious editions are recopied and illuminated; there is no lack of generosity in lending or of boldness in borrowing; there is brisk competition and liberal open rivalry. S. Alban's is especially rich in the collected materials that lie at the foundation of her great code of chronicles. At Peterborough Abbot Benedict is equally busy, directing transcription and compiling or editing his own recollections of S. Thomas; but every little monastery has its record: Crowland is thinking of hiring Peter of Blois, or some pretended Peter who borrows an illustrious name, to fabricate for her an apocryphal chronicle; at Ramsey there is an invaluable chronicle kept, going far back into the old English times, and there is the same at Ely conducted by a succession of learned and patriotic monks. But at Peterborough the pen has just dropped from the hand of the native annalists.

Coming to Lincoln, there is Walter Map with his poems and stories about the courtiers, acting as archdeacon or precentor; the wise S. Hugh himself, the bishop, has stories to tell at the high table in the hall, and admiring disciples anxious to gather up every word that falls from his lips.

So our friend goes on into Yorkshire; if he stays at Howden by the way he may be put under contribution by the rector and made to tell what marvellous tale he can tell about his own country; perhaps to compare notes about the news from Constantinople, or the study of the enchantment that guided the storms in the Gulf of Satalia, or the last enormity of Swerre-Birkbain and the fellow kings of Norway. For Roger of Hoveden is quite Herodotean both in the faithfulness of his personal relations and in the wish to incorporate in his chronicle all that he can gather touching the geography and history of strange lands. Going on to

York, the traveller finds himself in the midst of legal controversies; there had been good schools there once, but the
head master was lost in a storm at sea in 1177 and since then
the canons have taken to quarrelling. There have always
been two parties there and some black sheep in the flock.
The archbishop too, since Becket's death, has been under a
cloud, so the chapter is at sixes and sevens. Peter of Blois
looks in occasionally when in residence at Ripon, and Hubert
Walter, the dean, tries to keep matters fairly well, but there
are quarrels even within the precincts of the church, and
in more than one case there are rival claimants for the same
stall: on one solemn occasion the precentor stops the music to
spite the treasurer, the treasurer puts out the lights to be even
with the precentor. But, notwithstanding, there are quiet
pens taking notes; and a good deal of York news filters into
the general history. There is the biographer of the archbishops, one or more than one; not far off, at Newburgh, in
the Augustinian priory, is William, the little inquisitive and
intelligent canon, who is writing a history of England, not in
the mere receptive spirit of the annalist like Hoveden, nor
in the didactic style of William of Malmesbury, but like a
thoughtful man who wishes to trace the origins and tendencies
of the events that he records, who weighs his epithets and
suspends his judgments, and, whilst he admits the marvellous,
argues only when and where he has sufficient data. If
William of Newburgh ever comes up to York, depend upon it
he is well received by all the thoughtful men. The Prior of
Hexham too is *ex officio* a canon of York, and he also is, as his
predecessor was, a writer of history strikingly in advance of
the mere annotator of annals.

If the visitor can be prevailed on to go so far north as
Hexham, he may even reach Melrose, and there watch the
process of annal making, and come home by Durham. There
he will find a magnificent court under Bishop Hugh, the
great prince prelate of the period, who lives in three-quarters
independence between the kings of Scots and English; and
in his train poets, preachers and writers of histories, who
are one after another continuing the work which had been

begun by Bede, and continued after long breaks by Simeon and the Hexham writers. And so, having completely traversed the literary world of England, he may come south, through either the eastern or the western counties, sure to find at every monastery or cathedral he may visit some one employed in keeping up the record of public as well as local history, or otherwise attempting to keep alive the fire of literary zeal.

He would go away, I think, from such a view with the impression that, whatever drawbacks there might be to the full enjoyment of life, England was a paradise of clerks. True, the cruel legate, Hugeson, had betrayed them to the king, had actually yielded the point, that most important point, about the forest law, and allowed the king to prosecute clerical offenders against the peace of the king's venison, and have them hauled before the sheriffs in the county court, but that was the only drawback to the free enjoyment of clerical society. So far as books were concerned, there was such a supply of writers and readers as would be found nowhere else in Europe, except in the University of Paris itself. Such an impression, I take it, would not be far from the truth : for the extant remains of the literary work of the period are so great, that, if we suppose them to bear the ordinary proportion to the lost works of the same age, they would prove it to be enormously prolific. I do not claim for it such a distinction, because I think that most of what was really worth preserving has been preserved; preserved because the men whose task it was to take care of it were sensible that it was the work of an age of transcendent importance in every region of English life; constitutional, moral and intellectual.

The greater works of the time survived not only because they were the most famous works of the time, but because they were of really great value. Thus Glanville's work on the Laws became the manual and text-book of the lawyers; the Dialogus de Scaccario the standing order book of the high Court of Exchequer; the annals of Roger Hoveden the recognised book of authoritative chronicle record, to which, whenever a question of foreign policy or even domestic diplomacy arose, recourse might at once be had. That the lawyers and statesmen of the day were not above the study of history may be proved by the later use of these and the like chronicles; especially when Stephen Langton produced the Charter of Henry I before the barons at S. Paul's, or when Edward I consulted all the cathedral and monastic chronicles of England in order to ascertain the true nature and extent of his claims over Scotland; or when Edward III elaborated his claim to France; or when the Commission of Doctors at West-minster searched all chronicles for information on the pedigree of the house of Lancaster; or when Beaufort and Gloucester explored them to ascertain the constitutional position of a regent; or when, to crown all, poor Henry VI, who probably was the best historical scholar in his divided realm, was requested by the lords of his parliament to search, out of the chronicles which he had loved so well, the materials by which they might come to the conclusion that he was a traitor and a usurper.

There have been, as I said, losses; but it may well be that the great value of the works that have survived may lead us somewhat to exaggerate the worth of those which have perished; the Antiocheis of Joseph of Exeter, the Tricolumnis of Bishop Richard, the de Præstigiis Fortunæ of Peter of Blois, the Liber Facetiarum of Gervase of Tilbury may not have been so permanently important as we should suppose; but there is no question of the serious importance of the lost leaves of the Gesta Stephani or the Draco Normannicus.

I have, you may observe, given prominence in this lecture to certain names and certain sorts of names. I have given them prominence because it was desirable, even at the risk of repetition, to impress them on the memory, even if it should prove impossible to form or fix any individual con-ception of them: they are the greatest names, and the names of those who have left the most precious books behind them. But they are very far from all; a reference to some such book as Mr. Wright's Biographia Britannica Literaria would furnish a long list of names of men who have places in the bibliographies; both historians, philosophers and natu-ralists, according to the idea of those days. If we turn, too, to Leyser's Bibliotheca Poetica we find many names of English poets, Englishmen, that is, who wrote Latin verses, but of whom little else is really known, and whose verses are neither in manner nor matter so good as the poorest prose of the period. Geoffrey Vinsauf, who no doubt was the best known Latin poet of the time, has left no personal history; his work, framed on the Epistle to the Pisos, is by no means to be despised as a guide to the medieval idea of Latin poetry, nor is it a mean work in itself. But the average of the poetry, with that exception and the Trojan War of Joseph of Exeter, is low, whether we look at the classical forms followed by these writers and some of the satirists or at the rhymed Latin poems of which Walter Map was so fertile a producer. A great many of the good prose writers, however, attempted versification. We have, starting with Henry of Huntingdon, a generation earlier, a fair list of good scholars who thought verse the best medium of enthusiastic panegyric. John of Salisbury mingles encomium and sarcasm in his Entheticus, a book in which he has described in enigmatic language most of the courtiers of the time, with praise or dispraise. William Fitz-Stephen, the biographer of Becket, courted the ear of Henry II with a poem which he presented to him at Brill, and which seems to have been so far successful that the king pardoned him for his adherence to the archbishop; Giraldus Cambrensis wrote epigrams, Walter Map hymns and poems of edification as well as satires; the author of the Dialogus de Scaccario and the Latin biographer of Richard I both run into what would be doggerel if it were not Latin, apparently out of the very glee of their hearts and devotion to their subject-matter.

But as every one who could write prose thought that he could write verse, and as good Latin verse required a somewhat higher strain than passable Latin prose, it is not surprising that the verse has been mostly forgotten. The question then which this point seems to suggest, to what did it all come, what amount of real, critical, and literary culture does this great mass of Latin writing truly imply? must be answered thus: The Latin of the twelfth century is fairly good and grammatical Latin; adjective agrees with substantive and verb with its nominative case; *ut* governs the subjunctive, and the dependent sentence follows the mood and tense prescribed by the principal sentence. There is a great fertility of vocabulary, there are frequent and consistent uses of words which in classical Latin are somewhat rare, as if the writer prided himself on knowing how to use dumtaxat and quippe and utpote, and brought them in at every turn : but even here there is nothing that is laboured; the Latin, if too free, is scarcely ever unnatural. It is Latin written as by men who on literary matters talked and thought in Latin ; it is not a dead but a living language, senescent, perhaps, but in a green old age. The more pretentious writers, like Peter of Blois, wrote perhaps with fewer solecisms but with more pedantry, and certainly lost freedom by straining after elegance.

Just think now what this common familiarity with Latin implies. It implies almost as ready a hold on all the great works of antiquity as the power of reading English at the present day implies with respect to our own national classics. To John of Salisbury, after his twelve years of study, all the writings of the Latin historians, poets and orators, the Christian fathers, the legists and the canonists, were not more ready of access than they were to the practical administrator, who could write freely and plainly an account of the details of his official board. This facility of learning was limited only by the scarcity of books ; a very fatal limitation, but not half so fatal as the common fault of these days, when there are so many more books than there are readers with a will to read. All these writers of Latin were readers of Latin, and many of them read a great deal. John of Salisbury's reading certainly rivalled that of Burton, the author of the Anatomy of Melancholy, and his power of reference and quotation was assuredly not inferior. As he worked among the classics, Ralph de Diceto worked among the historians of the silver and later age ; Aulus Gellius and Seneca, I will venture to say, were commoner books in the hands of ordinary readers then than now : as for the poets, I have spoken before. The great Roman historians were, I fear, less directly known.

Some parts of Cæsar's Commentaries, Suetonius, Florus, Eutropius, Justin, were, I think, directly known; I question whether Livy or Tacitus was; except so much as had filtered through the Historia Miscella, or the translations and additions to the Chronicon of Eusebius. Seneca certainly was read and utilised; there is indeed a manuscript of Seneca which contains on a fly-leaf a trace of having been at the English court about this very time. But John of Salisbury's acquaintance with Roman literature can only be estimated by a careful reading of the Polycraticus; but we must remember that what he could read was at least within the reach of his contemporaries.

I have not said much in these lectures about the vernacular writers of the reign, whether of the Norman or English race; for indeed they can hardly as yet be said to be literary people. But I must not finish without a word about them, lest I should be thought to undervalue them. The poem of Jordan Fantosme, on the rebellion of the sons of Henry in 1173 and 1174; the poem on the Conquest of Ireland; the original French poem of Ambrose, on which the Gesta Ricardi are founded; the Life of S. Thomas of Canterbury, by Garnier of Pont S. Maxence; the valuable poetic chronicle of Benedict of S. Maur, are the beginnings of a new literature the value of which is prospective; predecessors of Villehardouin and Joinville and the Chronique d'Outremer, after the law, if there be such a law, that in the development of a vernacular literature poetry takes precedence of prose. I sometimes think that the growth of this school or schools of composition was owing to the increased interest taken by women in the history of their country; certainly the spread and strengthening of it tends to show that the classes to whom the use of Latin, except in the Church services, was becoming less and less familiar, were beginning to care to have a literature of their own. It shows, moreover, taken in connexion with that deadly liveliness of the Latin poetry which I have adverted to, that, whilst Latin was still a ready enough medium for serious writing, it was necessary to find something better and freer than Latin verse to interest people. Medieval Latin prose never dies out;

medieval Latin verse continues to live only as a pedantic and attenuated survival from the moment that either Norman French, or medieval English poetry comes into fashion. Into these fields of investigation I do not now propose to intrude. I shall have done something to reconcile myself with the perfunctory and superficial way in which alone my irksome duty on these occasions can be discharged, if I have called your attention to the literary side of a period of our history which, although it may be the fashion to regard it as obscure and barbarous, still contains the germination and early growth of institutions which are vital portions of our national existence. An age so important as that of Henry II in constitutional growth could not be an age of barrenness and deadness in any department of culture, altogether; that it was not is amply proved not only by the remains of literary work which are still preserved to us, but by the glimpse they give us into circles of scholar-like activity, a highly stimulated growth of literature, and an extent of education which we ought to be the last to undervalue.

VIII.

THE MEDIEVAL KINGDOMS OF CYPRUS AND ARMENIA.

(Oct. 26 and 29, 1878.)

I HOPE that I need not apologise for my choice of a subject. The events of the last two years can scarcely be called to mind without much misgiving, both as to the way in which they have been construed by contemporary readers, and as to the way in which they will be judged by history. I am not one of those who hold that the maintenance of an opinion contrary to their own belief, implies either moral delinquency or mental imbecility. I have been quite prepared to admit that two honest men, equally gifted and alike trying to be impartial, may come to diametrically opposite conclusions from the same evidence. But it is sickening to see the policy of a statesman, still more to see the question of a fact, debated, maintained or contradicted, by advocates whose arguments are not based upon attempts to find out the truth, but are simply weapons of attack and defence. 'This is to be believed because it suits the party; this is to be discredited because it would damage the party: this is true because Pericles has said it; this is false, or why should Alcibiades, or Cleon, or whoever it may be, have called heaven and earth to witness that it is true?' It will be a good thing if, after so much that is disheartening in the popular treatment of great questions, even one little benefit may be secured. Whatever may be thought of the Anglo-Turkish Convention, on whatever grounds, moral or political, we may determine that the salvation of Turkey is possible, or that Cyprus is an unhealthy island, a professor of History may draw some little comfort from

the fact that the attention of people has been called to a
portion of the history of Christendom of which little notice
has been taken of late years, and which is closely connected
with one of the greatest movements that ever affected the
history of the world.   Having said this I will add, that my
object in this lecture is not to ventilate dogmas, to impress
any principle, moral or political, or to justify any foregone conclusion.   I plead guilty to the charge brought against me of
choosing subjects which are of no importance to any human
being ; I wish simply to talk about a subject on which a good
deal of intelligent interest has arisen, and in the further
discussion of which many fresh points of interest may be
expected to present themselves.

It is right, however, that I should preface one word of
caution against myself.   The Crusades are not, in my mind,
either the popular delusions that our cheap literature has determined them to be, nor papal conspiracies against kings and
peoples, as they appear to the Protestant controversialist ;
nor the savage outbreaks of expiring barbarism thirsting for
blood and plunder, nor volcanic explosions of religious intolerance.   I believe them to have been, in their deep sources,
and in the minds of their best champions, and in the main
tendency of their results, capable of ample justification.   They
were the first great effort of medieval life to go beyond the
pursuit of selfish and isolated ambitions ; they were the trial-
feat of the young world, essaying to use, to the glory of God
and the benefit of man, the arms of its new knighthood.   That
they failed in their direct object is only what may be alleged
against almost every great design which the great disposer
of events has moulded to help the world's progress ; for the
world has grown wise by the experience of failure, rather than
by the winning of high aims.   That the good they did was
largely leavened with evil may be said of every war that
has ever been waged ; that bad men rose by them while
good men fell is, and must be, true wherever and whenever the race is to the swift and the battle to the strong.
But that in the end they were a benefit to the world no one
who reads can doubt ; and that in their course they brought

out a love for all that is heroic in human nature, the love of
freedom, the honour of prowess, sympathy with sorrow, perseverance to the last, and patient endurance without hope, the
chronicles of the age abundantly prove; proving, moreover,
that it was by the experience of those times that the forms
of those virtues were realised and presented to posterity.
This much I say, by way of a caution, that you may not accuse
me of an attempt to impose upon you. The history of the
Crusades has always had for me an interest that quite rivals
all the interest I could take in the history of the Greeks and
Romans; and very much of that interest is of the same sort;
a half archæological interest in a life and growth from which
we have ourselves received some great impulses, but almost
all the minutiæ of which are important only through their connexion with those great impulses.   Such a half archæological
interest I hope you may feel in the history of medieval Cyprus,
and what little is to be told of its sister kingdom.

The last decade of the twelfth century saw the establish-
ment of two small Christian kingdoms in the Levant, which
long outlived all other relics of the Crusades except the military
orders; and which, with very little help from the West, sustained a hazardous existence in complete contrast with almost
everything around them. The kingdoms of Cyprus and
Armenia have a history very closely intertwined, but their
origin and most of their circumstances were very different.

By Armenia as a kingdom, is meant little more than the
ancient Cilicia, the land between Taurus and the sea, from
the frontier of the principality of Antioch, eastward, to Kelen-
deris or Palæopolis, a little beyond Seleucia; this territory,
which was computed to contain sixteen days' journey in length,
measured from four miles of Antioch, by two in breadth, was
separated from the Greater Armenia, which before the period
on which we are employed had fallen under the sway of the
Seljuks, by the ridges of Taurus[1]. The population was com-

---

[1] The boundaries of Armenia at its greatest extension are thus given by
Du Laurier, in the Armenian volume of the Recueil des Historiens des
Croisades, pp. xix sq. :—Westward, Side or Eski-Adalieh; eastward, the
Pylæ Ciliciæ, or passes of the mountains close to the gulf of Alexandretta.

posed largely of the sweepings of Asia Minor, Christian tribes which had taken refuge in the mountains. Their religion was partly Greek, partly Armenian, for the Armenian Catholicos, after resting for a century and a half in Mesopotamia, took refuge at Sis, and founded there an independent or national Catholicate at the close of the thirteenth [1] century. Their rulers were princes descended from the house of the Bagratidæ, who had governed the Greater Armenia as kings from the year 885 to the reign of Constantine Monomachus, and had then merged their hazardous independence in the mass of the Greek empire [2]. After the seizure of Asia Minor by the Seljuks, the few of the Bagratidæ who had retained possession of the mountain fastnesses of Cilicia or the strongholds of Mesopotamia, acted as independent lords, showing little respect for Byzantium save where there was something to be gained. Such was the lord Taphnuz of Edessa, on whose inheritance Baldwin of Boulogne founded his principality; such were the lords Leo, Thoros, Melier, and Rupin of the Mountains, who ruled Cilicia during the twelfth century; trying to balance their position between the Byzantine and Latin influences on each

The custom-house, towards Iconium, was at Pilerga, and the passes Westward were at Germanicopolis and Claudiopolis.

[1] The Catholicate was without fixed residence from 1066-1114; it was then settled at Hrom-Gla, on the Euphrates, in the principality of Edessa, where it remained until 1292, when it settled at Sis.

[2] The Armenian historians describe the Greater Armenia after the fall of the Arsacidæ, under Arsaces IV, A.D. 387, as divided between Persia and Byzantium; the Arsacide rulers governing as tributaries until 428. From 428 to 625, it was governed by Persian governors, 'Marzbans,' frequently native Armenians of the house of the Bagratidæ; from 632 by a Curopalates or patrician named at Constantinople; sometimes by the patriarch, sometimes by the Khalif. In 885 the Bagratide, Aschod I, was recognised by the Khalif Motamed as king, and was crowned. His successors were Sempad I, 890; Aschod II, 914; Apas, 928; Aschod III, the Merciful, 952; Sempad II, 977; Kakig I, 989; John Sempad and Aschod IV, 1020; Interregnum, 1040; Kakig II, 1042. Kakig gave up his kingdom to Constantine Monomachus in 1045, and was murdered in 1079. These kings reigned at Ani. There was another principality at Kars, which surrendered to Constantine Ducas in 1064. Senekerim John, king of Vasburagan, had, in 1021, surrendered to Basil II, and received Sebaste in Cappadocia; and Abelgarib had Tarsus as a separate lordship from Constantine Monomachus in 1042.—The Bagratidæ claimed an Israelite origin. S. Martin, Mémoires Historiques et Géographiques sur l'Arménie.

side of them. Rupin of the Mountain was prince at the time of the capture of Jerusalem by Saladin ; he died in 1189, and his successor, Leo or Livon, after having successfully courted the favour of pope and emperor, was recognised as king of Armenia by the emperor Henry VI, and crowned by Conrad of Wittelsbach, archbishop of Mainz, in 1198. This act which, although Livon forfeited his position by obtaining recognition from Alexius Angelus, implied a cessation of the old dependence on Byzantium, and an ecclesiastical reconciliation with Rome, was the typical act of Armenian history; the whole of which, save and except the defence against the Saracens and the Tartars of a later date, was an attempt to secure independence by skilful balancing of Greek and Roman influences ; to obtain money from the West and arms from Constantinople, to obtain alternate alliances by royal marriages, and ecclesiastical freedom by regular variations between the two poles. For this latter policy the position of the Armenian Church was peculiarly fitted. It was so far schismatic as not to be integrally a portion of either Roman or Byzantine obedience, and so little heretical that its alliance was courted by both communions. Hence its importance in the conciliar history of the middle ages ; an importance which has no sufficient parallel in the secular history of Armenia.

The origin of the Latin kingdom of Cyprus is less obscure and more romantic. Cyprus had been seized by the Arabs in the early days of Islam (cir. 700—cir. 963), but recovered for the empire by Nicephorus Phocas, and ruled by dukes down to the reign of Manuel Comnenus. Its population was a mixed one ; there were Griffons or Greeks, Armenians, Georgians, Maronites, native Cypriots, Greek parœci, emancipated slaves, the descendants of Albanian soldiery of the empire, and of Venetian emigrants of the first Crusade. But the land was fertile, and they had dwelt together in peace. In the reign of Manuel the happy days of Cyprus ended and the period of calamity began. According to the anchorite Neophytus, who wrote the tract ' de Calamitatibus Cypri,' the native authority for the conquest by Richard Cœur de Lion, Isaac Comnenus, a nephew of the emperor Manuel, had been appointed by him to

rule the Armenian frontier; he had quarreled with the
Armenians, been taken prisoner and sold to the Latins ; that
is, to Bohemond III of Antioch, whose step-father, Reginald
of Châtillon, had many years before ravaged the isle of Cyprus
in revenge for the hostility of Manuel Comnenus. He was
ransomed from captivity by the emperor Andronicus, and,
about the year 1184, came to Cyprus and set up an independent
tyranny. He called himself βασιλεὺς, but ruled as a despot of
the worst order. All the better class of Greek inhabitants
fled to Constantinople ; and the state of Cyprus under Isaac
Comnenus was only paralleled by that of Jerusalem under
Saladin. On the evidence of Neophytus, Richard of England
came not as a freebooter, but as a deliverer from utter misery.
In this point there is a fair consensus of Eastern and Western
testimony. Richard seized Cyprus not as a pirate, but as
an avenger and emancipator. The story is short, or may be
made so.

After wintering at Messina, Richard having with him, in
his fleet, not in his ship, his betrothed wife Berengaria and
his sister, queen Johanna, of Sicily, sailed for Acre on the
10th of April, 1191 ; the fleet was dispersed by a storm on
Good Friday, April 12 ; and Richard, after being obliged to
land at Rhodes, was driven by a second storm on the 1st of
May into the Gulf of Satalia. Before this day the queens
had appeared off Cyprus, and found anchorage off Limasol.
Isaac had attempted by courteous offers to get them into his
power, but his hospitality was presented in so military a
fashion, that the guardians of the royal ladies took fright,
and avoided landing. On the very day on which they were
obliged to promise that they would go on shore, Richard's
ship came in sight. His first act was to demand from Isaac
an account of the treatment of the wrecked vessels which had
been driven on the coast of the island and plundered by the
emperor. Isaac replied contumeliously, and Richard landed in
force. On the 6th of May Limasol was taken : the emperor
was unhorsed by Richard in single combat, and fled to Nicosia.
On the 12th of May Richard and Berengaria were married at
Limasol ; and Berengaria was there crowned, not queen of

Cyprus, for the island was not yet taken or claimed, but queen of the English. Negotiations for peace and alliance were on foot, when Isaac suddenly broke off the deliberations and fled to Famagosta. Richard, who had now obtained the assistance of Guy of Lusignan and the prince of Antioch, and who was much pressed for time, left him no rest. Guy employed himself in capturing the chief strongholds; Richard, who was ill, after taking Buffevento, occupied Nicosia. There the emperor submitted to him on the 31st of May, and surrendered himself, his daughter and his treasures. Richard put him in silver chains, having promised that he would not put him in irons; placed the little girl under charge of the queen, and spent or distributed his treasure. Cyprus was conquered in a fortnight. Richard bestowed on the island the inestimable gift of his presence for five days after the emperor surrendered: Isaac he sent off under the charge of Ralph Fitz-Godfrey to Tripoli; he extorted from the Cypriots half their property, in return for a charter by which the laws of Manuel Comnenus were restored to them; constables were placed in the several castles, and Richard Camville and Robert of Turnham were left behind to govern Cyprus as justices and sheriffs on the English model [1]. What followed is not very clear. Before a month was over Camville was dead, and Turnham had been obliged to put down a revolt and hang a pretender. Richard found his new acquisition a burden; Neophytus briefly says that the 'Incliter' sold the island for 200,000 pounds of gold to the Latins. The Templars were the purchasers; they also found the burden a heavy one, especially at a moment when the war with Saladin demanded all their energies. The small garrison which they were able to keep in the island was shut up in Nicosia by the angry Griffons, and there was every chance that Cyprus would be lost as rapidly as it had been won. This was the state of affairs in May 1192, when Richard, by a piece of rough diplomacy, prevailed on Guy of Lusignan to surrender his claim to the shadowy crown of Jerusalem, and to accept the lordship of Cyprus instead. The Templars were glad enough to sell

[1] Ric. Divis. c. 61.

their rights, and Guy, with Richard's advice, bought them. A successful sally of the garrison of Nicosia saved the Latins from massacre, the alarm of which they avenged by an indiscriminate slaughter of the Greeks. Guy thus obtained his first hold on the island ; so much of the Greek population as was still spared fled in panic ; and way was thus made for the institution, in this remote corner of the Levant, of a dynasty and government of the straitest feudal character ; the introduction into a land, empty of all but the cultivating classes and slaves, of the fully developed and now crystallised block of feudal polity.

The house of Lusignan maintained itself in Cyprus for nearly three centuries, during which, although fallen somewhat from the blessedness which had been broken up by Isaac Comnenus, the island seems to have retained so much fertility and prosperity internally as to make its later history very dark by contrast. The flight of the Greek population, which had begun under Isaac and been completed after the massacre of Nicosia, left the island open to colonists from the West. The peculiar privileges of the Cypriot Church, which was autocephalous, made it easy for the remaining prelates and people to accept the Western obedience, and enabled the house of Lusignan to appeal confidently for the support of European Christendom. The short period too during which, under Guy and his successor, the administration of Cyprus was kept separate from that of the waning kingdom of Palestine, gave those kings a moment's breathing time, and this they improved with a success which the long continuance of their dynasty against fearful odds may be held to prove.

Guy, we are told, received Cyprus for life only, and did homage for the island to Richard. As he already bore the title of king, the question whether he should hold Cyprus as a kingdom does not seem to have arisen. He appears in the Lignages d'Outremer as ' seignor,' not as ' roi de Chypre ; ' and no coins occur on which he is called king of Cyprus. On his death, in April 1194, Richard putting in no claim for the reversion, his brother, Amalric of Lusignan, constable of Palestine, entered on the possession as his heir ; he was not as yet King of Jerusalem ; it was a matter of importance to him to be recognised as King of Cyprus ; and he accordingly did homage to the Emperor Henry VI. He was crowned by the Bishop of Hildesheim, who was sent over from Sicily to perform the ceremony ; this was done in 1197. Immediately after this, Amalric succeeded to the crown of Jerusalem ; the crown of Jerusalem which, after the year 1269, became permanently united with that of Cyprus, was an independent crown, and the king of Jerusalem an anointed king : the union of the crowns therefore seems to have precluded any question as to the tenure by which the kingdom of Cyprus should be held. The crown of Cyprus was conferred at Nicosia, that of Jerusalem at Tyre or at Acre, and, after the capture of Acre, at Famagosta. The homage then due to Richard, or to the crown of England, ceased at the death of Guy ; although the discontented barons of Cyprus are said to have revived the idea of such a relation when they wanted the aid of Edward I, in 1271. The homage secured to the Emperor by Amalric was possibly recognised until 1269, but was throughout complicated by the claims of Frederick II and his sons on the kingdom of Jerusalem. In 1459 the illegitimate pretender, James II, did homage to the Sultan of Egypt as suzerain of Cyprus ; but that act was not the recognition of a right ; it was only a bid for support, and was one of the immediate causes of the entire downfall of the house of Lusignan. Guy, however, does not seem to have troubled himself about his title. His reign lasted only two years, and his whole time was given to the restoration of something like prosperity in the desolate land [1]. According to the contemporary ' Chronique d'Outremer ' he opened an asylum for the dispossessed Franks of Armenia and Palestine. These, to

---

[1] There were five classes of native cultivators in Guy's time :—

   (1) Parici—πάροικοι—slave cultivators.

   (2) Lefteri—ἐλεύθεροι—freed folk.

   (3) Albanesi—descendants of Albanian soldiery.

   (4) Veneziani bianchi—descended from the soldiers of Vital Michaele in the first Crusade.

   (5) Perperiarii, enfranchised Paroeci—paying a tax of 15 perperi ; (cited from Bustron by Beugnot, Assizes of Jerusalem, i. 207).

the amount of 300 knights and 200 men-at-arms, with a great
number of bourgeois, he enfeoffed with estates of land in
Cyprus ; so liberal was he that he retained for himself only
twenty knights' fees. Possibly the truth was that he was
obliged to sell the land of the island to find the money due to
the Templars ; but the mode in which it was done proves that
the feudal idea, on which a few years later the Latin conquests
in Romania were apportioned, was full grown.   The arrangement however made by Guy had to be altered by Amalric
when he reached the dignity of kingship.   He threw himself
on the mercy of his vassals ; they responded liberally, and
surrendered to him so many of his brother's grants that at his
death a royal revenue of 200,000 byzants was forthcoming.
Guy had perhaps made as much as he cared to make of his life
interest, but he was, like his patron, careless in the spending
of money, whilst unlike Richard's, his opportunities of acquiring it were very limited.

Thus, however, the land system of Cyprus was restored ; the
300 knights, 200 men-at-arms, and extensive bourgeoisie, constituted one or two permanent estates of the kingdom.   The
nobles, who were, no doubt, included in the number of the
knights, were the numerous lords who had either fled before
Saladin, or were so little hopeful of the event of the Crusades,
that they thought it wise to look to Cyprus as a prospective
refuge.   Hence throughout the middle ages the Cypriot lords
retained the titles of their homes in Palestine ; and the Palestine titles, when the families of their possessors were extinct,
were conferred as a sort of life peerage at the will of the
kings.   Of the few Frank families that showed any vitality
the house of Ibelin was far the most prominent and prolific ;
the lords of Ibelin and Mirabel, sprung from the house of
Puiset, viscounts of Chartres, and closely connected with the
counts of Champagne and Blois [1], had played a conspicuous

---

[1] Balian le François, the first of the family, is described in the Lignages
d'Outremer as brother of Count Guillin de Chartres ; by which we are to
understand that he was a relation of Hugh de Puiset, count of Joppa, son of
Everard, and grandson of Geldewin, viscount of Chartres. His name Balian
is probably a softened form of Waleran ; see Du Cange on the Lignages,
pp. 360, 361. One lady of this house married an English knight, Hamo

part during the twelfth century in Palestine ; they were still
more prominent in Cyprus : from them the royal house received wives and guardians for the infant kings ; two of the
great recorders of the Assizes of Jerusalem were lords of Ibelin ;
one as regent or bailiff of Cyprus conducted the valiant resistance to the claims of Frederick II : and in fact, if any one
had cared to write it, the fortunes of the house of Ibelin
would have been as great part of the history of Cyprus as
those of the house of Lusignan. Other great families were
those of Gibeleth and Bethsan, named from Byblus and Beth-
shan or Scythopolis. The whole peerage of Cyprus however
contained only a few names, which sound strangely enough,
as they illustrate the geographical unity of history. There
were princes of Antioch, Galilee, and Montreal, lords of Bey-
rout, Sidon, Toron, Cæsarea, Tyre, and Tiberias ; counts of
Jaffa, Tripoli, and Carpasso ; there were also, as grand serjean-
ties, the double stewardships, constableships, and marshalships
of Cyprus and Jerusalem, and the chamberlainship of Cyprus ;
these are all, or nearly all. They constituted a high court of
baronage or parliament, as they had done in Palestine, and
were the supreme council of the king, of which we have so
much information in the Assizes of Jerusalem.

As for the ecclesiastical estate, tradition assigns also to
King Guy some trenchant measures which help to complete
the parallel or the contrast between him and William the
Conqueror. The old Cypriot church had an archbishop and
fourteen suffragans ; the archbishop was Archbishop of Cyprus,
and owed obedience to no patriarch. The flight or submission
of the Greeks left the field open to the Latin clergy ; and
Guy placed a Latin archbishop at Nicosia, with suffragans at
Famagosta, Limasol and Baffo. This arrangement was sanctioned by Celestine III in 1196. As time went on, the
Greek clergy returned, and Jacobites and Nestorians followed ;
very uneasy relations were produced between the two chief
hierarchies, one of which depended on Rome, whilst the other,

l'Estrange, who died in Palestine about 1272 ; this was Isabella, daughter of
the lord of Berytus and widow of the young king, Hugh III. See Assizes of
Jerusalem, ii. 449.

now seated at Famagosta, claimed the ancient prerogative of the Cypriot church. The schismatic clergy were, however, subjected by Honorius III to the Latin bishops, whilst Alexander IV, in the year 1260, went so far as to forbid the election of a Greek archbishop after the death of the reigning prelate, and reduced the number of Greek sees to four, Soli, Leucara, Arsinoe, and Carpasso; the bishops were also subjected to the Latin metropolitan, who was bound to administer justice among them. Probably Guy has obtained credit for some of the measures which properly belong to the popes and to a later date. The clergy of the island were as numerous as the difference of nationalities required. The Mendicant orders formed the strength of the Latin portion, the secular priests that of the Greek and Armenian. Monasteries abounded. In Nicosia alone were 250 churches.

These then being the estates of the realm, the powerful people were all Franks, the returning Greeks and Armenians would only creep into an equality of privilege, or return into the enjoyment of their old customs, as the governing race allowed; and, although they ultimately grew and prevailed while the governing race dwindled and perished, all political interest centres in the governing race. For them the existing polity of Palestine was transported across the sea; not as yet reduced to writing, for the system of Godfrey of Bouillon, 'the Letters of the Sepulchre,' if it were ever codified, had perished, and the Assizes had not yet taken their historic form. But the new kingdom was singularly rich in lawyers, and this was early recognised; in 1214 we find Lewis of France, son of Philip II, applying for a legal opinion on a point of procedure to Hugh I of Cyprus; the old lords of Palestine spent their leisure in Cyprus recording the customs of their lost inheritance, and the extant Assizes of Jerusalem were the result of their studies. The names of the great legists are Philip of Navarre, John and James of Ibelin, and Guy le Tort. John of Ibelin, who died in 1266, and bore the title of count of Jaffa, Ramlah (Rames), and Ascalon, drew up the existing Assize of the High Court. It is in exact symmetry with Western usage, that this great compilation was not received

as a code until the year 1369 : like the ' Siete Partidas ' of
Alfonso the Wise, it was but a body of jurisprudence, the use
of which depended on its own reasonableness, or a collection of
customs which were recorded because they were used, not
merely used because they were recorded. The Highest Law
was still ' the custom' recorded in the heart and mouth of the
' lawful man.'

The Assizes of Jerusalem, then, although no doubt they
describe what we may call the common law of the Cypriot
kingdom, so far as concerned the Franks, cannot be regarded
during the greater part of the period as an authoritative code ;
the native population of Cyprus, like the native Syrians of
Palestine, had laws and customs, such perhaps as the laws of
Manuel Comnenus for which they obtained Richard's confirmation ; and the city of Famagosta at a little later period,
after having been for some years under the government of the
Genoese, was allowed to retain the laws of Genoa. Within
the feudal fabric itself, custom, or perhaps principle, was more
dominant than law ; the lords of the great fiefs did not
accept the rules of the high court as binding unless they had
themselves consented to them ; the unity of feudal jurisprudence lay rather in ideas than in cogent uniformity. Add to
this the fact that the Frank population of Cyprus showed no
tendency to ordinary increase, but was either constantly diminishing or recruited by arrivals from the West, whilst the
Greek population was at home, strong, numerous, and wealthy ;
that the Latin Church accordingly, although powerful in the
protection of Rome and of the Cypriot crown, was surpassed
in wealth and historical greatness by the Greek and Armenian
communities ; and we cannot but conclude that in this, which
is regarded as the most flourishing period of Cypriot history,
there was little chance of strong government or administrative
development. The Assizes of Jerusalem lay like a crystal
block, a model of usages, incapable of enforcement and incapable of growth. The kings lived for the most part the
life of adventurers or knights-errant, playing their part in
the defence of Christendom, but still, like the great military
orders and fragmentary principalities of Palestine, only as an

isolated garrison in the middle of a world out of which they were being gradually driven ; no more, as Richard had hoped, an advance post in the great campaign by which the East was to be humbled before the West.

Hence, no doubt, it is that, notwithstanding the example of the kingdom of Naples, which was the nearest Catholic neighbour of Cyprus, we find no traces of a Cypriot parliament. There were councils of nobles and councils of bishops ; there were high courts and bourgeois courts ; and there were, as elsewhere, three estates well defined, clergy, nobles, and burghers ; but if there ever was any attempt to range these in an organised body either for legislation or for money grants, I have failed to discover it. The ' Bancs,' or ordinances, with which the customs of the Assizes were supplemented, were issued by the king's proclamation ; in two or three cases the participation of the court or of the barons is expressed. In 1362 we have an ordinance issued by the king, Peter I, by the assent of the men of his court. A few years before, his father, King Hugh, issued his laws by proclamation : ' Hear the ban of God and of my Lord the King, Hugh of Lusignan of the Kingdom of Jerusalem and of Cyprus ; know all men that on the 16th of May, 1355, the Lord King and his men ordained an assize.' Here it is possible there may be some reference to a general court or ' witenagemot,' but not, I think, to an assembly of estates. According to the Assizes of Jerusalem, every vassal who, whether immediately dependent on the king or on a mesne lord, had done homage to the king as chief lord, was a member of the royal court ; a usage which in so small a state must have crushed out every tendency to representative government[1]. In default of further evidence we must, I think, assume that, as in France before the institution of the states-general, the only check on the king was his court of vassals ; whereas, after the example had been set in the states-general, diets and parliaments of the West, the national life of Cyprus was too much attenuated to allow it to reproduce such institutions on an unfriendly soil. The Basse Cour or Court of Bourgeois, organised under the vis-

[1] Assizes, i. 254.

counts or sheriffs of Cyprus, with jurats and other machinery
of courts of law, was an organisation of tribunals of justice
and local government, not a legislative constitutional organisation : its assizes are therefore a book of procedure rather
than a code of laws, and, like the Assizes of the High Court,
rather a record of customs than a body of statutes. These
courts also, like the court of barons, may be regarded as
developments towards constitutional growth, arrested and
petrified at a certain stage.

But I have said more than enough upon a subject which,
somewhat repulsive by itself, needs severe study before it will
begin to be remunerative. The Assizes of Jerusalem will
always remain a mine of feudal principles and a treasure to
scientific jurists ; they reflect infinite lustre on the Cypriot
lawyers who, in an age of turmoil and exertion, continuous
and overwhelming, found time and labour for recording them.
We conceive that the lords of Ibelin must have been well
acclimatised in more ways than one ; it is certainly curious
that they supplied the main historical support to the kings of
Cyprus in marriage, war, and jurisprudence.

King Guy had a very short reign ; and most of the acts
that are ascribed to him I have already noted. After the
collapse of the third crusade and the three years' truce between
Richard and Saladin in 1192, he seems to have retired to
Cyprus, and to have died in April 1194 ; the same year the
old Emperor Isaac died in the custody of the Hospitallers at
Merkeb. Isaac's daughter was still wandering up and down
Christendom ; by the agreement for Richard's release she was
to have been handed over to Duke Leopold of Austria, her
kinsman, but when Baldwin of Bethune brought her to
Austria, she found Duke Leopold dead ; she was accordingly
brought back to Richard, and subsequently married to a
Flemish knight, who came to the East in the fourth crusade
in the retinue of John de Neesle, and, in her name, put in a
claim for Cyprus, which King Amalric summarily rejected.
The rights of Guy devolved upon his brother; or rather
Cyprus, for the reversion of which no arrangements had been
made, fell to the lot of the possessor.

Amalric of Lusignan had been, under his brother, constable of both kingdoms, and Prince of Tyre; he was thus in command of such military force as his brother had possessed, and succeeded quietly to his dominion : from Henry VI, as I said, he obtained recognition as king, and was crowned in 1197; in 1198 he obtained the crown of Jerusalem, marrying, as fourth husband, the lady Isabella of Anjou, who had carried the right of succession first to Henfrid of Toron, then to Conrad of Montferrat, and then to Henry of Champagne. The German chancellor, Bishop Conrad of Hildesheim, who had crowned the King of Cyprus, negotiated the marriage and succession, and Amalric, leaving Cyprus under the administration of the Hospitallers, transferred his court to Acre. We hear no moie of Cyprus during Amalric's reign. He was an able warrior, and as successful as mere warlike ability, coupled with very indifferent morality towards the infidels, could make him. With the aid of the German crusaders of 1197 he recovered Berytus, where the ceremony of his coronation took place ; he also took Byblus, and besieged Toron ; but the difficulty of keeping terms between the Germans, the Franks, and the military orders, was too great for him. The siege was raised, the Germans retired, and Amalric had to make a truce with Safadin.

The Crusade of Villehardouin passed over without any direct effect on either Cyprus or Palestine. Amalric died at Acre in April, 1205, and was buried in the church of S. Sophia at Nicosia. He left the crown of Cyprus to his eldest son Hugh, the son of his first wife, Eschiva of Ibelin, under the guardianship of Walter of Montbeliard, his brother-in-law. The crown of Jerusalem, the right of which depended on Queen Isabella, was left unclaimed: John of Ibelin, half-brother of Isabella, and uncle of the jurist, was lieutenant of that kingdom ; and he, after some years' searching, found a husband for Mary, the queen's eldest daughter by Conrad of Montferrat ; John of Brienne was accepted as king of Jerusalem in 1210. The queen's second daughter Alice, the child of Henry of Champagne, was given to the young king, Hugh of Cyprus. The event of the minority was a descent made by Walter of

Montbeliard on the coast of Asia Minor, the only result of which was booty. Hugh came of age in 1211, and was in that year crowned at Nicosia. His reign was short, and was devoted chiefly to the restoration of order and prosperity in Cyprus. He encouraged the study of law, and was so learned in it himself that Lewis of France applied to him for an opinion on legal procedure, which was held as authoritative by the feudal lawyers. From Palestine he seems to have stood aloof, partly perhaps owing to the fact that the death of Queen Mary, who, dying in 1212, left only an infant daughter, might seem to open the succession to his wife, Queen Alice. In 1217 however he joined the expedition against the fortress of Tabor, persuaded by King Andrew of Hungary, who visited Cyprus on purpose to engage his support. The attempt on Tabor was unsuccessful; and Hugh retired to Tripoli, where he died in February, 1218. It thus happened that neither the great Crusade of 1202 nor the expedition against Damietta in 1219 directly touched the fortunes of Cyprus; for the heir of King Hugh was an infant of nine months old; and the Queen Alice, who with the aid of the child's great uncles, the lords Philip and John of Ibelin, was guardian, seems to have avoided too close alliance with the new troops of Crusaders. Cyprus was, however, a regular station for the pilgrim fleets, and as regularly an object of attack whenever the Sultans saw an opportunity of unresisted devastation.

The little interest of the history runs rapidly on to the Crusade of the Emperor Frederick II, which brought about many other critical conjunctures in the history of Christendom. This particular portion of the history is of no small legal as well as historical interest. The kings of Jerusalem being men of action, practising little self-restraint and never taking care of themselves, generally died young, and left the fate of their kingdom in suspense on the life of their young children. Hence constant minorities, and the need of provisions for guardianship, a need which, as yet, had scarcely begun to be felt in the kingdoms of Europe. The practice therefore of the kingdom of Jerusalem in the matter of regency became a stock of legal cases, which, if not cited as occasion arose in

corresponding circumstances in the West, afford to us at least
a number of parallels. The earlier practice had been to give
the wardship of the person of the heir to the nearest relation
incapable of inheriting; that of the kingdom to the presumptive heir[1]. But the rule laid down in the Assizes, which
is really perhaps a generalisation from the earlier cases rather
than a deliberate constitution, was that the mother of the heir
should be his guardian; in case of her death, the next relation
on the side on which the kingdom moved, that is, the heir-
presumptive; in case no such person could be found, it was
for the barons of the kingdom to meet and choose a regent or
guardian. The practice seems to have been to leave the
queen-mother as regent with a bailiff or high-steward to do
the work of government.

In the year 1228 the case in Cyprus was this: the King
Henry, although old enough at seven to be crowned, was still
a minor. His mother, Queen Alice, had married a second
husband Bohemond V, heir of Antioch, and had quarreled
with the lords of Ibelin, who were not only her nearest relations, but the most powerful and cleverest of the acclimatised
baronage. These lords were the sons of that Balian of Ibelin
who was supposed, by going to mass instead of to battle, to
have ruined the chances of Guy of Lusignan at Nazareth in
May, 1187: he had married the widow of King Amalric I,
and his sons were thus half-brothers to the many-husbanded
Queen Isabella, great uncles to King Henry, and half-uncles
to Queen Alice. So long then as the family party hung
together, they formed a strong phalanx; when they quarreled,
all the internal strength of the kingdom was turned against
itself. The second marriage of Queen Alice probably broke up
the unity. Philip of Ibelin died in 1227; John of Ibelin,
lord of Berytus, naturally expected to succeed him as bailiff;
the queen proposed a baron named Amalric Barlais. John

---

[1] Assizes, i. 261. If a vassal die the custody of the ward is not to be in
the heir, but in the nearest kinsman on the side on which the fief cannot fall.
Cf. Glanville, vii. c. 11; Etablissemens, i. c. 117. If he is a sovereign or
suzerain, his men shall have care of his body and fortresses, the heir to guard
the heritage (i. 435). See Itinerar. R. R. p. xcvii.

succeeded in maintaining his position, and became bailiff or regent under the nominal guardianship of the queen. But the struggle was still proceeding when Frederick II, on his way to Palestine, arrived in the Levant. Frederick II, as I need not remind you, was already the 'Stupor mundi,' the man of unbounded ambition and almost ubiquitous versatility, who never did a great or truly kingly act, or followed any but a selfish aim. He was, as son of Henry VI, heir of imperial aspirations that coveted the whole world, and, as the husband of Yolanda of Brienne, father and guardian of the young heir of Palestine. Yolanda, who must have been a child when she married him, died in this same year 1228, leaving an only son, the luckless Conrad. When then Frederick reached the Peloponnesus, he was met by five Cypriot barons of the queen's party, who asked his aid against the lord of Berytus. The emperor, whether desirous as he might well be to make Cyprus available for military purposes, or simply wishing to assert his right as overlord, undertook to deal with John of Ibelin ; the barons told him that the revenues of Cyprus were large enough to secure the conquest of Palestine, and Frederick thought them worth a trial. He arrived at Limasol, and wrote to John as his dearest uncle, begging him to come to him with all his family and concert measures for the crusade. John called together his friends at Nicosia and consulted them : they told him that to admit Frederick was to betray the infant king, but advised him to return a courteous answer, to meet craft with craft. But this John would not do ; he swore that he would rather die than let the Crusade fail by his default ; and therefore presented himself to the emperor with all his force, and with the little king in his train. Frederick received him ostentatiously, made him change his black mourning robes for scarlet, and entertained him at dinner : after dinner, the usual time apparently for quarreling, he turned round upon him and insisted on the resignation of the lordship of Berytus, which was a fief of the crown of Jerusalem, and also of the office of bailiff of Cyprus. John boldly told the emperor that this treatment was only what his friends at Nicosia had bidden him expect. The emperor

changed colour at the reproach, which showed in what estimation his honour was held. But the friends of the Crusade
interfered, and an agreement was made that the question of
Berytus should be decided by the high court of Palestine, that
of the regency by the high court of Cyprus. This was not
carried into effect. John, dreading the emperor's treachery,
fled to Nicosia : there Frederick besieged him and forced him
to a compromise ; he did homage for Berytus, and the emperor
was allowed to receive the revenues of Cyprus until King
Henry reached the age of twenty-five, thus apparently exercising the rights, if not under the name, of an overlord ; but
whether he claimed the right as emperor or as king of Jerusalem, or as representing the nearest kinsman, is not clear[1].
Frederick left Cyprus under charge of five barons of the island,
and went on to Palestine. After his short stay in the Holy
Land, and his politic but not very far-sighted treaty with the
infidels, he left the East to take care of itself. For about
three years the arrangement continued in force ; but in 1231
the emperor's marshal and deputy, Richard Filangier, tried to
wrest Berytus from John of Ibelin, and threw him into open
rebellion. John equipped a fleet, and, with the young king,
landed in Cyprus. The marshal retired before him. John
occupied Famagosta ; the marshal retreated to Nicosia ; there
he was defeated and forced to disband his army, which passed
over into the service of the king of Armenia. Cherin held out
until Easter, 1233 ; and then the last remnant of Frederick's
army left Cyprus.

John of Ibelin died in 1236 ; the imperial power was by
that time broken up in Palestine as well as Cyprus ; and now
Queen Alice attempted to turn the tables on Frederick himself. The relics of the whole Crusading history were im-
perilled ; Frederick would accept no invitations, nor would he
send Conrad to assert the rights of Yolanda. Alice, therefore,
as heir of Jerusalem, put in her claim for the regency of

---

[1] That Hugh had to perform homage and swear fealty to Frederick II
appears from the letter of Innocent IV, releasing him from the oath in 1247.
See Mas-Latrie, Hist. de Chypre, vol. ii. p. 63. It is said that the barons
recognised the emperor as suzerain, but refused liege homage.

Palestine; the poor barons clung to a straw; they accepted her, and she named her third husband, Ralph of Soissons, bailiff of Jerusalem. No sooner was he appointed than he left his post and went back to France. Jerusalem had already fallen to the Sultan of Damascus in 1239; after a brief restoration in 1243, it fell to the Kharismians in 1244; to the Sultan of Egypt in the same year. The crown became a derelict; the title was borne after Conrad by his half-brother Henry, the son of Isabella of England; and subsequently by a number of ruling houses, who seem to have clung to the name far more faithfully than they had ever clung to the reality of the dominion. The remains of substantive power devolved with the title on Hugh the Great, King of Cyprus in 1269.

The rest of the history of King Henry is soon told. He came of age in 1232, married a daughter of the house of Montferrat, and lost her the same year; a second wife, Stephanie of Armenia, died in 1250, and he then married Placentia of Antioch. Henry took a subordinate part in the Crusade of the middle of the century. His action is obscure, as are all the details of the period. In the expedition of 1240 he seems to have borne no part: Richard of Cornwall does not mention a visit to Cyprus either going or returning; but Henry seems to have, in 1246, asserted his right to Jerusalem on the death of his mother, and to have been recognised as king by Innocent IV, who included King Conrad in his father's doom. In the Crusade of S. Lewis, Henry is said by the Cypriot historians to have shared both perils and glories; he certainly received the French king, and entertained him at Nicosia during the winter of 1248, which was so fatal to many of the French nobles. We are not told that King Henry furnished any part of the supplies that S. Lewis collected in Cyprus, the mountains of corn or the towers of wine casks; all these were furnished by the emperor and the Venetians. The King of Cyprus entered Damietta with the French king in triumph in 1249; but he did not, as has been asserted, share his captivity. After this we read no more of him; he died early in 1253, having been the sport of fortune all his

life, and leaving the inheritance of his history to a child of a
few months old, Hugh II, who reigned from 1253 to 1267.

The only incident of the reign of Hugh II turns, like that
in his father's reign, on the question of regency. Queen
Placentia acted as regent, but in the second year of the reign
went over to Palestine and married Balian of Ibelin, the
reigning lord of Arsouf. As Hugh was the last of the
Lusignans, the marriage seems to have been unpopular; and,
either in consequence of it, or after the death of the queen
herself, a new bailiff was appointed. This was Hugh of Antioch, son of Henry of Antioch, and grandson of Bohemond IV;
his mother Isabella was daughter of King Hugh I. He was
nearest in blood to King Hugh and his presumptive successor.
One military exploit signalised the regency: in 1265 he led
to the defence of Acre against the Sultan Bibars a fleet of
Cypriot vessels. Then, says Sanuto, was the military force of
Cyprus in great valour and of great prudence; there were in
the company 130 knights and much cavalry besides. The
contribution however helped the falling cause but little. All
in Palestine was going to ruin; already the Venetians and the
Genoese were at war; the Templars and the Hospitallers were
irreconcilable; the Frank princes were selling their estates
and returning westward. The lord of Sidon sold, in 1260,
Sidon and Belfort to the Templars; Balian sold Arsouf to the
Hospitallers. Henry of Antioch and his wife claimed the regency of Palestine as against the house of Brienne. In 1264
Bibars destroyed Cæsarea; and the defenders of Acre were
obliged, in self-defence, to lay waste their suburbs, and leave
open to the Saracens the great poliandrum or cemetery of
S. Nicolas, in which 124,000 men had been buried in one year
during the third Crusade. In 1261, the year before Hugh's
appointment to the regency, the Latin empire of Constantinople fell. All the older medieval things were passing away
in both East and West, and the tide which had led on the
Crusades was turning.

The child king, Hugh II, died in 1267; and the bailiff,
Hugh III, succeeded as king. Hugh II was the last of the
house of Lusignan who was left in the East; in the West

there were still many members of the prolific family. Our memory recurs most naturally to that large family of the Aliens, the half-brothers of our king, Henry III, who nine years before had been banished in consequence of their opposition to the Provisions of Oxford; their father, Hugh X of Lusignan, Count of la Marche, was nephew to the Kings Guy and Amalric. Hugh of Antioch, too, the new king, represented the house of Poictiers, being sprung from Raymond of Poictiers, the uncle of Queen Eleanor, the wife of Henry II. The reigning house of Lusignan in la Marche came to an end in 1303. But although this was the case, the Cypriot dynasty continued to bear the name of Lusignan, to which by a female descent it was entitled; and there are many Lusignans, in England as elsewhere, flourishing at the present day.

Hugh III, the new king, had the advantage of acquiring the throne when he had age and experience to fill it: and he reigned fourteen years, long enough to establish his own authority, and to see the downfall of all the Frank states around him. I will mention three points only in his history; for although he bore the title of the Great, ' Hugh the Great,' it was a very forlorn hope that he was called on to lead. He seems to have been the king of Cyprus to whom S. Thomas Aquinas dedicated the famous treatise ' De Regimine Principum;' a book which, owing to the great reputation of its author, and the ˙definiteness of the principles which it enunciates, became a handbook of the relations of Church and State in the middle ages. Of the work which we now possess under this name, only a book and a half out of the four books was the work of S. Thomas, the rest was added probably by Ptolemy of Lucca; but the book itself was a model which later publicists chose to follow or to comment upon. Many of these commentaries are found in our libraries; and down to the age of Sir John Fortescue, the book addressed to the King of Cyprus occupied a position of authority inferior only to the Politics of Aristotle. It is not improbable that the book was originally written for the education of the young King Hugh II; but it is certainly very curious that the composition both of the great Feudal Code of the Assizes, and of the manual of medieval politics, should have a direct relation to this remote little island. The second point to be noted is this :—

Hugh saw nearly all the Crusading conquests lost. In 1268 Antioch was taken, and the prince, Bohemond VI, retired to Tripoli. In 1269 Hugh claimed the crown of Jerusalem, and was crowned at Tyre on the 24th of September. But this empty honour was not obtained without competition. The king's great-aunt, Mary of Antioch, daughter of Bohemond IV, and grand-daughter of King Amalric, contested the title ; she carried her cause to Rome for the arbitration of the pope ; and unable to make good any claim herself, she sold in 1277 her rights to Jerusalem to Charles of Anjou, the King of Naples, the brother of S. Lewis, and head of that Angevin house which transmitted the crowns of Jerusalem and Sicily to René of Anjou, the father-in-law of our King Henry VI. Hugh III then was King of Jerusalem when Edward I made his crusade. In May 1271, and for several months later, the two kings were together at Acre ; and during their intimacy Hugh put before Edward a question which bore a signally close relation to that on which so much of the interest of Edward's own reign was to turn. The documents concerning it are preserved among the Assizes of Jerusalem. Unfortunately we have only the case, not the opinion which Edward gave. The question was, what obligation lay on the knights of Cyprus to feudal service within the kingdom of Jerusalem ; exactly parallel to the great question of 1297 in England, upon which the Confirmation of Charters resulted.

It was not decided by Edward, but John of Ibelin had laid down the rule : 'Three things are they bound to do outside the realm for the lord : 1. For the marriage of him or any of his children ; 2. To guard and defend his faith and honour ; 3. Por le besoing aparant de sa seignorie ou le comun profit de sa terre.' When we find a jurist named Accursi d'Arezzo practising at Acre in 1270, it becomes even probable that Edward picked up his friend Francesco there. It was possibly on this occasion that Edward laid down the rule that, for the recovery of the East, Egypt should be first occupied, then the Holy Land, and then Constantinople. When that was done, and not till then, would the Christian warriors, settled and established, be able to dwell safely. So at least says Marino Sanuto, writing in 1321.

But neither Edward's little army nor his legal skill could save King Hugh from discomfiture; in 1272 he was forced to submit to make a treaty with Bibars, which left him only Acre and the right of pilgrimage to Nazareth, and for this he had to thank, it was said, the diplomacy of Edward. After Edward's departure, and an attempt to sustain the Frank cause in Tripoli, Hugh seems to have devoted himself to the care of his island kingdom, which was itself threatened by the monstrous policy of Charles of Anjou. That wretched tyrant, by way of inaugurating his purchased sovereignty, wrested Acre from King Hugh in 1277. He did not live to recover it. After a siege of four months the Cypriot knights declared their term of service at an end, and the siege was raised. Hugh was a patron of learned men, and a founder of monasteries. Probably he saw that unless the Christians were unanimous he must be content to sit still. The Hospitallers supported him; the Templars spited him; the Genoese helped him; the Venetians thwarted him. So he stayed in Cyprus, where the people to a great extent prospered under his care, and had sons and daughters. His wife was a lady of the house of Ibelin: he died at Tyre in 1284; he was buried in the abbey of Lapais. His eldest son, John I, who succeeded him, died in 1285; his brother and successor, Henry II, reigned from 1285 to 1324; witnessing a period of transitional history which affected the East as well as the West, and which furnishes material of more curious if not wider interest.

So long as Acre held out against the Infidels, that is exactly a hundred years from the date when Richard restored it to Christendom, almost all the living interest of the Crusades centres in that curious stronghold; for it must have been a very strange encampment of fighting and praying men of all nations. There each of the great orders had its strong tower, palace, and appointed share of the wardship of the walls. There the Hospitallers and the Templars issued from their palaces the orders that governed their brethren throughout Christendom; the Genoese and the Pisans had their quarters in close neighbourhood; the Venetians had their Tower far off, between the Tower of the English and the ward of the Hospitallers; and the mendicant orders had each their house and church to themselves. Immensely strong, and able to draw in supplies constantly from the sea, Acre was a standing menace to the Eastern world; but without were fightings and within were fears. The very closeness in which the conflicting powers were encamped intensified the dangers of their disunion. There was still great appearance of strength; the King of Jerusalem and Cyprus was at least safe in the castle around which this fortified camp was spread; all along the coast northwards, of Syria and Armenia, were placed the strong munitions of the military orders; over the sea, a little way, was Cyprus, the great granary of Palestine, and within the lines of Palestine itself were strongholds of both the knights and the ' pullani,' or acclimatised Franks, which were fortified with great skill, and need indeed succumb to nothing short of famine. All this, however far short it fell of a well-administered state or a well-regulated camp, was still a strong power, when the fatal quarrels in the West, the downfall of the Hohenstaufen, the wicked policy of Charles of Anjou, the rivalry of the Venetians and the Genoese, combined to bring about the end.

Acre held out almost to the last; Antioch had fallen in 1268; all Palestine proper, save Acre and the road to Nazareth, had been surrendered in 1272; Tripoli was lost in 1289. Dependent on Acre were Tyre, Sidon, and Berytus, and a few straggling forts that must fall when Acre fell. That was on the 18th of May, 1291. The King of Jerusalem and Cyprus at the time was Henry II, the second son of Hugh III, who had succeeded his brother John in 1285, and had been duly crowned in 1286. The recovery of Acre from the forces of the King of Naples, which was effected before he could duly receive the crown of Jerusalem, was the one brilliant exploit of a long and otherwise unhappy reign. The assistance which the military orders afforded him on the occasion caused the regent of Naples to confiscate all the estates of those orders within the kingdom of Naples, which formed a precedent for the atrocious measures of Philip the Fair against the Templars. Five years afterwards the Sultan Khalil Ashraf besieged Acre: King Henry brought his forces to the rescue, but, on the day of the assault by the Mussulmans, lost heart and sailed away. For three days the luckless defenders struggled and perished, and on the fourth day the city was taken. I shall not dwell on the valour of the knights or on the atrocities of the captors. The same day at evening the Franks of Tyre embarked and set sail for the West. The Templars left Sidon and went to Cyprus; and the people of Berytus surrendered. The break up of the great camp was followed by a dispersion of the forces of the Cross. The kingdom of Armenia began to falter in its obedience to the Roman Church. The Armenian Catholics had to flee from Mesopotamia to Sis in 1292; and about the same time the relics of Antiochene chivalry took service under the Armenian king. The military orders were only kept in Cyprus by the gift of Limasol, which King Henry bestowed on them conjointly; but soon the Templars sought their Western preceptories, within a very few years to perish utterly; the Teutonic knights found work in the conversion of the North; the Hospitallers, maintaining a better heart, fitted out a new Crusade, and in 1308 seized the island of Rhodes, whence for two hundred and fifteen years they made the Mediterranean too hot to hold a Turkish fleet. The rest of the unattached Franks found a home in Cyprus.

Amongst these was one little known and obscure knightly order, which Englishmen need not be ashamed to recognise; the Order of the Knights of S. Thomas of Acre. This was a little body of men who had formed themselves into a semi-religious order on the model of the Hospitallers. In the third Crusade, one William, an English priest, chaplain to Ralph de Diceto, Dean of S. Paul's, had devoted himself to the work of burying the dead at Acre, as the Hospitallers had given themselves at first to the work of tending the sick. He had built himself a little chapel there, and bought ground for a cemetery; like a thorough Londoner of the period, he had called it after S. Thomas the Martyr; and, somehow or other, as his design was better known, the family of the martyr seem to have approved of it; the brother-in-law and sister of Becket became founders and benefactors, and a Hospital of S. Thomas the Martyr of Canterbury, of Acre, was built in London itself on the site of the house where the martyr was born [1]. Little indeed is known of the early days of the knights; they were not numerous, and probably poor; but when Peter des Roches, the Bishop of Winchester and ex-justiciar, was in Palestine in 1231, he placed them in a new church and under the rule of the Templars, giving them also in his will a legacy of 500 marks [2]. They had their proper dress and cross: according to Favin their habit was white, and the cross a full red cross charged with a white scallop; but the existing cartulary of the order describes the habit simply as a mantle with a cross of red and white [3]. They were building a new church when Edward was at Acre; and in 1278 we find him writing to the King of Cyprus on their behalf [4]. The Chronicle of the Teutonic knights, in relating the capture of Acre, places the knights of S. Thomas at the head of the 5000 soldiers whom the king of England had sent to Palestine [5], and Herman Corner, who however wrote

---

[1] In the ninth year of John, Oct. 13, 1207, messengers of the house of S. Thomas at Acre, being canons, had a safe-conduct. They had come to England to seek alms for the redemption of captives; Rot. Pat., ed. Hardy, i. 76. The 'Terra Sancti Thomæ' abutted on the land of the Temple at Casale Album, near Coquet; Paoli, Cod. Dipl. S. Joh., i. 468. Richard, the English tanner, at Acre, in 1273 sold two houses in the Street of the Tannery to the Hospitallers; ib. 195, 196.

[2] Matthew Paris, ed. Wats, p. 472.   [3] MS. Cotton, Tiberius C. V.

[4] Mas-Latrie, Hist. de Chypre, ii. 81, 82, where two documents are printed from the letters of Edward in the Public Record Office. In one of these the king commends Ralph de Coumbe, master of the Hospital of S. Thomas, to the good offices of Hugh of Lusignan, in Cyprus; in another, dated Sept. 15, 1279, Ralph de Cardolio and the brethren write to the king on the misfortunes of Palestine, and urge that the master of the Order should be sent into Syria. See the 7th Report of the Deputy Keeper of the Records, App. II. No. 2252; Royal Letters, MS. (Chancery), No. 4260.

[5] Matthæi, Vet. Ævi Analecta, x. 182; Eccard, Scriptores, i. 942.

a century later, mentions them amongst the defenders of Acre. We know from their cartulary that they had lands in Yorkshire, Middlesex, Surrey, and Ireland[1]; their Master was called Master of the whole Order of the Knighthood of S. Thomas the Martyr, in the kingdom of Cyprus, Apulia, Sicily, Calabria, Brundusium, England, Flanders, Brabant, Scotland, Wales, Ireland, and Cornwall. Some few noble names of the masters have been preserved; Ralph of Coumbe was master in or about 1278[2], Henry de Bedford in 1323, and Robert de Kendale in 1344. In 1350 the order was recognised as still existing by the German traveller Ludolf of Suchen. In 1357 Hugh de Curteys, the preceptor of Cyprus, invested one Richard of Tickhill with the habit

---

[1] At Wapping, Plumstead, Coulsdon, and Doncaster. The estate at Wapping was the gift of Tierri of Alegate; MS. Cott. fo. 156. Coulsdon was confirmed to the master of the knights by a charter of Henry III, in 1261; fo. 236: the Hospital of S. James, at Doncaster, was given by Peter de Mauley: 'Deo et militiæ beati Thomæ martyris de Acon;' fo. 258: the benefactors in Ireland are enumerated by Edward I in a grant of confirmation, 5th June, Ao. 17; Fulk de Villars, John de la Zouche, Edmund Bret, Gilbert Marshall, Walter Marshall, and Philip Horsey. James Butler, Earl of Ormond, was another at a later date.

[2] Frater Radulfus preceptor fratrum Sancti Thomæ de Acon in Anglia; A.D. 1249. William of Huntingfield 'magister militiæ hospitalis B. Thomæ Martyris de Acon Londini;' MS. Cotton, fo. 166. Richard of Southampton was master of the Hospital, 11 Edw. II; Thomas de Sallowe, 'magister domus,' 40 Edw. III.

Aug. 7, 1323, Henry de Bedford, master general of the order, creates John de Paris prior and custos of the Chapel of S. Nicholas of Nicosia; sealing with his seal for Cyprus.

June 17, 1324, William de Glastingebury, preceptor of the house of S. Thomas of Acre, in the diocese of Nicosia, with consent of the chapter of the house, to wit, Nicolas Clifton, John of Paris, and William of S. Bartholomew, appoints Nicolas Clifton proctor against a brother Henry, who calls himself master; 'actum Nicosiæ in capella Sancti Nicolai presentibus Henrico et Thoma presbyteris Anglicis et prædicto Johanne priore dictæ capellæ.'

Aug. 30, 1344, Robert Kendale, master of the whole order, appoints Henry of Colchester and William of Brunill to collect money for the order; 'dat. Nicosiæ' in the house of Guddefrid, archdeacon of the church of Famagosta, vicar of Philip, archbishop of Nicosia.

Feb. 2, 1357, Hugh Curteys invests Richard of Tickhill; 'actum in regno Cypri in Nicosia intra ecclesiam Beati Nicolai Anglicorum, præsentibus Francisco de Gave burgensi Nicosiæ, domino Rob. de Swillington canonico, domino Ricardo de Chatesby presbytero Anglico; Guillelmo Gaston de Anglia Turcopolo regis et pluribus aliis.'

of the order, in the presence of Robert Swillington, canon,
Sir Richard Chatesby, an English priest, and William Gaston
of England, Turcopolier to the king of Cyprus. The ceremony
was performed in the church of S. Nicolas of the English in
the city of Nicosia; one of the many churches which formerly,
according to Father Stephen of Lusignan, adorned that city,
of which the Venetians destroyed 130 in the process of fortification. [It is possible that it still exists, and is indeed that
church of S. Nicolas, which our dear friend the bishop of
Gibraltar tried to recover in 1879.] The hospital in London
became, probably at the fall of the Templars, a mere Augustinian Hospital. Its church, or one built on the site of it, is
now the chapel of the Mercers' Company[1].

England had not, with all her business under Henry III
and Edward I, forgotten Palestine : some of her sons fell
at Acre, and the remnant of the little order found a home
at Nicosia.   But the great king himself never forgot his
first love ; in fact all the nobler Plantagenets, Richard of
Cornwall, Edward I, Henry of Lancaster, Henry of Bolingbroke, Henry V, and Cardinal Beaufort, all either made the
pilgrimage or looked forward to a great crusade. To Edward I,
in or about 1303, was addressed the very amusing ' Libellus
de recuperatione Terræ Sanctæ [2],' the work of an ecclesiastical
judge in Aquitaine, whose name is unknown, but who specu-
lates like a special correspondent of the period ; a book which
shows a just sense of the evils which had rendered the united
action of Christendom impossible ; points out ways in which
all political dangers in Europe can be avoided ; stigmatises
the crime of war between Christian princes, the ruinous
discord between Venice, Pisa, and Genoa, and proposes to
settle the military orders chiefly in Cyprus, and employ them
in the recovery of the holy places. Curiously enough, one
of the remedial measures proposed by the writer, who is
especially strong on the subject of natural science, is that

---

[1] The history of the London house may be read in Newcourt, Repertorium,
i. 553 ; and Mon. Angl. vi. 645 : it must be carefully distinguished from the
Hospital of S. Thomas the Martyr in Southwark, the germ of the present
S. Thomas's Hospital. See also Itinerarium Regis Ricardi, præf. pp. cxii–cxiii.

[2] Printed at the end of the second volume of Bongars' *Gesta Dei per Francos.*

girls should be taught to practise medicine and surgery; they are to learn grammar, and logic also, natural principles, and mathematics, but it is that they may qualify as wives for the Oriental princes.

But to return to Cyprus: Edward, as I said, was not the only one of his family who remembered it: Henry III had proposed to the Bishop of Bethlehem a marriage between his son Edmund and the queen-mother Placentia in 1256; the young king was also to marry one of his daughters [1]. The records however, of both that reign and the next, contain more references to Armenia than to Cyprus; thus in 1260 Alexander IV exhorts Edward to defend Armenia against the Tartars; in 1280 the Bishop of Hebron, vicegerent of the patriarch, sends the thanks of the Franks, and adds that Armenia and Cyprus have been laid waste by a plague of locusts [2]; the same intelligence is sent by the master of S. Thomas from Acre; the wars of Charles of Anjou cut off all hope of succour, and the king of the Tartars had demanded provisions from Acre. Boniface VIII was unwearied in impressing on England the importance of these regions; in 1298 he urges the sending of a subsidy to Sembat, king of Armenia [3]; in 1300 he is negotiating a general confederacy which will include the princes of Armenia and Georgia. Edward cannot do much, but if he cannot send knights he will send missionaries. The king of the Tartars sends envoys to him, and one of them is baptized. The last measures of Edward I and the first of Edward II are to the same purpose. Edward I issues safe-conduct to the bishop of Lydda and other Dominicans who are going to convert the heathen; Edward II sends a warning to the king of the Tartars against Mahometanism. The kings of Armenia, who have apparently little else to do, send constant appeals for money. Faithful Armenia, says Sanuto, writing in 1321, lies among the wild beasts; on one side the lion, the Tartar; on another the leopard, the Sultan; on a third the wolf, the Turks; on the fourth the serpent, the Corsairs. But these I must notice by and by.

[1] Fœd. i. 341.   [2] Ib. 402, 586.
[3] Ib. 900, 742, 749, 902, 919.

Henry II of Cyprus reigned nominally from 1285 to 1324; but during great part of the time he was superseded by one or other of his brothers: his quarrels with them form the whole history of his reign ; at one time he was a prisoner in Armenia, whither his brother, Amalric, the prince of Tyre, had sent him ; another brother, Guy, the constable of Cyprus, was put to death by his orders for a conspiracy against him. The Popes were much exercised by this fraternal strife ; but it was not until after the death of Guy that Henry had peace. As so often happens after an unquiet reign, he outlived all his enemies, and died rather regretted than not. This was in 1324 : he was buried in the church of the Franciscans at Nicosia. When he had been able to exercise independent authority he had used it well ; he had welcomed the refugees from Acre and fortified Famagosta ; he contributed largely to the judicial decisions which form the supplement to the Assizes, and he established a strong judicature in Cyprus. But he was an epileptic, which perhaps accounts for his incapacity to retain the rule ; and he left no children.

With the accession of his nephew, Hugh IV, begins a more stirring, and, perhaps, the most interesting, period of the Cypriot history. Before however entering on the outline of this portion of our subject, we may just look back to Armenia, where the native kingdom and the native dynasty were nearly coming to an end. Leo I, the first king, who was regarded by the Armenian writers as a really great and patriotic ruler, died in 1219, leaving an infant daughter, who carried the crown to her husbands in succession ; Philip of Antioch first, who, failing to make himself agreeable on the Church question to the native lords, especially a great lord called Constantius, or Constantine, was put to death with his partisans. The second husband was Hayton, the son of Constantius, who reigned for nearly fifty years, at first under his father's directions, and after the year 1237 independently. Hayton was thus king during the whole of the crusading period of the thirteenth century, and had dealings with Lewis IX in his first Crusade, and with Edward of England during his stay in Palestine. He was moreover the king of

Armenia in whose time Marco Polo set out on his travels in Asia ; and it was through his means that the Western kings became acquainted with the Tartar dynasty at Samarcand and its tendencies to favour Christianity. For the Tartar rulers during this period were far from being committed to Islam ; they received and favoured missions and protected Christian doctrines in a liberal fashion, without understanding them or finally committing themselves[1]. Hayton may possibly have the credit of having stirred up the Mongols against the Khalifate of Bagdad, which Hulaku brought to an end in 1259. The alliance with the Tartars brought down the Sultan of Egypt on Armenia ; and, after the capture of Antioch, Hayton resigned his throne and retired to a monastery, where he took the name of Macarius, and died soon after. His brother, the constable of Armenia, Sempad, Sembat, or Sinibald, was the author of an Armenian chronological history of authority. A better known person, also of the royal house, was the monk Hayton, who about the year 1305 wrote a history called the Flower of the Histories of the East. Hayton's career is curious. He had been lord of Gorigos, or Corycus, on the Mediterranean coast, and had both fought in Palestine and negotiated among the Tartars, where the Armenian princes were constantly tantalised with the hope of converting the khans. About 1290 he went to Cyprus and became a Præmonstratensian canon, as Brother Antony. From Cyprus he turned westward and came to France, where the Pope was. It was at Poictiers that he dictated his history, which accordingly was written in Latin. It has been printed both in Latin and in a French translation of the same century, but contains more about the Tartars than about the Franks. It is not improbable that to Hayton's influence we may trace some of the interest shown in Armenia by Edward I and Edward II.

[1] Mosheim in his 'Historia Tartarorum' has collected all the notices accessible in his time of the attempts to convert the Tartars, which for a long time had a show of success. After dallying with Christianity, the Khans seem to have become finally Mahometan and hostile at the beginning of the 14th century. But the subject, since the publication of the Armenian authorities, has become susceptible of much more elucidation.

King Hayton, however, who died in 1271, was succeeded
on the Armenian throne by his son Leo II, who seems to
have clung to the Tartar alliance as against Egypt, and to
have come to an open rupture with the Pope on the other
side. He was likewise in close alliance with Byzantium, and,
although his history is obscure, he seems to have asserted an
independent position for which his successors toiled in vain.
He reigned eighteen years, and was followed by four of his
sons in succession. Of these Hayton II purchased the support
of the West by reconciling himself and his people to Rome ;
he was a poet and historian also, and ended in becoming a
Franciscan as Friar John. With his brother, Thoros, who
on his withdrawal became king, he went to Constantinople
to obtain help from Andronicus Paleologus. On their return
they found themselves unseated by a third brother, Sembat ;
fled to Cyprus first and then to Tartary, but were taken ;
Hayton was blinded and Thoros strangled. Sembat had
thrown over the Roman alliance and been crowned by the
Armenian Catholicos ; but, finding the Saracens still gaining
ground, he changed his tactics, and obtained from Boniface VIII a bull for a subsidy, which was circulated in
England in 1298 [1]. He was supplanted in his turn by his
brother Constantius. He, after a short reign, was succeeded
by Leo III, son of Thoros, who reigned under the guardianship
of his uncle, the blind brother John, who had been king as
Hayton II. Both Leo and his uncle were put to death by a
Tartar general, at the suggestion, according to the Roman
writers, of the discontented Armenians, who had been again
too summarily reconciled to the papacy in a council at Sis,
in 1307. Oissim, who succeeded in 1308, was another son
of Leo II. He was connected with the Cypriot history,
taking part with the brothers of King Henry against him ;
and he also obtained a confirmation of the union with the
Roman Church in 1316. Leo IV, who was the last of the
native dynasty, succeeded his father Oissim in 1320. His
whole reign was a continued struggle against the Moslems,
who were encroaching on every side, and his name became

[1] Fœd. i. 900.

very well known in the West. It was in his defence that
John XXII proclaimed a Crusade in 1333 ; and among other
helps Edward III, in 1335, allowed his ambassadors £40 from
the London subsidy. Leo found himself before his death
reduced to the few mountain fortresses from which his
ancestors had emerged two centuries before. He failed to
gain the support of the Armenians, and was thus thrown on
that of the Latins, who could really give him no aid. He
was assassinated about 1342, and his dynasty ended with
him. The five remaining Kings of Armenia sprang from a
branch of the Cypriot house of Lusignan, and were little
more than Latin exiles in the midst of several strange populations all alike hostile.

We have now to return to Hugh IV, King of Cyprus, a
prince who is known in literary history as the king to whom
Boccaccio dedicated his genealogy of the gods. He reigned
twenty-five years, and has the merit of setting on foot the
great alliance between the Venetians, the Pope, and the
Knights of Rhodes, to which the chief successes of his reign
and that of his son were due. It is true that these successes
wear to modern eyes the look of mere piratical exploits : but
we have two points to remember in this connexion. All
naval war, not only during the middle ages, but down to the
seventeenth century, was more or less piratical ; and the war
between the Christians and the Saracens, although interrupted
now and then by truces, which both parties felt ashamed to
make and took the first opportunity of breaking, was really
continuous and internecine. The coasts of Asia Minor had
been gradually lost to the Christians ; the coasts of Egypt
were to some extent open to reprisals. The fact that the
coast of Syria and Palestine afforded so few harbours had,
when once the fortified harbour of Acre had fallen into the
hands of the Saracens, the effect of removing the seat of war
to the Asiatic and Egyptian coasts. That was the deliberate
opinion of King Edward I, who had ruled that Egypt must
be the first point of attack, then Palestine, and then Constantinople. Hence the two attacks on Damietta in 1219
and 1249. Now, after a long period of defence, the Christians

took the initiative. The leaders and fighters in all this from
1308 to 1523 were the Knights of Rhodes, but Cyprus was
very frequently the head-quarters and source of supplies, and
the Western pilgrims were not chary of labour, blood, or
treasure. In all the great achievements of the time too
some English pilgrims were associated. The single exploit
however of King Hugh's reign was a descent on Smyrna in
1344. John of Biandra, Grand Prior of Lombardy, the head
of the expedition, made himself master of the citadel; and
Smyrna remained in the hands of the knights until the close
of the century. The King of Cyprus had contributed a con-
tingent towards the fleet, but, except by weakening the
Saracen power a little, he obtained no immediate benefit for
his state [1].

The great plague of 1349 fell with especial fatality on
Cyprus; only one castle, that of Dieudamour, was safe for
the king to dwell in; and the island got such a reputation
for unwholesome air that the trade almost ceased. The Frank
population especially diminished. In 1349 the traveller,
Ludolf of Suchen, described the barons of Cyprus as the
richest in the world: after the plague Hugh had to recruit
the ranks of the nobles by conferring titles on the merchant
class. The succours sought in Europe were only scantily
afforded. The King of Armenia cried louder and got more
sympathy than the King of Cyprus. Still some brave men
went out to the East. It is at least to this period that we
have to refer the pilgrimage and warlike exploits of Henry
of Lancaster, the great duke-palatine and father-in-law of
John of Gaunt. He, according to his biographer Capgrave,
about the year 1351 made his grand tour, and fought not
only in Prussia, where he went first, but also in Rhodes,
Cyprus, and the East, ending his military education with a
campaign in Granada. William Lord Roos of Hamlake,
died in 1352, either in Palestine or in Cyprus, on a more

---

[1] Paoli, Cod. Dipl. Ord. S. Joh. ii. 93, gives a commission from the Pope to
the Archbishop of Candia to recover from the King of Cyprus, the Grand-
Master of Rhodes and the Doge of Venice, the money covenanted for the
defence of Smyrna.

distinctly religious pilgrimage: to 1357 we have referred our last glimpse of the English order and their church at Nicosia. In 1352 Henry Lord Percy left by will 1000 marks sterling in florins of Florence for his son Henry to make the pilgrimage. But the French war in the West, and the struggles of the Venetians with the Genoese, prevented anything like national or united expeditions. In the midst of turmoil King Hugh died in 1359, and was buried in the Blackfriars' church at Nicosia. His eldest son, Guy, prince of Galilee and constable of Cyprus, had died before him, leaving a son, Hugh of Lusignan. He, on his grandfather's death, went into the West to obtain some support in his claim on the crown, which, owing to the fact that representation was not allowed by the laws of Cyprus, failed to obtain recognition. This is that Hugh of Cyprus whom the Pope in 1360 made senator of Rome, and who really ruled there from January to August 1361. He has been confounded by some of the Cypriot historians with his grandfather, who accordingly is made to abdicate and die at Rome. Hugh, having failed to find employment for his military genius at Rome, resigned the senatorship, and we hear no more of him [1].

The crown of Cyprus had been secured by Hugh IV to his second son Peter, whom he had had crowned, before his death, at Nicosia.

Peter, with apparently some characteristics of genius, had several more or less allied to insanity. He had made a vow of slaughter against all Mussulmans generally, and, for the purpose of keeping it, wore his naked sword hung round his neck. Our acquaintance with him is largely due to Froissart, who follows his exploits with some minuteness; but we have a more valuable record in the work written by Philip de Mazzeriis, chancellor of Cyprus, on the life of the legate Peter Thomas, whose period of activity nearly coincides with the reign of King Peter, 1361–1369 [2]. Peter Thomas was a native of Guienne, a born subject of Edward III, and was

---

[1] Gregorovius, Gesch. d. St. Rom., vi. 393; Theiner, Diplom. S. Sedis, ii. 391.

[2] Acta Sanctorum Boll. Jan. ii. 995–1023.

probably instrumental personally in creating the interest felt
in England and Guienne in the plans of the King of Cyprus.
He crowned Peter at Famagosta, and made an attempt to
bring over the Greek population of Cyprus to the Roman
obedience.   The first exploit of King Peter was the voyage
across the enchanted gulf to Satalia, and the capture of the
place, where, as Froissart tells us, he slew without exception
all the inhabitants of both sexes whom he found there.   In
this expedition he was assisted not only by the Catalans and
the fleet of Rhodes, but by an English force, or a force under
an English knight, whom the Italian historians name Robert
of Toulouse [1], and describe as sent into Armenia to demand
tribute from the princes.   If Robert of Toulouse was engaged
in the sack of Satalia, we must hope, for our national credit's
sake, that he was only an Englishman by courtesy, a Knight
of Rhodes of the langue of England, which would contain
knights drawn from the continental estates of the Plantagenets.   Having fleshed his maiden sword at Satalia, King
Peter set out on a mission westward, a general canvass of
Christendom.   Having gone by way of Rhodes to Venice, the
legate, making known the approach of the king, applied for
succour to the ' communitates, dominos et tyrannos ' of Lombardy, and then passed on to Avignon.   In March 1363, King
Peter himself reached Avignon, where the Pope gladly received
him, and determined to preach a new Crusade, of which King
John of France, who had just emerged from his prison in
England, should be the leader.   After settling this, the king
went to Prague, where he saw the emperor Charles IV, and so
to Juliers, Brussels and Bruges.   Everywhere he was received
with suppers and tournaments, in both of which he seems to
have played his part.   Whilst he was enjoying himself, the
legate was negotiating, and it was determined that the Crusade under King John should start from Marseilles in the
following March.   Froissart follows the movements of King
Peter through Picardy to Calais, and on to London.   At
London he was well entertained ; Queen Philippa made him

---

[1] The name is variously given : Dulaurier reads it Lusugnan ; it also appears
as Julassan, which looks like a corruption of an English name.

handsome presents; King Edward gave him a ship named the
Catharine. The mayor, Henry Picard, gave him a dinner, and
allowed him to win fifty marks at play : but as the poor king
did not lose with a good grace, the mayor gave him his money
back again. Of substantial aid he got little; and Edward
was not liberal even with promises ; he himself was too old to
go, but his sons and nobles might. Peter went back therefore
to France. Before he went he was robbed by some English
highwaymen ; as however Edward paid all his expenses, he
was probably no great loser.

King John had during this time returned to England,
where he took part in the festivities, but died soon after, in
April 1364, thus putting an end to one part of the great design ; and one of Peter's first acts after returning through
Guienne to Paris, was to attend King John's funeral, May 7,
1364, and the coronation of his successor. He seems then to
have revisited the emperor and the kings of Hungary and
Poland, a route which hindered him from reaching Venice
until the legate had left. The legate had been called away to
Cyprus to settle a quarrel between the Genoese and King
Peter's officers. Peter appeared at Venice rather forlorn ; but
he had obtained the support of some English lords, one of
whom, the Earl of Warwick, must, if the traditions of the
Beauchamps are to be trusted, have gone on before him ; for
in the great battle in Turkey, fought Nov. 1, 1364, he took
prisoner a son of the King of Lithuania, whom he brought
back to England and made a Christian. Two other Englishmen of distinction are known to have followed Peter ; John
Lord Grey of Codnor, and a knight of the house of Stapylton,
who had been especially impressed by the virtues of the
legate.

Having got together as many volunteers as he could, and a
considerable fleet, King Peter sailed from Venice and joined
the fleet of the Hospitallers. The great stroke to be made
was the capture of Alexandria. This was effected with no
small bloodshed and very rich spoils. Alexandria taken, the
next object was to strengthen the fortifications and make it
the head-quarters of a Crusade. But here the English

auxiliaries objected.   There can be no doubt that the story is
true, for it is from the pen of the legate himself: they refused
even to stay all night in Alexandria, and having conspired
with a certain prince, whose name the legate feels bound to
keep secret, set sail for Cyprus.   They sent word home too
that the city was only half taken [1].   It was a great disappointment to the ardent crusaders ; but no doubt the
English lords who had had experience in foreign warfare saw
that Alexandria was untenable, and the season, for it was now
the 10th of October, 1365, was too far advanced.   The failure
of the Crusade was bitterly commented on by Petrarch, who
in a letter to Boccaccio writes, at the time, in the severest
way of the greediness and irresolution of the Transalpines [2],
and many years after laments, in an epistle to Philip de Mazzeriis, the loss to Christendom, and the wretched effect produced, by the failure, on the character and fate of the king [3].
The English lords seem to have stayed sometime longer in
Cyprus : the legate died at Famagosta in January, 1366,
and they brought back to England the biography by Philip
the Chancellor, which has furnished the most certain details
of the story.   After the Alexandrian expedition the Venetians,
whose commerce was suffering, prevailed on Peter to treat for
a peace with Egypt, which was to establish Cypriot consulates
and reduce the customs in the ports of the Levant ; but the
attempt failed.   The next year, with the Genoese and the
Hospitallers, he ravaged the Syrian coast, but again had to
make peace.   He then visited Rome in search of succour, and

---

[1] ' Recesserunt Anglici qui videbantur fortiores, facta conspiratione cum
principe cujus ex parentela et dolosa sequela nomen tacere debeo ; ' P. de
Mazz. AA. SS. l. c. p. 1016.

[2] ' Siquidem Petrus Cypri rex Alexandriam cepit in Egypto, magnum opus
et memorabile nostræque religionis in immensum amplificandæ fundamentum
ingens, si quantum ad capiendam tantum ad servandam urbem animi fuis-
set ; qui certe non defuit, ut fama, nisi comitatus ejus ex transalpinis maxime
gentibus collectus, melioribus semper ad principia rerum quam ad exitus, illum
in medio præstantissimi operis deserentes, ut qui pium regem non pietate sed
cupiditate sequentes, collectis spoliis abiere piique voti impotem avari voti
compotes fecere ; ' Petrarch, Opp. p. 843 ; Ep. Senil. lib. 8. ep. 8.

[3] Ib. Lit. 13. ep. 2: 'Petrus rex Cypri, indigni vir exitus sed sacræ memoriæ
nisi,' etc.

returned finally to Cyprus in September 1368. The rest of King Peter's life was very wretched : he had left his queen during his long visit to the West, and she had proved faithless : he retaliated on the nobles who had been her favourites, and gave rein to his cruelty and lasciviousness. If he were not mad, as seems most probable, he was desperate ; and his family took the lead in getting rid of him. He was assassinated by a body of nobles, who acted with the concurrence of his brother John, the prince of Antioch, on the 16th of January, 1369. His wife was Eleanor of Aragon ; and it was this connexion, no doubt, that gave him a higher place than his predecessors had enjoyed in the estimation of the Western kings.

Peter II, who succeeded him, was a boy of thirteen ; his uncle John acted as regent. Peter reigned till 1382. He avenged his father's death by murdering his uncle in 1375. His reign witnessed a fatal rupture between the Venetians and Genoese, which accelerated the fate of Cyprus. The representatives of the two republics quarreled about precedence at the coronation : the court decided in favour of Venice. This was complicated by a quarrel between the queen-mother and the prince of Antioch. The Genoese took up arms and over-ran the whole island. The boy king was taken prisoner, and to secure his ransom had to pledge Famagosta to the Genoese. This great city and the port, which Sir John Mandeville thought the finest in the world, was permanently lost to the kings, for it was subsequently made over to the Genoese altogether in order to obtain the release of James, the king's uncle and successor, who had been detained as a hostage by the admiral Fregoso.

The particular interest which attaches to the struggle of Venice and Genoa,—a struggle which only ended when the Levant was left to the Turks, and was one great cause of the abridgment of Christendom at the close of the middle ages,— and the glorious exploits of the knights of Rhodes, however close to our subject, are far too wide and engrossing topics to be discussed incidentally. But the fate of Armenia, where the very succession of the kings is very obscure, demands a word. The first Latin king, according to the native historians, was John of Lusignan, also called Constantine, who reigned only a year ; his brother, Guy of Lusignan, who succeeded in 1343, was connected by marriage with the Cantacuzenes, and even addressed Edward III as cousin [1]. Both the brothers were little else than adventurers. Guy reigned for only three years. In 1347 his successor Constantius, or Constantine, was, through an envoy of the same name, collecting money in England by virtue of a brief issued by Clement VI [2]. He seems to be identical with Constantine, who, in 1351, was on the throne ; in his favour also alms were collected in England. He died in 1361. After an interval of three years, during which the crown was offered to Peter of Cyprus, and an unknown fourth king may possibly have reigned, Leo V appears on the throne in 1365. He had a hard fight for it ; from 1371 to 1373 he was lost to his people, concealed in a mountain fortress where he had been obliged to take refuge. A new king was sought for, a husband for the supposed widow, and Gregory XI offered the crown to Otto of Brunswick. He, however, preferred to marry Johanna of Naples, and Leo emerged from seclusion. But with little better prospects ; taken prisoner by the Egyptian sultan in 1375, he was released in 1382, to be thenceforth a wanderer and a pensioner on the Western princes. After his release he made the pilgrimage to Jerusalem, and went thence to Avignon and so to Spain. In Spain he obtained a provision. King John of Castile gave him three lordships, one of them Madrid ; and as lord of Madrid King Leo granted a charter to the burghers of the town. But he did not stay in Spain. In 1384 he was in France offering his services as a mediator between Charles VI and Richard II. His offers were not welcome to the English lords, who then held the king in tutelage. They refused him in the first instance his passport—said that though he proffered peace he only wanted money ; he was an illusor, and they would have nothing to do with him. Notwithstanding this he obtained not only a safe-conduct but a permit for a

[1] Fœd. ii. 1220.   [2] Ib. 1234; iii. 103.

cargo of French wine to be brought to England for him ; he made an eloquent speech before the king and council at the palace of Westminster; and received a pension of £1000 a year; the first instalment of which was paid into his own hands in gold nobles. He had a passport again in 1392, a few months before his death. His pension was still paid in 1391, in the fifteenth year of the unlucky king : at that time Leo, it was said, had been driven from his dominions ; the pension was to be continued until he regained them. Fortunately for the English exchequer, it was not required, for according to the epitaph of King Leo in the Church of the Celestines at Paris, the very noble and very excellent Prince Lyon of Lusignan, fifth Latin king of Armenia, rendered his soul to God Nov. 29, 1393. He left no legitimate issue, and his claims devolved on his cousin of Cyprus. The name of the kingdom of Armenia was thus familiar in English ears at this time. English sympathy had not flagged during these years. In 1383 another Lord de Roos, Thomas, son of the lord who died in 1352, had set out for the East, but died before he left England ; his son John fulfilled the vow, and having reached Cyprus, died at Paphos in 1393. A large party of English visitors had appeared there in that year.

James I, the uncle and successor of Peter II, reigned from 1382 to 1398, and was on excellent terms with England. There is a letter addressed by him to Richard II, in July, 1393 [1], in which he acknowledges the receipt of the epistle of commendation brought by Lord de Roos, and tells him that it was needless, because all the King of England's friends were welcome. He thanks him too for the message which he had received by his most noble cousin, Sir Henry Percy. We learn from this that Hotspur had made Cyprus a part of his great tour ; and, as the same year is fixed for the pilgrimage of Henry of Bolingbroke, we may surmise that they came in company. Henry of Bolingbroke, having sailed in July from Lynn, went by way of Prussia, Poland, Hungary, and Venice to Jerusalem ; on his return he visited Cyprus,

---

[1] Raine, Extracts from Northern Registers, p. 425.

and so back by Italy and Bohemia [1]. King James was a
kindly old man, but much tied up between the Venetians and
the Genoese. He had accumulated three crowns ; he had received that of Jerusalem at Nicosia, as Famagosta was now
lost ; in 1393 he received that of Armenia, which he handed
on to his successors. James had been a hostage or prisoner at
Genoa when the Cyprian crown fell to him ; he had been sent
thither when the perfidious Admiral Fregoso had seized the
island ; and at Genoa his son, King Janus or John II, was
born.

The reign of Janus, thirty-four years long, was one sad
struggle, with the Genoese on the one hand and the Turks on
the other. The main features of the story are these. King
Janus, with a very natural ambition, stimulated moreover by
hereditary and personal enmity, made it the first object to recover Famagosta from Genoa, and for this end, in the year
1402, prepared a force and fleet to besiege the Genoese there.
The days of Genoese greatness were over. In 1396 the Doge
Adorno had submitted to Charles VI of France, and Genoa
had become a French dependency. Famagosta had been won
by the Fregosi, the opposite faction to that of Adorno, but the
French were, as usual, ready to maintain their claim to conquests under whatever regime they were acquired. On the
alarm of war in Cyprus, they sent Marshal Boucicault with a
small fleet into the Levant. King Janus prepared for resistance, but the Grand-Master of Rhodes, Philibert of Naillac,
interposed as mediator, and a collision was avoided ; the poor
king had to pay 150,000 ducats for the expenses of the expedition. Peace was however made, and both parties turned
their arms against the Mahometan neighbours. The Genoese
ravaged the Syrian coast ; King Janus plundered the shore of
Egypt. Booty was abundant, but the inexorable vengeance
of the Sultans was aroused ; the ravaging of Syria ended in
the loss of the last fragments of Armenian sovereignty ; and
the plundering of Egypt drew down the Mameluke Sultan on
Cyprus. Truces and treaties were made, but were kept on
neither side. In the midst of war Cyprus was again, for the

[1] Capgrave, Illustrious Henries, p. 100.

third time since the Black Death, devastated by the plague; and the Sultan saw his opportunity; in 1417 he took and wrecked Limasol. In 1420 he swore the entire destruction of the Cypriots, and prepared for a final conquest. Four years after, during which King Janus, although he continued his policy of piratic expeditions, had made scarcely any preparation for defence, he attacked the island, including Cypriots and Genoese in a common purpose of extirpation. Famagosta was taken and pillaged. Two years later the king was defeated and taken prisoner, and Nicosia was sacked. The king's imprisonment lasted fifteen months; during which an attempt was made by an Italian, Sforza Pallavicino, to seize the government. In this he was defeated by the Queen Charlotte of Bourbon, who sent against him Carion of Ibelin, one of the last, if not the last of that great house, of whom anything historical is recorded. Ransomed at an enormous cost, Janus returned in 1427, but thoroughly broken in spirit and despairing of the fortunes of his house. One of his last acts was to marry his daughter Anne to Lewis of Savoy, a connexion which in the next generation helped to place the nominal crowns of Cyprus, Armenia and Jerusalem, among the honours of that aspiring house. He died in 1432, and with him the last sunset gleams of Cypriot glory vanished.

The native historians date the beginning of the downfall to the murder of King Peter in 1369; and if that date be taken we must allow that Petrarch, who thought that that event determined the loss of the East, was gifted with somewhat of prophetic spirit. But I think that, unfortunate as that event was for the Lusignan house, the doom of the Levantine principalities was already sealed. The great plague had swept off the old acclimatised Franks, especially those nobles who, like the lords of Ibelin, had increased and multiplied in the land. With all their faults these nobles were *bona fide* Crusaders; men who, like the first champions, were ready to cast in their lot in a Promised Land, and not, like the later adventurers, anxious merely to get all they could out of it, to make their fortunes. They were swept away. Then there was the antagonism of Genoa and Venice, a piece of history which, so long as history is read in books written in direct hostility to Venice, will be read two ways. Genoa had from the very early Crusades been the ally of France, as Pisa had been the ally of England. Venice had succeeded to the political connexions of Pisa; the tower of the English at Acre abutted on the ward of the Venetians and the Hospitallers; not that during these ages the English national power was of any weight in the Mediterranean, but a good deal of national piety and knight-errantry found expression in pilgrimages which now were conducted by way of Venice, in alliance with the Teutonic knights and the Hospitallers. The final acquisition of Cyprus by Venice, and the extremely unfair way in which it was acquired, seem to have afforded the grounds for supposing that the republic had long coveted the island, and that her policy had been for several generations directed to that end. This crooked policy is contrasted by the hostile writers with the open violence of the Genoese exemplified in the war of 1374, and the seizure of Famagosta. But I confess that I see little to choose between the two, and that what little there is seems in favour of Venice. Neither republic looked at the defence of Christendom as the great thing to be sought. The trading interest, or territorial ambition complicated with trading interest, was the main thing. If Venice profited most by the common policy, it is not so much a proof of previous diplomacy as a result of her longer tenure of power. That the Venetians however had an equal share with the Genoese in weakening the Frank kingdom it is impossible to prove: the Genoese hold on Famagosta was a fatal if not a mortal wound.

But still more powerful agencies were at work. The hands of Christendom were paralysed, and the barbarians were gaining strength and unity. The close of the fourteenth century, an exceptional but a very critical era, seems to show us all nations, all royalties, churches, religions, civilised and barbarous, in a cauldron or a whirlpool from which there was very small chance of emerging whole. A madman on the throne of France, an impotent drunkard claiming the crown of the Cæsars, a frantic absolutist overthrowing the constitution of

England ; the see of S. Peter divided between two, three, four Popes ; the Emperor of Constantinople begging money openly in the courts of the West ; the three barbarian powers pitted against each other—providentially, we may say, for who could have resisted their united force?—the Ottoman sultan the prisoner of Tamerlane ; the Mameluke sultan only sustained in independence by the contest between the Turks and the Tartars. Yet Europe does emerge ; the battle of Nicopolis puts an end to the Crusades ; the retreat of the Tartars enables the Ottomans to recover their ground ; Byzantium has a respite of half a century, and Egypt of more than a hundred years of Mameluke tyranny. It takes a century more to constitute the great national factors of modern history. But out of the whirlpool little states like Cyprus do not emerge ; and after the death of King Janus, the causes that were at work worked quickly and steadily. The immediate cause of the break-up was connected with the same sort of religious disputes which, after occupying half the century in councils and debates, left the Byzantine empire defenceless before the Ottomans. King John III, who succeeded in 1432, took for his second wife, in 1435, Helena, the daughter of the despot of the Peloponnese, Theodore Paleologus. The house of Lusignan had been hitherto, as a matter of necessity, devotedly Catholic ; the house of Paleologus was devotedly orthodox ; Cyprus was a Catholic kingdom with an orthodox population ; a Latin king with a Greek people ; the Latin Church was rich, and the Greek Church was not poor, but the political power was engrossed by the former. Helena would not see this. She determined, if she could, to make Cyprus orthodox ; she, through her husband, who was a weak and vicious man, refused the papal nominee to the archbishopric of Nicosia, imprisoned him, and was accused of poisoning him. The grand-master of Rhodes came in, as usual, in the part of a peace-maker, and prevailed on the king to receive the prelate ; and soon after, in 1458, both Helena and her husband died. But the quarrel had shaken the tottering kingdom ; the grand Caraman, the Turcoman ruler of Caramania, took the opportunity of these quarrels to seize Corycus, the last Frank stronghold of Armenia. The Cilician and Syrian begs with the Egyptian sultan formed a league for the conquest of Cyprus, which was foiled by the Rhodian galleys, or the Latin kingdom would have succumbed before the capture of Constantinople. The end was clearly coming, and it was not now a question between Venetians and Genoese, but between Christian and Moslem, which should take the island as a derelict. The royal house was nearly extinct. Charlotte of Lusignan, the only legitimate child of John III, succeeded him in 1458. She was the widow of John of Portugal, prince of Antioch, who had been poisoned by the creatures of Helena in 1457. She married, in 1459, her cousin Lewis count of Geneva, of the house of Savoy, who was crowned the same year. Her bastard brother, James, archbishop-elect of Nicosia, the son of a Greek lady, whose nose Queen Helena had bit off, was disappointed of the succession, and turned traitor. He aspired to the vain glory of sovereignty, and, having done homage to the sultan of Egypt, invaded Cyprus. For four years Queen Charlotte was besieged at Cherin; in 1464 she fled to Rhodes, and thence to Italy, where, in 1485, she made over her rights and the three crowns she wore to the house of Savoy. James II, a prince of some power, governed or commanded in Cyprus from 1464 to 1473, and to some extent justified his usurpation by taking Famagosta from the Genoese, but his reign was one long series of conspiracies. He was assassinated two years after his marriage with Caterina Cornaro (in 1471), who bore a son after her husband's death. This was King James III, who died when he was two years old. The Venetians held that the rights of the infant king devolved on his mother, and in her name governed Cyprus.

On the details of the Venetian title I cannot now enter; the whole history has been accepted on the evidence of the enemies of the republic, whose story is briefly this. In order to qualify Caterina for a foreign marriage she was declared the adopted daughter of S. Mark, and her husband the son-in-law of the republic. The republic, anxious for the succession, poisoned the son-in-law, who in his will entailed the crown on his children, posthumous and illegitimate, with remainder to the house of Lusignan. But this was set aside by the connivance of Caterina with the Venetians, who, after they had ruled Cyprus for fifteen years in her name, obtained from her a renunciation of her rights in favour of the republic; this was done in 1489; and then, formally as well as actually, Cyprus became a Venetian dependency, tributary to the Sultan of Egypt. Caterina herself retired to the Venetian territory, where she lived at the villa Paradiso in the Trevisan mountains, painted by Titian, and patronising the scholars of the renaissance, until the year of her death, 1510. After eighty-one years spent under Venice, Cyprus was conquered by the Turks in 1570. From the date then of Caterina's surrender, and indeed from the death of King James, the history of the island falls into the mass of that wonderful Venetian history of which we read so little, but which must contain so many lessons, and so many warnings for a nation like our own.

The titles of the several royalties which thus came to an end were claimed, as titles easily may be claimed, by other competitors: the Dukes of Savoy called themselves Kings of Cyprus and Jerusalem from the date of Queen Charlotte's settlement; the Kings of Naples had called themselves Kings of Jerusalem since the transfer of the rights of Mary of Antioch, in 1277, to Charles of Anjou; and the title has run on to the present day in the houses of Spain and Austria, the Dukes of Lorraine, and the successive dynasties of Naples. The kingdom of Armenia must, I think, have been dropped; but the Savoyard claim to Cyprus was held as an offence to the Venetian republic, a point of ceremonial which, in the seventeenth century, put a stop for thirty years to any diplomatic intercourse between Venice and Savoy. The successors of Richard I never put in a claim to the reversion; the quartering of the arms of Cyprus, which is said to appear on the tomb of Queen Elizabeth, being no doubt a part of the bearings derived from her great-grandmother, Jacquetta of Luxemburg, whose daughter, Elizabeth Wydville, carried the blood of the house of Brienne and the Dukes of Athens into

the line of York[1].   The Kings of Sardinia continued to strike
money as Kings of Cyprus and Jerusalem, until they became
Kings of Italy.   There is no recognised King of Cyprus now,
but there are two or three Kings of Jerusalem ; and the
Cypriot title is claimed, I believe, by some obscure branch of
the house of Lusignan, under the will of King James II.

So much for the archæology of the question.   The interest
of England in the affairs of the Levant did not come to an end
with the surrender of Cyprus to Venice ; for the Knights of
Rhodes maintained the defence of Christendom for half a century longer, and England was a close friend of the order until
Henry VIII confiscated its estates.   The Turcopolier of the
Knights Hospitallers was always an Englishman ; he was the
commander of the light infantry of the order.   I have found
no list of the Turcopoliers ; but in the fifteenth century we
have the names of Peter Holt, Thomas Launcleve, or Lang-
cliffe, Hugh Middleton, and John Kendall ; all of them would
seem North-countrymen.   In the last century a medal of
John Kendall was found in Knaresborough Forest, and it
would appear that he was a member of the family which was
particularly marked by its devotion to S. Wilfrid of Ripon.
The last known brother of the Order of S. Thomas of Acre,
Richard of Tickhill, must also have been a Yorkshire man.
The Cypriot king also had a Turcopolier, who, in 1357, was
an Englishman.   But these are trifles.

I said in beginning my lecture that I should draw no moral

---

[1] The descent is a long one, and there is a question whether the arms are
those of Cyprus at all.   But certain claims to represent the elder house of
Lusignan had come into the family of Luxemburg.   Jacquetta was daughter
of the Count Peter of S. Pol, whose mother, Marguerite of Enghien, carried
the representation of the Counts of Brienne to the Luxemburgs.   Mary,
daughter of Hugh I of Cyprus and his queen, married Walter IV of Brienne,
father of Hugh, and grandfather of Walter V, duke of Athens ; Walter V
had a daughter Isabel, who married Walter IV of Enghien, father of Lewis,
Count of Brienne and Conversano, and grandfather of Margaret, who was
the heiress of Enghien.   She married John of Luxemburg, and was mother
of Peter, Count of S. Pol.   As a claim to the throne of Cyprus, this descent
was worthless ; but it was a royal descent, and, after the extinction of the
Lusignans and the house of Antioch-Lusignan, might be thought to have a
value of its own.   Queen Elizabeth, however, was in no sense the heiress of
S. Pol, much less of Lusignan.

or political lesson from the history of Cyprus and Armenia. No lesson can safely be drawn from it, if by lesson we mean absolute instruction or warning that it would be foolish to despise. But it does suggest some generalisations and prompt some questions. We can see that the loss of the Levantine states in the middle ages, that is, the cessation of the defence of Christendom against Mahometanism, was mainly caused by the jealousies of the Christian powers themselves: the determination of the Venetians and the Genoese to set their respective commercial profits above all other considerations. Whilst the Teutonic knights were fighting in the North and the Rhodians in the South, Cyprus, the storehouse of Palestine, was left a prey to the evils out of which the Genoese and Venetians could make their market. It was so in the age that followed: the alliance between Francis I and Solyman paralysed all action by which Charles V and Ferdinand I would have defended the provinces on the Danube and Transylvania, and suffered the Turkish dominion to grow almost unimpeded, until the world began to think that the Turks had a vested interest in the lands they devastated. But the questions which arise are not easily stated, and not easily answered. How can the East be redeemed by the acclimatisation of Northern races? are the Northern races the only races that can redeem the East, and if so, how are they to be saved from the evils, moral, intellectual, and political, which acclimatisation seems invariably to bring with it? Are the Eastern races to be redeemed at all, or is that part of the aspiration of the Christian Church and of social philanthropists to be a vain dream? Is the task of empires to conquer or to colonise; the task of colonies to extirpate or to develope? Is a commercial or a military policy the surest agent of civilisation? Can a worn-out nation be revived and refreshed and recruited by a bracing treatment? can it be revived at all? Does the difference between European and Asiatic history consist in the vitality of the historic nations in Europe and the inexhaustibleness of the hive in Asia? If not, how is Europe to treat Asia, so that the march of civilisation may affect the lands in which the stream of history seems to have long been stayed? if it is so, how shall the East be rescued from the successive waves of barbarism which may be now impending, and how kept alive when those successive impulses are exhausted? Small as our subject was, it was a part of that which touches all, the world's government and the long patience of Providence. 'And I said, it is mine own infirmity, but I will remember the years of the right hand of the Most Highest.'

IX.

ON THE CHARACTERISTIC DIFFERENCES BETWEEN MEDIEVAL AND MODERN HISTORY.

(April 15, 1880.)

IF I were asked for what reason I have, in my teaching in this place, preferred medieval to later modern history, I should answer, because I think that for the training of the judgment, the former furnishes material more readily applicable to educational purposes than the latter. It is further removed from the arena of political controversy, and, whilst it possesses interest quite sufficient to awaken every sentiment that may lawfully affect the judgment, it stirs no emotion that could reasonably be expected to pervert or overbalance it. We find in it heroes and heroines quite heroic enough to justify hero-worship; we find in it questions of controversy quite sufficiently exciting to divide parties; and points of sufficiently continuing and permanent importance to kindle our zeal in a moderate degree in connexion with the questions and interests of to-day. The rights and wrongs of the political life of modern Europe are rooted in the medieval history of Europe, and we can trace sufficient connexion between the extreme past and the present, to give interest to the earliest investigations. So we try to train the judgment by investigating causes, effects, ideas and results, rights and wrongs, in a subject-matter sufficiently akin to modern life to engage lively feeling, and yet sufficiently apart from it to prevent party views from being predominant. I have said this so often on these occasions that I am almost ashamed to say it again; I must however go on until I can find some one to believe me. The use to which the trained student may put his judgment when he has educated it is a quite different thing: only I believe that whatever side he may take, or, even if he turn his back altogether on the line of study along which I have tried to lead him, he will approach questions of the day with a more balanced judgment ; he will be less disposed to see all good on one side of the great questions, and all evil on the other ; he will come to the strife of politics with his weapons more carefully chosen, better handled and better sharpened than if he had never passed through the training.

Medieval History is a history of rights and wrongs ; modern History as contrasted with medieval divides itself into two portions ; the first a history of powers, forces, and dynasties ; the second, a history in which ideas take the place of both rights and forces. The point of time at which we should mark the separation in the latter is the first French revolution. There is a continuity of life through the three ; the fundamental principle, which still holds its ground in the struggle of ideas, is distinctly traceable in the primitive struggle of rights and wrongs ; and far more and more distinctly in the more modern struggle of the balance of power ; but in the first and second period, ideas have little weight compared with rights and forces ; in the first rights are more potent than force, in the second forces are more potent than rights ; and now rights, forces, and ideas are matched in the arena of modern politics in such a way as to make right and force themselves ideas. At this moment—I use an illustration which ought properly to grow out of something that must show further on—Austria may be regarded as representing the more ancient form of right, Russia as representing the form of force, and Germany, Italy, and France different forms of leading idea. I do not mean that Austria is justified on appeal to right, or that Russia relies solely on force, or that the other three states have not ample grounds, both in right and force, for their present position, but that historically those are distinctions essentially characteristic.

You may wonder at my temerity in the use of such very abstract terms, and you have a right to bid me define more clearly the historical periods of which I am speaking ; I will then define medieval history for our present purpose as beginning with the eleventh century, and proceed to state next what sorts of rights, forces, and ideas, I consider, mark differentially the three periods at which I have been looking. It may almost provoke a smile that I should use words so, that I should speak of rights and wrongs in ages in which all was done with the strong hand, or of forces where intrigue and policy conspicuously take the place of violence and blood-shed, or of ideas in connexion with the present age at all. I do not care now to justify my use of these particular words, but I can tell you what I mean, and then, if you can supply me with better formulæ, I will use them.

Our first position then is, that the idea of right or rights was the leading idea of the middle ages. I say now right or rights, because, whilst in the greatest men of the period there was a conscious attempt to exalt law and a willingness to abide by it, there was in the inferior actors, in the worse men, a disposition to maintain their own rights within re-cognised limits, and, when they attacked the possessions or infringed the apparently equal rights of their opponents, to do it on the ground of legal pleas. We all know how enormous is the debt which English law owes to the great legislators of the twelfth, thirteenth, and fourteenth centuries; Henry II and Edward I are, both of them, conspicuous examples of both the tendencies which I have coupled under the term ; in their better actions defenders of the law, in their worse actions captious defenders of their right. The same is approximately true in other countries ; Lewis IX is not only the great legislator of France, but almost the single example of the period, in which the more powerful sovereign grants to his competitor, even in the hour of his utmost weakness, the full extent of his legal right; the treatment of Henry III by S. Lewis is a very striking example of the respect for rights that do not happen to be your own. As to generalities, I need only remark that the names of Frederick II and Alfonso the Wise stand by those of Edward and Lewis as the founders of the non-Roman jurisprudence of Europe, and that in Germany in the fourteenth century the two great legis-lators are the two champions of the rival houses, Lewis of

Bavaria on the one side, and Charles the IVth on the other ;
the codification of Bavarian law and the issue of the Golden
Bull were at all events attempts in the direction of civilisation
in accordance with the highest existing ideal.

The foundation of legal studies in the Universities, the attempts by legal means to control the customs of private war,—
private war being itself an example of the strength of the idea
of rights,—the proclamation of the public peace from time to
time in Germany by emperors who had the will but not the
power to enforce it, and the multiplication of central tribunals
in the place of local ones, are examples of the same. No doubt
they are developments, evolutions of the unconscious progress
of civilisation ; that I am not enough of a philosopher to
dogmatise about, but if they were, that is the line which the
development or evolution took. The middle ages proper, the
centuries from the year 1000 to the year 1500, from the Emperor
Henry II to the Emperor Maximilian, were ages of legal
growth, ages in which the idea of right, as embodied in law,
was the leading idea of statesmen, and the idea of rights
justified or justifiable by the letter of law, was a profound
influence with politicians. It may seem fanciful, but I cannot help adding a parallel illustration. The scholastic philosophy was an attempt to codify all existing knowledge under
laws or formulæ analogous to the general principles of justice.
It was no attempt, as is sometimes said, to bind all knowledge with chains to the rock of S. Peter, or even to the rock
of Aristotle ; just as right is one and indivisible, and all rights
are referable to it (if we only knew where to find it) as the
ultimate touchstone and arbiter, so Truth is one and indivisible, and the medieval philosophy found its work in
reconciling all existing knowledge logically with the One
Truth which it believed itself to possess. What logic was to
the philosopher legislation was to the statesman and moralist,
a practical, as the other was a theoretical, casuistry ; an
attempt to justify all its conclusions by direct reference to first
principles.

You may tell me, if this is true, the age of which you
are speaking ought to have been a scientific age, or at least

a mathematical age, and it was not. I reply that it was a scientific age in many respects, only it had misunderstood to some extent the character of its subject-matter; it applied scientific method to matters which were not capable of being scientifically treated, an error which it had in common with a good deal of the scientific philosophy of other ages, the present age not least signally. It used principles and applied demonstration in matter to which neither the principles nor the method were properly applicable; it argued too rashly from the known to the unknown, and relied too implicitly on its own implements. But that is by the way: our present parallel is simply, that in both philosophy and law the middle ages exemplified a like tendency to generalise and to syllogise; the names of Thomas Aquinas and Duns Scotus stand over against the names of Edward I and Lewis IX as leaders of thought, emancipators for the time, imprisoners for the future, in a far wider realm than that of practical legislation.

But this has taken me rather off the point. The great men, I have said, were law abiding; so also were the small men: and the same standing ground furnished the strength of both. Perhaps the easiest example to take is from the end of the period, the Emperor Frederick III; a man whose history, if it did not fall in a period of worn-out influences, in which the old order was vanishing in the twilight that ushered in the new, would be worthy of the deepest study. Here was a man, nominally the master of the world; a man capable of the highest aspirations for the future of his house, able to lay his plans and to compass designs which, read by the light of his existing means, look like the merest dreams of the merest visionary; a man of capacity and a man of ambition, but possessing with the crown of the Cæsars hardly a rood of land in his own undivided possession;—within his reach, with but an infant's life between, a great inheritance to which he might assert a colourable claim, and which ultimately fell to his descendants, yet silently, patiently waiting, and holding back his hand from all unrighteous aggression: his designs, dreams as they seem, come to fruition in the third generation, and his impoverished house becomes mistress of half, or more than half, the world. He contented himself with his right and his rights, and the idea was still so potent as to lay the basis for the powers of the next age. Unfortunately no one can be enthusiastic about Frederick III, but he has his place in the moral history of kings.

But to proceed; the continued existence of small states throughout the middle ages is a very important illustration of the subject before us; another is the extreme dislike, apparent in both continental and English history, to the forcible extinction of historical claims to territory. I do not mean to say that there were not some very remarkable instances of departure from this rule; indeed, as I shall show, two at least of the most important changes in the map of Europe, the most potential and far-reaching changes, were produced by the breach of it; but the rule as a rule was observed. In England we know how the long-suffering of the Plantagenet kings allowed the continuance of such houses as the Mowbrays, the Ferrers, the Mortimers, the Despensers; how, when generation after generation had proved that disaffection was a part of the hereditary constitution of the offending races, the heirs of the traitors were restored or rehabilitated, until, in the wars of the Roses, the opposing houses perished in one another's downfall. There was no fear of shedding blood, but there was great fear of destroying right. So, too, with small states abroad. The little principalities of the Low Countries subsisted side by side with their powerful neighbours; the small kingdoms of Spain united and separated according to the special law of inheritance that was recognised by each; and where an attempt at infringement was made, the aggressor found himself matched against a wide and powerful union of powers instinctively actuated by the intention of right. In France we see this exemplified, not merely by the long continuance of the Plantagenet inheritance in the South, but by the existence of Provence, by the toleration of the accumulations of the Burgundian inheritance, by the independence of Flanders and Lorraine. In all these cases there were conducing causes, but in each case there was also the plea of right. Proprietary right, we say; the recognition by kings that, if they do not recognise the proprietary rights of the weaker, then the stronger will not consider theirs ; proprietary rights, the leading idea that the tenant belongs to the land and the land to the landlord, and if the principle be broken down in one case, it cannot be maintained in another: proprietary right, I grant, but still right, still something that may be justified by law, not merely by the logic of the strong hand.

The whole history of Germany is, during this period, full of the same idea : small states continuing to exist side by side with larger ones ; each of them in one aspect a centre of light and political culture, in another a centre of intrigue and petty tyranny : I am not concerned to defend them, but to adduce them as facts. Italy can show parallels, but her history is, to a great extent, here, as elsewhere, exceptional, and may more instructively be made to furnish counter illustrations ; but the long struggle of the Hohenstaufen in the South, and of the Lombard cities in the North, is capable of being read in the same light : they would have perished before they did, if not as they did, if it had not been for the idea of right, inspiriting the weak, dismaying the strong, and affording a rallying point for the wronged from generation to generation.

But two great influences in the medieval world, the medieval empire and the medieval papacy, how are we to class them ? Is the permanent toleration of their existence to be accounted for by the fact of their legal claims, or by that sort of prestige which might seem to throw them into the class of ideas ; the inherited dignity of Cæsar and of Peter ? The imperial dignity, during a great part of the period before us, was shadowy in the extreme ; nay, during the whole period its substantive existence depended on the strength which the families who passed it on amongst themselves derived from their patrimonial estates. After the extinction of the Hohenstaufen, the imperial dignity became in itself an almost honorary distinction ; either shunned for its costliness or coveted for the chances which it gave to a second-rate house of increasing its power by such little windfalls as might come to it. Yet it continued to subsist when any one of the great vassals might with impunity not only have declared his own independence but have extinguished the dignity which had ceased to symbolise, not only universal empire, but even national unity.

From time to time the phantom empire clothes itself in power and strength; the house of Bavaria fails to hold the dignity, but, on legal pleas which, if their legality were contested, it could not vindicate by arms, possesses itself of two or three electorates, and founds a distinct family policy of most important consequence. The house of Luxemburg, a little county under Henry VII, gains in the third generation the superiority of the two non-Teutonic kingdoms, and under Sigismund, knight-errant and political pedant, sways the destinies, for the moment, of Christendom itself. The house of Austria, in the same way, lays thus the foundation of that empire which is to be one of the great forces of the next age ; not by fraud, not by violence, but here by a politic marriage, here by a well advocated inheritance, here by a claim on an imperial fief forfeited or escheated : honestly where the letter of the law is in her favour, by chicanery it may be here and there, but that a chicanery that wears a specious garb of right. The imperial idea was but a small influence compared with the superstructure of right, inheritance, and suzerainty, that legal instincts and a general acquiescence in legal forms had raised upon it. In the counter influence, that of the Roman see, there is perhaps more of the idea and less of the substantive right. I am speaking, of course, politically, and not theologically. The idea of the Petrine succession was a developing idea, that of the Cæsarean succession was a waning and diminishing one : the latter was the declining from a great fact, the ancient dignity and power of imperial Rome; the former was the growth into a great fiction, the temporal supremacy of papal Rome.

The empire astonishes us with the vitality which the universal acquiescence in its rights, however attenuated, conserves to it : the papacy appals us by the arrogance and grandeur of assumption which it raises on a foundation that seems to be itself a hypothesis, to say the least. Yet, as the languishing empire lives by law, the aspiring papacy must live by law, and rights and proprietary rights too. So the forged donations of Italian territory, the baseless claims to feudal supremacy within the Sicilian kingdom ; the spiritual position based on the false decretals ; all of them attempts to supply to the rising power the sort of strength that sustained the falling power. When the point of substantive independence is reached, how are the wider claims made to rest on the firmer basis of spiritual and religious obedience : the law of papal Rome becomes the living voice of the Catholic Church, the voice of the pope in cathedra an infallible utterance ; the jurisprudence of the decretals a universal jurisprudence ; the sovereignty of Innocent III and Boniface VIII, a sovereignty which it is blasphemous to deny, criminal to gainsay. But when the idea has gained recognition, far be it from us to say that the power so won was used unlawfully. No, the spiritual claims of the papacy, however unjustifiable in their early history, were to a large extent justified by the beneficial use to which they were put by the better pontiffs. The Court of Rome was a tribunal for international arbitrament, the efficiency of which was one great proof of the law-abiding character of the ages which it influenced. I do not forget the wars of the medieval papacy, wars, some of them, which were encouraged and even prompted by those who were ex officio the peace-makers of the world : but when we consider how, with all those exceptions, the influence of the Church, during these ages worked from the Roman centre, was as a rule employed for the prevention of war, for the shortening of inevitable struggles, and for the healing of wounds that could not otherwise have been healed, we cannot deny to it such justification as belongs to men who believe themselves to be the ministers of a higher than human righteousness.

But I have no wish to touch more on controversial points : let papal Rome, as the law-giver of the medieval Church, have all the credit of her great achievements : however based, on law or on idea, her position was a standing protest against brutal force, a standing offer of peace and goodwill to those who could pay for it ; a great office of incipient diplomacy, a

great treasury of legal chicanery, but still a refuge against
overbearing violence. The position of both empire and papacy
is historically maintained by a public sense of law and right.

But perhaps the field in which the most abundant illustrations of the thesis will be found is that in which a priori we
should be least inclined to look for it ; in the region of war ;
in the drum and trumpet territory in which, according to the
new reading of history, so little can be found to indicate the
growth of human thought or the development of national
character and life. Medieval wars are, as a rule, wars of
rights : they are seldom wars of unprovoked, never wars of
absolutely unjustifiable, aggression ; they are not wars of idea,
of liberation, or of glory, or of nationality, or of propa-
gandism. Ah, you will say to me, you are wrong there ; how
about the Crusades, how about the Norman Conquest, how
about Scottish independence, how about Lewis of Bavaria and
John XXII, how about the Hundred Years' War? Not one
of these was simply a war of aggression which those who
waged it felt it to be without justification, except perhaps the
Norman Conquest ; and we all know what an amount of special
pleading was thought necessary to justify that. Do not mistake me : if I had meant to say that law and right were the
ruling ideas of medieval politicians, I should have said so at
first ; but I could only have proved my thesis by showing that
there was no war at all. There was war in abundance, public
war and private war : the Temple of Janus could not have
been shut for all those centuries, if it had been still standing
and put to its mythical purpose. What was meant was not
that men loved law, but that they did so far respect it as to
wish to seem to have it always on their side. They did not
attack their neighbours because they wanted glory ; or because
they could not bear rivalry, or because their neighbours' armies
were too strong for their safety, or because their neighbours'
armies were so ill equipped that they might be an easy conquest ; but they alleged a legal claim or a legal grievance ;
and in the majority of cases really legal claims and really
legal grievances. Of course, if law had been supreme, the
wrong-doer would have yielded at once, the false claimant

would have hid his diminished head at the first expression of
the opinion of a competent counsel or an authorised judge;
we know how often that is done in these days in quarrels great
and small. But I make no such claim for these ages; I only
say that, when a man coveted his neighbour's vineyard, he
went as it were to law for it, and did not simply take it by
force. The Norman Conquest of England, I need hardly say,
is scarcely a fair illustration. It is at least as much a
viking invasion as a war waged according to the international law of the age; yet the pleas of bequest, the legacy
of Edward the Confessor, the papal sanction, the oath of
Harold, the legal election by the witenagemot of the humbled
race, alike the inventions and the ceremonial of the succession,
were a concession to a public sense of right. Take the other
great wars; of England first: we cannot doubt that in all the
quarrels arising from the Norman, Angevin, and Poictevin
inheritances, the right of proprietary succession was on both
sides distinctly recognised: the wars arose not on account of
the mere wish of France to revindicate her alienated provinces,
but on account of the disputed right to a feudal superiority, or
the possession of a debateable frontier, or the division between
two co-heiresses, or the existence of a custom of representation.
When, as under Philip Augustus, the design of aggression
was strong enough to take a more decided line, still it was on
no false pretext that war was waged, and on no merely imaginary process that forfeiture was decreed; the barons of
Poictou legally impleaded John for his treatment of the Count
of la Marche, the barons of Brittany legally arraigned him
for the destruction of Arthur: as his feudal lord, Philip summoned him, and John, as a contumacious vassal, suffered judgment by default. In the execution of the sentence Philip had
on his side, not only the popular hatred of his competitor,
but the conscious recognition that legally John had lost his
cause. Normandy and Anjou were practically undefended;
Philip's victories were justified by the recognition of the
countries which renounced their old rulers for sound and lawful
reasons. There were no nonjuring bishops in Normandy and
Anjou. It would not be difficult to show how the legal aspect

of the Poictevin succession affected the different fate of
Guienne and Gascony ; but I pass on, for I have mentioned
that already in reference to Henry III and S. Lewis ; I
may just add that when Lewis, in 1259, obtained from his
brother-in law a final surrender of Normandy and homage and
fealty for Guienne, Henry formally acknowledged the justice of
the sentence under which his father had forfeited the former,
and Lewis practically acknowledged the justice of the claim
by which Henry retained his hold upon the latter. A piece
of legal formalism this, we say ; yet it was so powerful a piece
of formalism that it unquestionably made the breach between
Simon de Montfort and the royal party an irreparable breach,
and led directly to the catastrophes of Lewes and Evesham.

We come next to the French and Scottish wars of Edward I.
The claim of the Scottish overlordship was made with every
pretence to legality, and, there can be little doubt, was believed
by the king himself and accepted by the lords of Scotland as
long as they remained hopeless of their national independence
or blind to their chances of escape. John Balliol's forfeiture,
his renunciation of homage, his cession of the crown to Edward,
were all legal acts : the attempt of Philip the Fair to exert
over Edward the same sort of jurisdiction that Philip Augustus
had successfully exercised over John, was foiled by Edward,
but was in itself an almost exact parallel to his treatment of
Balliol. The Scottish war was again, in his eyes, an attempt
not to choke national independence, but to enforce legal right.
As the age advances, we find Philip of Valois and Edward III
comparing pedigrees before they go to war ; for more than a
century two rival kings, Philip and Charles, kings of the
French, and Edward, Richard and the Henries, kings of France,
dispute the sovereignty of a great nation which is not consulted under which lord it will live, but has to abide by the
conflicting judgments of varying courts appellate on the field
of battle.

After that come the wars of the Roses ; wars which were
at once fought out in battle, camp and court, pamphlet, book
and parliament. In the wars of York and Lancaster, just as
in the war of Stephen and Matilda, the legal recognition

of the rightful king; the existence of the king de facto as a bar to the recognition of the king de jure; the solemn character of the ties that unite the baronage to the head, which they are determined to disown, but will not disown without a formal legal sentence; the parallels furnished by the cession of Edward II and Richard II, the curious pedantic circumstantiality of processes which, before they reached the stage of reality, had cost the lives of thousands; all these mark not merely the legal character and instinct of Englishmen, but the characteristic of the long medieval centuries, the conscience that war is justifiable only by law.

If we turn to Germany, the great struggle of the Investitures is in its outer aspect a struggle about legal forms : there were deeper causes at work, the national schism between Saxony and Swabia, caused by the legal wrongs which the Saxons believed themselves to have endured from Henry III, and the religious schism which arose from the rival ambitions, personal and ideal, of Henry IV and the popes; but the bone of contention was a legal claim. The struggle of the Welf and the Hohenstaufen was a legal struggle; although the weaker went to the wall, his cause was capable of very definite defence; the sentence under which he fell, although unrighteous, was formally legal. Other illustrations are furnished by the dealings of the Hohenstaufen with the popes; the great house falls by manœuvres and expedients of much the same sort as those by which it had destroyed the Welfs : the papacy expands the principles on which it had claimed the inheritance of the countess Matilda, and at the same time formulates the claims by which in the fourteenth century it was to cripple the central power of Europe and reduce, itself an exile, the rival influence to the shadow of a shade.

Let these, however, suffice for the pattern wars; the same characteristics belong in varying intensity to all the minor quarrels, down to the lowest grades of recognised private wars; war for the right of a bridge-toll, a mill or a pigeon-cote. War was, in one aspect, a sublime ordeal, but, like the ordeal, it was attended with all the forms and ceremonies of law : public war was an ordeal resorted to when all inferior tribunals had failed to satisfy the litigants; and private war was little else, except that there the coercive power of the tribunals which should have been appealed to was greater, and the waging of war in contempt or despite of them a bolder defiance of the laws of human society. Public war was not, like private war, branded as a social crime, because the one tribunal which might have decided the questions at issue without blood-shed was both dishonest and weak. Private war was not only a contempt of competent jurisdiction but a sin against social order. Yet down to the close of the period, the habit of private war was in a great part of Europe unbroken and unrepressed: in the empire the successive proclamations of the peace were inoperative; in the other states the custom was extinguished only with the independence of the powers that practised it: wherever there was disorganisation, wherever the feudal spirit broke the bonds in which constitutional rule had limited its powers, there private war was regarded as the ultimate appeal: men went to law to avenge their wrongs and to vindicate rights, and, when they could not get law that was strong enough to enforce itself, they went to war.

Lastly, look at the Crusades. The Crusades were the great exception to the rule as I have stated it ; they were not wars waged for proprietary rights ; they scarcely even pretended to be so. The Holy Land, the patrimony of the Crucified, as the Crusaders called it, was not theirs by any title of law ; histori-cally the only power which had a legal claim to Palestine was the Byzantine empire, but the territorial claims of the Comneni were, throughout the crusading period, defied where they were not ignored ; the Crusaders believed the Greek emperors to be either in league with the Moslems, ready to betray Christen-dom for a price, or else, as schismatics, one shade more or less culpable than the Mahometans. The Crusades were, more-over, at least in the commencement, originated not by the national authority, king or emperor, of a Christian state, but by adventurers, who might for the purpose be called private adventurers, acting under the exhortations of the popes. In one aspect they were wars of speculation, in another wars of re-ligion, in another wars of defence. The first Crusade was perhaps more than the others a war of speculation, the second a war of religion, the third a war of defence; in the fourth, again, speculation under Venetian influence threw both religion and defence into the shade: and all the later Crusades were wars of defence. Yet, although to say this is a partial condemnation, I cannot go further. The conquest of Palestine was to Robert of Normandy, Raymond of Toulouse, Bohemond of Tarentum, a sanctified experiment of vikingism; but to Godfrey of Bouillon, to the great mass of the Crusading armies, to the popes even, it was something far different. It was a war of idea; a going forth to recover the heritage of Christ, the land, as they termed it, on which His feet had stood: it was a going out of the petty range of proprietary rights and wrongs, out of the petty interests of armed litigation. As I have said before in this place, the Crusades, with all their drawbacks, were the trial feat of a new world, a reconstituted Christendom, striving after a better ideal than that of piracy and fraternal bloodshed. In the character of wars of defence they need not be defended: they stemmed the tide that but for them must have covered Europe, as it had covered Asia, with desolation.

Perhaps I need go no further; but there is one class of wars which I have not yet noticed, and which yet are very characteristic in their history of the principle for which I have been contending. The civil wars which were waged for national liberties were not in any great measure wars for ideas, but wars for rights. I do not mean to say that this was quite the case in Italy: in Italy the question of rights had become so complicated that nothing but the infusion of an element of idea could have produced even a semblance of order out of the chaos. The old sway of Rome, the successive deluges of Goth, Lombard, Greek and German, had thrown rights and wrongs into an inextricable hotchpot. The restoration of order was the initiation of liberty; with liberty, or the idea of it, came new forms of organisation, democracies, aristocracies, municipalities, tyrannies, monarchies: each formulating rights and laws as they arose, but less bound by laws of rights and obligations because for the most part they lacked historic basis. What

the faction of to-day might set up, the faction of to-morrow
might pull down : the exiles of to-day were the governors of
to-morrow, the forfeitures of to-day only the reprisals of the
forfeitures of yesterday. In England it is very different.
Here the rights struggled for are historical rights, and the
liberties secured are historical liberties. Step by step, from
precedent to precedent, the national growth asserts itself, and
the kings, yielding their consent, recognise the justice of the
claim, or, exchanging resistance for sympathy, throw new but
still historical energies into the common growth. We have
in the medieval growth of our constitution little to be ashamed
of ; little of conspiracy, little of fanaticism, little—as little as
there can be in the essential character of a politician—of self-
seeking. There is enough of the idea of liberty and sound
government to lift the struggle out of the region of mere legal
resistance to mere legal oppression : there is a growth towards
liberty in all the vindication of even class rights and special
privileges: a growth towards liberty so spontaneous, I had
almost said so little self-conscious, as to show that it is a
natural, not a factitious growth : it is not taught by philosophers, it is not extorted by agitators, it is the outgrowth of
law and a law-abiding spirit, tending by its very nature to
freedom and order conjointly. The transition from medieval
to modern history is in this department of national life not an
abrupt transition, but a growth befitting a land of settled
government ;

> A land of just and old renown,
> Where Freedom broadens slowly down
>   From precedent to precedent ;
> Where faction seldom gathers head,
> But, by degrees to fulness wrought,
> The strength of some diffusive thought
> Hath time and space to work and spread.

X.

ON THE CHARACTERISTIC DIFFERENCES BETWEEN MEDIEVAL AND MODERN HISTORY.

(April 17, 1880.)

IN the lecture which I gave the other day, and of which the present is a continuation, I made an attempt to show what I meant by a distinction which I had drawn between medieval and modern history in the two divisions into which it is separated by the gulf of the French revolution. I had begun by a little self-justification in the preference of medieval to modern history as an instrument of education, and, while treating the subject from a higher point of view than that of mere utility, had run off into a disquisition on the distinguishing characteristics of the divisions in question. On the remark which I have made elsewhere that the leading influence of early medieval history was the strong insistance on law and right, I had founded a somewhat rambling examination of the main points of the history of the middle ages, the characters of their great men, the permanence of their institutions, and the peculiar character of their wars. I had marked the characteristics of the second division as power or force, and that of the third as the influence of ideas. I now proceed to explain what I meant by this and to illustrate it, leaving my hearers to infer, as I proceed, what my reasons have been for preferring the earlier portion as the subject of my own teaching. When I have said what will no doubt appear to you to be more than enough about that, I shall venture to make some remarks on the influence of the ideas by which at the present day politics and politicians seem or profess to be guided. In that division of the subject I may seem to become somewhat political myself; if I do, I shall not ask your pardon. I have never been ashamed to express my convictions where they happened to differ from those of my friends with whom on most other subjects I should be willing to agree. I shall not, therefore, I think, rightly be thought rash or disputatious if I venture to express difference from those modern political schools with which I feel that I cannot sympathise at all.

So now to the subject. Almost any student who has read the usual books, if he were asked to mark what was the foremost idea of the three centuries that intervene between the year 1500 and the year 1800, would reply that it was the idea of the balance of power. The balance of power, however it be defined, i.e. whatever the powers were between which it was necessary to maintain such equilibrium, that the weaker should not be crushed by the union of the stronger, is the principle which gives unity to the political plot of modern European history. Whether the balance is to be maintained against the preponderance of the house of Hapsburg, or the preponderance of France, or the preponderance of Catholic powers as opposed to Protestant ones; this is the key to the plot.

But it is not the existence of the key or the character of the plot, but the existence of the drama of modern European politics, that is the first feature of our sketch : the existence of the powers by whom the drama is played and between whom the balance is maintained. Medieval history may, it is true, be read as a drama, but it is not one in which the plot is obvious; it is rather more a series of dramas which may be combined, like Greek trilogies, but have unities and plots of their own. The history of each great nation is a drama by itself; the blending of the several dramas may be so read as to show how the nations were severally being educated for work on a stage in which they should appear together: in the modern life of Europe they do appear together, and take each the part for which it has been educated in the earlier stage. But that early preparation had been carried on, to a great extent, separately. England and France had been no doubt training one another for centuries, but the balance of power between England and France never came into the great plot of later days; the discipline of Spain had been worked out within the walls of the peninsula; between France and Germany there had never been a great war; between Germany and Italy, as nationalities, no struggle had as yet been possible; and the border warfare of the border states had been carried on without any great amount of interest or interference from the greater or growing agglomerations of territory which under the name of nations, states or dynasties, now come to the front. The Crusades had been a common field of work and a common stage of action, but the nationalities which in the Crusades had fought side by side in union or in rivalry, had long retired from the uncongenial work, and all the zeal of the best popes and the most heroic kings had been unequal to the task of uniting Christendom again for the common emancipation.

There was, however, no great crash at the passing away of the old things and the coming in of the new. The new influences, many and various in character, quickly combine to produce the new actors and to clear the common stage. The concentration of power in the royal hands in France, under Charles VII and Lewis XI; the creation of a compact and solid kingdom out of a number of rival and hostile feudal provinces or dynastic appanages, a concentration for which, during the whole of the medieval period from Lewis VI onwards, the kings had been working, but which only became possible when the long struggle with England had made it necessary; a concentration of power which signified not only territorial union, but administrative autocracy; which reduced all powers except that of the crown, states general, parliament, clergy, feudatories, all to a shadow; a concentration in which, in the language of the time, France emerged from tutelage and attained to such maturity of manhood as might be expressed in the later formula 'The state, it is I myself.' This compactness, this concentration, equipped France for her part.

Just at the same moment England emerged from the terrible dynastic struggle in which, with the competing houses, the very bone and sinew of liberty seemed to have perished. The baronage, attenuated to a shadow of its former bulk, and with its power as attenuated as its numbers, the Commons wearied, exhausted with political struggles, turning their back on politics altogether to seek new and more profitable interests in new channels, and to leave the battle of rights and wrongs to settle itself; the clergy, on the one side left alone among the estates to continue the tradition of liberty, but on the other declining rapidly from their function of the national conscience and memory, to be mere officials, servants of the great monarchical administrative unity that towered so high over the prostrate estates; all three alike in isolation or in pitiful sympathy left the national action at the disposal of a king, a king like Henry VII, who would be a tyrant only in self-defence, to be succeeded by a son who would be a tyrant in very self-will. England, growing rich in the peace which its politic king and its busy people alike left all else to cultivate, growing stronger in wealth and union and abeyance of liberty, was likewise ready to act as a force at the will of one man.

Spain had finished the seven centuries of her crusade, and the two rival kingdoms, rid at last of the enemy, met and were united in the Catholic couple. In Germany Maximilian had at last concentrated in his own hands the territorial acquisitions of his house, had united Austria and her outlying states, had obtained for his son the accumulation of Burgundian fiefs, and for his grandsons the crown of Spain and Sicily, the reversion of Hungary and Bohemia besides. The Hapsburg power is a union of many unions, ill compacted, heterogeneous, uncongenial, but of extremely great might, a power consolidated by legal titles, happy and unhappy marriages, legal windfalls, traditional pretensions, but yet the most important factor for many years to come in the welfare of Europe. The strength of France is in her compactness and concentration, that of Charles V, for in him the Austrian force is first impersonated, in its extent and universality. To that extent and universality the discovery and the rapid pouring in of the wealth of America gave still new weapons and greater opportunities. France and Austria were both equipped for their struggle.

The minor actors had somehow girt up their loins also: the popes, giving up their place as the overseers of a too wide dominion, had begun to accumulate the territorial aggregate of provinces in which they also could call themselves the state. Gustavus Vasa was reconstructing Sweden; although the attempt to unite the Scandinavian kingdoms had failed, the same influence that was knotting up the south into bundles was knotting up the north.

And so the struggle of powers begins. First comes the rivalry of Francis I and Charles V ; with Henry VIII and the popes hovering round the combatants, aspiring to hold the balance between them, and made alternately their tools and scapegoats. The struggle is a curious one : the older idea of rights to be fought for has not altogether disappeared, but now the interest is not in the right, but in the battle. So it has been since Charles VIII, marching into Italy, had opened the new drama. Rights were sought out and put forward as the pretexts of the struggle, but the struggle was for superiority and the hold on power. The action of the house of Austria was in itself defensive action ; on every side its spreading dominions were at the mercy of the strong enemy whom they seemed to hem in ; the action of Francis and Henry II was necessarily aggressive ; wherever they turned, except seawards, there were the forces of Austria watching them; over the Pyrenees, over the Alps, over the Rhone, over the Rhine, within the historic limits of France, northwards and eastwards, there was the rival power, and even on the sea-board there were the hostile fleets.

Next comes the Reformation, a struggle it may be said of ideas, as the Hapsburg struggle with France is a struggle of rights, but primarily a struggle of powers ; the rights in the one case, the ideas in the other, being the occasion rather than the essential ingredients of the rivalry.

But setting the idea side of the Reformation for the moment in the background, follow the rivalry of the foremost powers. In this aspect the Reformation cuts curiously across the earlier dividing lines : it breaks up such unity of German action as has yet existed, and gives France its first great advantage : the strange alliance of Henry II with the Protestant powers, an alliance most distinctly of force, not of idea, strikes the first hard blow at the preponderance of Austria, and the irrecoverable loss of the three bishoprics is one of the mortal wounds of the empire. The next act is the rebellion of the Netherlands and the contemporary wars of the league in France; the Austrian heritage is broken in two, but the family interest and alliance for a time supplies the place of personal union. For a generation, however, Austria proper stands outside the struggle of the balance; she has to repress the movements towards religious reformation, and to ward off the attacks of the Turks on the side of Hungary. Where her weight is at all operative it is thrown on the side of Spain. Spain is the overshadowing, all-threatening force; France doing her best to produce the disruption of the Netherlands, Spain doing her best to produce the disruption of France; again the reformed party, acting as a force rather than a sentiment; for although on Philip's side the interests of Spain and religion are at one, France is persecuting at home the very ideas for which she intrigues abroad.

After a while the balance wavers: the strong hand of Philip II is taken off, the unworthy hand of the Valois lets fall the sceptre which it had held with so weak and vacillating grasp. Henry IV becomes the dominating influence. Henry IV is a man of ideas, a man of sentiment, a man of force; not of much sense of law and right. To his mind a reconstituted Europe was the ideal; not of course to accept as his the minute remodelling of the map which was once ascribed to him and his advisers, we can yet see enough of his design to know that he planned a forcible partition of the Hapsburg inheritances, the erection of a counterpoise to the empire in Germany itself, and the rearrangement of the minor states in a way which would have left France the civil and religious arbiter of Christendom. His day is but a short one, and the ideas which he or his counsellors conceived came to bearing in the struggle of forces which occupied the long reign of his grandson.

But the scene of the drama changes at the same time. The United Provinces have gained recognition; the action of Spain is becoming languid, and its energy bears no proportion to its still subsisting power and mass. The great act is now in Germany, the Thirty Years War: a war of two forces, two rights, two ideas : Austria against the princes, Catholic against Protestant, ancient territorial right as against new territorial force. Here too the religious influence produces cross division ; the Lutheran and the Calvinist will not fight side by side ; the Bavarian sets Catholicism before imperialism ; Austria sets the family interest before either ; yet Austria is as Catholic as the Jesuits and as imperial as the jurists can make her. But notwithstanding this cross influence of rights and ideas, the Thirty Years War is mainly a war of force, a war for determining the balance, not between ideas or rights, not between competing religions or competing liberties, but between armed sovereignties and territorial aggregations. Make the utmost of the idealism of Gustavus Adolphus, the legal pretexts of his interference are even worse founded than those under which Denmark in the earlier stage of the war had thrown in her lot as against the empire ; and the idealism of Gustavus, his high and noble purpose of coming down as the saviour of religion, ends in the artificial aggrandisement of Sweden, as the luckless intriguing policy of Christian ends in the complete humiliation of Denmark. The interference of France, without sympathy of idea, without pretext of legality, is a simple intrusion of force. But I pass on.

The Thirty Years War exhausted Germany, even the victorious powers were worn out, much more the defeated ones : the stage is left clear for the glories of Lewis XIV. 'The state is myself.' 'The right is the glory of France.' Perhaps the lurid glare of the glories of this act, the act of the Great Monarch, throws a shade on minor actors and less prominent motives, but it can scarcely be misread ; it is the triumph of force over both old rights and new ideas ; a régime in which might is construed as right. The dominance of the idea of force in the aggression produces a corresponding influence in the resisting powers. They are bound not by sympathy but by necessity ; the alliances that resist the great monarch are alliances of expediency, not of principle, and when the resistance is past they are ever ready for new combinations.

The struggle of the Spanish succession followed, a struggle in which ancestral right was matched against the doctrine of the balance, and the force of the stronger determined the verdict. The struggle of the Imperial succession next led on to the triumphant career of Frederick II, and that unmistakeably to the new forms of political combination and antagonism which emerged from the French Revolution. Lewis XIV and Frederick the Great impersonate the two principles, or aspects of the one principle, that might gives right; Frederick was far the greater man, of course; Frederick had rights; he had claims old and legal on Silesia, and the old question of the Cleves Juliers inheritance had been a burning question for a century before he began to fight; and he had ideas—who so many? Lewis XIV had scarcely any plea of right for his aggressions, and his sole idea, as his sole policy, was himself, his interest and glory and that of France in him. But it all came to the same thing. Frederick knew that he was strong, and revived old pleas that his father had let slumber. Lewis knew that he was strong: the rival powers at both conjunctures were exhausted; war, policy, money, philosophy, intrigue, rights and ideas, all gave way or led on to the triumph of force. The right, the idea, the balance of power, was on the side of the strongest battalions.

But now I must turn back to the Reformation, for there can be no question that, in the changes that brought about and resulted from that crisis, both rights and ideas were very strong within certain circles of their own, and to make the balance of power, the struggle of material forces, the sole lesson of this portion of history, would be a serious mistake. Yet I think even here we shall see that the principle of the idea was less operative than the principle of force, the policy of force more effective than the policy of idea. The crisis of the Reformation is not less remarkable for its results than for its causes. The throwing off of the Roman supremacy, in doctrine and ecclesiastical government, was, in those countries in which it was permanently effected, a most complex proceeding. No doubt there was throughout Europe much religious disaffection at the opening of the sixteenth century; but for a century before there had been even more prominent doctrinal disaffection, and

only just a century before the Church had passed through a
most dangerous schism, which threatened its substantial
organisation as well as its doctrine. The desired reformation
in head and members had been familiar all this time. But it
did not come till now; till the stage had, as we have seen,
been cleared for the new actors. We might conjecture that
whilst the concentration of the new powers gave them in
themselves greater vitality and more manageable force, it
would exhaust the vitality of the older organisation, which
had kept them together whilst the divisions were smaller and
the common action less vivid. Whilst all the powers of
Christendom were busy with their own internal rights and
border quarrels, a languid acquiescence in the undivided
supremacy of Rome was more a powerful influence than it
could be when two or three new and well girt combatants
were ready to assert their own αὐτάρκεια; still more, when the
new combatants saw the truth that they must be lords in
their own houses. As we saw, the concentration of power in
Spain, France, and Germany meant more than the absorption
of weaker states; it meant the absorption of inferior powers in
the state. The strong actors in the new drama must be strong
governors at home as well as strong combatants abroad. Great
designs, great rivalries, demanded concentrated energies, determined wills. Strong government came in with the sixteenth
century, and strong government was a very strong element in
reformation history, for it weakened the solidarity of the
Catholic Church and prepared the way for the formula ' cujus
regio ejus religio,' the disruption of national churches as well.

But neither these causes, religious disaffection and the dis-
integration of the weak church organisation by the growing
strength of absolutism, nor the ideas of the new learning, nor
the rivalries of political rulers fostering abroad forms of discontent which they persecuted at home, nor the lust of enlarged territory, nor the coveting of ecclesiastical wealth, nor
the envy of unprivileged classes, nor the new power of the
press, would alone have sufficed to do the work that was done.
Who could have reckoned on the coincidence of the Indulgence
agitation in Germany, the divorce agitation in England, the

growth of Huguenotism in France, the rising up of men like
Luther, Zwingli, Calvin and Knox in such rapid succession, and
with such marked differences, and such diverse contributions to
such a complex result ? There was unquestionably, in conjunction with the yearnings for spiritual change, a deep and
strong impulse for breaking with the past; breaking with
national traditions and with religious traditions ; a tendency
which would, if it had been unchecked, unobstructed, or not
diverted into other channels, almost of necessity have amounted
to revolution.

Strong government had not come too soon ; but for that,
with all its oppressions, its repressions, and its persecutions,
there would have been a period of anarchy in the breaking up
of the deeps of old society.   Well, however it was to be met,
reformation came ; the absorption of a great part of the lands
of the churches followed or accompanied reformation ; either,
as in England, by the seizure and surrender of monastic
estates, or in Germany by the adoption of transparent fictions
which enabled Protestant princes to lay on ecclesiastical
positions a hold which was never to be relaxed ; or, as in
Scotland, by sweeping away the old fabric altogether.   The
ancient right of territorial ownership was weakened, and the
process of secularisation, which was in Germany completed at
the peace of Westphalia, set the seal of legality on the status
quo.

Protestantism had done its utmost to shift the balance
of power.   Yet, as I said before, it had really done little more
than produce a cross division in the conflicting parties.
Where Protestantism was an idea only, as in Spain and Italy,
it was crushed out by the Inquisition ; where, in conjunction
with political power and sustained by ecclesiastical confiscation, it became a physical force, there it was lasting.   It is
not a pleasant view to take of the doctrinal change to see that,
where the movement towards it was pure and unworldly, it
failed ; where it was seconded by territorial greed and political
animosity, it succeeded.   But so it has been with many of the
changes by which in the long run both Church and world have
been benefited.   In the case of the English reformation, it is

certain that without the redistribution of monastic estates the change must have been long delayed, and might have been suddenly and permanently reversed. Anarchy and confusion were imminent under the puritan rule of Edward VI, as well as under the papal reaction of Mary. If Elizabeth and her advisers had leaned to either, the flood must have poured in; unsympathetic as is the Elizabethan Church rule, little as we can find to love among the men whom she set up as Fathers to the Church, it was their strong rule that saved England from revolution far more dangerous, far more calamitous, than all the mistakes, the terrors, the persecutions, the reactions, of the so-called rebellion and revolution periods of the seventeenth century. But again the subject is one that tempts to too wide digression : only, after what I have said, whether you agree with me or no, you will see why I have thought it better to treat the Reformation under the aspect of force rather than idea.

We must not, however, imagine that in any but the extremest cases of change, political, territorial, or religious, the old landmarks were so entirely swept away that none of the earlier ideas of rights remained. No: it was the conflict between the old influence of right and the new influence of force, between old legality and new strong government that forced into existence the diplomacy of the sixteenth and following centuries,—diplomacy, in its beginning a sort of kriegspiel, in which threats and bribes on paper took the place of mobilisations and marches, sieges and invasions. Most curious are the beginnings of the diplomatic policy of Wolsey and his master ; the restless attempts to make the political force felt without the cost of exerting it ; how as soon as they have concluded an alliance, do they begin to work for a counter alliance ; how they seem to conclude treaties with one high conflicting party that overlap the treaties they have just made with the other ; what secrecy, what mystery, what bribery, what intimidation ; and amid all, a little sour grain of conscience, that the old law-abiding, treaty-keeping faith and loyalty would have been better. A plea must be sought for every aggression ; no compact must

be broken without hesitation unless a flaw can be found.
Whether it be true that Charles V justified the imprisonment
of Philip the Magnanimous by the misreading of a single
letter in the word which had induced him to surrender, I do
not know; the story may be false, but the moral is true;
men were loth to own themselves actuated by simple greed.
And as diplomacy was in its beginnings, so it lasted for a long
time; the ambassador was the man who was sent to lie abroad
for the good of his country. Rights, pleas, grudges, were
registered against the time when strength would accrue to
make them real weapons of argument and instruments of
aggression.

But as the old influence of right lingered on, the new
influence of idea was from time to time giving distinct
warnings of a further change. There was an idea of religion,
there was an idea of liberty, struggles for the vindication of
historical nationalities, although, as ideas, they were overborne
or absorbed by the mightier forces which played around them.
It could scarcely be but that strong government should force
up premature longings for liberty, or that religious repression
should compel a desire for tolerance. Yet we must not make
too much of the first glimmerings of the changes that were
coming. The revolt of the Netherlands was perhaps the
most resolute attempt at liberty that had been seen since the
middle ages opened; the idea of nationality was strong in the
Spanish provinces of the Hapsburg inheritance and in the
Bohemia of the Thirty Years War. But they never became
ruling principles; nor were they likely to do so until they
were emancipated from the mere selfish and localised interests
with which they were bound up. Class liberties, isolated
nationalities, local privileges, may keep up the memory, the
tradition of liberty, nationality, and privilege, but they do
not become leading ideas until they have been accepted as
universally just and desireable, until they can command assent
and inspire sympathy. The religions that demanded toleration but meant tyranny were no true exponents of religious
liberty: the classes that would limit royal prerogative to
lay their hand heavier on their own vassals, were no true

exponents of constitutional government.   The hand that
cherishes nationality in Italy, and represses it in Greece, is no
true defender of nationality.

But the clock and the limit of my paper warn me to proceed at once, imperfectly as I must have indicated or suggested my view, to the third portion of the subject.   Later
modern history, the history of the last hundred years, seems
to me to differ from that of the two preceding divisions,
by the prominence and real importance of ideas, as compared
with the earlier reigns of right and force.   I need not
repeat that the prominence and real importance, the theoretical and practical weight of political ideas being admitted,
we need not suppose either of the preceding principles
to be extinguished; nor, on the other hand, need we suppose
that the ideas which latterly come to the forefront were either
unknown or unappreciated in the earlier periods.   I have just
said that liberty, nationality, and the like were strong agents
before they became the strongest ; we may freely admit that
both force and right still exercise a strong influence, though
not the strongest, in modern politics.   Keeping this in mind,
you will not expect me to discuss the origin and growth of the
ideas in question ; rather it will be enough to indicate the
point at which they seem to take such hold on the political
mind as to presage their future importance.

It seems to me that the partition of Poland, in the last century, was the event that forced the idea of nationality upon
the world, and the revolt of the American provinces of the
British empire forced the idea of self-government, not as a local
British invention, but as a sort of political gospel, upon general
belief.   You will not suspect me of being a believer in the
' rights of man,' or in the legal position of the American
revolutionists ; you will not, I trust, suspect me of believing
that territorial right can ever be made a justification of moral
iniquity or of abandoned misgovernment and tyranny : and
yet I may insist more strongly on territorial right and believe
more strongly in the universality of true principles than
others who talk politics more fluently than I can deliver
public statutory lectures.

But to stick to facts : as the suppression of Poland, on
the one side, forced on the world the conscience that nationality is more than a geographical formula, on the other
hand, it showed how easily force and fraud could remove
the ancient landmarks of territorial right. It was, therefore,
a two-edged experiment, and no doubt it cut the hands of
all the intermeddling powers. As the vindication of American
liberties made a precedent for the ideas of the French Revolution, the partition of Poland pointed to the reconstruction
of the map of Europe; the destruction of that kingdom
was a precedent for the destruction of any kingdom; the
extinction of that nationality aroused a sympathy, awakened
an idea of the importance of nationality as a reconstituting
idea in reformed society.

Well, the French Revolution set at liberty all the disrup-
tive influences that existed in the weakly governed states
of the continent, and roused to a somewhat rash, hurried,
and incautious hostility the instincts of the strongly governed
but ill-prepared powers like Prussia, Austria, Russia, and
England. And the first attempts at a propaganda of liberty,
and the first attempts at a propaganda of nationality, were
marked by great excesses and great mistakes : excesses and
mistakes so potential that the propaganda of the two influences together determined in the Napoleonic empire,
the tyranny and glory of France and the privilege of all
nations to acknowledge and toil under the shadow of her
supremacy. Liberties were enunciated in fulsome language,
nationalities were carved out with amusing caprice; but glory
and victory were the real aim; force exerted itself as strongly
under Napoleon as under Peter the Great and Frederick the
Great and Lewis the Great. By and by came the recoil.
Napoleon was humbled; the map of Europe was reformed on
a plan which showed a respect for territorial rights, and a
just recognition both of the earnings of force and of the growth
of ideas. But the end was not yet; liberty, though recognised, was distrusted; nationality, though allowed some
weight, was everywhere set beneath territorial right and
material power : and self-government made very little way

in the world for at least fifteen years after the battle of
Waterloo.

When the world had rested, when politics began to move
again, both these ideas came to the front: the nationality of Greece; the independence of Belgium, a distinct
nationality as regarded the state with which it had been
bound up: these were the first notes of the triumph of one
idea: the second French Revolution cannot be said to have
opened the campaign of self-government, for the revolt of the
Spanish and Portuguese colonies had done that; but it was an
important contribution to the cause among the old countries
of Europe: the German principalities had to hasten the gift
of constitutional governments which had been long deferred,
and were, even when granted, to a great extent illusory.

An uneasy time of peace and repression were the seventeen
years that followed: since 1848 the action of the drama has
been exciting and unintermitting. France, dissatisfied with her
government, threw Europe again into turmoil; again there
was a cry of liberty and nationality, again force and legality
were equal to the occasion, and society was saved. France
sank under a military despotism which subsisted by keeping
the world in arms. But the ideas were stronger at each
revolution and each struggle. France went to war for the
idea when she had nothing else to go to war for; and, having
bound liberty hand and foot at home, proclaimed herself again
the apostle of liberty. It was liberty for your friends, humiliation for your enemies, as usual: but the result far outran
the intention.

After the Crimean War, of which I will not trust myself
to speak further than to say that I believe it to have been
a profound misunderstanding of the current of the world's
progress, a mistake of legality, a miscalculation of force, a
misconception of idea, but which had the sole merit of teaching the generation of soldiers to fight and of diplomatists to
conjure; after the Crimean War we get, first, the reconstruction of Italy on the principles of nationality and with a free
constitution; then the reconstruction of Germany, then the
reconstruction of Austria; of Germany on a principle of nation-

ality and self-government which has yet to find a balance for the preponderance of force, and in Austria on a principle of nationality and self-government that has yet to determine its relations to the older rules of legality on which historically the unity of Austria depends. And within the last two years the world has been kept alive by the struggle for nationality and freedom, between Russian force and Turkish tyranny.

Out of the crucible, out of the fiery furnace, against the will of the potent actors, as if by a law that may not be broken, the victory of the idea is rapidly being realised. There are, of course, other ideas, counter ideas, ideas which are only the old legality and the old material force disguised under new names. Such ideas may be Pansclavism, or Internationalism, or Nihilism, if it be anything but a negation of ideas. Such ideas may be that of Russia at Constantinople, of a restored Poland, of a free church in a free state, of universal voluntaryism, of scientific frontiers. I am not here to justify or to condemn, much less to prophesy ; and whatever it is that is coming, I am sure we are only at the beginning of it. At present Russia stands before the world, really as representing force, in pretension,—pretension which I am far from believing to be insincere,—as the liberator of the Christian races of the East. Austria is far the most conspicuous defender of historic territorial right ; and all those who are not afraid of the nickname of reactionists will be slow to condemn her for the maintenance of a principle on which she has grown into power, and which she is doing her best to reconcile with more potent ideas and influences more likely to be permanent. France to some extent represents democracy, to a far greater extent she still, as ever, represents the old claim to arbitrate in Europe. Prussia or Germany, in the same way, represents the force which, relying on the strength of nationality, has for the moment made her the leading power in Christendom. For the perishing remnants of Turkey a faint plea of territorial possession has gone forth, but the conscience of friend and the determination of foes have alike repudiated it as an excuse for misgovernment and palliation of tyranny. There is no idea, no such justification for that curse of Christendom. Turkey means nothing, represents nothing but butchery, barbarism, and the vilest slavery. What does England represent? What is she to represent in the future? What would we wish for her but clear-sighted justice and living sympathy with what is good and sound in the progress of the world?

Having achieved that sentiment, I must now slip into bathos. I have preferred medieval history to modern in my own teaching, partly because I believe the study of rights is more wholesome as an educational study than that of the balance of forces, partly because I think it a safer study altogether than the theoretical study of political ideas. Political ideas are apt to lay hold on the fancy and on the affections, and to make men partisans before they are at all competent to weigh the merits of parties, to adjust the balance between order and progress, between historical right and historical growth : and there is in the study of them very little training. Educationally, I prefer the first division. I may also be turned towards it by certain legal tendencies and documentary tastes of my own. I am only justifying myself, not laying down a law for others. There are other sorts of studies here besides law and history. I can conceive the man who has spent his terms here on philosophy taking more naturally to the examination and analysis of ideas, and the mathematician being more charmed by the thought of reading national complications as illustrations of the parallelogram of forces : the student of physical science will no doubt soon be able to infer the national idiosyncrasy of races from the shape of their skulls. With all this I am so far from finding fault that I rejoice and delight in the thought of so many minds and so many studies working towards my truth. But I plead for a toleration which I have done my best to justify.

XI.

THE REIGN OF HENRY VIII.

(June 7, 1881.)

I SHALL not trouble you with any detailed reasons for my choice of a subject for this Term's statutory lectures ; it is enough to observe that I have been busily employed upon the reign of Henry VIII for some months of ordinary lecturing, and that there is every probability that I may have to work upon him for some months to come. You will at once admit that Henry VIII is too big a subject to admit any rival on the same canvas, or under the same hand ; whoever undertakes him at all must be content to devote himself for the time entirely to him. This being said, you must further concede to me that, although the subject is interesting enough, two lectures, in which anything like a bird's-eye view can be offered, must be very dry ; I will not say dull, but so concentrated as not to allow much extraneous illustration. That granted, I propose to put before you, in as concise a form as possible, the main points of importance in the reign, in some degree adopting the method which I have followed in the analytical chapters of my Constitutional History. If, in doing this, I succeed only in drawing out a plan on which the long history of the reign may be arranged for subsequent reading, I feel that I shall have done something. I intend to try to do more, but I may not, in the further aim, satisfy you, and I certainly shall not satisfy myself.

My plan will be to offer you, at the beginning and end of the lectures, some general remarks on the position and character of England and her king at the beginning and end of the reign ;

but to devote the main part of our discussion to the definite arrangement of the particular acts and measures of the period, saying as little as possible about external matters, but fixing as accurately as we can the framework of internal history; its principal changes and their tendency. I will not now anticipate any general conclusions, but simply propose an arrangement under the ordinary heads of taxation, legislation, administrative action, ecclesiastical reform, and parliamentary history.

The position of England at the opening of Modern History, the position which she had assumed under Henry VII and in which Henry VIII found her at his accession, was that of a young, well concentrated and well equipped, but untrained, actor for the great drama of European politics. England had had more than twenty years of such peace as amounted to a disuse of warfare; that is, her yeomanry had only maintained the use of arms as a part of their education, they had no practical acquaintance with military tactics or with blood and iron. But in other respects she was well furnished; she had money, and good intelligence, and astute ministers, men of wide mind like Wolsey, and of minute experience, and of no small ambitions. I am not going to say that England came upon the stage with more real wisdom or with more honesty of purpose than the other powers: her diplomacy seems to have partaken quite as much of the character of chicanery as did that of Spain, France, or Austria : but her interests in the struggle of European forces, which is now commencing, were not so direct as theirs; her sympathies were not definitely with either the one side or the other; and, if her hereditary antipathy to France might seem likely to throw her too unreservedly on the side of France's enemies, the cool way in which, on all occasions except when money was wanted, her attentions were received by the Imperial administration in Spain and the Netherlands, was quite enough to repel any approach to sympathy.

So, as a rule, throughout the reign of Henry VIII, the cool heads among English politicians dreamed of nothing more for their country than the position of an arbitrator, an umpire between great rival parties on the Continent, from whose humiliation nothing was to be gained, and from whose over-exaltation something was to be feared. Henry VIII might sometimes dream of the Empire, or of the recovery of Normandy and Aquitaine, as Wolsey might dream of the papacy; but the wiser heads contemplated no such shadows; nor, I think, had those aims more than a slight and momentary influence on the king and cardinal; the people were not unwilling, up to a certain point, to fight and, up to a certain point, to pay : but they did not care to sacrifice their blood and money, and win neither spoils nor glory. So, although there was much talk of war, and much money spent on armaments, money well spent perhaps in part, for the armed power of England was a not unimportant qualification for her position as arbitrator, there was very little real war ; there were countless treaties, leagues, unions, truces, armistices, sufferances, neutralities and abstentions, but the expeditions of Dorset and Howard to Spain and France in 1512, the king's expedition to Tournay in 1513, the invasion of France by the Duke of Suffolk in 1523, and the expedition of Henry to Boulogne in 1543, are the sum and substance of Henry's military doings outside of Great Britain.

A momentary effort, a little advantage gained, time taken to secure it, and the utmost terms exacted for the surrender of it, is the whole story. In spite of many leagues with France, the sword is never really drawn against Charles ; and, in spite of many leagues with Charles, war of England against France has no other direct object than the acquisition of a stronghold on or near the coast. Money is spent in loans, or dangled in the shape of promises, there are threats of diversion and plans of united campaigns which come to nothing more. England claiming to be an arbitrator is really a make-weight.

I cannot therefore agree with those who would extol the foreign policy of England in the beginning and end of the reign as a masterpiece of diplomacy. Honesty would have been the simpler, the wiser, and the cheaper policy; and so I think the nation itself felt. Far more would really have been gained by letting the competitors fight out their quarrel and exhaust themselves; and the position of England could have been made safe at a tenth of the cost. But it was a new game, a new drama, and England as represented by Henry must have a leading part.

Within the borders of the island, the old struggle of Scotland, allied with and prompted by France, is a matter of secondary interest; and the two great crises, the battle of Flodden in 1513 and the death of James V in 1542, great as they are in picturesque and personal interest, scarcely trouble the current of peace at home; the border warfare, seldom intermitted, the party struggles of the Scots themselves, whether the time is one of truce or of hostility, furnish opportunity for military and administrative occupation, and for the energies of uneasy men. I pass then rapidly and generally over these external points in which so much of contemporary history is expended, and prefer to look more closely at home.

And let us first look at the king. I am not one of those critics who incline to a very disparaging estimate of Henry VIII. He was not, as a man, more vicious than many kings who have maintained a very fair reputation in history. In force of character there are few indeed that come near him; if he seems to act upon pure self-will, he is able to give a reason for his acts, and that such a reason as we cannot on mere prejudice determine to be unreasonable; he makes his way with good men and bad men alike, and, with a few notable exceptions, he is able to overrule all protest. On mature consideration, I am inclined to regard Henry himself as the main originator of the greatest and most critical changes of his reign; and I am sure that, after the fall of Wolsey, there is no minister, great or small, who can claim anything like an original share in determining the royal policy. He could keep More as his chancellor, and Warham as his archbishop, whilst he was pushing measures which they abhorred; he could send Cromwell to the block the moment he discovered that he was pursuing designs of a colour which did not recommend itself to him; and to Audley and Wriothesley no one would dream of giving the name of an independent or original minister. Cranmer and Gardiner he tolerated alike

and in turn, but Cranmer kept his place by abstention from
politics and by the facility with which Henry could use him
when he wanted; whilst Gardiner, on the other hand, sank the
ecclesiastic in the politician until his time came.

So, for all the critical years of the reign, Henry's strong
will threw the advice or agency of any subordinate politician
into the shade.   Henry was every inch a king; the king, the
whole king, and nothing but the king.   Another of our kings,
George IV, I think, who also had matrimonial troubles, in
writing to his ministers used to employ an expressive phrase to
describe a contingency which it was useless to contemplate.
' If I were an individual,' he writes, ' I might, should, or would
do so and so.'   Now Henry VIII in that sense was never an
individual: he was always a king, looking on himself as a
thing apart from mankind, on kingship as an end in itself,
on kingly volition as the only and ample reason for anything
whatever; on his dignity as such a complete vice-Deity that,
under his fiat, municipal law rose, without any further sanction,
to the level of divine revelation.   His marriages are royal
marriages, his murders royal murders, his diseases royal diseases.
There is nothing to hide, nothing to be ashamed of.   Bessie
Blount is as much a fact as Anne Boleyn, and Anne Boleyn as
Katharine of Aragon.   If they are to his taste they are
honoured and worshipped with him; if he is tired of them the
country is tired of them too; they are abominable; they
confess themselves guilty of impossible sins; send them by
parliamentary petition to the block.

What is strange in all this is not the idea itself, which
George IV may have had as strongly as Henry VIII: it is
the force of character that makes the idea tolerable to other
men; that makes More, Warham, Cranmer, Gardiner, Cromwell, faithful administrators of the idea; and that forces,
against their will evidently, but still effectively forces, Parliament and Convocation, Lords, Clergy and Commons, to register
simply the peremptory orders of the king as their own wishes.
There were cliques and parties at Henry's court during the
whole of his reign, there was a strong party against Wolsey,
there was a protestant and a catholic party, and a Norfolk and

a Suffolk party; but I am sure that it is a mistake to regard Henry as pulled by one or other of these alternately; or to think that the changes of his policy, and I am not at all sure that the changes were at all so great as they are commonly re- garded, were dictated by any other than his own despotic will : he used, I think, the parties, not they him ; what influence he allowed them was allowed for his ends, and the moment he saw them pursuing their own ends he stopped them.

Of course such a theory about him, if true, necessitates the belief of great development of design and new purpose in the king himself : but that I think is the most natural solution of most of the critical questions of the reign. The words which More addressed to Cromwell, soon after he resigned the chan- cellorship, seem to be a key, almost prophetic in simplicity, to the after-history. 'Master Cromwell,' he says, 'you are now en- tered into the service of a most noble, wise, and liberal prince : if you will follow my poor advice, you shall in your counsel- giving to his grace, ever tell him what he ought to do, but never what he is able to do.' 'For if a lion knew his own strength, hard were it for any man to rule him.'

From the very beginning of his reign, he is finding out what he can do ; from the fall of Wolsey, and especially after the sacrifice of More, he is coming to regard what he can do as the only measure of what he ought to do : he is becoming the king for whom the kingdom is, the tyrant whose every caprice is wise and sacred : he turns the theory of kingship into action ; the king can do no wrong ; therefore men shall call right all that he does : he is the king, not an individual ; what in an individual would be theft, is no theft in him ; all property is the king's, he can take it, and he takes it ; all that proceeds from his mouth is law ; the king's heart is in the hand of the Lord, therefore all that comes out of the king's heart is the Lord's doing.

Yet with all his grotesque and inhuman self-absorption, the miserable and growing result of the long tenure of irrespon- sible power, we cannot wisely deny the king some great qualities besides mere force. Contemporary foreigners, the justice of whose general judgment is amply proved by later history, and whose opinion, according to Lord Bacon's dictum,

is generally that which future ages will be found to confirm,
are unanimous in their glorification of Henry's personal and
mental gifts. His beauty was of that sort that commended
itself to the taste of those times. And more than that : for the
painters of his portrait have succeeded in giving him an indi-
viduality and a humanity which shows either that he possessed
a remarkable physique, or that they took more pains with him
than they did with his wives—the deadly-lively sort of ladies
whose portraits are, if not a justification, at least a colourable
occasion for understanding the readiness with which he put
them away. Henry's portrait, I said, would fill any canvas ;
and, allowing for what must be allowed for, dress, expression,
and attitude, it must be allowed to be the portrait of a per-
sonable king.

His mental abilities I rank very high : he had been carefully
educated by good scholars, and had made remarkable progress ;
not so great, Lord Bacon tells us, as his brother Arthur ; but
still remarkable at a remarkable time : he did not let his
knowledge acquired in boyhood fade out of his mind : after his
accession he must have continued his reading ; his book against
Luther, which, whatever assistance he may have received, was in
conception and execution entirely his own, was an extraordinary
work for a young king ; and the intelligent interest which,
down to the last, he showed in religious and other ecclesiastical questions, even when he was most capricious and peremptory, evinces both memory and a real appreciation of subjects on
which contemporary kings thought it sinful to think at all.
If it were not for the miserable self-will and self-worship
which runs through these, there might be something to
admire.

Well, it is not for us to judge. The king is apart from
other men in his opportunities, in his excuses, in his temptations ; even in his responsibility for the direct results of his
acts ; and he must stand alone in the judgment. But I will
leave the remaining sentiments or reflexions which suggest
themselves, to be justified after the review of the reign which
I propose to take now.

The first question, who were Henry's responsible advisers, is capable of a very short answer considering the length of his reign : he succeeded a king who had been his own first minister, and who had under him two sorts of secondary ministers ; one set, like Warham and Fox, trustworthy men to whom he gave official confidence, that confidence which a self-confident autocrat can afford to give to men whose interests are the same as his own; and another set, like Empson and Dudley, whom he used as tools, responsible tools, to be used as long as they were useful, but to be held responsible the moment their use was over or the outcry they provoked became more noxious than the ends they served were advanta-geous. Henry VIII, doing everything on a larger scale than his father, had the same ideas of ministerial usefulness : during a reign of thirty-eight years he had only five chancellors, Warham, Wolsey, More, Audley, and Wriothesley ; and the office of lord high treasurer was held by two dukes of Norfolk in succession during the whole reign. Of the chancellors, Wolsey alone was displaced against his will; Warham had been long anxious to retire; More resigned in disgust; Audley retained the seals to his death, and Wriothesley was chancellor when the king died. Of these seven ministers we may sum-marily conclude thus : the two Norfolks and Warham were in position ministers of the old type, official and confidential, but not leaders of political parties, until, after the fall of Wolsey and, in the later years of the reign, after the fall of Cromwell, the second duke undertook the more onerous and critical position which in the end was so nearly fatal to him.

Wolsey was too great a man, and More too good a man, to be tools of Henry, especially after the inclination towards tyrannic caprice became more pronounced; Audley and Wriothesley were tools, either altogether selfish and un-principled, or, like Cromwell, able to combine self-aggrandise-ment and servility with some quantum of ulterior political design, which raises them above that common herd into which Empson and Dudley fall.

Besides these ostensible ministers, Henry had a council, in which perhaps more influential advisers might be looked for :

such as were his brother-in-law, friend, and boon companion
Suffolk, who, worthless enough himself, still was no man's
enemy; Cromwell, the greatest and most famous, whose character
and career are even more mysterious than his master's; and the
men who made their position and reputation by their share in
the business of the divorce, such as Cranmer, of whom, in this
aspect, the less said the better, and Gardiner, the rough and
ready, faithful, skilful, imperious yet adroit minister, on whose
back history has laid so great burdens. It is no doubt within the
walls of the council chamber that we have to look for the suggestions of such parts of the royal policy as were not due to
Henry himself: we can hardly, except in the cases of Wolsey
and Cromwell, very distinctly lay our hand on the authorship
of a particular scheme: and it is quite certain that, when a
particular scheme that pleased the king was started, he
adopted it as his own with an ardour and pertinacity fully in
keeping with his own idea of his infallibility. So, although
for a time Wolsey, and after him Norfolk, and after him
Cromwell, and after him Norfolk again, seem to be the prime
ministers of a country in which for at least two centuries
such prime ministers had been constitutional facts, and
although there was in the council a fertile seminary of
politicians creeping into power, yet on the whole Henry was
his own chief counsellor; in spite of his inconsistencies the
most consistent, and in spite of his changes and caprices the
most persistent, of all the men who changed, at this great
critical juncture, the whole face and attitude of England.
What more need be noted, in such a brief outline as I am now
drawing of these things, of the vast industry and broad views
of Wolsey, of the wisdom and virtue of More, of the mysterious unconscientiousness of Cromwell, and the like, may be
taken as we proceed.

The first region of constitutional action that lies before us
is the finance of the reign; a subject on which we have
abundant, though not very conclusive data, in the acts of the
parliaments which now begin to put on record the amounts
expected from the several grants; in the subsidy rolls, which
show how the sums granted were assessed and collected, in

the correspondence of the period, which sets before us what the estimated expenditure was from time to time, and in the incidental references of the annalists which tell us how the imposts were from time to time felt by the people. Of the thirty-eight years of the reign, twenty-one passed away without a parliament, and therefore without a budget; and long prorogations had now become so much the rule, that only nine new parliaments, nine general elections, were held during the whole time; the country therefore had not much opportunity of showing a change of feeling in this respect.

It is thus comparatively simple to state the parliamentary grants: tonnage and poundage, and the subsidy on wool, wool-fells and leather, were, in the first parliament of the reign, granted to the king for his life: the ancient vote of tenths and fifteenths was made on eleven occasions, sometimes as a sufficient grant and sometimes as a supplementary grant when a more grasping exaction had disappointed the officers of the Exchequer; and nine several subsidies of a new kind, a graduated income and property tax, were levied at more critical periods, as for the expeditions of 1512 and 1513, for the payment of expenses in 1515, and for the warlike preparations made in 1523, 1539, and 1543. These latter taxes were exactions on lands and goods according to fixed scale, minutely drawn out in each of the acts that sanctioned them: but, as the impost invariably fell short of the amount expected from it, we must conclude that, like the old tenths and fifteenths, it was assessed on fancy valuations and produced no very pressing hardships; judging from the existing returns it pressed very lightly upon individual payers, from the highest class to the lowest.

Besides these legal taxes from the laity, the king had votes from convocation following those of parliament in due proportion, the clergy paying a tenth whenever the parliament voted a tenth and fifteenth, adding a subsidy when the parliament granted a subsidy; and, after the parliament of 1534, paying to the king a whole tenth annually, which had been previously paid, almost if not quite regularly, as a contribution to the funds of the papacy. These were the regular and constitutional sources of income.

Besides these, we have to include in the list of the king's
resources, first the heavy loans which were exacted by a regular process, not very far removed from compulsion, in the years
1522–8 and 1542, and which were so fully remitted by the parliaments of 1529 and 1543, that even those unlucky creditors
whom the king had paid were obliged to refund the money;
secondly, the exactions from the clergy under the threat of
præmunire in 1531, amounting to about £120,000; thirdly,
the very large payments of tribute from France under the
treaties of Edward IV and Henry VII; and, fourthly, the
enormous revenue, enormous at the lowest estimate, which
accrued during the last years of the reign from the spoils of
the shrines and the plunder of the monasteries. Besides these,
there was an occasional devotion money, like that collected
in 1544 nominally for war against the Turks; a benevolence,
or amicable contribution, such as in 1525 produced considerable disaffection in the country; and lastly, enormous sums
raised under occasional forfeitures. I shall not attempt a
summary of these taxes, but may mention a few data that
may be relied upon: the value of a tenth and fifteenth was
£30,000; of a clerical tenth, £10,000; the estimated amount
of the subsidy of 1513 was £160,000; the estimate for the royal
expedition made in 1522, £372,404 18s. 4d.; the estimated
sum of the loans of 1523 was £260,000; the income from the
monasteries cannot be stated in reasonable figures; but of
this a considerable part was during the few years that it
accrued expended in pensions. Of estimated outlays we have
but a few illustrations; the expenses of the household were a
little over £20,000 a year, but these of course represent only
the fixed charges, not the king's lavish personal expenditure;
Wolsey's estimate for the war of 1513 was £640,000; and
when we find Giustiniani estimating the outlay at half of the
ten millions of ducats which was the treasure supposed to be
left by Henry VII, we are inclined to conclude that the estimate was not below the mark; anyhow the cost of the expedition to Tournay was such as to recommend a peace policy
for several years.

The time may come when these accounts may be subjected

to a formal historical audit, that is when the researches at
the Record Office furnish us with a complete view of extant
material; but it would be very rash now to define with
any exactness either income or outlay for a reign of such
abnormal character. The only general conclusion that I can
come to is that, in despite of Wolsey's financial ability, and
the cleverness of the agents who were trained under him,
the policy of the whole reign in this respect was a hand-to-
mouth policy, assisted by occasional godsends in the shape of
forfeitures and benevolences. In this department the parliaments showed some spirit, as we shall see; the result of that
was the grant of subsidies to reach over several years; under
these subsidy-acts the king collected as much as he could, and
then collected money in other ways until, the patience of the
lenders being exhausted, a new parliament was got together
to wipe off the old debt or promise a new subsidy. There can
be little doubt that some of the most important legislative acts
were carried, at least through the Commons, by the inducement that the king would be able to dispense with direct taxation; and although that undertaking was a fallacious one,
men could be found to overawe opposition or make a show of
self-sacrifice which was sure of subsequent reward. I may note
some of the parliamentary methods when I reach that part of
our subject: for this is the only point on which Henry in his
parliaments had any real difficulty.

A hand-to-mouth policy has this drawback; that, on
critical occasions, it involves critical demands, and critical
demands produce special irritation. That rule is exemplified
very clearly in the reign of Henry VII, whose financial
policy was much safer than his son's; it was not a hand-
to-mouth policy, but a severely economical one; and both poli-
cies coincide in having nothing to spare for emergencies;
accordingly we find, on every imposition of a subsidy in
the reign of Henry VII, an outbreak of popular disaffection,
taking hold of some political quarrel. There was under
Henry VIII something of the same sort; but it was, as a
rule, more easily localised, and put down at once; the restoration of law and order by his father had borne this good fruit.

In 1497 a rising in Devonshire caused by an income tax, utilised by a faction, and facilitated by the weakness of local organisation, could affect all Southern England, and force the king into the field. In 1536, even a great religious movement like the Pilgrimage of Grace sinks into a local and provincial rising, an abortive tumult. It is not necessary, however, at this point to formulate a general conclusion as to the oppressive character of Henry's financial administration: the legal taxes were not excessively heavy, and the illegal exactions were condoned by subservient parliaments. The question of the high-handed confiscations leads on to further questions.

I do not wish in these lectures to give more than its proper prominence to the great question of the divorce; even to give it its proper prominence would involve discussions far more lengthy than I have time for now; I shall therefore hope that you will take as read all the details of the negotiations concerning it, and simply look upon it as a force, or the application of an impact, which had much greater consequences, and originated a larger developing series of measures, than could have possibly been calculated on. In a word, to use Sir Thomas More's expressive formula, it opened the eyes of the lion as to what he could do; not all at once, but by a very gradual process, which may indeed be traced most distinctly with reference to the Reformation history, but is also apparent in the other departments of administration.

It is clear, from the beginning of his reign, that Henry was a prince who had only to learn the extent of his powers, in order to attempt to exercise them. If we may believe the law reporters, as early as 1515 he had declared himself determined not to allow any superiority of external spiritual courts in a country of which he was sovereign; and there are signs, in Wolsey's history, that the imminent danger of the king's taking advantage of the Statute of Præmunire was in his mind long before he was actually sacrificed. But the earlier years of the reign were remarkably free from occasions on which any great constitutional crisis could arise. Henry's ambition, like Wolsey's, was mainly set upon an influential place in the councils of Europe,

and among the people at large there was contentment. Henry
had been brought up very strictly, and married, very young,
to a wife, to whom he gave his full affection; the good impressions of his training were, at least for several years, strong
enough to keep him out of the domestic scandals that divide
courts; and although Bessie Blount and the Duke of Richmond
became prominent about ten years after the reign begins, it is
not until 1524 or 1525 that the divorce question even looms
in the distance.   Up to that time the want of constitutional
principle in the king and his minister has been chiefly apparent in the matter of money-getting.   Soon after this Henry
seems to have fallen in love with Anne Boleyn, and to have
begun to contemplate the divorce.   The mere formalities of
obtaining such a divorce were not formidable; but the parties
interested in preventing it were very formidable indeed.   The
emperor was the queen's nephew.   The pope's power was
being rudely shaken both in Germany and in Italy.   To be
brief; the pope was prevailed on to commission Wolsey and
Campegio to determine the validity of the king's marriage;
when the trial had begun, the cause was called back to Rome;
Henry felt that his only chance of getting the divorce was to
have it tried in England; the pope felt that the only chance
of avoiding a crisis, in which between Henry and Charles he
must certainly either temporally or spiritually be ruined, was
to keep the discussion languidly dragging on at Rome until
the parties were tired, or something else turned up.   This,
thus early, Henry had the sense to see; he therefore destroyed
Wolsey, and that by the very Statute of Præmunire at the
evasion of which he had so long connived: his eyes were
opened to the powers of the Præmunire, and in his confiscation
of Wolsey's estates he had his first taste of spoil.   He saw that
the Præmunire made him absolutely master of the clergy, and,
as absolute master, the primary owner of all Church property.
Hence the great chain of ecclesiastical statutes follows in an
order that we might almost dignify by the name of Evolution.
As lord and master of the Church, he could utilise Church
machinery to obtain the divorce and the marriage on which
he had set his king's heart; and, when he was tired of the

second wife, he could obtain, from the archbishop he had made,
an annulling of that marriage as easily as he could obtain a
Bill of Attainder from the parliament; and, when in time he
married another woman whom he did not like, he could by a
commission to the national synod obtain another judgment of
nullity of marriage, and by negotiating with parliament
another petition for another marriage. This wonderful Præmunire, of which the foreign residents at the English court
speak with horror as a mystery of which the king alone possessed the key, might be a lash brandished over laity and clergy
alike so long as the papal supremacy was admitted by either.

Thus the desire of spoil, the ambition of uncontrolled sovereignty, and the facilities of gaining his own immediate ends
in marriage, urged on the king in the line of doing, not what
he ought, but what he could. In 1531, by the threat of Præmunire he compelled the clergy to recognise him as the
supreme head on earth of the Church of England, and to pay
him £118,840 by votes of Convocation: he tried the same
policy with the Commons; endeavouring to compel them to
purchase their exemption from the same sentence, if not by
votes of money, at least by modifications of the land laws in
the direction of wills and uses. In this he was for the moment
defeated by the vigilance of the Commons, but he kept this
line of legislation before his eyes, and with singular pertinacity; the Statute of Uses was delayed until 1536 and
the Statute of Wills until 1540, but both statutes were promulgated in 1532, and formed part of a policy which we may
compare, not favourably, with that of Edward I; but which
has a special legal side of such importance, that only the
superior importance of the ecclesiastical questions of the time
can account for its being overlooked. It is true that, in their
later results, the two statutes of which I have spoken seem
small and beneficial as compared with the mischievous results
of the Church policy, but they were, like it, distinct puttings
out of the claws of the awakened lion, which would have gone
much further and held much tighter if they could.

But I proceed with the ecclesiastical evolution. The recognition of the king in 1531 as supreme head on earth of the

Church of England was closely connected with the appro-
priation of the £118,840 by the supreme head. But the
facility with which the Church parted with its money opened
the supreme eyes a little wider. If they will pay money they
will surrender power: a form of three articles is sent to Convocation in 1532 by which the clergy are to renounce their
right of spiritual legislation without royal licence, and consent
to a reform of the canon law under the king's authority. After
some discussion, with the fear of another Præmunire, the
clergy consent to that also. By crafty dealing with the
House of Commons, the Court, in which Cromwell is now becoming a leading man, obtains an address complaining of the
ecclesiastical courts, their use of canon law on the one side
and their practical abuses on the other; if the commons will
help the king against the pope, the king will help the commons against the spiritual courts; he will not press the
Statutes of Uses and Wills if they will agree that he shall
forbid the payment of annates. The commons resist, but
their strong men have gone over to the king. The Annates
Bill is passed; the Submission of the clergy is exacted; and
More, the good and wise chancellor, resigns the seals. He
and the foreign ambassadors saw which way the Lion was
looking better than the Lion himself. If the clergy accept
the Submission, says the Imperial resident, they will for the
future have less power than the shoemakers, who at least can
make regulations for their own craft. That was done however.

In the autumn Archbishop Warham died; it became clear
to the king that, if he appointed Cranmer, who was already
committed to him in the question of the marriage, that
long-standing difficulty could be got over. As yet there
was no formal breach with Rome, his hand had lain heavy
only on his own Church; the Annates Bill even had not been
confirmed yet. Cranmer should be regularly consecrated,
commissioned, and made legate, and then called on to act up
to his expressed convictions. So certain was the king of his
power, that, in anticipation of the sentence, he married Anne
Boleyn; appointed Cranmer archbishop, obtained from him a

sentence of the nullity of his previous marriage and of the validity of his new marriage, and got opinions from the divines and canonists in convocation which had a similar effect. Then, and not before, he confirmed the act about Annates, and defied the papal power.

But, having gone so far, why not go a little further? In the parliament of 1533 he obtained the passing of the Statute of Appeals, founded on what seems to be the true theory of Church and State; forbidding the carrying of appeals to Rome at all, and providing sufficient machinery for appeals at home: the Annates Bill had provided for the confirmation and consecration of bishops, and the two together proclaimed with one breath the emancipation of the Church from Roman supremacy, and its competence for complete internal administration under the supremacy of the king. But from this moment the ecclesiastical reforms became involved more and more with the king's marriage policy. Anne Boleyn, her father, and Cranmer, who seems to have been their family counsellor, were bent on further measures of hostility to Rome; and Cromwell, who was the king's minister rather than the queen's, was likewise politically a protestant. The year 1534 saw the clergy, both secular and regular, compelled to make a new submission, to recognise the validity of the marriage and the succession, and to admit a new and comprehensive oath for the maintenance of the two. A new statute of appeals, founded on the Submission of 1532, modified the appellate jurisdiction, and furnished a recourse to the king in chancery as the final reference which in the former statute had been left to the Archbishop and, in causes touching the king, to the Upper House of Convocation; a new statute on Annates reformed the regulations for the appointment of bishops; the synodical declaration which denied the authority of Rome, and a statute which forbade all payments to Rome, swept away all signs of the old subjection.

But there is no step, in parliament at least, towards doctrinal change: the law of heresy is reformed but not made less stringent, and it is no longer heretical to speak against the pope. Even in the Articles of 1536 the progress towards change is defined by the simple elimination of distinctive papal doctrine ; the convocation urges an authorised translation of Holy Scripture as the best antidote to heresy. But events were proceeding more rapidly than ideas : the oath of succession necessitated the imprisonment of More and Fisher ; a second session in the autumn of 1534 gave the secular recognition to the king's style as supreme head on earth of the Church of England ; that title was publicly promulgated by letters patent in January, 1535 ; and the accusation of attempting to deprive the king of this designation brought the two worthiest men in England to the block during the summer of that year. The death of Fisher, the confidential friend of his father and grandmother, and that of More, who represented all that was good in his own early experience, whether they were wrung from him by the importunities of his wife, or coldly acquiesced in as cases in which all human feeling must be sunk before the self-idolatry of the theoretic kingship, seem to prove and to have proved to the king himself that no scruples should ever hereafter touch him.

The next step of change was the dissolution of the smaller monasteries : Wolsey, in his great scheme for church reforms, had led the way to this. He had seen the increasing importance of the great towns of England, and the increasing mischief caused by the incurable uselessness of the monastic foundations ; and he had obtained bulls of legation from Rome enabling him to suppress convents and establish bishoprics. That had opened the king's eyes to a new possibility, and, although he waited several years before he executed his scheme, all that was good in the scheme was Wolsey's, all that was bad in it wears an unfortunate air of having been done by Cromwell. But it was almost a point of honour with Henry to show that without the pope he could do all that Wolsey had been empowered to do. So in the autumn of 1535 Cromwell and his agents effected a visitation of the monasteries, the report of which insured their condemnation ; and, in the last session of the Long Parliament in 1536, the dissolution of the smaller houses was decreed. A new court, the Court of Augmentations, was founded to manage the property which by the same act was vested in the king and his heirs. The greater monasteries survived a little longer, and in their case the process of surrender took the place of a general and compulsory dissolution. In the session of 1539, however, a similar act vested in the king the property of the surrendered houses, and in that year the abbots disappeared from parliament. At the same time the king was empowered to establish new bishoprics; suffragan bishops had been the subject of legislation in 1534, when the act was passed which supplied to the more aged and busy prelates the assistance that had been hitherto furnished by titular bishops *in partibus* commissioned at Rome.

These acts very nearly complete the series by which Henry evolved the idea of a regal papacy out of the royal supremacy. For some subordinate purposes, as for dispensations and faculties, he allowed the Archbishop of Canterbury to exercise a quasi-legatine authority under himself, and with a check in Chancery on his proceedings; but in all such matters he was himself the fountain of power. The climax was reached when, by the appointment of Cromwell as Vicar-General, with an authority and precedence above all prelates and nobles, he emulated the papal assumption of exercising direct powers through a legate *a latere*. Unluckily for himself and for Henry also, the royal legate *a latere* proved too great a power to manage; meddled with too many things, provoked too much hostility, got his feet entangled in the marriage net he had provided for the old lion, and perished more sadly, because more ignominiously, than his predecessors in power and ruin.

I have spoken thus far mainly of Henry's ecclesiastical measures as they affected endowments and jurisdictions; but there is a side, the side of doctrine, which is not less important. He never forgot that he was the defender of the faith; nor, whatever were his eccentricities and aberrations in minor particulars, does he seem ever to have gone in this region further in the direction of change than the more enlightened popes and cardinals of his own age would have gone. Wolsey

would have agreed with him in the dissolution of the monasteries ; the convocation had petitioned for a translation of the
Bible ; the worship of the saints and the excessive devotions at
their shrines had long been a burden to the souls of men, not
merely men like Erasmus, but of far more unimpeachable
orthodoxy. The supremacy of the chair of S. Peter was by
no means as yet an article of unquestioning faith ; even the
marriage of the clergy was a point not beyond discussion.
But there were things which, quite irrespective of the pope
and his claims, could not be touched without the taint of
heresy. And of these Henry, with all his inconsistencies,
was a constant defender. He might tolerate a certain evan-
gelical obliquity in Boleyn's eyes ; he might choose to be
blind to Cromwell's sympathies with foreign protestantism ;
he might tolerate Mrs. Cranmer, as he had not looked too
curiously into the semi-matrimonial connexions of the great
cardinal ; he might even go the length of marrying a lady
like Anne of Cleves, in whom, through the phlegmatic im-
penetrability of the Flanders mare, some instincts of unortho-
dox skittishness might be detected. But Henry was royally
orthodox. If, for any purpose of the moment, he relaxed the
stringency of the courts, he kept the law very strong against
heresy. This acted in a curious way. The king's idea that
he was supreme in Church and State, whilst in some regions
it led him to maintain the administrative machinery of the
two severely separate, in others led him to some mixture of
his functions. In his first act of heresy he repealed the
statute of Henry IV ' de hereticis comburendis ' which seemed
to give too much power to the bishops, but re-enacted those of
Richard II and Henry V which tended to make heresy an
offence at common law. A similar intention is clear in the
Act of Six Articles of 1539, and with this light upon it, in
the several modifications of the Six Articles which were proposed in the later parliaments. I shall not speculate on the
possibility that, if he had lived longer, he might have
developed more in the direction of protestant doctrine ; I
think however that it is unlikely ; doctrinally, although quite
able to maintain his own line, he clearly symbolised con-

sistently with Gardiner and not with Cranmer. The extinction of the Norfolk interest might have led him to further
negotiations with protestantism abroad, but with domestic
puritanism, such as that by which Somerset palliated his
greed for confiscation, there is no trace in Henry. For spoil
however the old lion went on yearning to the last; the
dissolution of chantries and colleges, to follow that of the
monasteries, was one of the measures of his last parliament.

It may strike some of us that the process of change had
now gone far enough; the English Church was freed from
the yoke of Rome, but she retained all her proper framework
and at least half of her old endowments; I say at least half, I
should not like to commit myself to a statement that there
was much more. She had obtained the Bible in English
and the use of the chief forms of prayer in the vernacular,
and was preparing for a revision in form of the Sacramental
Services; she had rid herself of a mass of superstitious usages.
It is true that the king remained a believer in Roman Catholic
forms of doctrine; but it must always be remembered that
those forms had not yet, by the Tridentine decrees, been
hardened into their later inflexibility; and, when we consider
the terrible risks which, in the next reign, the Church of
England ran, of losing all sense or desire of continuity, identity, or communion with the historic Catholic Christendom,
we may feel thankful that such risk was run under a weak
king and feeble ministers, not under the influence of a strong
will and strong hand like Henry's.

You will see thus that I believe him to have been a man of
purpose; not the mere capricious tyrant who found it a pleasant
exercise of despotic power to burn Catholics and Protestants on
the same day, or found a malicious gratification in making
Cranmer support the Catholic doctrine of the Eucharist and
Gardiner the doctrine of unlimited obedience: further than this
I do not go. I believe him to have been a man of unbounded
selfishness; a man to whom the acquisition of power was
precious mainly as a step towards the acquisition of greater
power; a man of whom we may say, as I said at first, that
he was the king, the whole king, and nothing but the king;

that he wished to be, with regard to the Church of England, the pope, the whole pope, and something more than pope. You remember how in his early days Maximilian had tempted him with the offer of the Empire, he himself to retire on the popedom with an inchoate claim to canonization. Henry was determined to have in England at least both Empire and Papacy, to make the best, or rather the most, of both worlds.

I have said more than in proper proportion I ought to have said with reference to Henry's ecclesiastical policy, and left but little time for the analogous features that may be traced in his temporal policy: one reason for that is the greater interest we all feel in the religious question of the Reformation; another is in the fact that his ecclesiastical measures had a much more lasting consequence than his temporal ones. We have long rid ourselves of all the secular burdens imposed by what we call the Tudor dictatorship, but we are still living under religious or ecclesiastical conditions that owe very much, even of their present form, to the hand of Henry. You will, I hope, know me too well to misinterpret me in these expressions; you will not suspect me of making Henry VIII the founder of the Church of England; but I do not conceal from myself that, under the Divine power which brings good out of evil and over-rules the wrath of man to the praise of God, we have received good as well as evil through the means of this ' majestic lord who broke the bonds of Rome.'

If now we attempt to find in Henry's treatment of the temporalty a reflexion of the principles on which he dealt thus summarily with the spiritualty, what do we find? The answer to one important part of that question I propose to take in the next lecture, in which I shall work with rather more detail than is possible in so wide a *résumé* as I have attempted in this, an examination of his dealings with the administrative machinery of the parliaments. But in a general way I will attempt to state the answer now. As for taxation, we have seen how, by his early as well as his late policy, the real hold on the purse-strings was wrested from the hand of

the nation. A king who had over his parliaments the strong
hold that Henry had, who could dictate to them the measures
he wished to pass, even down to the smallest details, and
even make them petition for acts when he was the only man
in the kingdom that desired them, might, we think, have
contented himself with taking money through the overawed
or subservient Commons. But he did not; he chose to exact
money by loan and then to come to the nation that lent the
money for exoneration; the very fact that he went about the
loan by exactly the same process of assessment and collection
that he used in assessing and collecting a legal tax, shows
that he saw what he was doing: he saw that he had the
power, and he used it. Wolsey might dislike the idea of
meeting a parliament that might speak unreservedly about
himself; Henry had no such dislike; he could browbeat, or
bribe, or bully, or divide, or balance parties, but he never could
have doubted for a moment that in the end he should get his
own way.

Next to taxation, perhaps even more important than taxation, was the right of legislation; legislation of the temporalty
could at no time be carried through without the king's
enacting words; and the submission of the clergy in 1532,
embodied in the Statute of Appeals in 1534, had established the same rule for the spiritualty. But this did not
content the Lion. In the Proclamation Act of 1539 the
parliament is made to surrender to the king the power of
legislation; as head on earth of the Church he might already
issue, and had issued, proclamations touching Christian faith;
and by the natural power of king he had issued proclamations
for the public peace: but, O strange wilfulness of human
nature! men had not much minded: these proclamations
alike were set at nought by those who would not consider
the divinity of royalty; therefore, lest the king should be
tempted to become a tyrant, lest the king should be compelled by the wilfulness of his subjects to extend beyond their
natural limits the liberty and supremacy of his royal power
and dignity, what was to be done? Was he to renounce the
power of proclaiming, and bind the parliament to codify the

temporal law, as he had promised to the spiritualty to codify and reform the canon law? Quite the reverse; in order that he might not be tempted to usurp the functions of legislator, the parliament was to invest him with those functions, and, provided his proclamations did not contravene the existing laws, to give to them the full force and virtue of acts of the whole body of the realm. Here was a 'lex regia' indeed; a dictatorship which, with all conceivable limitations, left the 'king master and only master' in his own house.

The security of life and property was of course worth little when such things were possible: but Henry had a strong executive force at his disposal, and the actual working of this despotism did not affect the body of the people so much as might be expected. The clergy were of course in constant terror of the shadow of a præmunire; the reformers, alternately flattered and banished, had no easy time of it; and the position of even a bishop's lady must have been, to say the least, peculiar. But on the great men, the taller poppies, the actual pressure occasionally fell. The nation had fought hard for justice in the tribunals and for the limitation of the doctrine of treasons. Bills of attainder, trials in Star Chamber, and multiplication of treasons, form the dark side of the policy of Henry VII; they come to full development under Henry VIII.

Edmund de la Pole, Buckingham, Wolsey, Fisher, More, Anne Boleyn, Cromwell, the Marquess of Exeter, the Countess of Salisbury, Montacute, and last of all Surrey and his father, were victims of a system, of various contrivances but of one purport, for destroying without law, or without trial, or without defence, those whom the king determined, from whatever motive of policy or of caprice, of jealousy or of satiety, to sacrifice. Add to these the religious or ecclesiastical holocausts, and the number of inferior victims who were involved in the fall of the great ones, and for whom there was no need to violate laws that could so easily be manipulated. The liberty of the subject to act or speak, or even to think, was reduced to a minimum under an executive familiar with constructive treasons.

But it is time to close this part of our discussion; and I

must leave some, especially of the legal measures of the reign
which would most naturally have fallen in with the line of
this lecture, for the more formal treatment, which I propose to
take in the next lecture, of Henry's dealings with parliament.
Perhaps when we have looked at these, we may find time to
inquire to what extent he really fulfilled the office of dictator,
anticipated the line of history, or carried with him the wishes
of the nation.

XII.

PARLIAMENT UNDER HENRY VIII.

(June 9, 1881.)

THE great question of the reign of Henry VIII is, no doubt, this: to what extent did he, in the remarkable career of destruction and reconstruction, of public and private self-will, of commingled revolutionism and conservatism, carry with him the assent and goodwill of his people? then, when we have determined to what extent the national participation in his measures is to be admitted, would be the time to ask by what means he obtained that assent and goodwill. I do not flatter myself that I am going to answer the question or to solve the problem, either to your satisfaction or to my own. Far too many considerations are concerned in both, far too many facts of doubtful interpretation, and certainly too many historical theories. All that I can undertake to do is to prepare the clearing of the way for some later and more fully equipped investigator; more fully equipped, I say, because, as you will see, there is every reason to hope that in a few years, owing to the labours of the scholars employed in calendaring the State papers, many of the facts which are now capable of contradictory interpretations will be set forth in their true light and relation to one another.

In the former lecture I confined myself to such illustrations of the subject as belong to the royal character of Henry VIII himself; and you will not have mistaken my provisional conclusion that the great factor in the whole complication is the strong, intelligent, self-willed force of the king; that that alone seems to give purpose and consistency to the eventful policy of the period; that Henry VIII is neither the puppet of parties, nor the victim of circumstances, nor the shifty politician, nor the capricious tyrant, but a man of light and leading, of power, force and foresight, a man of opportunities, stratagems, and surprises, but not the less of iron will and determined purpose ; purpose not at once realised or systematised, but widening, deepening, and strengthening as the way opens before it ; a man accordingly who might have been very great, and could under no circumstances be accounted less than great, but who would have been infinitely greater, and better, and more fortunate, if he would have lived for his people, and not for himself.

But the subject of the present lecture is the parliamentary history of the reign ; and I will keep back any general or personal remarks until that has been treated as it can be treated in a public lecture.   It helps to answer the question and problem which I have stated, for it is through the Parliament that Henry inquires of the goodwill and support of the nation, as it is through the Convocation he inquires of the goodwill and support of the clergy.   If we believe the Acts of Parliament, we shall find the nation not merely acquiescing in but petitioning for measures, some of which had no importance except as fulfilling the wishes of the king, others of which were in strong opposition to all that is known of national feeling both in and out of parliament ; if we look at the early ecclesiastical measures we find the same acquiescence in great constitutional changes, abdications of power which could not be spontaneous, and acknowledgements of the truth of statements and principles which, if true at all, were far too novel to have been accepted without discussion. We may, if we please, admit the conclusion that the nation accepted the king's action as that of a divinely constituted dictator ; a theory which involves the assumption, which is altogether groundless, that the nation saw, or thought they saw, the existing circumstances to be such as demanded a dictatorship.   I do not think they did, and I am persuaded that the theory is based on that process of reading history backward, which it has been my fate, in this Chair, to have constantly to struggle against.

There was nothing in the circumstances of Europe during the whole life of Henry VIII, such as there was under Queen Elizabeth, which might persuade people then living of the need of such an extraordinary officer. We, looking back on the time, may see how dangerous a time it was, how full of pitfalls and snares, and how, in the result, a great advantage was gained by England having had such a hand as even the blood-stained hand of Henry to guide her through : but the critical character of the time was not apparent to the time, or to the leading men of England during it ; and the later reading of it cannot be made to account for the condition of feeling and action that we are now contemplating.

The opposite view, that Henry and his advisers concocted the parliamentary acts and manifestos in such a way as to make them embody a national adhesion, sympathy, and even enthusiasm, by the simple process of falsification, is, on the other hand, too arbitrary, too shameful, for us to contemplate with equanimity: history may be, and ought to be, tested at every turn ; acts of parliament, when they are tested, may, and often do, turn out very unsound and unsatisfactory in their statements of fact, and disputable and inconsistent in their statements of law ; but, if we could believe in such a wholesale perversion of evidences as this theory involves, we must resign all theories of history at once, and relegate the inquiring world to a combination of natural laws with historical novels. The fact of the matter, I take it, we may accept : that the nation and the Church accepted, acquiesced in, and petitioned for, in parliament and in convocation, the things which the acts of parliament and convocation declare that they accepted, acquiesced in, and petitioned for ; but the question remains how we are to interpret that co-operation, and by what means the conceivable measure of co-operation was obtained. With so much preface, more than I intended, let us approach this branch of the subject, the history, modifications, and alterations of the government by parliament and convocation, as it appears to be modified and altered or maintained during the great changes of the reign.

I have already mentioned that Henry VIII held nine parliaments in his thirty-eight years, and that of those one was extended over the best part of seven years, that is the great organic parliament, which began in 1529 and ran on to the spring of 1536 : a parliament which, both on account of its length and for the importance of its acts, may deserve the title of the Long Parliament of Henry VIII. Of the other eight parliaments, two, that summoned in 1512 and that summoned in 1542, ran over three years with short sessions ; the others are all shorter, of one or two sessions. All these parliaments were held in London, either at Westminster or, in one instance and possibly an occasional sitting, at Blackfriars, and in the old places of assembly; the convocation of Canterbury met at S. Paul's, and so continued to meet, as it still does on the first day of the session. In 1523 Wolsey summoned it to Westminster ; and, after the Submission in 1532, it was frequently adjourned from S. Paul's to Westminster for the convenience of the bishops, whose hands were full of business in both chambers. The House of Lords continued to meet in the parliament chamber, and the Commons sat in the chapter-house or refectory of the Abbey until the end of the reign ; Edward VI, in his first parliament, took the Commons to S. Stephen's Chapel. The parliament chamber, or the chamber of the Holy Cross, the situation of which is unknown to me unless it was the Painted Chamber under a new name, was the place of opening the session under Henry VII and Henry VIII.

Our first question, however, is concerned with the personal composition of the assembly. The House of Lords is the chamber that undergoes the greatest modifications during the period. We take the lords spiritual first ; the parliaments of Henry VII had contained two archbishops, nineteen bishops, and twenty-eight abbots ; Henry VIII added three abbots, the abbot of Tewkesbury in 1512, the abbot of Tavistock in 1514, and the abbot of Burton in 1534 ; and after the foundation of the new bishoprics, he added the six new bishops of Oxford, Peterborough, Gloucester, Bristol, Chester, and Westminster: but before that was done the abbots had disappeared from parliament ; so at the beginning of the reign the number of spiritual peers was 49; at the maximum in 1534 it was 52, and, after the dissolution of the monasteries, it fell to 26.   The number of lay peers varied little, for there were few new creations except where an old peerage had been extinguished.   The minimum number was called in 1523, being only 28, several of the peers being that year employed in military affairs abroad ; the maximum was in 1536, in the parliament called to approve of the destruction of Anne Boleyn, and the number was 51. In the other parliaments it varied between 36 and 46.   It will be thus observed that, until the dissolution of the monasteries, the spiritual lords were always in a numerical majority, but that the tendency was decided towards an equalisation ; a tendency which is ocularly perceptible in the journals where, in the list of attendances which from 1515 onwards are marked daily, the two bodies are arranged in parallel columns. It would, however, be wrong to infer from this that there was an equality of voting bodies, for of the clerical members the attendance was throughout the reign very irregular ; and the proportion, on most critical occasions, seems to have been about 20 bishops and abbots to 30 lay lords.   It is true they both had the power of giving proxies, but the irregularity of attendance does not seem to be compensated by the proxies : the prelate who is attendant one day is absent the next, doubtless without proxy ; and some are absent for whole sessions.

Convocation during the whole reign sits at the same time with the parliament; and generally the Friday in each week, sometimes the Tuesday also, is marked by adjournment that the prelates may attend convocation, the Wednesday in some cases being likewise surrendered for the session of the Star Chamber.   No doubt the business of the Upper House of Convocation engrossed the time of most of the absent bishops and abbots, for that assembly was, before the dissolution, a very large body, nearly as large as the House of Commons ; it included, as is seen in the great divisions on the divorce, between two and three hundred abbots and priors ; and much of the business undertaken in it was of a far more critical character than that which was gone through in the Parliament.

The House of Commons was a little, only a little, so far as concerns England proper, modified by Henry VIII : Preston, Lancaster, Thetford, Orford, Berwick, and possibly one or two more towns, gained the privilege of representation ; but by bestowing representation on the towns and counties of Wales, Calais, and Chester, Henry added in 1543 thirty-two members, knights and burgesses, to the old number.

The suffrage, as we know from the case of Leicester, was in the corporate towns being altogether appropriated by the councillors and other officers who constituted the corporation. This loss of distinctly representative importance is accompanied by a certain rise in the position of the borough members. Up to this time the office of Speaker has been engrossed by the knights of the shire, and the only names of men who have taken a prominent part in the debates of the Commons have been those of county members. In this reign, however, Humfrey Wingfield, member for Yarmouth, was chosen Speaker in succession to Audley; and the only persons who are found taking a leading part in the discussions of the Long Parliament of 1529–1536 are Thomas Cromwell, member for Taunton, who before he placed himself in the king's service had succeeded in throwing out the bill of attainder against Wolsey, and Mr. Temys, the member for Westbury, who had proposed that the king should be asked to give up his plan for divorce.

Still we do not possess journals of the proceedings of the Commons before the year 1547. Those of the Lords begin in 1509, and furnish us with much of the information that we have looked for in vain in the older Rolls of Parliament. From them we learn to how large an extent the use of proxies prevailed in the House of Lords, notwithstanding the careful way in which it was limited and tested ; a usage which shows how it was so easy for the king, by dealing with one or two of the more prominent prelates, generally to secure an ecclesiastical majority in parliament, and even in convocation. In the Lower House the Speaker of the Tudor reigns is in very much the same position as the Chancellor in the Upper House; he is the manager of business on the part of the crown, and probably the nominee either of the king himself or of the chancellor. Although the forms of election, apology and protest, of address to the king and royal admission, were maintained and developed, we know both from Sir Thomas Smith and from Coke that the king appointed the Speaker: even in the House of Lords the sovereign exercised the same right when the chancellor was not a peer; in 1529, as we learn from Chapuys' dispatches, that Warham was elected, but set aside as too old. The result was that the Speaker, instead of being the defender of the liberties of the house, had often to reduce it to an order that meant obsequious reticence or sullen submission. Happily it was not every Speaker that was like Rich, whose extant addresses to the king are nauseous compliments on his majesty's gifts of nature, fortune, and grace, the beauty of his person, the felicity of his enterprises, the perfect virtue of his character; compliments which the king deprecates with a modest reference to the Giver of all good gifts, but with a conscious acquiescence as ridiculous as the mock humility of the Speaker. But where even More himself had the greatest difficulty in behaving with decent independence, so poor a creature as Rich may stand excused.

The Speakers of the reign were Sir Thomas Englefield, M.P. for Berks; Sir Thomas Sheffield, for Lincolnshire; Sir Thomas Nevill, probably for Kent; all men of dignity and simplicity. The Speaker of 1523 was Sir Thomas More; he was succeeded in the parliament of 1529 by Audley, who succeeded him also as Chancellor in 1532. Humfrey Wingfield, whom I have mentioned, succeeded Audley; Rich was Speaker in 1536, Sir Nicolas Hare in 1539, and Sir Thomas Moyle in 1542. Moyle's speeches were formed on the model of Rich's; Hare's speech in 1540, although scarcely less complimentary, was better put together; he congratulated the realm on the felicity of having such a king as Henry, who had won, a boon which had fallen to the lot of no other Christian commonwealth, the distinction that under him, without any single

calamity, the land had not only flourished but had been restored to her perfect freedom. These words had a meaning ;
no doubt the absence of external calamity was a feature of
Henry's reign, and was one cause of his influence with the
people : on the other hand, the recovery of what seemed to
the age to be spiritual liberty from Rome was a real thing in
Hare's mind, not the mere compliment that was designed in
the comparison by which Rich equalled Henry with Solomon,
Samson and Absalom ; or with the sun itself, as drying up
noxious vapours and cherishing the growth of all good seeds.
Hare, however, had a difficult part to play, for, just before he
made this speech, he had been sent to the Tower for offending
against the king's prerogative; he had regained his liberty
and his appointment as Speaker by a complete submission.
There is no evidence, so far as I know, that the Commons had
treated this imprisonment as a matter of privilege.

It would be easy to parallel from the speeches of the
chancellor the fulsome compliments of the Speakers, but I
must hasten on to the more important questions of the direct
dealings of the king or his prime ministers with the two
houses ; and as it would be impossible to go into any thorough
details on this, I must content myself with occasional illustrations. Henry was generally present at the opening and
closing of the sessions, but he did not, in his later years, scruple
to interpose from time to time in the deliberations of either
house, and influence the voting. The first sensational event of
the kind is Wolsey's adventure in the parliament of 1523,
when More was Speaker. The great chancellor had in the
usual way come down to the Commons and told them that
the king's needs amounted to a sum of £800,000, and to
raise that amount a subsidy of a fifth would be required, payable in five years. After the Cardinal's departure a discussion
arose on particulars, which is amusingly described by Cromwell
as a communing on war, peace, strife, contention, debate,
murmur, grudge, riches, poverty, penury, truth, falsehood,
justice, equity, deceit, oppression, magnanimity, force, activity,
temperance, treason, murder, felony, and how a commonwealth
might be edified and continued in our realm. But the eco-

nomical discussions were pulled up by the announcement of
another visit from the chancellor. Then arose the question,
how is he to come; is he to come as chancellor, or as cardinal
in state; let him come as cardinal, for then, if there should be
a riot, the blame can be laid on his attendants. So he comes
in state, and asks an answer about the subsidy. He is met
with sullen silence; not even Mr. Marney, who is just going
to be made a baron, and whom Wolsey applies to directly,
will utter a word. Then poor More, on his knees, has to represent to the cardinal, who had made him Speaker, that this
manner of coming, on which, you observe, he and the House
had already calculated, was not expedient or in conformity
with ancient liberties. So the cardinal had to go away in a
rage; the Commons were willing to listen to him, but would
not debate in his presence. Still the visit was not in vain;
the deliberation was resumed, and a very heavy impost was
agreed to, when Sir John Hussey, the member for Lincolnshire, who also was made a peer soon after, proposed a substantial addition on the tax from land; only eleven or twelve
members voted for it, but, notwithstanding the abstention of
the majority, it was allowed to be added; then the session was
prorogued. After the vacation it was proposed by the knights
of the shire to extend to goods the tax which Hussey had
fixed on the land; a division took place with the curious result that all the county members voted one way and all the
burgesses the other; yet, notwithstanding the enormous
majority against the tax, More in his capacity of the king's
agent, prevailed on the House to pass the bill.

Here you have a very illustrative case of the way in which
even a most unpopular measure could be forced through parliament; well might Cromwell conclude the letter in which
he describes the session, 'after seventeen weeks of discussion
we have done as our predecessors have been wont to do, that
is to say as well as we might, and have left off where we
began.' I do not think that any of the fourteenth century
parliaments would have stood this; Wolsey can have been no
believer in parliaments, for this is the only one that was held
whilst he was chancellor.

I pass on to the Long Parliament of 1529–1536, of the
early doings of which, thanks to the chronicle of Hall and
the reports of the Imperial ambassador, we know more minute
detail than we do of any preceding session.   Cromwell's defence of Wolsey in the first session, which prevented the
passing of the bill of attainder in the House of Commons, is
a fact which rests on historical testimony too good to be
rejected ; but the circumstances in which it took place are
obscure ; there can be little doubt that Henry acquiesced in,
perhaps prompted the rejection ; and it is quite certain that
to have forced it through parliament would have made a
serious addition to his already awkward complications.

There were two other pieces of debateable policy in the short
session of 1529 : the remittal of the loans of 1523–8, and the
opening of the attack on the minor privileges of the clergy.
The convocation passed the bill of remittal, and it was likewise
read three times by the Lords ; the Commons however were
sorely perplexed by it ; hitherto the royal receipt and promise to
repay had been regarded as good security ; new debts had been
incurred on the strength of it and men had left it to their
children as an adequate and safe provision.   Now it was proposed to deprive pay, receipts and bonds, of all validity ; the
Commons refused to pass the bill without conditions, and
the only condition to be got was a general pardon, out of
which the penalties for præmunire, which had been so fatal to
Wolsey, were omitted : the nominal victory was with the
Commons, the substantial fruits were with the king, who saw
his way to the great exaction from the clergy obtained in the
next session.

The other contest involves more interest and more questions.   Already Henry was beginning to feel his way against
the clergy ; the clergy themselves were discussing points
of reform, and these points were even hinted at in the
opening speech of the Chancellor More.   The points raised
seem to us, in the light of the later history, only small
points ; the expenses of probate and mortuaries, non-residence
and pluralities, and the interference of the clergy as farmers
and tanners with the trade of the laity.   But unfortunately

they were points that divided the ecclesiastical interest: the bishops were willing to enforce discipline on the lower clergy; the lower clergy were willing to reduce the profits of probate which went to the officials of the bishops; but the lower clergy would defend their trade and their benefices, and the bishops could not allow the profits of their courts to be touched. Both would have agreed in strong measures against heresy; and both agreed in regarding the discussion of these things in parliament as an attack, as indeed they were, on the Church itself. Bishop Fisher, in his apprehension, proclaimed that lack of faith ruins the country in which it prevails, as it was ruining Bohemia. This imputation roused the spirit of the faithful Commons; the Speaker Audley and thirty other members were sent to complain to the king, and the bishop had to explain that he meant only to refer to Bohemia. Archbishop Warham and six other bishops attesting this apology, the king accepted the excuse and reported it to the Commons. Fanning the flame of dissension, he then suggested that the Commons should pass the two most obnoxious bills, strike a blow at the bishops by the bill on probate, and at the parochial clergy by the bill against mortuaries. This was done. The other points, non-residence, pluralities, and trading, were decided likewise: the lords spiritual by their majority in the upper house rejected the bills; the Commons insisted on pressing them; the king suggested a conference, in Star Chamber, of eight members from each house; the lay lords on the committee voted with the Commons, and by this contrivance the bills were passed. This little trick shows that it was not by force alone that the parliament was manipulated to pass the king's bills. More as chancellor must, in this business, as in 1523, when he was Speaker, have acted as the king's agent, but the burden was already too heavy for his back.

If I were now tracing the progress of the Reformation, I might say more on the antagonism thus established between the clergy and the commons; it is enough however to observe that Henry had clearly got a parliament on which he could depend; and that every point he now gained became a fresh vantage-ground from which he could grasp at more.

In 1530 there was no parliamentary session ; the king and his agents were busily collecting opinions about the divorce ; and the constitutional struggle begins again in 1531. Not even now did the king think matters ripe for discussion of the divorce in parliament; and, in the council which was held preparatory to the session, it was determined that the queen's business should not be brought forward ; the chief thing proposed was the exaction of money from the clergy under the threat of præmunire. The Duke of Norfolk, who was to all intents and purposes the prime minister, was negotiating with the emperor, and is said to have sworn that nothing in that parliament should be done against Katharine; Anne Boleyn and her father were drawing to the Protestants, but their time was not yet come. All the important business was done in convocation. Parliament, as the imperial envoy remarked, were employed on nothing more serious than crossbows and hand-guns. But in the convocation matters were important indeed ; the king was the only person who had the skill to understand, or the will to define, the doctrine of præmunire, and it was not by præmunire alone that he could manipulate the clergy ; he tried to tamper with Warham, threatened intrigue with the German Protestants, or the restraint of mortmain, or the appointment of a council of heresy which would take that question out of the hands of convocation, and other things which, vague threats at first, became realities of oppression as soon as they were familiarised to his mind. By threats and blandishments he obtained the Recognition of his headship of the Church, and the payment of £100,000. It was not done all at once ; the clergy kicked against the pricks very hard : they offered 160,000 ducats, the king insisted on 400,000 ; the papal nuncio was pressed into the service, and even forced his way into the lower house of convocation : but the clergy, following the example of the commons of 1523, stopped their ears, and bade him negotiate in the right way through the Archbishop : as yet there was no breach with Clement VII, and in the delay of the divorce both parties were for the moment at peace. At last the clergy granted the king's terms ; but they did not like

the form of Recognition, and in the end it was passed by an
evasion for which Warham must answer.   He proposed the
form suggested by Lord Rochford, and, in putting it to the
vote, added, ' qui tacet consentire videtur.'   The clergy by an
anticipation of Jesuitic subterfuge, and by a practical Irish
bull, cried out, ' Itaque tacemus omnes.'   By this levity the
great act was consummated, which was to be the fulcrum for
the whole ecclesiastical policy of the future ; the Recognition
was understood to be passed unanimously.

But not even here were matters completely arranged ; the
king now haggled about the præmunire ; the clergy threatened
to withdraw their promise to pay unless this mysterious monster were defined as well as remitted.   It ended however as I
have said ; the clergy voted the money and the king promised
the pardon.   But the pardon must be secured by the confirmation of parliament ; and, when the bill came before the
Commons they soon saw that it did not comprise the laity, and
refused to pass it.   The king's agents urged that this opposition would damage the clergy and not benefit the Commons ;
that the king could not be compelled to pardon, and that,
without their consent, he could pass the pardon under the
great seal.   The Speaker and a committee attended the king,
and, getting no other answer, went away sorrowing and declaring that Cromwell had betrayed their proceedings to
Henry.   Then there was some bitter talking about the exactions and the remittal of the loan ; but at last the king issued
the pardon, and the Commons, knowing that something would
be taken for the boon, sulkily accepted it.

The next day the chancellor laid before them the documents
touching the divorce, and the Commons were enlightened by
speeches on the subject from the Bishops of London and Bath.
But they remained sulky ; whether it was that the king was
not prepared to go further, or that the attitude of parliament,
still faithful to the queen and indisposed to quarrel with the
Pope, dismayed him, there the matter stayed, and the Commons were ordered to carry down to their constituencies the
information laid before them.   So the session ended, and the
convocation, which had engaged on the reform of grammar

schools and the publishing of a uniform Latin grammar, in
addition to the restoration of discipline and the translation
of the Scriptures, was prorogued at the same time.   The same
measures which passed the Canterbury Convocation were likewise adopted at York; that is the clergy remitted the loans,
paid £18,840 for the pardon, and acknowledged the supremacy.   Bishop Tunstall however made a protest against the
form of Recognition, and proposed that for fear of misinter-
pretation by heretics, the words *in temporalibus post Christum*
should be inserted; but this had only the effect of offending
the king, who directed that the bishop's house at Auckland
should be searched for heretical books; and also, according to
Chapuys, omitted to summon him to the next session of
parliament.

   I go on now to that third session of the Long Parliament;
it opened on the 22nd of January 1532.   Its events are extremely important, and fortunately are illustrated fairly well
by contemporary evidence.   It was understood, says the imperial resident, to have been called for two purposes, money and
the divorce.   The king wanted 2,000,000 ducats; Rochford and
Anne Boleyn were apparently given *carte blanche* as to their
dealing with the clergy for the divorce;   Henry, however,
keeping watch, and ready to make the most of an opportunity.
The clergy were now having their eyes opened; a bold
attempt made by the Boleyns to 'suborn,' that is, I suppose,
to bribe Archbishop Warham, at last shook the old man's
faith in the stability of things.   Norfolk and Rochford, who
were now acting together, proposed that matrimonial causes
should be declared a matter of temporal jurisdiction.   Warham,
as an old lawyer, protested in a formal document against all
legislation which might be enacted against ecclesiastical or
papal power.   This protest seems to have had the effect of
deterring any further procedure on the divorce itself during
the archbishop's life, but to have provoked the king to more
trenchant action against the constitutional arrangements
which Warham and his party now saw to be assailed.

   The history of the session falls into two sections, divided by
a short recess at Easter for about a fortnight.   The first portion

was devoted to the question of supplies, the second to that of Church reform : convocation sat during the whole time. The measures proposed by the king with a view to increase the royal revenue were fair enough, and were, as it seems to me, in strict analogy with the policy of his greatest ancestor, Edward I. The first was the bill for the withdrawal of Annates from the pope ; a measure intended to secure for the king the profits and firstfruits on all appointments to bishoprics ; the act allowed the king to compound with the pope for all reasonable payments, and also provided for the confirmation and consecration of bishops without recourse to Rome. As a companion to this measure the king introduced bills of the same purport affecting the laity ; just as on the transmission of ecclesiastical property the firstfruits went to Rome, so, on the transmission of lay property in land, by the operation of the doctrine of wills and uses, the king lost his reliefs and primer seisins ; accordingly he proposed two measures, or one measure with double purpose,—a statute of wills, allowing a man to devise half his land by will, provided the other half, left to the heir, secured the king in his feudal rights ; and a statute of uses, intended to take the force out of the old practice of feoffment to uses. Both these statutes ultimately passed in a modified form, the Statute of Uses in 1536 and the Statute of Wills in 1540. By that time it would seem it was discovered that they might be accepted as boons, now they were vehemently objected to, and the opposition they excited threw the Commons for the moment on the side of the pope, and into opposition to the Annates Bill. The latter bill was presented to the Commons as a measure of their own : the king protested and pretended, sending Norfolk to assure the imperial ambassador that the Commons had called for it ; that he himself was borne on and overpowered by their zeal for reform ; the prelates had refused their consent, but the people willed to have it ; at last by the 19th of March, after two personal visitations, the king forced it through the Lords ; all the bishops and two abbots voted against it ; of the lay peers only one lord, Arundel, had the courage to support them ; thirty lay lords formed a majority for the bill and it went down to the Commons. There also the king's presence was required; in the house the noes had it. Then Henry insisted on a division; a taking of single votes which, from some other illustrations which it would be tedious now to refer to, we infer to have been as yet an exceptional method of ascertaining the sense of the house. Partly by promising that there should be no more acts against the pope, partly by the terror of his majestic eyes, he obtained a majority; men could not comfortably vote in the presence of the definer of all præmunires. This much was accomplished before the Easter adjournment; the Statutes of Wills and Uses passed the Lords but were rejected by the Commons, and the king did not press them at the time.

The question of the Annates had opened his eyes to his power of obtaining further concessions. In the beginning of March, by the contrivance of Rochford, the parliament was discussing the possibility of transferring to the king all the power and authority of the archbishops and bishops: the divorce question was simmering in both houses; and Warham had plucked up spirit to speak up for the queen. This was not to be endured. Accordingly the old antagonism of the Commons to the spiritual courts was utilised, and an address drawn up by the king's secretaries was put in their hands to be delivered to the king as the prayer of the Commons. Audley, as Speaker, and a number of his own servile party presented it; it contained a bitter attack on the canon law and ecclesiastical jurisdictions generally, and, in twelve clauses, some of greater and some of less importance, singled out points for reform. The king received it on the 18th of March, and, as soon as Easter was over, it was laid before convocation for an answer. Both Houses of convocation discussed it in detail; the Upper House prepared an answer on the points that touched the bishops; the Lower on those touching the parochial clergy: both agreed in demanding a specific statement instead of general charges. The answer was sent to the king about the 27th of April; and the king was of course prepared to find it unsatisfactory.

On the 30th his Majesty sent for the speaker and showed him the answer, referring it, as a very slender production, to the consideration of that 'grete sorte of wise men to be found in the House of Commons.' There were indeed both wise men and foolish in that assembly; and both had the divorce business in their minds. They were again busy on the supplies: Henry wanted money to fortify the border and the coast: they offered a tenth and fifteenth, £28,000; that was not enough; the Statutes of Wills and Uses were again broached and rejected. Independent members went further, Mr. Thomas Temys, M.P. for Westbury, proposed, and found a seconder, that the king should be asked to take back his wife; 'if he would, there would be no danger from the emperor; if he would not, fortification would be useless.' The king could not stand that: he sent for Audley, and through him explained to the Commons what a horrible conscience a man had who married his brother's wife. The question of the divorce was not before them: if they would mind their own business he would help them against the clergy; if not, not.

Whilst this was going on in Parliament convocation was asked for a grant: the clergy discussed the subject, and determined to send to the king a supplication for help. They were in a strait; the Commons were insisting on severer measures against heresy, and still were impugning the laws and courts, by which only heresy could be extirpated. Rochford and Cromwell were intriguing with the heretics; Henry himself, pretending to stand aloof, was watching every point of vantage. But they got little comfort: in answer to their supplication, the king sent down to them in a bill the three points of submission, the abdication of the right to legislate in convocation, the consent to the reform of ecclesiastical law, and the sufferance of existing canons only under the king's approval. The day after this bill was sent to the clergy, Henry, still intent on exciting the Commons against them, summoned Audley and his friends, and put before him the oath taken by the prelates to the pope on appointment; an oath which he declared incompatible with their allegiance to himself. That was something for the Commons to consider: the Lords were consulted on the points which had been laid before convocation. The imperial ambassador was on the watch for results: the king was proposing, he heard, to abolish synods and synodal legislation, and to take into his own hands all coercive jurisdiction on heresy; the bishops might have the souls of the sinners, he would have their bodies; it was a strange thing; priests would be of less account than shoemakers, who at least might regulate their own trade. The Venetian ambassador foresaw a new præmunire, and fixed the amount of money that the king would take, 400,000 crowns from the clergy, a vote of a fifteenth, and a year's income as succession duty. Evidently a storm was rising. The royal propositions were, however, on the 15th of May, accepted by convocation, after brisk discussion and several significant divisions. In the House of Lords the chancellor and the bishops opposed them, and prevented them from becoming law as yet. The great Lion was nearer a defeat than he had ever been before: and, when More resigned the great seal, which he did on the day that the Submission was presented, the king became very sulky. On the day of prorogation he would not show himself: as for the grant of money, the fifteenth, he did not care about it; he would neither accept nor refuse, and the clergy would not now grant more; as a matter of fact no subsidy was granted. But the clergy were brought to their knees, and the king lost his wisest and most faithful adviser. The session ended on the 14th of May; convocation was prorogued on the 15th, and on the 16th More resigned. His successor was the Speaker Audley; a change indeed.

After losing More, Henry seems to have acted more and more on the counsels of the Boleyns; and circumstances rapidly accelerated the course of events. Gardiner, who was probably his near kinsman and who certainly had helped him in every way until now, left the court, and was in disgrace for refusing to preach in favour of the divorce. Warham's death, in the following August, removed the last of the old party whose advice had any chance of being listened to. A visit to Francis I in the next month seems to have determined the king to cut the knot by peremptory action. Immediately on his return he is said to have married Anne Boleyn. As each old

friend dropped off Cromwell rose a step, and the royal determination increased. Cranmer was designated for the primacy;
Audley from being Lord Keeper was raised to the Chancellorship; the parliament, which had been prorogued to November,
was adjourned to January, and in January both Houses and
convocation met.

For the session of 1533 we have no journals, and the
reports of the Venetian ambassador do not supply the gap
caused by the imperfect continuation of the Austrian dispatches. Two subjects, however, alone occupied both the
secular and the ecclesiastical assemblies: the divorce and the
abolition of appeals to Rome. In parliament the divorce business proceeded slowly; the king visited it more than once
with a view to expediting that, and the provision of an army
against the Scots; but the month of February passed over
without any real business being done. At last Henry resumed the plan by which he had succeeded in 1532, putting
the initiation of his own measures in the mouth of a private
member of the Commons; on the 15th of March a London
member was found to propose that the judges of the divorce
should be appointed in England. Immediately after this
Cranmer was consecrated, and he undertook to deal with
convocation. In convocation the two questions on which
the divorce turned were debated in the manner of University
disputations; the theologians disputed as to the dispensability
of a marriage with a brother's widow, the canonists on the
facts of Arthur's marriage with Katharine: there were formal
divisions, but the conclusion was foregone, the bishop of
Rochester was the only steady opponent. In the same way
the York convocation was dealt with by Archbishop Lee.

Notwithstanding the acquiescence of convocation, the Commons as late as April 10 were still reluctant. We are told
that one of the members for London offered to raise £200,000
if the king would refer the question of the divorce to a general
council. But in vain. The servility of Cranmer and Lee
had provided a short and easy method; on the 23rd of May,
at Dunstable, Cranmer, on the strength of the opinions thus
obtained, pronounced in favour of the divorce and Boleyn

marriage; and on the 1st of June Anne Boleyn was crowned; parliament having adjourned from April 12 to June 7.

The other great act of the year was the statute of Appeals, of the discussion of which we have few data. On the 14th of March, according to Chapuys, it was proposed in parliament to make a statute declaring that the pope has no authority in this kingdom; the king was set upon it and was arranging all his policy to that end. On the 30th it is mentioned in the Venetian dispatches as being then pushed in convocation. The next day the imperial envoy announces that the convocation has passed the Divorce Bill, but the House of Commons has refused to pass the Statute of Appeals, mainly on the ground that, if the pope were offended, he might injure the wool trade. But before the 10th of April he has to record that the opposition has given way before the king's threat to enforce the penalties of præmunire against the laity. A week later he reports that he has remonstrated with Henry and put him in a rage. Yet raging, still he was not without hope; he had sent to tell the pope that if, even now, he would send a dispensation for the second marriage, he would undo all that, in his wish to please his people, he had done against Rome. It is no doubt an exaggeration of Chapuys when he says that the nation would have welcomed the emperor as a deliverer, but there can be no reason to question his statements as to the sincerity of the opposition. The work of the year ended there; no business session was again attempted; the question of supplies, which had been brought forward in February, dropped and no grant was made.

The next session, that of January 1534, was a heavy one: we have the Lords' Journals, but very scanty details about convocation, which is unfortunate as the most important business was ecclesiastical. We know, however, from the Lords' Journals, that the clerical assembly sat on regular days, every Friday and sometimes on Tuesdays, the lords adjourning on those days for the convenience of the prelates, and on the Wednesdays for the session of Star Chamber. The attendance of prelates in the House of Lords was very scanty, and they were generally outnumbered two to one by the lay lords:

there were discussions and differences of opinion between the
Lords and Commons; a Bill on the consecration of bishops
sent up from the Commons was rejected by the Lords, and a
new Bill drawn by the Lords was passed by the Commons.
The Submission Bill or second Statute of Appeals was presented by the Commons in a body on the 27th of March, and
passed on the 30th. In convocation, on the 31st, the question
that the pope has no more power than any other bishop was
determined; this being probably regarded as their formal
judgment on more than one of the statutes which had
passed the Commons. We look in vain for any more determined or resolute action on either side. And again the
session passes without a money grant. A second session was
held in November mainly for this purpose; and a second
meeting of convocation, in which the king was petitioned to
expedite the authoritative translation of the Bible. I enumerated I think in the last lecture the important acts of these
sessions.

There was no session in 1535. The Long Parliament
came to an end in 1536. Of its last session we have no
definite details, simply the Acts which it passed: the Journals
of Convocation deal only with the question of the subsidy.
Henry had, we may presume, quelled all opposition in Parliament; and, if contemporary annotators had been minded
to preserve particulars, they were lost in the grand and
tragic interest of public events. The dissolution of the
monasteries, the death of Queen Katharine, the awful tragedy
that closed the career of the Boleyns, the pilgrimage of grace,
and mutterings of rebellion in north and south, fill the pages
of the annalists.

For the second Parliament of 1536, that newly elected
after the fall of Anne Boleyn, we have much material: it
sat for six weeks, and has left full journals, as has convocation also. There is no reaction traceable in either.
If the Seymours inherited the influence of the Boleyns,
they were even more zealous for change and plunder
than their predecessors: but the real hero of the hour is
Cromwell, doing his master's work with zeal. Cromwell, as

the king's vicegerent, claims for himself or his deputy the presidency of Convocation, and by his presence there invests the proceedings of that body with an importance that Cranmer could not have given. All that he proposes in the way of change is passed without show of division; and, even in the direction of doctrinal reform, he carries things as far as the king allowed. The legislation in parliament likewise is mainly ecclesiastical; and the journals record nothing but assents.

I must pass on very rapidly now. The session of 1539, in which the dissolution of the greater monasteries was accomplished and the Bill of Six Articles passed, was likewise held under the predominating power of Cromwell, who had, however, learned to sink his protestant tendencies before his master's stern orthodoxy. Convocation again worked with the Parliament, and there are traces also that the clergy attended under the præmunientes clause; but the new prelates of Henry's nomination now outnumbered the old, and in both assemblies the abbots and priors knew that they appeared for the last time.

Yet abject as was the condition of a parliament which could pass the Proclamation Act, there were still two parties at work in it. The secret history of the Six Articles, when it is known, will show that Cromwell's influence was already shaken. The king proposes to abolish the diversities of religion; Cromwell, the two archbishops, and six bishops, are named as a committee on the 3rd of May. On the 16th the Duke of Norfolk announces that the committee cannot agree, and proposes that the Six Articles be discussed in parliament. After some delay two committees are, on the 23rd, appointed to draw up alternative schemes for the king's approval on the following Sunday; the king approves apparently that which is subsequently chosen. It goes down in Cromwell's hand to the Convocation and is accepted there on June 2. Between June 7 and June 16 it passes the Lords, and the Commons also adopt it before the 28th, on which day the session ends. Of the other important acts of the session that which empowered the king to create new sees was passed through the whole of its stages in both houses in one day: the Proclamation Act and another for the rehabilitation of the religious, were, on the other hand, rejected by the Commons, redrawn and passed after several days' discussion.

I must now pass very briefly over the incident of the remaining parliaments. In that of 1540 the king's matrimonial relations with Anne of Cleves were, by petition of parliament, referred to and discussed in the convocations: the abbots finally disappeared from parliament; the House of Lords agreed that Mondays, Wednesdays, and Fridays should be devoted, by the Royal Commissioners appointed for the purpose, to the preparation of measures of religious reform. Bishop Tunstall is bold enough to draw up a protest against the subsidy, but this is the only trace of opposition. Cromwell's fall was sudden and without sympathy; the Bill of Attainder for treason passed the House of Lords without an opposing vote; the Commons added attaint for heresy as well as for treason; not a voice seems to have been raised for him. Nay, in the House of Lords not a single measure of the king's was opposed at all, and it is left on record in the most unsentimental of all registers, the Journals of the Lords, that not a single division occurred during the whole session. In 1542, in the same way, no protest is made against the sacrifice of Catherine Howard. But the king is not satisfied with silent acquiescence; he does not hesitate to urge both houses to work harder at that and other public business; again we find Tunstall protesting alone against some minor measure: the most remarkable event, from our point of view, is the withdrawal from the House of Lords, at the request of convocation, of a bill allowing laymen to act as ecclesiastical judges; a measure which, though withdrawn now, became law in 1545. The convocation itself was very busy in the matter of the translation of the Bible and Scriptural formulæ of prayer and belief. The same work occupied the session of 1543, in which we find Lord Mountjoy voting by himself against the amplification of the Proclamation Act; and four bishops opposing the Bill for Collectors and Receivers. Clearly the independent spirit has nearly evaporated. The

ecclesiastical bills pass without a protest, but the Lords are
not reduced so low as they were in 1540.. The remaining
sessions, those of 1544, 1545, and 1546, furnish nothing that
illustrates our subject : the journals record no opposition or
protest ; the king has his own way in everything.

Time would fail me if I were to attempt to go into the
minor parliamentary cases of privilege, or to clothe or colour
the dry facts that I have been retailing to you; or I might
describe how, when the Duke of Suffolk opened parliament, all
the members, every time the king's name occurred, bowed
until their heads all but touched the ground; or how Henry
himself closed the session of 1545 with a sermon on charity;
how in 1515 parliament and convocation were so comfortably at one that Taylor, the clerk of the parliament,
was prolocutor of the Lower House of Canterbury : or how
ecstatically Hare and Moyle praised the beauty of their royal
master ; or how, when he brought the news of the king's
death, the rough old Wriothesley could not speak for tears :
or how weary the clerk of the parliament was of Audley's
speeches, which took such a long time to deliver, and so much
more to write out and read.

All our authorities, even the dry journals themselves, furnish matters of amusement to inquiring minds. But time
has failed me already, and I must wind up with a few words
of sentiment.

I think, that after what I have said, you will allow me
to say that I have grounds for believing that Henry VIII
was the master, and in no sense the minister, of his
people : that, where he carried their good will with him,
it was by forcing not by anticipating or even educating it.
I am obliged altogether to reject the notion that he was the
interpreter in any sense of the wishes of his people : the
utmost that he did in this direction was to manipulate and
utilise their prejudices to his own purposes. I allow fully the
truth of the theory that one great principle of his policy was
to obtain for his measures, for all his measures, the acquiescence of his people, and thus to invest them with a safe,
irrefragable authority; but I must add that he knew how to

turn opposition into acquiescence, or to take acquiescence for granted. Further, I am convinced, as I said in the last lecture, that he was his own chief, I might say sole, counsellor, not one of his other advisers, after the fall of Wolsey, succeeding in becoming anything more than the instrument of a grand, imperious, ever encroaching will.

And now let me confess that I do not think so badly of Henry VIII as the received views of either his advocates or his enemies would suggest. The unhappy, most unhappy history of his wives, has brought upon him an amount of moral hatred which is excessive. Nine kings out of any ten whom you may pick out of the list would have saved their character for humanity by simple self-indulgence. No absolutely profligate king could have got into the miserable abyss in which we find Henry VIII struggling during the latter half of his reign. I do not believe that he was abnormally profligate : in this region of morality he was not better perhaps than Charles V, but he was much better than Francis I, and Philip II, and Henry IV. But he was cruelly, royally vindictive ; there was in him an ever-increasing, ever-encroaching self-will, ever grasping and grasping more and more of power : a self-will guided by a high intellect, and that sort of sincerity which arises from a thorough belief in himself. I am not prepared to deny that deep, cunning, unscrupulous men, like Cromwell, traded on their knowledge of his character ; but not one of those who tried to work their own ends through Henry escaped the doom to which false friends and open foes alike found their way.

Well, you say, you would not wish to see him worse cursed. I do not condemn him. God forbid, in whose hand are the hearts of kings. I do not believe him to have been a monster of lust and blood, as so many of the Roman Catholic writers regard him. I cannot accept at all the picture which Mr. Froude has drawn. I think that even Lord Herbert's estimate of him is deficient in the perception of his surpassing self-wilfulness. I do not attempt to pourtray him after my own idea ; but I seem to see in him a grand gross figure, very far removed from ordinary human sympathies, self-engrossed, self-confident, self-willed ; unscrupulous in act, violent and crafty, but justifying to himself, by his belief in himself, both unscrupulousness, violence, and craft.   A man who regarded himself as the highest justice, and who looked on mercy as a mere human weakness.   And with all this, as needs must have been, a very unhappy man, wretched in his family, wretched in his friends, wretched in his servants, most wretched in his loneliness : that awful loneliness in which a king lives, and which the worst as well as the best of despots realises.   Have I drawn the outline of a monster? Well, perhaps ; but not the popular notion of this particular portent.   A strong, high-spirited, ruthless, disappointed, solitary creature ; a thing to hate, or to pity, or to smile at, or to shudder at, or to wonder at, but not to judge.

XIII.

THE HISTORY OF THE CANON LAW IN ENGLAND.

(April 19, 1882.)

IT requires no small amount of moral courage to approach a subject of legal history without being either a lawyer or a philosopher. A lawyer, no doubt, would make short work of it, and pronounce a definitive judgment, without misgiving, on any subject, historical or other, human or divine, on which he had evidence before him ; and a philosopher would systematise to his own satisfaction any accumulation of details that could possibly be referred to the categories of cause and effect. The student of history has not, ex officio, any such privilege of infallibility ; the highest point to which he can rise is the entire conviction of his own ignorance and incapacity before the vast material of his investigation ; the highest approach to infallibility is the willingness to learn and correct his own mistakes. If he wishes to learn something of a subject his best policy is to write a book upon it, or to deliver two public statutory lectures. Here then you have my motive ; wanting to know something of the history of Canonical Jurisprudence, I undertake to lecture upon it. I shall be wiser, that is, more convinced of my own ignorance, before I have done.

If I were a philosopher I should begin thus : The legal history of a nation or institution must be the history of the successive stages by which it develops or adopts laws, according to the stages of its social, or moral, or political, or religious development ; or thus: As a nation develops in civilisation, or foreign policy, or in specialised ambitions, or in consciousness of nationality, or in peculiar constitutional

identity, it has to develop new branches or systems of law,
or to borrow them ready-made from nations whose polity is
in advance of its own, who have made themselves representative nations in the particular branch of sociology in
which it desires to regulate itself. Hence, in England, on
the original superstructure of ancient popular law is superinduced, in the age of the Conquest, the jus honorarium of
the royal courts; and, when the royal courts have become
the courts of common law, on their rigour is superinduced
the moderating influence of Equity and Appeal: on the
conversion of the nation to Christianity a religious discipline
is a necessity, and on that religious discipline, as the framework of the Church is built up, there is based a canonical
jurisprudence; if the nation is in close communication with
foreign churches or a great Catholic religion, it naturally
adopts, from them or it, its religious legislation; if not in
such close intercourse, it develops a system of its own, and,
when the intercourse becomes closer, modifies its own until it
is more or less in harmony with that of the nations round it,
always retaining more or less of its own home growth. Or
again, still as the philosopher, I might say: Religion, Law
and Morality cover the area of human action with rules and
sanctions, and, with different origins, motives, and machinery,
regulate regions of common energy, a number of acts that fall
within reach of each or all. The fact that they spring from
different sources necessitates the formation of distinct systems;
the fact that they cover the same ground accounts for the
possibility of conflicting operation; the fact that, whilst
they overlap one another, their proper areas nowhere coincide,
necessitates some sort of definition and limitation of the
scope and system of each, which definition and limitation
must be supplied either by a concordat between them or by
the subordination of one to the other. And once more:
within the region of religious activity itself there are provinces which demand varying degrees of distinctness in
definition and graduation of discipline; there are matters of
doctrine, of discipline proper, of property and of judicature;
there are legislation, jurisdiction, administration; there are

functions for the theologian, the casuist, the canonist, and the civilian; questions of doctrine for the theologian, of morals for the casuist, of discipline for the canonist, of procedure for the civil lawyer.

Well, philosophical or not, these considerations seem to give us a clue to the method of our investigation, and suggest a division into two heads: first, the tracing of the growth of the ecclesiastical law, including both the material and the scientific study; and secondly, the history of its working in competition with and in general relations to the other systems of law. In such a cursory attempt to examine these heads as is possible in such a lecture as this, it is necessary to limit the field of survey as much as possible. I shall therefore restrict myself chiefly to the history of ecclesiastical jurisprudence in England, taking liberty, where it is necessary, to go beyond, but not attempting any general treatment. I have, you will observe, coupled together four topics under two heads; I propose to take the two heads separately, but to discuss the two topics that fall under each conjointly.

The first head is the growth of ecclesiastical law, and its two branches are the materials and the study. The materials arrange themselves thus: the New Testament contains not only all doctrine necessary to salvation, but all necessary moral teaching, and as much social teaching as was needed for the age in which it was propounded, and for the society which in the first instance was embodied under apostolic government. But in the very nature of things, and you must here recollect that I am trying to look at the subject rather as a philosopher than as a divine, Christianity, as a growing religion, was certain to require an expansion, in expanding circumstances, of the principles which were clearly enough stated in the Gospel, but the application of which had to be regulated by some other process than the will of the individual. The moral teaching had to be expanded authoritatively, the dogmatic teaching had to be fenced by definitions, the administrative machinery had to be framed with some attempt at uniformity, so that, whilst the Christian

society remained a simple voluntary society with no power
of enforcing its own precepts by material sanctions, it should
have a common jurisprudence recognised by the conscience
of its members and by their general consent. Hence from
the days of the apostles there were councils, and canons, and
constitutions, and books of discipline; at first the canons,
councils, and books of discipline covered all the ground of
which I have spoken—doctrine, discipline, and administration,
although some councils may be more famous for their decisions on one point than on another. Not perhaps to speak
of the Apostolic Constitutions, take the council of Nicea for
an example, and remember that we owe to it not only a
formulated creed, but directions about consecration of bishops
and ordination of priests, and likewise rules for the treatment
of the lapsed and apostates, and the prohibition of usury.
The legislation of Constantine added a new element which
worked itself into all these three; giving a coercive and
material force to rules which had been hitherto matters of
conscience and consensus; the church was empowered to
enforce her doctrinal decisions, her rules of discipline, and
her frame of administration; and that so completely that
from this date the ecclesiastical administration in Christian
countries under the empire became so wedded to the secular
administration as to be at times almost indistinguishable
from it except on close investigation. From this date then
our materials begin to sort themselves: the doctrinal definitions are embodied in the Creeds, and need not be pursued
further than the fourth, or, at the outside, the sixth general
council: but the canons of discipline and administration are
worked into great detail for a long period and in many
countries. And here I must take a new point: the coercive
authority given to the churches in matters of morals becomes
henceforth a branch of jurisdiction, but there still remain
branches of moral discipline which depend on voluntary
obedience, in which a powerful offender, or a man who does
not choose to confess, may defy law and order. For the
latter were invented what may be called manuals of casuistry,
the Penitentials; for the jurisdiction proper there remained

the can ns of the councils, now possessing cogent authority,
and the laws of the empire, now framed on a strict conformity
between church and state.

Here then we reach the historical materials on which is
based the later canon law; and almost at the same time the
date at which the conversion of England began. In the
middle of the sixth century Dionysius Exiguus, a Roman
abbot, compiled the collection of canons which was the germ
and model of all later collections. Nearly at the same time,
both in the Eastern Church under John the Faster, and in
the extreme West under the Irish and other Celtic missionaries, began the compilation of Penitentials; and in the
same century the emperor Justinian completed the great body
of the civil law. Thus you get the three conjoint systems
of jurisprudence: not distinct in fact from each other; over-
lapping everywhere, and even containing much common
matter, but distinct in basis. Take the Penitential first:
that was in reality a list of sins and their penances; sins so
ticketed and valued as to please even the most abstract
philosopher; permutated and combined to mathematical pre-
cision. This sort of literature, belonging especially to ages
and nations brought into close contact with heathen abomina-
tions, was very important in the last converted countries
of East and West; Archbishop Theodore of Canterbury, the
Venerable Bede, Egbert of York, and among the Celts Colum-
banus, Cummian, Vinniaus, and Adamnan, founded the
penitential system here: from them the Frank and German
churches adopted their rules, and by and by, when Anglo-
Saxon literature was borrowing from the Continent, our
scholars translated back with interest the developed systems
which their predecessors had sent abroad. These rules of
penance continue to be elaborated in England to the time
of the Conquest; and bear some analogy to the early laws
of the Anglo-Saxon kings, which consist so largely of definitions of crimes and penalties. It is to be remembered,
however, that the Penitentials were private compilations, the
authority of which depended on the estimation or dignity
of their authors, and not on any legislative sanction; but,

notwithstanding that, there is sufficient harmony amongst
them to show that they incorporate the rules on which the
episcopal jurisdiction pure and simple generally proceeded;
they were a sort of customary church law for their own
province.   But over and above these there were the canons,
or authorised church law; and of these also there was a
series of important collections.   I am unable to say how far
the collection of Dionysius Exiguus was received in England
and Ireland at first: but from the beginning of the Church
History of United England, a series of new canons began
to be added to the early collections: Theodore himself added
the decisions of Roman and Byzantine councils to the re-
solutions of his own national synods: a great and important
succession of Anglo-Saxon councils issued canons which were
received with great respect in all the Western churches, as
we know from S. Boniface's letters and the remains of the
canons themselves.   From Ireland likewise proceeded a great
collection of canons—the famous Collatio Hibernica, which,
beginning with the edicts of S. Patrick, went on to embody
the results of ecclesiastical legislation in West and East, and,
by the time of Dunstan, whose copy of it we possess in the
Bodleian, had added by successive accretions all that was
thought worth preserving even in the capitularies of the
Frank kings.   The Anglo-Saxon Church possessed no such
comprehensive collection of its own ; but abroad the codification of church law proceeded rapidly.   I have seen in
the National Library at Paris some invaluable MS. collections
earlier than the date of the forged decretals ; and the forged
decretals themselves were probably not the work of one man
or one generation.   Not however to tread again this well-
trodden path, pass on to the collectors of genuine or less
suspected canons : of whom the most important is Burchard
of Worms.   He, at the beginning of the eleventh century,
got together and arranged systematically all the materials
he could find : borrowing authoritative determinations from
the penitentials, the canons of councils, articles of the civil
law as known to him by the Theodosian code, and the
capitularies of the emperors.   A century later, bishop Ivo of

Chartres produced the Pannormia, a similar collection, improved on that of Burchard by the use of the Digest and Code of Justinian. Ivo was a contemporary of Henry I of England, and his date carries us past the Norman Conquest and the Hildebrandine period.

We must revert to the third element of church law, the religious laws of the kings. Of these the history in England is straightforward enough. The Anglo-Saxon sovereigns, acting in the closest union with their bishops, made ecclesiastical laws which clothed the spiritual enactments with coercive authority, and sometimes seemed to ignore the lines which separate the two legislatures; such sacred laws of Alfred, Canute, and Ethelred only affect our subject so far as they operated on the common law of the country in such matters as tithes, observance of holy days, and the like; they do not become by themselves a part of the later church law. On the Continent there is this difference:—the Theodosian code had to a great extent won its way over Western Europe; it enters into the codes of the barbarians, into the law of the Pays du droit écrit, and into the canon law of France; the capitularies of Charles the Great and his successors, even to a greater extent than the Anglo-Saxon laws, combine ecclesiastical with secular dooms; and such of them as are accepted find their way into the Church law. But, over and above this infiltration, comes the necessary requirement of developing jurisprudence. The New Testament, the canons of the General Councils, the Penitentials, the Decretals, did not invent new systems of procedure. Where the Roman courts existed they became the model of the Church courts, and where they did not the ecclesiastical procedure followed the lines of the national and customary tribunals. Hence, wherever the Theodosian code spread, it carried the Roman procedure as a part of church administration; where, as in England, only faint scintillæ of the civil law were to be found, the Church courts must have proceeded on much the same rules as the popular courts. And this is a matter to be seriously noted as we reach the critical point of the Norman Conquest. It is true we know very little about ecclesiastical procedure before this date, and what we do know is not very clear ; we may however affirm pretty confidently that there was, over and above the strictly private discipline of the Confessional, a system of church judicature with properly designated judges, and a recognised though not well-defined area of subject-matter in persons and things. To put it very briefly, sacred persons and sacred things, men in orders, monks and nuns, sacred places, churches and churchyards, sacred property, lands, books and the furniture of churches, were under the special protection, and, as protection implied jurisdiction, under the jurisdiction of the bishops, who likewise had authority in matrimonial and like causes. There was a territorial episcopate, and the bishops exercised their judicial powers with the help of archdeacons and deans. But, it would appear, these judicial matters were transacted in the ordinary gemots of the hundred and the shire. Just as the court baron, court leet, and court customary of a manor are held together, so the court spiritual and the hundred or county court were held together ; and the proceedings were probably in strict analogy. Just as suretyship was the rule in the hundred court, it was in the bishop's court ; so also compurgation and ordeal, the law of witness, and the claim of the mundborh over the person of the litigant. I am not prepared to say that through intercourse with the French Church some portions of the Roman procedure may not already have crept in, but, so far as I can see, I am inclined to the belief that, whilst there was a customary canonical law and a substantially canonical judicature, the character of the procedure was customary and primitive, and differed in nothing materially from the lay procedure. The bishop declared the ecclesiastical law as the ealdorman did the secular, the assessors determined the point on which evidence or oaths were to be taken, and the suitors were technically the judges Of course all this is stated subject to correction : but this I suppose to be the case at the Conquest, and more or less the case until the close of the reign of Henry I, for the changes introduced by the Conqueror were not instantaneous in their effects.

And we come now to the consideration of the effects of the Conquest on this branch of our constitutional system. Here we have to remember two things : first, that the Norman Conquest coincided in time with the Hildebrandine revival ; and secondly, that the Conqueror carried through his most important measures of change by the work of Norman ecclesiastics, many of them lawyers rather than theologians ; of whom Lanfranc, the representative of a family of Lombard lawyers, was the chief. These two points enable us at once to estimate the importance of the act by which William separated the work of the bishops' courts from the work of the sheriffs' courts, and promised the assistance of the royal or secular justice in carrying into effect the sentences of the episcopal laws. In the first place he had substituted for the native bishops, used to national law and customary procedure, foreign bishops learned in the Hildebrandine jurisprudence and the Roman procedure : and in the second he had liberated the Church judicature from its association with the popular judicature. But, you will observe, much still remained to be done ; for not yet had either Ivo or Gratian collected the Decretum, nor had Irnerius and the Bolognese lawyers begun to lecture on the Pandects ; there was not as yet a recognised canon law or a complete civil law procedure.

One immediate result more I will notice, the breaking up of the dioceses into archdeaconries ; for up to this time the bishops had done most of their own work. Dunstan had sat at the south door of Canterbury Cathedral and had administered supreme justice ; and one archdeacon, generally in deacon's orders, had been a sufficient eye for the bishop where he could not be personally present. The Norman bishops wanted more than one eye, and, almost immediately after the Conqueror's legislative separation of the courts, we find that the archidiaconal service is formed on the plan of that of the sheriffs ; the larger dioceses, such as Lincoln and London, being broken up into many archdeaconries ; and the smaller ones, such as Norwich, following the example. There was a vast increase in ecclesiastical litigation, great profits and

fees to be made out of it; a craving for canonical jurisprudence and reformed judicature analogous to the development
of constitutional machinery; and with it the accompanying
evils of ill-trained judges and an ill-understood system of
law. This continued to be the case throughout the twelfth
century, and very conspicuously so in the earlier part of it.
The archdeacons were worldly, mercenary, and unjust; the
law was uncertain and unauthoritative; the procedure was
hurried and irregular. The evils were not confined to England,
although they were here intensified by the fact of the novelty
of the system.

On this condition of things a new light arose in the
middle of the century; the resuscitation of the jurisprudence
of Justinian and the codification of the canons by Gratian.
The one supplied the necessary procedure, the other the necessary law. I place them together, because their operation
reaches England nearly at the same time; more minutely,
the civil law revival precedes the canon law revival by about
forty years. I must say also that, when I speak of the civil
law as remodelling procedure, I do not mean that it introduced any sudden changes, but that it supplied principles and
precedents for the due development of the older Roman
procedure, which had become as much a matter of custom
as that of the popular jurisprudence was. The real founder
of the medieval canon law jurisprudence in England was
Theobald, Archbishop of Canterbury, who was consecrated in
1139 and ruled the Church until 1161; he is best known
popularly as the rival of Henry of Blois, Bishop of Winchester, and as the patron of Thomas Becket; but his real
importance is irrespective of personal matters. He saw the
mischief which the maladministration of the archdeacons was
doing, and instituted a nearer official of greater authority
and more direct responsibility. John of Salisbury, the philosopher and historian, was, as secretary to Archbishop Theobald,
the ancestor of the diocesan chancellors, officials and vicar-
generals, who begin to execute with more regularity and
intelligence the law of the Church. Henry of Blois when
legate had, as we are told, greatly encouraged the practice of

appeals ; and an immense proportion of John of Salisbury's letters, written in the name of Theobald, are concerned with questions of appeal, on the rights of advowsons, and other branches of clerical discipline. But that was not all. In the year 1149 Theobald brought from Lombardy and settled at Oxford as a teacher Master Vacarius, who had given himself to the study of the Code and Digest, and drawn up handbooks of procedure sufficient to settle all the quarrels of the law schools. Stephen, the reigning king, set himself stedfastly against this new teaching and expelled Vacarius; he had on his side the unintelligent dislike of foreign manners, the prudent conservatism of the elder prelates, and the personal jealousies of his brother Henry, whose opponent in political matters Theobald was. Accordingly the civil law was for the time banished. In the year 1151 Gratian completed the Decretum, the concordance of the canon laws ; and they shortly found their way to England, where however they were scarcely more warmly received than the civil laws had been, but were not directly banished. It is curious that both Prynne and Selden, not to mention Coke, have confounded the teaching of Vacarius with the attempt to introduce canon law. It is certain that what Vacarius taught was the Corpus Juris of Justinian ; but the two systems are thus closely joined together both in time and in essential character. And from this time dates in England that extremely close connexion between the two systems which is recognised in the ' Utriusque juris doctoratus ' and in the fact that every great canonist throughout the middle ages in England was also a great civilian.

The first result perhaps of these novelties, so far as English law is concerned, was the improvement in legal education. Although Bologna and Pavia could not be suffered to come to England, England might go to Bologna ; and a stream of young archdeacons, at the age at which in England a boy is articled to an attorney, poured forth to the Italian law schools. Many and varied were their experiences ; but invariably they get into debt and write home for money ; some of them fall in love and become the quasi-husbands of Italian ladies ; some get a bad character for learning the Italian art of poisoning ; some are killed in frays with the natives ; some remain abroad and become professors ; all more or less illustrate the scholastic question which John of Salisbury propounds, Is it possible for an archdeacon to be saved ? There are some few exceptions, but they seem to be generally of the men who stuck to theology and went for their education no further than Paris. The scrapes of the archdeacons however I have spoken of before ; they are a really amusing feature of the epistolary correspondence of the time. I pass on to something more important.

Great as the advantages might be of an improved code of laws and system of procedure, neither the canon law nor the civil law was accepted here ; they were rejected not only by the stubborn obscurantism of Stephen, but by the bright and sagacious intellect of Henry II. Now, considering the close political connexion between Theobald and the Plantagenet party, it is not at all impossible that Henry II may have been among the pupils of Vacarius : certainly he was more of a lawyer than mere empirical education could make him, and, as certainly, he was awake to the difficulties to which too ready acceptance of the reformed jurisprudence would expose him. How great a lawyer he was I need not tell you ; how directly his difficulties were owing to the new doctrines of the canon lawyers we know from the history of Becket. I will only mention two points that illustrate his permanent relation to the subject : first, his Assize of Darrein Presentment re-moved all questions of advowsons and presentations from the ecclesiastical courts where they were the source of constant appeals to Rome ; and secondly, by the Constitutions of Clarendon he did his best to limit the powers of the ecclesi-astical lawyers in criminal matters and in all points touching secular interests. Against this must be set the fact that to his days must be fixed the final sliding of testamentary juris-diction into the hands of the bishops, which was by the legis-lation of the next century permanently left there, in a way which, however accordant with the policy of the papacy, was an exception to the rule of the rest of Christendom. Henry, although not by any known assize or constitution, must have restrained the ecclesiastical judicature from interfering in secular matters, except in the two points of matrimony, which was closely connected with a sacramental theory, and of testamentary business. These two, however, furnished matter sufficiently remunerative for a school of church lawyers; and the more distinctly ecclesiastical jurisdiction over spiritual things and persons provided much more. A thoroughly learned class of civil and canon lawyers is required over and above the thoroughly learned class of common law and (to anticipate a little) chancery lawyers of the royal courts.

Here then we begin to mark signs of increasing divergence. The common lawyers of England, the men who tread in the steps of Glanville, who are closely allied with the baronage and with the customary theories of prerogative, are opposed to the introduction of either branch of the Roman law. Glanville, anticipating the decision of the Statute of Merton on the question of legitimisation of children by the subsequent marriage of their parents, speaks of the 'canones legesque Romanorum' with the same tone of aversion. The ecclesiastics who followed the common law were as adverse to the Roman law as were the knights and barons who learned secular jurisprudence in the discharge of executive office: and very rarely do we find a great judge of the courts of Westminster taken from the ranks of canonists or civilians. Yet the educational influence of these two great systems was making itself felt very early indeed. Not only does Glanville, in the preface to his manual, cite from the Institutes the language in which he addresses his master, but large importations from the civil law procedure must have come in as the jurisprudence developed; and Bracton, who wrote a century after Glanville, makes direct citations from the compilations of Justinian. If I were not afraid of the lawyers, I should venture to say that the whole theory of Appeals and the whole subject of Equity are strange to the national growth of the common law, and, although widely differing in details, far more akin to the civil law, the practice of which in ecclesiastical causes was steadily before men's eyes whilst they were developing the

new systems. But I dare not venture to say this without
more authority.

As we proceed, however, we are struck more and more with
the prominence of the scientific element in legal education.
The great compilations are not received as having any
authority in England, but they are the sole legal teaching
which is to be obtained in the schools where Englishmen go
to learn law. The common law judges may not be canonists
or civilians, but the statesmen, in many cases at least, are;
certainly archbishops Langton and Boniface and Peckham
and Winchelsey. And even of the common lawyers it must
be affirmed that their teaching, such as they had, was not
merely empirical, not the mere knowledge of customs and the
few statutes that were as yet incorporated in the common law
code ; but scientific, that is, learned from the writings of
jurists who treated not merely of the letter or the case, but of
the spirit and reason of legislation. Glanville's is indeed but
a book of procedure, but Bracton, Fleta, and Britton are
jurists, and whilst they illustrate and explain the common
law, bring to the interpretation an intelligence and authority
that look to something far higher than precedent. We see
how long the old doctrine of the authority that is in the
mouth of the judge stands out against the new doctrine that
is in the letter of the law. Like the ' decretum,' like the
' responsa prudentum' of the Pandects, the work of Bracton is
a scientific rather than an authoritative text-book. But I am
anticipating what I ought to put in proper order somewhat
later.

Whilst the study of these foreign systems was becoming
increasingly important and increasingly common, the popular
dislike of foreign law was not in the least diminished. I
must here couple the two Roman systems together, for to all
purposes of domestic litigation they were inseparable : the
' canones legesque Romanorum' were classed together and
worked together, mainly because it was only on ecclesiastical
questions that the civil law touched Englishmen at all, but also
because without the machinery of the civil law the canon law
could not be worked ; if you take any well-drawn case of litiga-

tion in the middle ages, such as that of the monks of Canterbury against the archbishops, you will find that its citations from the Code and Digest are at least as numerous as from the Decretum. Moreover the accretions of the Decretum, the Extravagants as they were called, that is the authoritative sentences of the Popes which were not yet codified, were many of them conveyed in answers to English bishops, or brought at once to England by the clergy with the same avidity that lawyers now read the terminal reports in the Law Journal. The famous decision which Glanville quotes about legitimation is embodied in what then was an Extravagant of Alexander III, delivered to the bishop of Exeter in 1172, founded no doubt on a Novel of Justinian but not till now distinctly made a part of church law. And this point further illustrates what I was saying: for it is the point on which the great dictum of the council of Merton turns in 1236. The English hatred of the foreigners was in that year fanned to white heat by the importation of the king's half-brothers and the new queen's uncles: it was an unlucky moment for Grosseteste and the bishops to press that the English law of bastardy should be altered to suit the canon and civil law of Rome. The murmurs were already rising that William of Valence was going to change the constitution. Notwithstanding the influence of Grosseteste, the king and the barons declared 'Nolumus leges Angliae mutari.' That is a well-known story; but it is perhaps not equally well known that the king had just a year before issued an order which stands in close parallelism with the banishment of Vacarius. By a letter to the Lord Mayor of London, dated Dec. 11, 1234, he had directed that no one should be allowed to hold law schools in the city of London or teach the LAWS. What laws were these? Coke thought that the king referred to Magna Carta and the Carta de Forestis; but Selden, and Prynne after him, pointed out that this was inconceivable; and that doubtless the LAWS were the canon laws. I think that under the term Leges both civil and canon law were intended, but certainly at the moment the danger from the canon law was greater. In the year 1230 Gregory IX had approved of the five books of Decretals codified by Raymund of Pennafort from the Extravagants of the recent Popes and added to the Decretum of Gratian. In 1235 Matthew Paris tells us the Pope was urging the adoption of them throughout Christendom. But they were not received in England, although they continued to be the code by which English causes were decided at Rome, and began to be an integral part of the education of English canonists. And here again we have to distinguish between the scientific or implicit and the explicit authority of these books. Great as the influence of Justinian's code has been, there are very few countries in Europe where it has been received as more than a treasury of jurisprudence ; the 'Siete partidas' of Alfonso the Wise was a book of jurisprudence, not a code of law ; the independence of the Gallican Church turns, as a historical question, on the non-reception of Roman decrees, the acceptance of the council of Basel, and the non-reception of portions of the Tridentine canons, the incidental working of which must, notwithstanding, have been irresistible and undeniable. So in England neither the civil law nor the canon law was ever received as authoritative, except educationally, and as furnishing scientific confirmation for empiric argument ; or, in other words, where expressly or accidentally it agrees with the law of the land. Nay, the scientific treatment itself serves to confuse men's minds as to the real value of the text ; and in both laws the opinions of the glossers are often cited as of equal authority with the letter of the law or canon.

But this same date 1236 brings me to another point ; the beginning of the Codex receptus of Canon Law in England ; in spite of the Council of Merton and the closing of the law schools of London. Since the Conquest most of the archbishops had held provincial synods and issued provincial canons ; but many of these were acts of a temporary character only, and, even when they received support and confirmation from the kings, seldom amounted to more than the enforcement of discipline which had previously been authorised by papal or conciliar decrees. These canons are extant in the pages of the annalists, but remain rather among the Responsa Prudentum than as materials for a code. Just, however, as the statute law of England begins with the reign of Henry III, so does the codification of the national canon law. Archbishop Langton's Constitutions may be set first, but next in order, and even of greater authority, come the Constitutions of the legate Otho, which were passed in a national council of 1237. After these come Constitutions of the successive archbishops, especially Boniface of Savoy and Peckham, which were drawn up in a very aggressive spirit; Boniface taking advantage of Henry III's weakness to urge every claim that the English law had not yet cut down, and Peckham going beyond him in asserting the right of the Church against even the statutable enactments of the state. Between Boniface and Peckham in the year 1268 come the Constitutions of Othobon, which were confirmed by Peckham at Lambeth in 1281, and which, with those of Otho, were the first codified and glossed portions of the national church law. In the reign of Edward III, John of Ayton, canon of Lincoln, an Oxford jurist it is said, collected the canons adopted since Langton's time and largely annotated the Constitutions of Otho and Othobon. Contemporaneously with this accumulation of national materials, the Corpus Juris of the Church of Rome was increasing; Boniface VIII added the sixth book to the five of Gregory IX, and John XXII added the Clementines in 1318; and his own decisions, with those of the succeeding popes, were from time to time added as Extravagants unsystematised. The seventh book of the Decretals was drawn up under Sixtus V as late as 1588; so that practically it lies outside our comparative view. Of course very much of the spirit of both the Sixth and the Clementines found its way into England, but the statute law was increasing in vigour, the kings were increasing in vigilance, and after the pontificate of Clement V the hold of the papacy on the nation was relaxing. Occasionally we find an archbishop like Stratford using the papal authority and asserting high ecclesiastical claims against the king, but the age of the Statutes of Præmunire and Provisors was come, and no wholesale importation of foreign law was possible. Not to multiply details, I will summarily state that in the reign of Henry V William Lyndwood, the Dean of the Arches, collected, arranged, and annotated the accepted Constitutions of the Church of England in his Provinciale, which, with the collections of John of Ayton generally found in the same volume, became the authoritative canon law of the realm. It of course was proper in the first instance to the province of Canterbury, but in 1462 the Convocation of York accepted the Constitutions of the southern province as authoritative wherever they did not differ from those of York, and from the earlier date the compilation was received as the treasury of law and practice. Nor were any very material additions made to it before the Reformation ; for although the Church of England was deeply involved in the transactions of the Council of Basel, and might, if the matter had been broached as distinctly as it was in France, have formally accepted its canons, no such incorporation of those canons ever took place here as was accomplished in the Pragmatic Sanction of Bourges in 1438.

Still, authoritative as Lyndwood's code undoubtedly was, it was rather as the work of an expert than as a body of statutes that it had its chief force. The study of the canon law was a scientific and professional, not merely mechanical study ; and just as much was the study of the civil law also. I think that I am right in repeating that it was mainly as a branch of church law that the civil law was studied at all; but I do not mean that it was so exclusively. In the infancy of international law and the administration of both admiralty and martial law, the English jurists had to go beyond their insular practice, and to no other source could they apply themselves ; hence the association which to the present day has subsisted between the curiously unconnected departments of maritime and matrimonial jurisdiction. It is really owing to the distinction between scientifically and empirically trained lawyers. Of the indirect influence of scientific jurisprudence on the common law and chancery I have spoken already.

England has then for at least two centuries before the Reformation a body of law and a body of judges, for ecclesiastical and allied questions, quite apart from the law and judicial staff of the secular courts ; and, with the growth of the Universities, she begins to have educational machinery for training her lawyers. In this department of work, however, the scientific study has a long start and advantage over the empirical. The common law has to be learned by practising in the courts, or by attending on their sessions. The apprentices and serjeants of the Inns of Court learn their work in London; their study is in the year books and the statute book, a valuable and even curiously interesting accumulation of material, but thoroughly insular, or less than that, simply English. The canonists and civilians have also their house in London, the 'Hospitium dominorum advocatorum de arcubus,' but they are scarcely less at home at Rome and Avignon. The canonist and civilian learn the legal language of entire Christendom; the London lawyer sticks to his Norman-French. The Norman-French of Westminster is unintelligible beyond the Channel and beyond the border. Scotland, the sister kingdom, is toiling without a common law system at all until, in the sixteenth century, James V introduces the law of Justinian as her treasury of common law, and thus gains University training and foreign experience for her lawyers: but England has an ancient system and is content with her own superiority; her common law is of native growth, strengthening with the strength of her people; she sees the nations that have accepted the civil law sinking under absolutism; as distinctly as ever 'non vult leges Angliæ mutari.' But she has ceased to banish the skilled jurist. Oxford and Cambridge have their schools of both the faculties. The civil law at Oxford had its schools from the fourteenth century in Cat Street, on the north of S. Mary's, in Schidyard Street, and in the great civil law school in S. Edward's parish where Archbishop Warham learned law. The canon law school was in the neighbourhood of S. Edward's church also, and was rebuilt in 1489 by subscription of the canonists. Wood enumerates no less than seven distinct sets of Scholæ Legum, the majority being for civil law. In the colleges legal study has its proper endowments. At Merton the study of the canon law is by the founder's statutes permitted to four or five of his scholars, that of the civil law is allowed to the canonists as subsidiary

to their proper study, *pro utilitate ecclesiastici regiminis.* At
Oriel five or six fellows, with consent of the seniors, might
read the canon law, and by dispensation of the provost, the
civil law also. At Exeter, one of Stapledon's fellows was to
study Scripture or the Canon Law. We learn from Mr. Mul-
linger's invaluable book on Cambridge, that at Gonville Hall,
founded about seventy years after Merton, each fellow was
allowed to study canon law for two years. It might be possible to trace in the successive foundations vestiges of the old
subsisting and often revived jealousy of the studies; for
Merton was founded at a time when, as Roger Bacon tells us,
the civil law was looked on with jealousy as a mere professional or money-making study, whilst before the foundation
of Gonville Hall the conflict between John XXII and Lewis
of Bavaria had made the political tendencies of these studies
more important and obvious. At Trinity Hall, which was
nearly of the same date as Gonville, ten civilians and seven
canonists were seventeen out of the twenty statutory fellows.
At New College, out of seventy there were to be ten civilians
and ten canonists, but these were reduced by Waynflete to two
civilians and four canonists. At All Souls, sixteen out of
forty were to be lawyers; at King's College, Cambridge, out
of seventy, two civilians and four canonists; while at Catharine
Hall both the canon and civil law were excluded. These
variations depend no doubt on the special intentions of the
founders to promote scientific study, or to insure the worldly
advancement of their pupils, and, to some extent, on the
varying relations between theology and law of which I must
speak in the next lecture. It is however clear, at the lowest
estimate, that abundant encouragement and opportunities for
the study could be found in both the seats of learning.
Closely allied as the canon and civil laws were, they composed
two faculties; with regular schemes of lectures, fees, and exercises; the doctor of the civil law had to prove his knowledge
of the Digest and the Institutes; the doctor of the canon law
must have worked three years at the Digest and three at the
Decretals, and studied theology also for two years. It is, you
observe, not the national church law, but the universal or

scientific material, on which he is employed. In a great number of cases the degrees were taken at the same time, but as the era of the Reformation approaches the canonists become more numerous than the civilians at Cambridge, and probably at Oxford also. But these points belong to a view of the subject on which I cannot pretend to enter now; and indeed it is in the conflict of laws rather than the conflict of studies that the present interest of the subject lies. In the next lecture I shall have to recur for some points to the ground which I have attempted to cover in this, for the struggles and jealousies of the rival and allied systems of jurisprudence do not date from the Reformation only. Here, however, I stop now, having in a cursory way traced the history of the materials of the canonical jurisprudence so far down. We shall have to begin by looking at the later history from the theological as well as from the legal side, and to follow it through the Reformation period, steering clear, as much as possible, of questions of modern controversy.

XIV.

THE HISTORY OF THE CANON LAW IN ENGLAND.

(April 20, 1882.)

IN the first of these two public lectures I attempted to give a sketch of the growth of the Canon Law ; its origin and materials, its introduction into England and the limits of authority which it attained here, its relation to the civil law of Rome, and the distinction between the scientific study of the Decretals in the Universities and the professional use of the Provinciale in the Ecclesiastical Courts. The second branch of the subject, as I proposed to treat it in opening the lecture, is the history of its working in competition with and in general relations to other systems of law : a branch of the discussion which compels us at once to go back to the very root of the subject. Canon law as a code, and the civil law of Rome as a treasury of procedure, working together in the hands of ecclesiastical lawyers, may be for the moment looked at together ; and the first aspect which our subject then takes is the attitude of the system towards theology on the one side and to the national, or, as lawyers would perhaps call it, municipal law on the other. From the Conquest to the Reformation canon law, proceeding by civilian method, and being able to call on the municipal executive to put its sentences in force, is a strong link between theology and national discipline ; but a link with so much intricate workmanship employed upon it as to be offensive in many ways both to theology and to the common law. The theologian saw the great commandments of God, and the statutes of the Church, and the voice of conscience, lowered by being made dependent for their cogency on an elaborate system of human

invention which fettered freedom of action, and in some
respects freedom of thought also ; which reduced moral obligations to a system of penances, pecuniary commutations,
monitions, and excommunications, and which made use of the
sacraments of the Church as the mere means and appliances
of a coercion to external good behaviour, which ought to be a
free-will offering and the instinctive product of a sincere
heart.   Do not think that I am exaggerating the attitude of
repulsion in which the pure theologian and the pure moralist
stood to the ecclesiastical lawyer who was making money out
of the practice of the Courts Christian.   You remember how
John of Salisbury had doubted whether an archdeacon could
be saved : Roger Bacon declares that the study of the civil
law, attracting the clever men among the clergy, threw the
study of theology into a second place, and secularised the
clerical character, making the priest as much a layman as
the common lawyer ; while Richard of Bury, the author of
the Philobiblion, and Holcot the great scholastic, declared,
the one that the civilian, although he gained the friendship of
the world, was an enemy of God ; the other, that under existing relations the handmaid Hagar, despising the true wife,
was in apt analogy to the contempt under which neglected
theology sank in the estimation of the world as compared with
the law.   It is true that these remarks have a primary
reference to the civil law, but, as I showed, the civil law was
learned chiefly as the executive of the canon law, and it was
by its relations to the canon law that it became practical and
remunerative.   I need not go into much detail about this,
but, if I am speaking to any who attended my lectures on
Ockham and Marsilius, they will remember how not only
those great writers, but a crowd of minor ones, attack the
canon law and its professors as the great enemies, not only of
civil government but of vital religion : an exaggeration no
doubt, but founded on a true principle.   ' Who,' says John of
Salisbury, himself a canonist, ' ever rises pricked at heart from
the reading of the laws, or even of the canons[1] ? '   The
practice of these studies stood to theology, stood to religion

[1] Joh. Salisb. i. 196, epist. 138.

itself, in the relation in which the casuistry of the confessional stood to true moral teaching.

When however we turn, as we must do, to consider the attitude of the national law and the national lawyers, we see more distinctly how incompatible were the systems which, for four hundred years, from the Conquest to the Reformation, stood side by side, with rival bodies of administrators and rival or conflicting processes. Look first at the area of matters with which the canon law assumed to deal : it claimed jurisdiction over everything that had to do with the souls of men, and I think there is scarcely a region of social obligation into which, so defined, it would not claim to enter. It claimed authority over the clergy, in matters civil and criminal, in doctrine and practice, in morals and in manners, education and dress, in church and out. It claimed authority over all suits in which clergymen were parties, or in which ecclesiastical property was involved ; I say, mark you, claimed, rather than exercised, for some of these are the points in which the struggle with the national law arises. It claimed authority over the belief and morals of the laity, in the most comprehensive way. The whole of the matrimonial jurisdiction, the whole of the testamentary jurisdiction was, we know, specially regarded as a branch of canon law ; but by its jurisdiction for correction of life, ' pro salute animae,' it entered into every man's house; attempted to regulate his servants, to secure his attendance at church, to make him pay his debts, to make him observe his oaths, to make him by spiritual censures, which by the alliance with the State had coercive force, by the dread of a writ of *capias excommunicatum*, to keep all the weightier matters of the law, not only judgment, mercy, and truth, but faith, hope, and charity also. Now the common law of the land was quite competent to deal first with ecclesiastical property, temporalities, advowsons, and the right to tithes ; the canon law dealt with the qualifications of presentees and the exaction of tithes : the common law was competent to deal with matters of debt or theft ; the canon law claimed to deal with matters of credit or dishonesty in legal and moral as in spiritual obligations : the common law dealt with dower, the canon law with matrimony; the common law with succession to property, the canon law with legitimacy. So over great regions of property law, and over the whole domain of moral delinquency, the medieval world had two sets of courts at which they might sue, and two sets of lawyers to keep alive with fees and retainers. The canonists affirm that a suit may be brought in the ecclesiastical court for every matter which is not cognisable in the courts of secular law, and for a great many matters which are so cognisable. There is surely an ample claim. I do not want to go into detail, but I will just point out one particular; the commissary of the Bishop of London entertained suits exactly analogous to those of the trades unions of the present day, turning on the question how far it is a breach of oath for the sworn member of a guild to impart the arts and mysteries of his guild to outsiders.

Here then you see the elements of a pretty conflict; between the jurists as a matter of scientific or empiric lore, between the practising lawyers a conflict for practice and for profits; and you can see how degrading the practical part of the profession was to the theological student, or to the parish priest. Over and above this, there was the natural jealousy of the crown and the parliament. If the canon law had restricted itself to really spiritual questions, matters of belief or of morals for which the national code had no provision, it is not likely that the kings would have been jealous of papal or archiepiscopal enactments, or would have stood on their rights when the exact line was occasionally overstepped. But the extravagance of ecclesiastical claims provoked them to opposition and justified it. When the archbishops of Henry III's reign claimed exclusive jurisdiction in suits of advowsons, the right to exact personal tithes, and to try all questions of credit granted ' fide interposita,' even so gentle a worm as the king turned again; and we find among his letters, and still more among those of his son, constant cautions to the primates and their convocations not to attempt anything to the prejudice of the crown and customs of the land, as well as innumerable prohibitions to ecclesiastical judges against their trying other

civil suits than those which touch testamentary or matrimonial matters.   Edward II had to prohibit the employment
of imperial notaries. In the spiritual matters proper, the kings
seldom interfered; only where a political motive was suspected, or where a servant of the crown was attacked, or where
the spiritual judge had clearly gone beyond his discretion.
The Church history of the thirteenth and fourteenth centuries
is full of cautions and prohibitions, and of struggles between
the officers who had thus to interfere with one another; and
the definitions of the ' Articuli Cleri' under Edward II which
prescribed the points on which prohibitions were to be granted,
and the Statute of Præmunire under Edward III, which forbade the multiplication of appeals to Rome, did little to
ameliorate relations.   When however heresy became a matter
of litigation, the two systems deliberately worked together;
and, although there were many hitches, during the whole of
the Lancastrian period there was more definite co-operation
and less conflict.   The common law was really becoming more
a matter of scientific treatment, and the greatest judges were
men who had had scientific education on both sides. Sometimes
there was, as was natural, a little inconsistency and awkwardness; the bowsprit got mixed up with the rudder; as when
Morton, at once archbishop and chancellor, allowed his judgment on a fraudulent executor to be modified by the reflexion
that he would be ' damnée in hell.'   But this may have been
exceptional.

It must not however be supposed that the fault in this
rivalry was altogether to be ascribed to the canonists.   The
English-trained lawyer was as infallible in that age as in this;
and when we find him, and his brethren in the parliament,
constantly hampering the legitimate work of the church, we
see that there were two sides to the question; when in the
fourteenth century the Commons petition that the clergy may
not make in their convocation canons to bind the laity, it is
rather a relief to find that the canons in question relate to
tithe of underwood: but when in 1446 we find the clergy
remonstrating that the professional lawyers ' pretended privilege, by what right,' they say, ' we know not, to interpret

acts of parliament and explain the mind of the legis-
lature, and by thus practising upon the statutes sometimes
ground their opinion on mysterious and unintelligible reasons,
and so wrest the laws contrary to the meaning and intention of parliament;' or petitioning that the judges who
showed such strong bias should no longer issue prohibitions,
but, when questions arose concerning the limits and jurisdiction of the rival courts, indifferent persons should be
pitched upon to judge them; or the lawyers, on the other
hand, striking at the root of all ecclesiastical jurisdiction as
if it were a transgression of the Statute of Præmunire[1],—
well, when we look at these things, we shall see that there
were questions unsettled even before the Council of Trent,
and hear opinions and complaints that sound like echoes
beforehand of voices with which in these days our ears are
too familiar.

I must, however, now proceed to the Reformation, and
endeavour to determine, as strongly and as clearly as I can,
the bearing of that most critical era on our subject. Henry
VIII had, as early as 1515, seen a struggle between the
secular and ecclesiastical jurisdictions in Standish's case, in
the course of which he is said to have expressed himself as
determined to endure no division of sovereignty in his own
realm. Whether that was really said or merely put into his
mouth afterwards, I cannot say; but certainly no scheme of
change in the relation between Church and State was set on
foot for nearly seventeen years. Then the business of the
divorce at Rome, and the discontent of the king with the
half-hearted support of the clergy at home, completed his
disgust, and he set out in the course of radical change.
Having in 1531 compelled the clergy by the threat of præmunire to recognise him as supreme head 'quantum per
Christi legem licet,' he induced the Commons in 1532 to
present a petition or remonstrance against the whole theory
and practice of the canon law. They attacked the power of
the clergy to make canons in convocation, they protested
against the exaction of fees and mortuaries, and deliberately

[1] Wilkins, iii. 555 (1447); Parker's Antiquitates, 429.

impugned the honesty and purity of the episcopal courts in all their branches and with reference both to jurisdiction and to procedure. This petition had two results; the parliament passed bills to limit the benefit of clergy and forbid feoffments to the use of churches. An earlier session in 1529 had attempted to deal with probate and mortuaries; this, by the Statute of Citations, cut down the power of the Archbishop of Canterbury to entertain suits from other dioceses except by appeal or on request, and so struck at the root of the universal jurisdiction enjoyed by the Court of Arches and its advocates. The same term—the second result of the king's policy—the Convocation was compelled to surrender its right of meeting and legislating, and to consent to a revision of the canon law to be carried into execution by a mixed body of clergy and laity whom the king should appoint. This last concession sealed the fate of the old scientific study of the canon law, which, as we have seen, was a distinctly popish study; and, if it had not been accompanied by a limiting clause, allowing the old canons, so far as they were not opposed to the law of the land, to stand until the revision was published, there would have been an entire abolition of ecclesiastical jurisdiction of any kind. In 1535 Cromwell, as the king's vicegerent, visited the two Universities, and in both issued injunctions, that both the old scholastic teaching of the Sentences should cease, and that the teaching in the Decretals and the conferring of degrees in canon law should be abolished. What the exact legal force of Cromwell's legal injunctions was has never been determined; but in these points they were obeyed: the Universities ceased to teach the systematic theology of the Schools and the systematic jurisprudence of the Decretals; and the ancient degrees of bachelor and doctor of the canon law are known, except during the reign of Mary, no more. How did this affect the civil law? you ask: well, just as it might be expected; the scientific study was abolished, the old canons were in abeyance, but the courts continued to practise, the civil law procedure was as lively as ever; and students who intended to practise as advocates took degrees in civil law instead of in both. Oxford dropped the canon law degree altogether; Cambridge, by adopting a more general form, retained a shadowy presentment of the double honour.

And now we come again to an Act which shows the continuity of the inherent rivalry between two systems which, for the sake of mutual profit, had so long worked together. In 1541 a bill was introduced into parliament which enabled married D.C.L.'s to exercise ecclesiastical jurisdiction as chancellors and commissaries; it did not pass in that year, being withdrawn on the request of Convocation, but was reintroduced and passed in 1545. So long as the two degrees were granted together the D.C.L.'s were, as doctors of decrees, bound by the canon which forbade a married man to act as an ecclesiastical judge; but now the right of the D.C.L. simple, both to marry and to act as a judge, was secured: as the civil doctors of Bologna had done in the thirteenth century, their successors in England now married; before this they were probably, as a rule, in minor orders.

I must pass over the more important of Henry VIII's other acts, especially the Statutes of Appeals and Submission, except just to recall the fact that in the preamble to the former of those Acts passed in 1533 he had expressed himself confident that the realm of England would, as it always had done, provide a sufficient number of spiritual men to decide spiritual questions, and of secular men to decide secular questions, under his own supreme authority and to the exclusion of any foreign jurisdiction. The other matters in which those statutes affected ecclesiastical jurisdiction lie somewhat deeper than our present speculations.

We are not however to suppose that, when the king practically abolished the canon law, he intended to hand the clergy over to the common lawyers. The procedure was, as we have seen, still kept in the hands of the civilians; but the theologians were a body of men whose functions had been to some extent usurped by the canonists, and who now for some years, under Tudor and Puritan and Laudian influences, were to come to the front. The theologians or divines divided with the canonico-civilians the authority of the ecclesiastical jurisdiction: the character of a bishop in itself was that of a divine, not of a lawyer, and we might almost say that whilst questions of application of law and procedure belonged to the lawyer, the interpretation was claimed for the divine. In cases of heresy, for instance, the theologians formulated the definition, whilst the canonists and civilians examined the teaching of the accused and determined how far he had contravened the definition. So in the question of Henry's divorce, the divines had been called on to define ' Can the pope dispense with a marriage with a deceased brother's wife ? ' the canonists had to determine whether the marriage between Arthur and Katharine was such a marriage as precluded the dispensation. This rule of combining theologians with canonists or civilians for commissions on ecclesiastical suits continued long after the Reformation, and ought never to have been disused.

These measures of change, sufficiently drastic one would think, had in this department satisfied Henry VIII ; the scheme for revising the canon law hung fire ; the powers granted to the king in 1534 were renewed for three years in 1536, and again for his life in 1544, but nothing was done in the matter during the remainder of the reign. But what had sufficed Henry VIII did not suffice Somerset or Northumberland, or the poor boy-king who succeeded him. The second statute of the first year of Edward VI went as near as possible to extinguish the episcopate ; there were still to be bishops, but they were to be nominated by the king without any form of election ; they were as a matter of fact appointed during good behaviour ; and their jurisdiction was henceforth to be exercised in the king's name. In him all ecclesiastical authority was vested, they were to be his ministers, their writs were to be issued in his name, their seals were to bear the royal arms ; and it was only to such of them as he pleased that even such authority was to be intrusted. It was proposed, though not passed, that a Court of Chancery should be erected for ecclesiastical causes. The revision of the canon law was to be urged on, and the Universities were to be further purged from the old leaven. All this was done : in vain the Protestant bishops pleaded in the

House of Lords that their position was intolerable and their
dignity a mere mockery, that the moral discipline of clergy
and people was entirely broken down ; no act for rehabi-
litating them was got through parliament ; the dominant
interests were opposed to it. The injunctions sent to the
Universities prescribed some renewal of studies ; the poor
canonists of course were left out in the cold, although not
treated as if they were illegal or irregular : the civilians were
authorised to read the Institutes, and the D.C.L., when he
had reached that dignity, was exhorted to devote himself
more zealously to the study of the king's laws, both temporal
and ecclesiastical. And work was to be found for him : bills
were introduced to lodge ecclesiastical jurisdiction in the
hands of students of the Universities, who were admitted by
the archbishop. By these, however, all special privileges of
the advocates were endangered and the bills dropped after
passing most stages : four bills on this point were before the
parliament of 1550. But again the revision of the canons
was dragging behind. The king's power of nominating
revisers was asserted by an act of 1550 to last for three
years, and an abortive attempt was made in the session of
1552 to renew or enlarge it ; but whether it was that Cranmer
found it impossible to obtain skilled assistants, or that the
division of parties prevented a joint effort, it was not until
near the end of the reign that the project was carried on :
in 1551 and 1552 Edward issued two commissions of thirty-
two, composed of equal numbers of bishops, divines, civilians,
and common lawyers ; the number thirty-two was reduced
to eight ; practically the work was done by Peter Martyr,
the Oxford Professor of Divinity, under Cranmer's eye, and
the result was the compilation known as the *Reformatio
Legum ;* a curious congeries of old and new material which
really pleased no party ; showing too much respect for
antiquity and divine ordinance to please the Puritan, and
too little to satisfy the men who had guided the Reformation under Henry VIII and those who were to do so under
Elizabeth.

The legislation and policy of Mary were directed to uproot

everything that Edward VI had originated; his bishops appointed 'quamdiu se bene gesserint,' were dispossessed without a struggle; his laws were repealed, many of them never to be revived; his advisers, where they would not comply, were exiled or burned: but the efforts to reinstate the old system were not successful; the monastic property could not be restored; the ranks of the lower clergy, reduced to a fraction by the abolition of chauntries and private masses, could not be recruited; and all the restored fabric hung on the life of a woman and a few worn-out old men. For the moment the canon lawyers lifted up their heads, and a few civilians took the doctorate of decrees at Oxford and Cambridge; but the complete extinction of reactionary forces, on Mary's death, showed that the Papal system, with all that was dangerous to national life contained in it, was, so far as England was concerned, practically extinct: six years of blood and fire, of tears and prayers, of cruel jealousies and heartbreaking divisions, wrought this; and Elizabeth for some years after her accession had before her a task, not certainly easy, but not encumbered with insuperable difficulties.

The subject which we are treating now contracts its limits; for to attempt anything like circumstantial discussion of the legal history of a period into which ecclesiastical quarrels so largely enter, would be to lose oneself at once in a wilderness of controversy. I must content myself with a few generalisations and a few significant facts. The Elizabethan settlement in Church and State was a compromise, satisfactory to no party, and very unsatisfactory indeed to the constitutional lawyer or historian; but, possibly, the best arrangement compatible with circumstances. She began her reign, of course, by a reversal of her sister's legislation; but she did not restore the Edwardian system; she did not revive the Act of Henry VIII which had asserted the king's headship of the Church, or the Act of Edward which deprived the bishops of all original jurisdiction: the doctrine of the headship was opposed both by the Puritans and by the Catholic party; the abolition of all the high functions of the episcopate which was aimed at by Edward's advisers was a measure which contemporary history was showing to be dangerous. But, whilst she minimised the definition of authority, she retained the virtual exercise of it: her explanation of her supreme governorship might have satisfied every one but the most Tridentine papist, but she re-enacted the most stringent part of her father's act of supremacy; and, whilst she allowed the continuance of the church jurisdiction, she kept all control over the religious discipline of clergy and laity under the hands of the Court of High Commission. The Court of High Commission, consisting of a large number of lawyers and laymen and a small number of bishops and divines, stands to the Church in much the same relation as the Court of Star Chamber stands to the Courts of Common Law, and the Court of Requests to Chancery, a legal but most unconstitutional relation, and one which, however long it might be tolerated, was sure in the long run to endanger the whole fabric. As for legislation, Elizabeth acted, as we know, on a high principle of supremacy; such measures of church discipline as required coercive authority she allowed the parliaments to pass, but she forbade any interference whatever where that authority was not necessary. As for the ecclesiastical legislation in Convocation, she exercised her veto, i.e. she granted or withheld the consent which would make it valid, according to her own views of high policy. The rulers of the Church, who were not free from the same humiliating bondage of adulation that influenced all around the great queen, tolerated a system which gave them the substance of power, although in an unpopular and unhistorical shape. Their legislative authority was paralysed, but they could exercise a real authority as the queen's advisers; and the jurisdiction, which they had difficulties in enforcing through their own courts, they could enforce as members of the High Commission Court. But the ecclesiastical law—how did it fare under the circumstances? In the first place the forms of the courts were maintained, and were enough to sustain the civilians who worked in them; the Prerogative Court and the consistory courts lived on the testamentary and matrimonial jurisdiction; and before the spiritual courts were tried the smaller cases of discipline which were not important enough for the High Commission Court. Doctors' Commons, which had dwelt before in Paternoster Row or at the Queen's Head, under the auspices of Dr. Henry Harvey, built itself a new home, with hall and library and plate and privileges for importing wine. Knowledge of canon and civil law was in parliament, as in 1585, regarded as a special qualification for service in the House of Commons on committees. In the parliaments of 1559 and 1563 were introduced bills to make a University degree necessary for ecclesiastical judges. And the canon law, as drawn up by Lyndwood, and the civilian procedure, subsisted, for the revision which had been completed by Edward's commissioners did not approve itself to Elizabeth or her advisers, and after an abortive attempt to carry it through the parliament of 1559, took its place on the shelf of broken projects. Even the Court of High Commission, novel as its functions were and unfettered as it was in the exercise of them, condescended to borrow from the canonical jurisprudence some of its most offensive details, its *ex officio* oath and the censures by which it would enforce its sentences.

It was a strange composite system, perhaps the only one possible consistently with the retention of historic continuity, but obviously and most certainly tolerable only for a time. What was the attitude of theologians, of common lawyers, and of canonists towards this critically-balanced structure? To the true theologians, whether Catholic or Puritan, the whole was repulsive: we see this in the half-hearted, almost despairing adhesion of Archbishop Parker, and in the strong and justifiable protests of the Puritans; and I mention them with respect here, because this opposition to unconstitutional tyranny is the only point in which I have any sympathy with them; their tenets I hold to be untenable, and their methods of promoting them by calumny, detraction, and coarse ribaldry I think entirely detestable; but I do think they were right in denouncing the Court of High Commission and all its works. Even conservative churchmen like Hooker, in their defence of the ecclesiastical system, are hampered by the consciousness that much of what existed was indefensible. The bishops saw their position as bishops ignored, and the Puritans saw the power which they thought should be exercised by their own ministers exercised through a royal commission : the bishops however had the power and endured the ignominy, the Puritans suffered and waited for their turn to persecute.

The lawyers were not all of one mind ; Coke the great lawyer was himself of two minds ; he liked the crown better than the episcopate, but he loved the common law better than the crown ; and his inconsistency produces some curious results on his teaching. This leads us to two or three facts. From 1587 to 1591 the famous Cawdrey's case drew its grievous length along. The High Commission had deprived Cawdrey for nonconformity; the question arose, had the Commission under the terms of the Act of the queen's first year exceeded its authority? The resolution finally adopted by all the judges, and recorded and approved by Coke, affirmed that the ecclesiastical prerogative of the crown was such that the powers of a commission issued by it were not limited by that statute, but covered the whole range of ecclesiastical jurisdiction ; and therefore the sentence was good. The judgment in Cawdrey's case, full of bad law and worse history, is often referred to even now by lawyers with a respect which it does not merit ; here it is useful as showing to what lengths the common lawyers under Elizabeth would go in support of the authority of the crown over things ecclesiastical. It stimulated the Puritans in and out of the Church to bitterer action, and disabled the hands of the bishops who, like Andrewes, would rather have taken the responsibility of their own acts. Twenty years later Coke himself declared against the constitutional character of the Court of High Commission, and, by refusing to act upon it, paved the way for its downfall. But Coke was then in opposition to the king's advisers, and made it his account to be an independent judge. But I am anticipating.

The change of Elizabeth for James I was a critical event in English Church history. James's dealings with the Church

are not among the strongest, but are perhaps among the
least reprehensible parts of his administration.   He willingly
confirmed the canons of 1604, which make a substantive
addition to the canonical lore of the clergy.   He failed to
secure co-operation between the House of Commons and the
Convocation, or between the bishops and the Puritan divines.
But this is no wonder.   A House of Commons which could
listen to Sir Herbert Crofts declaring that the Church had
declined ever since doctors began to wear boots ; or could
expel Mr. Sheppard, M.P. for Shaftesbury, for explaining
that 'dies Sabbati' meant not the Sabaoth as they called it,
but Saturday, and suggesting that as David danced before
the ark, the legality of dancing was a question on which
the bishops might decide before it was altogether forbidden,
—such a House of Commons was not likely to impress men
like Hooker or Andrewes with respect, or King James either.
It is clear I think that, if the Puritan party had been well
represented at the Hampton Court Conference, James would
have seen justice done to them ; but he saw their intolerance
and their frivolity, and the balance remained unredressed.
One of their minor complaints, against the issuing of ecclesiastical sentences by lay chancellors, touches directly on our
subject: their idea was to give all the disciplinary power to
the clergy, but to their own clergy: the prelates of the time
chose to maintain the *status quo* which left the power where
it was.   On this point the civilians were peremptory.   Some
of the prelates, either wishful to promote their sons or willing
to lodge Church discipline in clerical hands, appointed clergymen to be chancellors.   The doctors took umbrage at this,
petitioned King Charles I in 1625, and obtained from him
an order to remove the intruding officials and to substitute
qualified civilians.

Another interesting point arises at James's accession.   In
the hurry of his first parliament the Act of Mary which repealed the 1 Edw. VI. c. 2, by which the *conge d'eslire* and
the independent jurisdiction of the bishops were abolished,
was itself repealed ; and the lawyers, or some of them,
held that the Edwardian law was revived, that the whole

episcopate was intrusive, and the whole of the Church courts illegal. This was long in controversy, and it was only in 1637 that the judges finally resolved that the law of Edward, as contravening a law of Henry VIII which had been formally re-enacted, was not revived by the repeal of the Marian statute. If that resolution had not been accepted, the whole existing fabric of the Church must, so far as secular interests were concerned, have fallen to the ground.

But the opening of James I's reign is important for a third critical question. In 1605 Archbishop Bancroft presented from Convocation a series of articles against the proceedings of the common law judges in issuing prohibitions and claiming the exclusive right to interpret acts of parliament touching the Church. The long argument on this subject, which is to Coke's Second Institute what Cawdrey's case is to the Reports, is of considerably greater weight; no doubt there was much to be said on both sides, and the voice of the Convocation of 1605 was in harmony with that of 1559 and 1446, where the claims of the theologians to interpret acts that touched theology were fairly stated; but Coke embellishes the report with words that have an amusing cogency even in the present day; ' for judges expounding of statutes that concern the ecclesiastical government or proceedings, it belongeth unto the temporal judges, and we think they have been expounded as much to the clergy's advantage as either the letter or intention of laws would or could allow of: and when they have been expounded to their liking then they could approve of it, but if the exposition be not for their purpose then they will say as now they do that it appertaineth not unto us to determine of them.' Anyhow the judges agreed that they were the proper interpreters of the acts of parliament; and as the whole liturgy, and indeed the Bible also, might be brought under those terms, there was practically no limit to their assumption of infallibility; for the common law judges could not, like theologians, afford to leave any question unsolved.

Well, Coke was right as to the bishops, as was proved in 1612, when the common lawyers allowed bishops King and

Neill to burn two heretics under a common law writ, for which Coke's authority might be pleaded, although all the earlier legislation against heretical pravity had been abrogated. The invulnerability of the common law which had maintained the High Commission in Cawdrey's case, now treated the issue of the writ 'de heretico comburendo' as a matter of its own, and brought equal shame on theology and jurisprudence. The heretics who were burned were men whom the Puritans did not care to defend ; they would have burned them as willingly as they would have done the bishops.

And here let me say by the way, great as the horrors of religious persecution are, they cannot be properly estimated without some consideration of the value set upon human life both at the period in which they occur and at other times : I believe that I could show that all the executions for religious causes in England, by all sides and during all time, are not so many as were the sentences of death passed in one year of the reign of George III for one single sort of crime, the forging of bank-notes.

But I must pass on, leaving the Laudian period altogether out of sight : and indeed it is not, for our purpose, so important as the earlier portion : Laud and Charles were, neither of them, men who were satisfied with such things as the High Commission Court, and the sinking of ecclesiastical discipline in the state administration ; but they did not make their way to any better system, and supported that which was to them for the time the only possible system. With the opening of the struggle in 1641 the Court of High Commission fell to the ground, and at the Restoration its abolition was confirmed by the first parliament of Charles II.

During the Elizabethan and Jacobean period the study of church law had not been neglected ; for it had shared the benefit of the great historical and antiquarian revival of which Parker was the first leader, to which Spelman belonged, and which reached its climax in Selden and Prynne. Both of these eminent writers studied canon law from antagonistic

grounds: Selden regarded it as a philosopher ardent for
liberty; Prynne as an enthusiast, who had his own persecution to avenge and the thesis of royal prerogative to defend with all the zeal and learning of a convert. Selden
was a real jurist; Prynne an indefatigable searcher of
records. But, when at the Restoration the removal of the
incubus of the High Commission, and the political education
which the Caroline divines had gone through, enabled them
to restore the old ecclesiastical jurisdiction with some hope
of honest and successful issue, the canonists and civilians
showed that life was still in them. The old black-letter
Lyndwood was taken down from the shelf, rebound, and
annotated. Dr. Sharrock in 1664 abridged the Provincial
for the use of students, and in 1679 the Oxford edition, which
rapidly displaced the black-letter, was published with all
Lyndwood's commentaries and Ayton's work on the Constitutions. The study of the civil law needed no revival;
it had been kept up by the antiquaries and admiralty in the
worst times; and, in the Universities, the faculty fellowships
secured at least a languid succession of law degrees. The
D.C.L. of Oxford too had achieved the dignity which now
belongs to the honorary degrees at Commemoration; and in
1649, at what Antony Wood calls the Fairfaxian Creation,
both Fairfax and Cromwell were made doctors of the civil
law. According to Wood, in 1659 Nicolas Staughton, of
Exeter College, was admitted doctor both of civil and canon
law; and it is not impossible that there were other attempts
to revive the canon law doctorate as an adjunct to the degree
in civil law. Cambridge had always retained the shadow of
the double degree, for the Leges or LL. to which she admits
her doctors are a possible survival of the 'Utrumque Jus' of the
old University system; and in 1669, Richard Pearson, brother
of Bishop Pearson the commentator on the Creed, claimed to be
admitted in distinct terms to both faculties. The Archbishop
of Canterbury also, under the Dispensation Act, has the un-
questioned right to make a doctor of canon law, although
I am not sure that it has ever been exercised. But at Oxford
the designation of the degree had latterly come to be restricted

to civil law; and when in 1715, or thereabouts, Mr. Charles Browne of Balliol College applied to the Vice-Chancellor, Dr. Gardiner, for leave to proceed as bachelor and doctor of the canon law, he was told that he could not be prevented from doing so if he wished it, but that it would give the University a great deal of trouble; and the poor man died before he achieved the object of his ambition.

These notes are, however, of little importance, except as illustrating the revival of the ancient study, and the attention which the ecclesiastical questions of the day were calling to ancient practice. In point of fact, the whole of the second and last act of the Stewart dynasty was full of ecclesiastical questionings and excitements, which, though they did not directly touch our subject, stimulated the studies most closely connected with it. The struggle under James II, the position of the Nonjurors, the relation of Convocation to Parliament, the Whistonian and Bangorian controversies, all drew in lively partisans to the investigation of legal and ecclesiastical problems. The names of Hody, Kennet, Atterbury, Wake, and Gibson, all leading Oxford men, and men of deep research and minute if not accurate reading, are conspicuous in this regard; and, as for constitutional purposes it may be said that the very dust of their writings is gold, it would be ungrateful indeed to speak of their earnestness in the main object as misplaced. Gibson stands out more distinctly than any of the others as a great canonist, and his Codex or Collection of English Church Statutes is still the standard work and treasury of all sorts of such lore. There were too Johnson, Wilkins, and many other honest and subordinate workers on the theological as well as on the legal side. But the history of this department of law draws quickly to an end. The Hanoverian policy with regard to the Church and Convocation fell on all politico-ecclesiastical life as a blight. The Nonjurors were left out of the pale of the recognised laity, the common lawyers edged the theologians out of the court of delegates, the Convocations were silenced, and the bishops, almost as much as in Elizabeth's time, made their position in the House of Lords the fulcrum of all the force they ventured to exercise. Except for testamentary causes, and rare occasions of matrimonial and slanderous causes, the Church jurisdiction ceased to exist, and so continued dormant until in our times, in 1849 and in 1850, the Gorham case roused the attention of both lawyers and clergymen to the fact that without knowing it they had let the centre of ecclesiastical gravity become seriously misplaced. Into this region of discussion, for many reasons, I must not attempt now to make my way.

A few years after the Gorham controversy, a change or series of changes set in from another quarter: the matrimonial jurisdiction was remodelled when the facilities for divorce were increased, and the whole testamentary jurisdiction was withdrawn from the nominal superintendence of the archbishops. The Courts, the profits and privileges of which had so long maintained the close corporation of Doctors' Commons, and had caused the study of canon law in some at least of its branches to be languidly pursued, were radically and fundamentally changed; and, although it was difficult at once to improvise new forms and rules of procedure to take the place of the ancient forms and those which had grown out of them, these forms also were doomed. In the still more recent remodelling of the whole judicial system further changes have forced themselves in; and where the lawyers could find it their policy to acquiesce in the consolidation of the common law and chancery, they could without the slightest reluctance throw the ecclesiastical and admiralty law into the same cauldron. Out of that cauldron arises a new supreme judicature, which requires, every two or three years, to be amended and strengthened. It is supposed that thereby justice is quickened and law made so cheap, that any man, poor or rich, may ruin himself with a light heart. It yet remains to be seen whether this amended system, easier and less intricate than the old, supplies as good material for training or provides as sound schools of lawyers. It is no doubt philosophically more capable of perfection. The lore of Coke and Selden, like the lore of Eldon and Stowell, is for the present at a discount. Of course looking on all this

with a historical eye, one is apt to be a little disconsolate ;
but time will avenge them, and the neo-legal jurisprudence
will soon have an array of reports and decisions that will
outweigh, physically at least, the Year-books and Institutes.
As for the ecclesiastical law, which by its very nature, if it
loses continuity, loses identity, in the present changing aspect
of the world's politics, I for my part do not intend to prophesy. No one can investigate the letter and working of
the canon law without being struck by the marvellous mixture
of lofty and eternal principles of right, with arbitrary and
disingenuous evasions of obligation : it reads as if the jurists,
finding that the Church could not be ruled by the true
principles, were determined to rule by special pleadings and
artful circumventions. For the future the theologians must
look to the true principles, and let the canonists and civilians
pass with their evasions and circumventions into the twilight
of archæology. Whether that will be so or not, or how soon,
we may some of us live to see.

XV.

THE REIGN OF HENRY VII.

(April 24, 1883.)

M Y kindest friends will hardly be able this year to charge me with having chosen the subject of my public statutory lectures with a view of attracting an audience. I never, in the course of a long historical experience, met with any one who wished to attend a second course of lectures on Henry VII, or indeed with any one who expressed any interest in him at all. It is just possible that I may be suspected of a design to attract the admirers of the lady Margaret, by advertising a discourse upon her son; but, although the idea did occur to me, I set it aside as feeling it my duty to guard against any over-sanguine expectations. No; I chose the subject because I have to lecture, and, after sixteen successive ceremonies of humiliation, I thought that I had a right to throw some part of the imputation of dulness off myself upon my subject. If the men will not come, let it be as much Henry VII's fault as mine.

Yet, to begin with, it is a curious thing that the subject should be so dull; and perhaps my first point should be to account for that. I do not question the fact. It is so; but why? The period is full of interest: it is the beginning of modern as distinguished from medieval history; it exhibits to us, in their first definite and specialised forms, the forces which constitute the dramatic elements of the state of society in which we are living; the great powers in their newly consolidated condition, the balance of which makes up European history ever since. It is the age of the discovery of the

New World, the age of the birth of modern commerce and colonisation ; it is the eve of the Reformation, and of that wonderful renaissance which I believe exists at the present day, in prize essays and schools examinations, much more vividly, and alas in much greater solid bulk than it ever had in the most flourishing days *in rerum natura*. And it is a period too in which we begin to have, more distinctly and more numerously than before, representative men as they are called ; that is, men whose greatness and prominence consists not in their being exceptions to or protests against, or glories or shames to the age in which they lived, but in concentrating in themselves and giving force to the ideas, the accomplishments, the hopes and aspirations, the greatnesses and littlenesses of their own times. In the play of character also there should be something interesting in a period which embraces Ferdinand and Isabella the Catholic, the delightful old Frederick III, and the still more charming Maximilian ; the age of Charles VIII and Philip the handsome, not to speak of the Borgias, the Medici, and the Farnesi.

Yet the reign of Henry VII is dull. Look at it in relation to English history ; there also it should be important ; there also it comes between the ancient and the modern ; bridges over the strait between the Wars of the Roses and the Reformation, between England isolated and England taking a first place in the counsels of Europe, between England weak and England strong. The reign itself may be almost exactly divided between fifteenth century influences and sixteenth century influences ; the one series winding up in final bloodshed, the other opening with initial intrigue. We are really able to trace the last links of the chain of political murders which had begun when Warwick and Lancaster slew Piers Gaveston, and which ends or almost ends with the sacrifice of Edward of Warwick and the de la Poles ; and we trace the first links of the policy which grew and strengthened in intensity to the days of Waterloo.

But still it is dull: we do not much care about the effete struggles of the dynastic parties, and we cannot get up a lively interest in the negotiations for the Scottish or Spanish marriage. It is our own fault perhaps that we want more sensationalism. But there is a lack of it notwithstanding.

One reason I will shortly dismiss. I verily believe that one reason why this period is dull is that it was the period of the discovery and development of printing, and of the use of paper instead of parchment. Men began to write freely and to destroy freely; instead of writing for private purposes of record, they wrote for other men to read ; they wrote not what was worth writing, but what would catch readers ; they wrote what it was safe to write when every one could read ; they wrote because they could write, not because there was a necessity for them to write ; that is, anybody wrote, and few wrote what was worth preserving. One popular book destroyed a thousand chances of having invaluable records of timid private annals. And, when destruction began, it found paper more easy to dispose of than parchment : the age that could make tailors' measures out of Magna Carta, lighted its fires with State papers. Growing criticism, careful public administration, even before the age of destruction began, had not learned to be careful as to what should be preserved and what should be destroyed. And when the age of destruction did come, it was divided between the Roman Catholic force that destroyed everything new, and the Puritan force that destroyed everything old. So it is not so much a wonder that we have so little documentary remains of Henry VII's reign, as that we have anything at all. The only strictly contemporary account of the king's life and character is to be found in a few half-rotten, half-legible paper sheets in the Cottonian Library. All the more circumstantial parts of the history have to be worked out of the annalists of the next generation.

But there must have been a deeper cause. Why should a king with a good character and a romantic career subside into a historical fogey ? Look closely at Frederick III, the splendid old gipsy, in name governor of the world, ever august, and increaser of the empire, yet owning no more territory than an English alderman ; sitting in his study elaborating a horoscope with destiny of universal dominion

for his grandchildren unborn, inventing the motto of empire
for an Austria that was yet in embryo : honourable, perhaps,
and careless about selfish gains, but a dreamer, about whom
the strange thing is that so many of his dreams came
true.   Look at Maximilian, the most delightfully unprincipled hero of the age of transition; always in every
feast and every fray, always wanting money and selling himself for promises, and never getting the money and never
keeping his engagements ; a good deal of the rake and a
good deal of the knight-errant; to himself a portentous
politician, a reformer of Church and empire, yet willing to
set Church and empire to sale, and himself to retire from the
Cæsarship, to accept the chair of S. Peter, and provide before
his death for his own canonization ; yet with all that the
founder of one of the great powers of modern history, grandfather of Charles V, and contriver of the scheme which
placed half Christendom under his grandson's sceptre. I
have often thought of Maximilian in contrast with Henry
VII ; all the balance of real goodness, what measure there is
of politic honesty, purity of life, reality of character, straight-
forwardness in religion, intelligent appreciation of his people's
needs, every moral consideration is in favour of Henry Tudor :
yet we like Maximilian better. With all his undeniable faults,
his absurd dishonesty which did more harm to himself than to
any one else, his grotesque pretensions, the astounding inconsistency between his undertakings and his fulfilments ; there
is an attractiveness about him which there is not about Henry
VII.   We will not stay to compare him with Charles VIII
or Ferdinand the Catholic ; I do not know that we can care
much for either, but we do care very little for Henry VII.

Yet, again, here is the uniter of the Roses, the founder of
the Tudor dictatorship which steered England through the
age of the Reformation, which projected and secured the union
with Scotland, which started England in the race of commercial enterprise ; here is the hero of romance, in whom the
prophetic eye of the saintly Henry of Lancaster had seen the
Joash of the British Zion ; the child of exile, hunted, like
David, as a partridge on the mountains ; the knight-errant

coming to rescue the distressed lady, as Perseus to Andromeda ; the avenger of blood at Bosworth field ; the Hercules of the twelve labours ; who overcame the Nemean lion in Edward IV ; the Erymanthian boar in Richard III ; the Arcadian stag in John of Lincoln ; the Cretan bull in James of Scotland ; the mares of Diomedes in Martin Swart ; whose hydra had been the civil wars ; who had put down the Stymphalian birds by the agency of the Star Chamber ; had thwarted in Margaret of York the host of the Amazons ; and found the three heads of Geryon in Maximilian, the archduke Philip, and the dowager of Burgundy ; who had beaten Cacus in Perkin Warbeck, and Cerberus in three still more insignificant enemies, and by overcoming Max's opposition to the French alliance had lulled the dragon and made his way into the garden of the Hesperides. It is not every Hercules who answers so precisely to the archetype.

And then think of him as the eligible *parti* of Europe ; the young pretender of fifty looking out for a wife ; thinking of the queen of Naples as very practicable, and at all events worth very minute inquiries as to teeth and stay-laces ; or perhaps Margaret of Austria, who could make him arbiter of the Netherlands, and possibly of Spain ; or Johanna of Castile, if she could have been consoled for the death of the archduke ; or that delightful duchess of Angoulême, Louise of Savoy, the mother of Francis I, and destroyer of the Constable of Bourbon ; or last, but not least, Katharine of Aragon, his own daughter-in-law, if the pope, whose conscience was elastic enough to dispense a marriage with a brother's wife, could so far stretch a point of infallibility as to connive at such a politic enormity. Well, the lady Margaret, poor thing, had four husbands, and Henry VIII had six wives ; matrimony was clearly a feature in the germinating policy of the Magians of the renaissance. And then, did ever English king receive, like Henry VII, three caps and swords from three successive popes,—from Innocent VIII, Alexander VI, and Julius II ? And last, but not least, Francis Bacon for a biographer ! And yet we want something more !

But it is time to be serious. If it is fair to estimate the importance of a reign by the contrast which may be drawn between the two that precede and follow it, the reign of Henry VII should be regarded as one of the most important, and in some respects the most important reign in English History. But to argue thus would really be a mistake ; really much of the importance that does attach to it is not its own, but arises from the general character of the age in which it fell, the critical, transitional age, which would have been very much what it was whatever sort of king was on the throne of England.

If the points which English History has thus in common with general European History during this period be left out of consideration, both the interest and the real significance of the actual events of the history of England fall into the background. Such interest as it has becomes a dreary and commonplace interest ; its dramatic action, if it can be said to have any, is extremely slow ; there is little that calls for sympathy in men or institutions, and the pages of the annalist are dry and jejune to an exceptional degree. And what interest it has in the nature of personal incident, is apart from the life of the nation. With the single exception of that part of the incident which concerns the conspiracies and pretensions of the Yorkist faction, which again derives its interest from the tragedy of the preceding reign, the pages of the annalist, where there are any, are so dull that we scarcely complain of their jejuneness. We have no temptation to follow the humdrum movements of the court as we trace the military itinerary of Edward I or the judicial itinerary of Henry II ; and it is by an effort that we have to remind ourselves what great things, irrespective of political events, were going on in England during these years ; how it was the period of the great activity of Caxton and his early fol-lowers, the period of the foundation or development of colleges in Oxford and Cambridge, of the renewal of old studies, of the friendship of Erasmus and More ; of discovery of a new world, and of unexampled development of commercial enterprise.

It is curious how little notice is taken of these things

in the contemporary annals; they lie, for the most part, outside of the limited area that we are wont to take for constitutional history. But we do not doubt that an immense part of the life of the next age was wrapped up in these things. Certainly the invention of printing, not less than the agglomeration of the new factors of the European balance, was a starting-point of a new stage of History; and the freedoms and jealousies of commerce and conquest in the New World were factors in the new drama second only in importance to the accumulations of power and territory in Europe. But they are both of them events of a class which finds for contemporaries too much work to allow of much talk or many contemplative jottings. Few very busy men keep minute or accurate diaries; few very busy ages possess very picturesque or very circumstantial chronicles. The early printers and the early discoverers left material enough for the next generation to dispute about, but did little in record of their own exploits. Many navigators lived and died and perished from memory before Columbus, and even the continent which he discovered is not called by his name. The inventor of printing is still unknown, and we cannot tell when, or very distinctly where, even Caxton set up the first English press; they were too busy.

And yet more might be expected in the way of history. Caxton himself was a compiler of history; the old monasteries, like Crowland, still contained men capable of writing annals, and of combining annals into chronicles, and of drawing out of chronicles the lessons of History. There is no *a priori* reason why the English history of the age should be sought in Bernard Andreas of Toulouse, or in Polydore Vergil of Urbino, or from the relations of foreign ambassadors. We conclude that the really important things, in which the critical change was, were things that did not come easily into historical contemporaneous exposition. Perhaps too it was hardly safe to write history when the printing-press might diffuse it to distances that would be dangerous; kings and courts would read, and woe to those who wrote what would not please them; or perhaps the revival of ancient literature engrossed the minds of those who, without such employment, might have continued the roll of ancient scholars.

It was not history alone, but theology and science also, that languished under the sudden revival of classical learning; men lost themselves in the history of early Rome who might have told us something worth knowing about their own England; or satisfied themselves with simple attempts to write fine Latin, not troubling themselves much as to whether they had anything to say; or with pronouncing eulogistic orations fit for kings and chancellors to read. But you will be thinking that is just what I am doing now; it is too obvious that a public statutory lecture is not a labour of love.

It is clear, then, not from the distinct enunciations of the time, but from the lessons of preceding and following reigns, what England wanted, and what it got in Henry VII. England did not want to become territorially one, as France, Spain, and Germany did before the new drama of politics began. England had long been territorially one; but it required constitutional and governmental consistency. It required an equability of the execution of law, the abolition of local partisanships, the abeyance of political questionings and controversies, thorough concentration in the hands of strong kings and able ministers. Such a king Henry VII was; such a king Henry VIII was during the better part of his reign, and to some extent Elizabeth was a successor of the same kind; strong in will, strong in wealth, strong in definite personal aims, but even stronger in the way in which their absolute power could be manipulated. It wanted too such things as, first, the vindication of a dynastic title to the throne by the victory of the king over the Yorkist party, by the union of family titles in his marriage, by the securing of every possible lawful guarantee to the succession, so that there might be no more Wars of the Roses; and consequent upon this, the enriching of the crown to such an extent as to make the King almost, if not entirely, independent of taxation for purposes of ordinary expenditure: or, secondly, the humiliation of the baronage by exhaustion, impoverishment, and reduction of numbers, leaving scarcely a trace of the divisions of party between the adherents of the two Roses, extinguishing the hereditary politics of the great houses and almost extinguishing the constitutional powers of the House of Lords. The concentration of power in the hands of a royal council of nominees was another result of the abject condition of the smaller and southern nobles. Even the greatest magnates were content to serve in the council as ministers and advisers, rather than to act up to their position constitutionally as members of a great estate in parliament.

Or, thirdly, the humiliation of proper ecclesiastical independence, which resulted from the isolation of Church power in the face of the throne. The papacy, which might have lent strength to the clerical estate, was itself weak, and changing its front, becoming more of an Italian power and less of an ecumenical arbitrator and influence, just at the moment when in England the clergy alone remained united enough to withstand the royal will. The clerical estate did not at first feel what was happening to it; for Henry VII had no quarrel with it, and possibly had no design of secularising the powers that should have been, first of all, moral and spiritual: he chose his ministers from churchmen, and made bishops of his ministers; until the bishops forgot that they were anything but ministers; sadly to the depression of religion, and sadly to the depression of learning, as the revival showed when it threw the learning of the country into the party of innovation, notwithstanding the influence of such men as Morton, More, Warham, Colet, and even Wolsey. The Church was sitting at the foot of a dynasty which ere long was to kick it over and to trample on it.

And fourthly, there was the people, weary of dynastic parties and politics, and set on a new pursuit of money-making, loving peace and hating taxation, and willing to endure anything from kings who would so far humour them: not altogether content, but discontented in a way that showed that heart and treasure went together: for, true as some of the charges of financial chicanery against Henry VII are, they owe their real practical weight to the fact that the people who groaned under them were rapidly growing in acquisitive power and economic wisdom ; they knew they had something worth conserving.

Thus England, with her once turbulent baronage depressed and silent, her Church kept subservient by the bestowal of political influence to the loss of religious power, her people in good humour so long as they were not overtaxed, was, under kings with determinate views, rich and ambitious, collected enough and manageable enough to enter as an efficient actor into the international drama. If she wanted leaders, guides, dictators in the coming struggle, she found them in the race which Henry VII founded and impressed with a strong will, a strong policy, and a strong energetic activity that gave her unmistakeably her place in modern history.

It would be very difficult, more difficult than in the case of a reign which has a plot, or a dramatic complexity or unity, to attempt a chronological account of the development of any principle or principles in this reign. I have said it is naturally divided into two great sections; and those two are subdivided in their turn.

I am afraid that, having spent all my generalisations in the preamble, I must in the remainder of this and the following lecture descend to the level of tabular computations, pedigrees, acts of parliament, and treaties. But we will hope for the best. As I am not aware that there is anything in the statute under which I am lecturing which makes it incumbent on me to offer on these occasions a substantive original contribution to history, I shall not apologise for taking my hearers over well known and well trodden ground.

The first point, of course, that occurs to us in a survey of the reign is the nature of Henry VII's title to the throne. On this no little controversy has been raised, and yet very trenchant opinions are given. We are not uncommonly told that Henry VII had not in his own person a shadow of hereditary right ; that is a view not uncommonly taken in the schools ; it is concise, and not hard to remember. But it is not exactly true. The whole question of the title of the house of Lancaster is a matter of dispute ; and the title of the house of York has always, curiously enough, been a point on which extreme legitimists and extreme advocates of popular right have agreed. Edward IV was heir general of Edward III, therefore he pleases the legitimists ; he came to the throne by a revolution, therefore he satisfies their extreme opponents. From a legal point of view it is different ; Henry VI was the heir, in the male line of succession, of Edward III, and also, by descent from Henry IV, was heir male of a new purchaser under a new and parliamentary title. Henry VII's title was of course very debateable. With relation to Edward III, he was not heir general, for that place belonged to the daughters of Edward IV : nor was he heir in the male line of succession, because the line was broken in the person of his mother. With relation to John of Gaunt, accepting the legitimation of the Beauforts by king, pope, and parliament, he was heir general ; whilst with reference to Henry IV, he can hardly be said to have been heir by collateral descent or heir at all.

But a question arises, on what analogy does the royal succession proceed. If on the analogy of a private estate, then Henry VII, as the nearest kinsman to Henry VI on the side of the purchaser Henry IV, had a claim to succeed : that claim was barred, it is said, by reason of the half-blood ; and to that the answer is given that the doctrine of the half-blood does not affect the royal succession. If, on the other hand, we take for analogy the descent of peerages limited to heirs male, there can be no question that the Earl of Warwick was the right heir through the line of York, irrespective of the line of Clarence ; but Warwick's claim and that of all the line of York was crossed by attainder : so also was the claim of Lancaster.

Well, all this argument serves not to prove that Henry VII had a hereditary claim, but to explain what he meant when he said he had. And, although not *very* important, it is as well to try to understand it. In truth, the law of royal succession, except where it has been settled by parliament, has never been very certain. Mary I and Elizabeth were akin by the half-blood only to Edward VI, yet they claimed hereditary right : disputable, perhaps, in itself, that position was strengthened by Henry VIII's will and acts of settlement. But Edward VI's will was set aside, and, although conflicting opinions did conflict, the crown descended in the natural and legal order to James I. There can, I think, be no doubt that Henry VII was legitimately Duke of Lancaster, if we suppose that such a title could pass through a female, notwithstanding the half-blood. It is quite possible to maintain that he was king of England by hereditary right.

Anyhow, he said he was. In his first address to the collected parliament, Nov. 9, 1485, he declared that he had come to the crown by just title of inheritance, and by the true judgment of God in giving him the victory over his enemy : the parliament accepted the fact, and passed a statute, in avoiding all ambiguities and questionings, ordaining, establishing, and enacting that the inheritance of the crowns of England and France, and so on, be, rest and remain, in the person of our now sovereign lord and in the heirs of his body. You may think that this was enough, but the pope clenched the matter in a bull of March 27, 1486, declaring that Henry was king not only by the right of war, and by the notorious and undoubted nearest title of succession, but also by the choice and vote of all the prelates, peers, magnates, nobles, and of the whole realm of England, and by ordinance, decree, and statute of the three estates of the realm called the parliament, for this purpose publicly and generally held. Perhaps the good old man swore a little too hard ; the accumulation of reasons may show that Innocent VIII had some misgiving.

Trebly certain, however, as all this was, by a scale of verdicts rising from the king's own assertion, to the parliament, to the pope, and to the judgment of the Almighty, the king would make assurance doubly sure by marrying the equally undoubted heiress of the rival line. He was espoused to Elizabeth of York on the 18th of January, 1486. He had not waited for her to be crowned with him ; he himself had been crowned on the 30th of October : and he was in no great hurry to admit her to a share of his dignity. She was not crowned until the 25th of November, 1487, and a great deal had happened in the meantime. I am not sure that the marriage was a very happy one. *A priori*, there was no reason why it should, although I believe it is certain that husband and wife were faithful. But Elizabeth was a silly woman, and Henry was not a sympathetic man. It was said she would have married her uncle, and certainly her marriage with Henry was a marriage of convenience. Their family politics must have been very much opposed; that is if we suppose them to have had any family affections at all, which is rather a strong effort to suppose in the case of kings and queens in the fifteenth century. But it is still more certain that they both had mothers alive, and there would be, according to all analogies, no love lost. Henry was an affectionate and obedient son to a pious and noble mother : Elizabeth had a mother who had not much sense or discretion, and was constantly in disgrace. The lady Margaret was strict and stately, and a woman of great experience, of many husbands and good advisers : the queen dowager may have learned, in the romantic seclusion to which her son-in-law consigned her, some lessons that would counteract the influences of the court in which she had reigned during her false, fair husband's lifetime, and she may have profited by the sweet uses of adversity ; but she inherited the characteristic features of her mother Jacquetta, and her own early career was one of vanity and foolish ambition. Any how, the lady Margaret had the upper hand; she kept her son straight and the court fairly pure, both during his wife's life and after her death, when the discipline was so close that poor Katharine of Aragon had to write home to her father that she could not get a mouthful of meat in Lent.

The history of the first half of the reign is the story of the struggle with which this trebly attested title to the throne was maintained ; a bloody story, it is true, but, take it all in all, scarcely to be compared with what goes before and follows. The struggle is not altogether dynastic ; it is not in all its details a contest of competitors ; and, in fact, each of the incidents in it has a shade of its own, common as the colouring seems at a distance. There were dynastic rivalries, there were personal intrigues and party blood feuds that made use of the dynastic rivalries to secure their victory or revenge, and there were administrative difficulties emerging in discontents which had little to do with either dynastic or hereditary struggles, but lent aid to both and borrowed pretext from both.

It is hardly necessary for me perhaps to recall to your minds what roots of dynastic bitterness still subsisted : but for the sake of clearness I will enumerate them. There was the Dowager Margaret of Burgundy, ready to say or do or believe anything for the sake of revenge ; there was the son of Clarence, a prisoner in the king's hands ; there were the De la Poles, the five sons of John, Duke of Suffolk, by Elizabeth of York, the eldest of whom had been recognised by Richard III as his presumptive heir ; and there was the doubt that hung over the death of Edward V and his brother Richard. It is curious to trace the intertwining of these really incompatible and inconsistent interests, and yet the only conclusion at which we can fairly arrive is the utterly desperate and unprincipled character of the Yorkist intrigues.

The first rising is perhaps the most desperate ; in April 1486 the Viscount Lovel, and Humfrey and Thomas Stafford, rose in Worcestershire ; the king, as Bacon tells us, thought it a mere rag of Bosworth : although at one time it seemed to be becoming formidable, it collapsed before the king's offer of pardon. Lovel escaped to the Duchess Margaret, Humfrey Stafford was executed, and Thomas was pardoned. Whether the original motive of the rising was the despair of the attainted leaders, or an intrigue of the as yet unreconciled Yorkist remnant, it is, by the agency of Lord Lovel, linked on with the second rising, that of 1487, in the name of Lambert Simnel. The idea of dethroning the new king by setting up as claimant a person, who pretended to be another person, who was well known to be a prisoner in the king's hands, is not only desperate but unprincipled, and, if I can say it without offence, not only unprincipled and desperate, but Irish. Lambert Simnel, a boy of twelve years old, the son of an organ-maker at Oxford, educated by a clever priest named Symonds, a name still known here, was presented to the

world as Edward Earl of Warwick; was received in Ireland
in February 1487, crowned at Dublin in May, brought to
England in June, and taken prisoner at Stoke near Newark
on the 16th of that month. In this most extravagant imposture the Yorkist remnant was thoroughly implicated:
the Duchess Margaret was represented by Martin Swart and
his men; the Earl of Lincoln, the cousin of Warwick, was
slain fighting for Simnel; the Lord Lovel, 'the dog' minister
of Richard, disappeared on the field, and Henry's suspicions
were so strongly excited against his mother-in-law that he
had to send her to a nunnery, and her son Lord Dorset to
the Tower. The third rising, that in Yorkshire in 1489,. was
not directly connected with the dynastic quarrel, but was provoked by the taxation voted in the preceding parliament:
Egremont, however, the leader of the rioters who killed the
Earl of Northumberland at Thirsk, was a Yorkist partisan,
and found a refuge in his exile with the intransigent Duchess
of Burgundy. After this we get on for three years without
overt trouble. The year 1492 is marked by another Yorkshire
battle, that of Acworth, between the Earl of Surrey and certain rebels, whose occasion of rising is not known; and it
would therefore be of little use to argue whether or no it was
connected with the imminent conspiracy for Perkin Warbeck,
or a result of local discontent of which there may have been
other cases not recorded at all.

Next comes the grand episode or tragedy of Perkin, which
covers seven years of disturbance, and connects the Yorkist intrigues with the social discontents in a way more striking than
any of the previous outbursts. I will only just indicate the dates
and points of contact. Perkin, whose prompters, wiser than
Lambert Simnel's, identified him with a claimant who could be
more easily counterfeited, and who is said to have been educated
by the Duchess Margaret to appear as her nephew Richard of
York, lands at Cork probably in 1491, certainly by February
1492. According to Bacon, he himself was not at first quite
sure who he was, a sort of doubt that has affected the minds
of his adherents ever since; but, if there was any hesitation on
his part, it must have been assumed for the purpose of ascer-

taining under what title he would be most likely to make a good start. After having exhibited himself for some time in Ireland and France without much affecting the political feeling of England, he returned to Flanders in August 1493, and his supporters for a while had to content themselves with intrigue. So thoroughly, however, was the scheme worked, that in 1494 the Yorkist lords in England sent over Sir Robert Clifford to ascertain the truth of the story that was put in Perkin's mouth; and Clifford, after having familiarised himself with the conditions of the party at home, was brought over to the king's side, turned against his employers and gave up their names to the government. Several of these were of the old Yorkist connexion, and were executed in the autumn of 1494; the greatest victim, however, was Sir William Stanley the chamberlain, brother of the lady Margaret's husband, the Earl of Derby, and one of the most able of the adherents who had placed Henry of Richmond on the throne. He had, from some idea apparently that his own services were ill requited, entangled himself in the plot, and, although he must have been undeceived as to the identity of the impostor, was not therefore spared; he perished in February 1495.

The increasing severity of the king's proceedings, and the success of his counter intrigues, thus warned the rest of the plotters that no time must be lost. In July of this year Perkin attempted a landing at Sandwich; this failing, he went again to Ireland, and then to Scotland, where he obtained full recognition and a noble wife. Henry was now pursuing the course which Edward IV had adopted with regard to himself in his boyhood, and endeavouring to obtain by diplomatic agencies the expulsion of the claimant from the territories of the neighbour princes. Early in 1496 he concluded a treaty with Burgundy, which forbade the entertainment of Perkin there; and in 1497, on the approach of a peace with Scotland, he negotiated for his surrender. The king of Scots, who in November 1496 had made a raid into the north in his behalf, was still prepared to support him and refused to betray him; but he thought it best to be rid of him: sent him to Ireland in July, and, after another invasion and defeat, concluded in September a truce for seven years, with which any overt support of the Pretender would have been incompatible.

Before the truce was actually signed Perkin's career was over. In its last act the plot connects itself with the social discontent. In the January parliament a new subsidy had been voted, and this, when it came to be collected, provoked a rising in Corn-wall. The men of Cornwall rose under the local hero Flam-mock, who, declaring the law on his side, and insisting on delivering a petition to the king, started them for London. Picking up as their leader a disaffected nobleman, Lord Audley, on the way, they pushed on to Blackheath, where they were defeated with great loss on the 22nd of June. The king's severity was somewhat arbitrary, but the effect was to quicken Perkin's movements and to point to the part of England where he was most likely to win support. He landed near Penzance in September, pushed to Taunton where he was put to flight, took sanctuary at Beaulieu, and on the 5th of October was surrendered to the king. Henry was inclined to spare him, possibly having some doubt as to his real identity; he was however imprisoned, and his escape in June 1498, his recapture, and further involvement in the plot which was made an excuse for implicating the Earl of Warwick, ended in the execution of the two in November 1499 : a cruelty for which other motives and other influences besides the sense of actual danger, are probably accountable.

After the extinction of these two, the false and the true competitors, the king had only the De la Poles to doubt about. The eldest of these, Edmund, who after his brother's death at Stoke had been the head of the branch, and who after his father's death in 1491 had been allowed to sur-render his estate of Duke and subside into Earl of Suffolk, quitted England with his brother Richard, in August 1501. What intelligence they may have had of the means by which Ferdinand the Catholic was likely to insure the succession of his son-in-law Arthur; or whether Edmund, who had been fairly well treated by the king, but had taken offence at a humiliation which he had, so far as it was real, brought upon himself, acted on mere impulse and carried his brother with him, we cannot decide;—they fled together to their aunt Margaret and constituted the dynastic bugbear for the rest of the reign. It was not the first escapade. Edmund had been indicted for murder in 1498; he had been pardoned, but notwithstanding had run away to Flanders. He had, however, then returned, apologised, and been received into favour. Just before the celebration of the marriage of Arthur he made this second flight; on the invitation of Maximilian, who was engaged in one of his unaccountable intrigues, he went from Flanders and joined him in Tyrol; the emperor offering to put him at the head of a large force to secure his rights, but really playing him as a card in his diplomatic game with Henry and Ferdinand. In 1502 he was planning an invasion of England to start from Denmark, and was implicated in the attempt on Guisnes which brought Sir James Tyrrell to the block. The same year Henry, by promising Maximilian 10,000 marks for his war against the Turks, prevailed on him to expel the English malcontents, whilst Ferdinand and Isabella as well as Lewis XII joined in urging the proscription. Edmund fled then to the Count Palatine, and in 1504, venturing into Guelders, was taken prisoner by the duke. The same year he was attainted with fifty-two of his adherents. The next year the duke gave him up to the Archduke Philip, under whose care he made some very brave show of claims against Henry VII for the estates and dignities of his father. Unfortunately for him, when the archduke, in 1506, was forced by the weather to land in England, Henry made a point with him that Edmund should be surrendered. Philip, who like his father was quite equal to playing a game of the sort that Henry loved, was on this occasion at the mercy of his host. He promised to surrender the prisoner on the strict understanding that his life should be spared. He was surrendered and his life was spared, so long as Henry VII lived. He came to the Tower in March 1506. In 1513 he was beheaded by Henry VIII. According to Lord Herbert, Henry VII had left it in charge to his son that, although he had sworn not to execute him, his successor should and would be wise to do it. Whether or no this is true, Henry VIII's cruelty was no doubt stimulated by finding Richard De la Pole, the younger brother, fighting in the army of France against him. Richard continued to be a thorn in the side of England—the White Rose of York as he was called—until in 1525 he was killed fighting for Francis I at Pavia.

Margaret of Burgundy lived until 1503, but her power and wealth as well as her zeal had diminished, and after the failure of Perkin she had been almost innocuous. This finishes the dynastic complications of the reign of Henry VII. In the next lecture I shall devote myself chiefly to the constitutional points of importance in connexion with domestic and foreign history.

XVI.

THE REIGN OF HENRY VII.

(April 25, 1883.)

IN the first of these two public statutory lectures, I opened my subject with some vain remarks on the want of attractiveness which may be said to characterise the personal and political history of Henry VII : and then, having divided the reign into two portions, nearly coinciding with the change of century, I very briefly marked the series of dynastic quarrels, struggles, and disturbances, the interest of which belongs mainly to the first half of the reign. There remains to us some investigation of the constitutional and diplomatic history of a period which falls between two great constitutional periods, and lays the foundation of a great diplomatic, political, and commercial fabric ; or rather I should say opens a great diplomatic, political and commercial period, which constitutes modern history in its general acceptation.

With regard to the constitutional history proper, nearly the same line may be drawn as in the other case, for, as only one parliament was called between the year 1497 and the end of the reign, the greatest part of what little constitutional history there is belongs to the earlier half. It cannot however be said that, with the exception of two or three very distinct pieces of legislation, and a very distinct purpose of raising and storing money, there is much constitutional material to deal with. There is a great poverty of record. The Rolls of the Parliaments tell us scarcely anything more than the dates of opening, the subject of the chancellor's address, the name of the Speaker, and the titles of the Acts passed, including the subsidies. There are no details of deliberation, or discussions on petitions. There are no Journals of either House ; there is nothing in the shape of writs or returns to indicate the composition of the House of Commons; and little, if indeed anything, to show how the composition of the House of Lords was able to influence legislation or administration. Not that we are entirely in the dark as to these matters: we know from the character of the Acts passed, and from the nature of the political measures of the reign, what sort of influences must have been at work: but we have no documentary details, nothing of personal or sensational import.

The ministerial changes of the reign are not in themselves important: the chancellorship, after having been held for a few months by Bishop Alcock, early in 1486 devolves upon Archbishop Morton, who is the minister of the reign: he retains the great seal as long as he lives, and during the rest of the reign it is held only by Dene and Warham, successively archbishops of Canterbury. The treasury in the same way sees few alterations; whilst Alcock is chancellor, Sir Reginald Bray is treasurer; under Morton, Lord Dynham; and from 1500 to 1509 Thomas Howard, who, as Earl of Surrey and Duke of Norfolk, remains at the head of finance during his life and leaves the position to his son, who holds it until 1546.

The tenure of these great offices by prelates and magnates of this sort, of course, implies that a great deal of the business of the country was conducted by means of subordinate officials; it also means that the king and his council took such direct part in it, that the nominal ministers had a somewhat diminished responsibility; and it probably means further, under Henry VII at least, that the king dealt directly with the subordinate officials without much concert with his nominal ministers. This is especially the case as the reign proceeds; during the first half Archbishop Morton, who was both a distinguished lawyer and, in popular opinion, a too active financier, really did ministerial work. After his death the king seems to have employed men like Empson and Dudley for measures which men like Archbishop Warham and the Earl of Surrey could certainly not have approved, but which they were helpless to prevent, and perhaps without courage to remonstrate about. There is not then much to be said about ministerial history.

The next point to note is the composition of the House of
Lords.   We are open to some risk of exaggeration in relation
to this, because of the slaughters and proscriptions connected
with the Wars of the Roses.   But, great as were the effects of
those quarrels on the personality of the baronage, the effect was
far greater on the political status and influence of the peerage.
It was attenuated in power and prestige rather than in numbers.   Even the bloodshed and attainder fall within a narrow
circle ; generation after generation perishes out of a few great
houses ; the majority continue in succession and either escape
ruin or soon recover.   It is as well to be particular as to this,
because it has a real bearing on the character of the Tudor
despotism or dictatorship; and we are liable to be misled both
by striking catastrophes and by untested generalisations.   If
we compare the last parliament of Edward IV with the first of
Henry VII, we find a great difference on the face of it : in
1483 there are forty-five lords summoned to parliament ; in
1485 there are only twenty-nine.   But for this diminution
the recent change of dynasty is only very partially the cause :
only six peers are attainted as yet, three of whom, the late
King Richard, the Duke of Norfolk, and the Lord Ferrers,
had fallen at Bosworth field ; and a fourth was Surrey, the son
of the Duke of Norfolk.   Of the other missing lords, some
had perished under Richard's own tyranny, some two or three
were now represented by minors, and about half-a-dozen seem
to have had their summons suspended during either the whole
reign or a great part of it.   Of these suspended peers, who all
reappear either in the later parliaments or in the first parliament of Henry VIII, the chief are the Ogle, Dacre, and
Scrope lords, who rule in the north country, and whose absence, which is not necessarily to be accounted for on political
grounds, is a point that has not been satisfactorily investigated.   In this way, however, not by proscription or execution, the list is diminished.   In the later parliaments not
only do many of these suspended peerages revive, the empty
places being filled by the restoration of the heirs of Richard's
victims, but even the attainders of 1485 are cancelled ; the
Howards return to favour and power in 1489, Ferrers in 1487,

Zouch in 1495; Lovel perishes, the viscount himself who fell at Stoke leaving only coheiresses.

A proof of what I have been saying is seen also in the fact that during the whole reign only five new peerages were created; one of these, the earldom of Bath, held by a foreigner, does not seem to have entitled its possessor to a summons; another is an Irish earldom, Ormond; the other three are Daubeny, Cheney, and Burgh. Yet notwithstanding this economy and the later attainders of the reign, the subsequent parliaments contain a lay peerage of forty members, which is not below the average of the century and was not increased materially until Henry VIII brought up the number of lay lords to that of the spiritual lords, before he finally reduced the latter to half their tale by getting rid of the abbots.

This point, like that of the composition of the House of Commons, on which we have no information, would be more important if we knew anything of the parliamentary history. As we do not, and find that the king in that august assembly had things very much as he pleased, we conclude, as we have other reasons for concluding, either that the assembled estates were cowed into complaisance, or else that they were too busy about other matters to care for the excitement of a quarrelsome debate.

There were seven parliaments during the reign of twenty-four years; and of these seven, one had three sessions and another two; six of them fall before the close of 1497, and before the end of Archbishop Morton's life. I think that, if we had nothing else to judge by, we should infer from this, that so long as Morton was minister the king retained the Lancastrian idea of ruling mainly through parliaments; whilst, during the nine years that followed the archbishop's death, he reigned chiefly through councils and held but one parliament. Morton was indeed a thorough Lancastrian, though not of the type of Archbishop Arundel. He had been the mainstay of the party in evil times, and the leader of intrigue under Edward IV and Richard III; but the old political game of Lancaster had long been played out, and, although Morton probably retained the attachment to forms which marked it to the last, he, either as a politician or as overborne by the king, was not in his financial administration faithful to the constitutional principle. This matter touches, however, a point of character in which master and minister alike suffer. Henry VII is constantly accused of avarice, and Morton to the popular mind is best known as the inventor of the fork, Morton's fork, the dilemma by which he proved the necessity of the benevolences, to the great dissatisfaction of the payers: if you spend much you have plenty; if you spend little you must have saved; out of your plenty, or out of your savings, you must pay.

I do not know that I am concerned to defend Morton, who was certainly not an avaricious man himself, and who, if he incurs a part of his master's shame, incurs it as a too faithful servant; but it is worth while speculating on Henry's own character for avarice. He was a man who had a fair intelligence and a fair knowledge of history: he had been very poor himself, and he had learned that poverty and want of economic governance had ruined the great house to which Henry V had imparted so much glory. He knew, from the first, that he must save in order to get on at all; and when he had begun to save, and when, by the forfeitures of the early years, he had managed to save to some purpose, not only did the love of money increase as the money itself accumulated, but he found it pleasant to rule without having to ask parliament for money; and finally found it pleasant, through Empson and Dudley, both to rule and to gather money without the trouble of parliament. However that may have been, the seven parliaments each had a subsidy or a budget; and the financial history is capable of a brief summary.

In the first parliament Henry succeeded in obtaining a revenue for life; Bishop Alcock had made a moving speech on the text, ' Good luck have thou with thine honour, ride on; ' in which he adduced the fable of the belly and members, the properties of bees, Isidore on the virtues of royalty, S. Ambrose in the Hexaemeron, and Ovid on the Golden Age; with the usual application. After the approval of the Speaker, the king addressed the Commons with a declaration of his title and pro-

mises of good government: and they responded with a liberal
vote of tunnage, poundage, and the custom on leather for
life ; apportioning £14,000 to the household, £10,000 odd to
Calais, and £2105 19*s*. 11*d*. to the wardrobe ; there was likewise an act of resumption.

In the session of 1487 Morton preached on 'Cease to do evil,
learn to do well :' a wonderful sermon in four heads, subdivided
each into three arguments, illustrated from Cicero and other
gentile philosophers, the moral of which was the vote of two
tenths and fifteenths, and a poll-tax upon aliens, payable at
the next Easter.   In 1489 the text was 'The eyes of the Lord
are over the righteous ; ' the sermon a miracle of subdivision :
the demand a lump sum of £100,000.   To meet this, by a
curious departure from the rule which is always supposed to
have been long established, the Lords, by themselves, grant
a tenth of their income from land ; the Commons, with the
advice and consent of the Lords, offer to raise £75,000 by a
tenth on lands not belonging to the lords, and twenty-pence
on every ten marks of goods.   This must have been seen to
be a dangerous experiment.   An attempt to collect the tax
caused the outbreak at Thirsk, in which the Earl of Northumberland was slain ; the sums collected from the Commons only
reached the amount of £27,000, and in the third session early
in 1490 the grant of a tenth and fifteenth was substituted for
the balance.   The object of the budget was the maintenance
of the army, which was being raised for the defence of
Brittany against France, a design which culminates and
terminates in the expedition to Boulogne in October 1492.
Before this expedition took place another parliament in the
autumn of 1491 and January of 1492 was asked for a vote.
Morton chose his text from Jeremiah, and his illustrations
from Sallust on the war with Jugurtha ; the bill was two
entire tenths and fifteenths, and a third if the king himself
should go to the war.   He did go to the war and made peace.
And this carried him on to 1495.

I should say here that the parliamentary grants were each
year supplemented by ecclesiastical grants made in the Convocations of the two provinces, and generally consisting of one

entire tenth from each; the tenth of the Southern province was about £10,000 and that of York about £3,000, I think. In 1489, when the estates, as we have just seen, proposed separate grants, the share of the Canterbury clergy was fixed at £25,000, about the same sum as that offered by the House of Lords; but it finally took the form of two entire tenths.

Well, the grants of 1491, which extended over a year, proved insufficient for the king's needs, and he had recourse to the exaction of a benevolence; indeed the commissions for the benevolence were issued before the parliament sat, and are supposed to have been authorised by a Great Council which sat in the June previous. This must have been a very liberal contribution, if the subscriptions of the country bore any proportion to the sum raised in London, which was £9682 17s. 4d. But I am not aware that any exact account of it exists. No doubt the commissions were executed in the usual way, but the authority given to the commissioners is only that they should intimate the king's purpose to the subjects, and move, exhort, and require them to assist him, in contemplation of the war with France. The commission was worked to some purpose, for the short expedition did not cost so much as might have been expected, and it was not until 1495 that the king found it necessary to call a parliament. It is then to this period that we must fix the application of Morton's fork, and to it Lord Bacon assigns the beginning of the penurious or saving habits which later on grew so strong in the king. I will just add that, as it was the subsidy of 1489 that provoked the riot at Thirsk, it was in all probability the subsidy of 1491 and the exaction of the benevolence that caused the struggle at Acworth in 1492.

In the parliament of 1495 no new tax was asked for; the archbishop's sermon was a lecture on law, which he divided into the law of Nature, the law of Nations, the Mosaic, Civil, Evangelic, and Canon law, with an application of the subject to the regulations of trade and commerce. These have a visible outcome in the sixty-five Acts that the parliament passed. For our present point but one of these is important; the tenth statute, on the Benevolence: divers persons have granted

benevolences for the expedition to France ; some have paid
what they promised, some have not ; the crown is empowered
to enforce the fulfilment of the promises. There can be little
doubt after this as to the great value of the benevolence ; no
further demand is made of the parliament, but the clergy
grant an entire tenth.

The next session was not so happy. It was in January,
1497 ; the archbishop lectured this time on Roman history,
Scipio, Curtius, Scævola, Regulus, Julius Cæsar and S.
Augustine: the occasion was really pressing : the Scots king
was making a succession of raids, and the invasion by Perkin
was impending. And a very exceptional grant was made, two
fifteenths and tenths first, and then another sum of the same
amount, reaching, according to Lord Bacon, to £120,000, and
no doubt contributing to the disaffection which brought the
Cornishmen to Blackheath and encouraged Perkin to land at
Penzance. The clergy are asked for £40,000, of which the
king remits £10,000. This is the last great tax of the reign :
peace is practically insured, and the king finds other ways of
enriching himself. Nevertheless, in 1502 the clergy pay a
tenth, or thereabouts, for the expedition against the Turks,
that is to say, the subsidy promised to Maximilian for his
expulsion of Edmund de la Pole ; and in 1504 the parliament
granted £40,000 as an aid on the knighting of the king's
eldest son and marriage of his eldest daughter. This was the
last session of the reign. Morton had died four years before ;
and archbishop Warham opened the parliament with a discourse
on moral philosophy from Aristotle and Cicero, of a much more
florid and less scholastic type than the sermons of his predecessor, and probably in better Latin.

This closes the financial history of the reign except in one
point. Henry VII is said to have left behind him £1,800,000
sterling, a great part of which must have been the result of
savings from royal demesne and forfeitures, but which was
partially, and in popular belief principally, accumulated by
exactions made by Empson and Dudley. These two men,
acting as members of the royal council and under the direct
control of the king, had reduced to a system the extraction of

money on false or exaggerated charges. They had revived old sentences and ancient worn-out claims, and had the king's connivance in exacting the pettiest sums. In the year 1504 so great was the outcry against them that the king, suffering at the time from illness and taking a spell of penitence, issued letters ordering that all who had any reason to complain of injury inflicted in the king's name, should come forward and have a hearing. But no real good was done, and the abuses continued to the end of the reign : the culprits had imprisoned men without chance of hearing until they had paid their fines ; they had compelled others to recognise themselves as tenants in chief and so liable for feudal aids ; they had refused livery of seisin to wards, except on payment of enormous reliefs ; exacted two years' income from outlaws before they could sue for pardons ; they had heard and disposed of matters that belonged to the courts of law, and had imprisoned and fined a jury. These charges against them are in exact parallel with the abuses practised by William Rufus and remedied by Henry I and in Magna Carta. Yet they pleaded royal authority and the letter of the law, and, when the time of vengeance came, as it did at the very opening of the next reign, they perished on a charge of conspiring to govern the king and council, very much analogous to that which had been brought against the Despensers two centuries before, not on the ground of their real offences.

The next point to take is the legislation of the reign, on which I do not propose to say much, as it would be very tedious to repeat the dates and occasions of the parliaments, whilst to go into the social questions touched by the new laws would be impossible. I will, however, take the principal measures in the order of time. It is not necessary to recur to the acts of attainder and restoration, which occupy so large a part of the pages of the statute book, further than to remark that, although it was doubtless a piece of legal pettifogging to antedate the beginning of the reign by a day in order to include Richard's supporters at Bosworth under the title of rebels, it can scarcely be said to have been an unreasonable proceeding in the new Conqueror to treat them as such. The

large number of forfeitures, and the large sums exacted as
fines on restoration, show that scarcely any amount of political
guilt was beyond forgiveness, if the repentance were accompanied by a handsome sum down. On the whole, where
society was just recovering from a condition in which nothing
was certain for two days together, and nearly every household
was divided against itself, anything like settled peace was
worth paying for, and the people generally justified by
acquiescence in fact, however much and rightly they might
in words complain of the mercenary policy of the court.
Parliament itself acquiesced without complaint.

Leaving then these acts out of sight, I will mention the
most important laws of permanent interest. In the session of
1485 were passed the act of succession, establishing the king's
title, an act which allowed the bishops to imprison incontinent
clergy without applying to the sheriffs to arrest them, and an
act against unlawful hunting. In 1487 the act which founded
the Court of Star Chamber was passed, as a remedy for the
evils of maintenance, the misconduct of sheriffs, and riots and
unlawful assemblies. The court so founded was to consist of
the chancellor, treasurer and privy seal, taking to themselves a
bishop, a lord temporal and the two chief justices. This tribunal,
which took its name from the Camera Stellata, the chamber
in which the council generally sat, subsequently developed
into a judicial meeting of councillors and peers which has a
great history of its own; but there is no reason to question
its historic identity throughout, or that this was the occasion
of its foundation. This is the great judicial measure of the
reign, and was intended to meet acknowledged evils.

Blackstone has recorded his impression that every act of the
reign was intended for the benefit of the exchequer; perhaps
we may allow that, under certain conditions, there is no price too
heavy to pay for peace and order. The chief acts of 1489 and
1490 are commercial; cap. 13 limits the benefit of clergy, which
is to be allowed only once to persons not in holy orders;
murderers are to be marked with an M., other felons with a T.;
and a second claim is not to be admitted unless the Letters of
Orders are produced. Cap. 19 forbids the pulling down of

'towns,' and laying to pasture lands previously in tillage and tithable : church and realm are alike impoverished by the devastation that is going on ; owners of farm-houses, to which a holding of 20 acres is attached, are bound to keep them in repair or forfeit half the profits to the king.   The great importance of this matter is the burden of the History of John Rous, the Warwick historian, who does not otherwise add to our knowledge of the reign.   These two statutes are of great social significance ; signs of the times of which men like Morton and More took heed.   Cap. 24, the statute for proclamation of fines, has had a reputation of greater importance than it deserves, being supposed formerly to have given the power of alienating entailed lands, and so allowing the great landowners to ruin themselves.   This Hallam shows to be a mistake, and the statute accordingly becomes a minor legal detail.

Most of the acts of the year 1491–2 are connected with the expedition to France, which came off in the latter year ; the securing of the rights of absentees who took part in it, and a number of restorations from attainder.   Those of 1495 have a greater reputation in the law books, and especially cap. 1, which enacts that persons going with the king for the time being to war are not to be attaint of treason therefore ; an act passed in a true spirit of equity, but, I fear, quite inadequate to secure its end in critical times.   Perhaps as a historical landmark and as enunciating a principle of public law it has its chief importance ; anyhow, it shows that the king felt himself so secure that he need not speculate for a fall.   Cap. 2 is a law on the disposal of 'vacabunds and beggars,' who are to be sent to their hundreds ; if a university man is found begging he must produce a letter of the chancellor identifying his status, or else must go as a 'vacabund.'   Cap. 17 forbids the taking of pheasants and partridges on other men's lands, an early definite game law on which I will simply observe that a popular error makes the introduction of pheasants much more modern than it was ; the canons of Waltham had pheasants in the eleventh century, by Harold's ordinance, every festival day from Michaelmas to Lent.

Another act, cap. 22, settled servants' wages, and that at a rate
which it would not be wise to mention to modern economists,
unless we presume there was a handsome margin for per-
quisites ; the wages, for instance, of a bailiff are 26*s*. 8*d*. a year ;
and those of the agricultural labourer 4*d*. or 3*d*. a day according
to the season, his meat and drink being assumed to be worth
2*d*. or 1½*d*. a day : perhaps the proportion was not so bad.
Most of the other acts of 1495 are what we should call private
acts ; the exceptions dealing with dishonesty in tradesmen,
sheriffs, officers and jurors.

The acts of 1497 are few and not important ; cap. 3 repeals the
wages act of the session of 1495 ; cap. 6 relieves the merchant
adventurers of England from the fines imposed by the merchant adventurers of London, who claimed, under colour of a
fraternity of S. Thomas of Canterbury, to tax them for dealing
in foreign marts : the most significant acts concern the money
grants.

This brings us to the last parliament, that of 1504. This
assembly passed forty statutes, some of them comprehensive
and historical enough, as cap. 34, which enumerates with names
and dates the successive revolts and conspiracies which had been
visited with attainder ; others are acts of reconciliation and
restoration.   The more important statutes I can only name
now ; cap. 14 is on maintenance and livery, increasing penalties
and extending the power of the Star Chamber ; cap. 15 is on
Uses, a step in the growth of the doctrine afterwards fully
enunciated in the statute of Henry VIII ; cap. 27 settles the
custom on wool taken at Calais for the payment of the garrison, to the amount of £10,022 4*s*. 8*d*. for the next sixteen
years.

Other statutes are interesting mainly in relation to details
of trade and to minute points of legal proceedings, and do
in their particulars throw light on a few social questions on
which light is much needed.   Still, on the whole, the survey of the legislation of the reign does not much impress
us ; in spite of the one or two really important notes we
have marked, there is no trace of a grand or constructive
genius such as might be looked for in the opening of a new

era ; it is really business-like and humdrum, the work of men who welcomed legislation only just so far as it helped them to get on steadily in the course, the quiet course which they had marked out for themselves. There is nothing, more-over, in the record, either of the financial or legal proceedings, that suggests any political struggles in the parliament itself ; the story that Sir Thomas More in a parliament in 1502 pre-vented the Commons from granting an aid for the marriage of Margaret, although told on good authority, falls to the ground, for the good reason that no parliament was held in 1502 and that in 1504 the grant was actually made. More probably was instrumental in limiting the sum. Outside of the circle of attainders and restorations very little was done which was likely to excite opposition or obstruction ; and as to the little that was done at all, it seems that Lord Bacon's dictum is too much to say for it : that such was the excellency of the king's laws that he may be justly celebrated for the best Lawgiver to this nation after King Edward I. It is not well to analyse the words of an express panegyric, but Bacon's theory of government must have been, to say the least, peculiar, if he overlooked the great statutes of Edward III on taxation and on church liberties, not to speak of the elaborate legislation of the next reign. Richard II was, however, no great lawgiver, and Edward III's good laws were mainly con-cessions to popular demands ; if the words I have quoted refer to the king's possible personal agency in legislation, they may have a meaning, otherwise not. I have already mentioned Blackstone's very different opinion, that all the laws were calculated for the benefit of the exchequer.

I must now pass on to the foreign transactions and negotia-tions of the reign, which are most important and most tedious ; most important because they are closely connected with the opening of the new drama, the equipment of England for her part on the stage ; most tedious because they go on without crisises and without issues, like a game at chess which has a charm only for an adept, or a well contested game at croquet which never comes to an end. If I cannot help being tedious about this, I will at all risks be brief.

At the opening of the reign of HenryVII there were, I think, only two points at which English foreign politics touched the interests of the continent, Brittany and Burgundy. Brittany Henry was, for substantial reasons of personal gratitude, bound to help; and a marriage with the heiress Anne, supposing that he was not obliged to marry Elizabeth of York, was a conceivable contingency. Burgundy under Maximilian was likewise involved in the alliances of Brittany; both were hostile to, or afraid of France which, under Anne of Beaujeu and Charles VIII, was rather preparing for than actually engaged in her scheme of aggrandisement. From 1485 to 1491 Brittany is the point round which English diplomacy moves. Maximilian is unable to go to war: Henry is unwilling to go to war; France is able and willing; but it requires at least two combatants to fight a respectable battle. Duke Francis, who had been Henry's friend in his exile, had been constantly opposed to Lewis XI, and was intent on securing the succession for his daughter. By receiving Orleans and Dunois in 1485, he had set himself against Anne of Beaujeu; in 1486 he had prevailed on the estates to settle the succession; in 1487 he had been openly attacked by Charles VIII, and had betrothed his daughter to Maximilian. Henry had not as yet moved; he was busy in negotiations all round, but he did allow Edward Wydville to collect volunteers for a campaign in 1488 against the French, followed, as Henry's few campaigns always were, by an immediate truce. That year Duke Francis died. For the three following years Henry talked of war, and war really went on occasionally as if it was stimulated by the little peaces that interrupted it. In 1489, Charles and Maximilian made peace at Frankfort, and Brittany joined. In 1490, Henry made a league with Maximilian and the Catholic Sovereigns to defend Brittany if it were attacked; in 1491 it was attacked and they did not defend it. That year Charles VIII took Nantes and married Anne of Brittany. Then, in fulfilment of his engagements, as well as in compliance with the wish of the nation, Henry, in good time, made his expedition to Boulogne in the Autumn of 1492, which ended in the peace of Etaples concluded in November.

The peace of Etaples is an epoch in more senses than one ; it was the most definite peace that had been made between England and France since the reign of Edward I. It was the closing of the Brittany business which had been the door by which England entered the arena of the new politics ; and it allowed Charles VIII to begin his Italian expedition, which usually is regarded as the starting-point of the new drama. Henry, moreover, made a great deal of money by it. It was to last during the lives of both kings, and practically did so. For, in 1498, after Charles' death it was renewed with Lewis XII, and notwithstanding jealousies, intrigues and counter intrigues, remained unbroken until the next reign.

Scotland, which had been and was still to be the facile tool of France, had a policy of her own during these years. James III, who recognised in Henry VII a friend and kinsman representing the Lancaster interest, which he had always supported, perished in 1488, and from that year to 1498 the relations of the two countries consisted of an uneasy succession of truces broken by inroads of the Scots into the north, which, during the period of the activity of Perkin Warbeck, threatened to develop into active warfare.

In 1491, we find Henry intriguing to get the young king James IV into his own hands, as Henry IV had James I : in 1493, a treaty for seven years was concluded but not kept : in 1495, the marriage of James with the king's daughter Margaret was proposed. In 1498, by the good offices of the Spanish ambassador, a treaty for seven years was concluded which was shortly turned into a peace for life, cemented by the marriage which really came off in 1502. Thus, about the same time, although by a different process, the king secured himself, so far as negotiations could secure him, in peace for life with his two national and ancestral foes. In 1502 was made a treaty of perpetual peace with both.

The direct negotiations between England and Spain, which, like those between Henry and Maximilian, arose on the Brittany business, began, in 1489 and 1490, with the alliance for the defence of the duchy, and so early comprised a purpose of marriage between Arthur and Katharine of Aragon. The marriage itself was not concluded until 1501; and, on Arthur's death early in 1502, the scheme for her marriage with Henry was set on foot; out of which so great results were to come. The design was not, however, carried into effect until the next reign; and the intervening years are full of correspondence on points connected with dowry and dispensation. The earlier years of the Spanish negotiations contain no incidents independent of the general action of Europe, in which Henry, like Ferdinand and Isabella, was content to play a waiting game.

I have left to the last the negotiations with Flanders, first under Maximilian, and after the year 1494 under his son Philip. These, so far as they concerned the dynastic quarrels, are so closely interwoven with the French and Breton relations, that I need not recur to them.

In 1496, was concluded the great commercial treaty called *Intercursus magnus*, which was intended to secure the freedom of trade intercourse between England and the Netherlands, as well as the exclusion of Perkin Warbeck. The peaceful relations were not broken even whilst Maximilian and Philip were lending questionable support and making promises to Edmund de la Pole. The network of the family alliance, by which Ferdinand and Maximilian were uniting the great inheritances, might have led to a wavering of the balance under a more energetic hand than that of Henry; but, even if it had been endangered, the danger would have been averted by the arrangement concluded by the archduke on his forced visit to England in 1506; this, besides some advantage gained in the way of commerce which led the Flemings to call it *Intercursus malus*, not only secured the surrender of Edmund de la Pole, but opened a series of fresh marriage schemes, which entertained the king during the short remainder of his life. The most important of these was the engagement of the lady Mary to the archduke Charles; but the king himself, who had lost his wife in 1503, was in the matrimonial market, and his adventures contribute the one semi-comic element to this severely business-like reign.

The death of the archduke Philip in 1506, the advanced

years of Ferdinand, and the proved impracticability of Maximilian, seemed to be opening out a career for a new leader in Europe; and many eyes were turned on Henry. He was willing enough to marry, perhaps the queen dowager of Naples; perhaps the archduchess Margaret; the latter marriage would have given him a direct hold on the Netherlands and a possible claim on the regency of Castile, especially if the young Charles should become his son-in-law. With two such competitors, however, as Ferdinand and Maximilian the diplomatic game was slow and cautious. And in the midst of it Henry died, on April 21st, 1509.

I cannot now presume to enter upon two remaining aspects of the reign, the social and the religious, although both of them furnish us with details not less important, and scarcely more entertaining than those which we have now gone through. As for the social history, I can only say that it must be read chiefly in the Statutes concerning trade, labour, and agriculture, and the slightly increasing store of such letters as we have in the Paston and Plumpton collections: the letters of Erasmus and the scholars of the time, More's Utopia, and a very few other sorts of materials, add a little to the light that is beginning to shine towards the close of the reign. Ecclesiastically Archbishop Morton's design of visiting and reforming the monasteries was a partial anticipation of the much greater scheme of Cardinal Wolsey. There is little or no religious persecution; there is little or no literary or ecclesiastical activity, although there are, now and then, small flashes of anticipation of what is coming: the reign of Henry VIII would not in any respect have been what it was, if he had not had a predecessor like Henry VII; but, such as it was, it gathers up and concentrates in itself all the interest that would properly belong to that of his father.

I have said enough about the political importance of the reign, and perhaps in the last lecture more than enough about personal incidents and characteristics. To the last, however, Henry VII remains somewhat of an enigma to us. Was he a great king? If it be enough to constitute a great king, to have reigned twenty-four years without a single important

war, and to have united in apparent peace a number of
dynastic forces that had been struggling for a century; to
have found England weak and poor, and divided against herself and isolated in Europe, drenched in blood and impotent in
internal government; and to have left her rich, and at peace
with herself, and growing in contentment, and well administered; having a place in the councils of Europe second to
none, courted on every side and able to make her weight felt
perceptibly in the balance; to leave a full treasury and an
uncontested title to his successor, and a reputation stained by
nothing that in the eyes of his contemporaries bore the guilt
of crime; then the reign of Henry VII was a great reign, and
perhaps Henry VII himself was a great king.

If we look rather on the moral of the reign we may somewhat modify our opinion. We look in vain for anything that
would constitute him a hero or a benefactor. We find no great
fault except his avarice, but even that cannot be regarded as
the vulgar appetite for hoarding: and avarice, in a king who
keeps within the letter of the law and the constitution, is perhaps really, and certainly in a land which had suffered from royal
prodigality for three centuries, a less fault than extravagance.
Even avarice is not always fatal to the heroic character, if
there be the rudiments of the true heroic character there
at all. Henry VII was a virtuous man, sober, temperate,
and chaste, withstanding great temptations to vice and an
abundant store of loose example. His household was kept
frugally and severely; all his advisers, except Empson and
Dudley, were men of character unstained, if not energetic for
good. For one better or greater king, there are in European
history fifty smaller and worse. But still—is there any of
that self-denying devotion which gives itself for the people?
Is there any true conception of the duty of a shepherd of the
host? Is there any impulsive well-doing? I can see none.
I see a cold, steady, strongly-purposed man, patient, secret,
circumspect; with not many scruples, yet not regardless of
men's opinions; very clear sighted; very willing to wait for
reconciliation where there is a chance, and not hasty where
vengeance is the only course; but ruthless where his own

purpose is directly endangered, and sparing neither friend nor
foe where he is not strong enough to rely on himself alone.
It may have been a nature too cold to care for popular love;
or too self-contained to condescend to court it; there is no
evidence that Henry VII ever dreamed of winning it. In his
domestic life there is little that calls for remark. He cannot
have cared much about his wife or any of her relations: he
honoured and trusted his mother, and may have been in
some matters guided by the advice which natural acuteness
and varied experience helped her to give him. But this is
a minor matter, and would count for little in the picture of a
man of whose real character we knew enough to enable us to
judge of him. I said in the former lecture there is nothing
attractive about him, with all his virtues and all the great
consequences of his work. There is surely always something
attractive about either greatness or goodness, unless they fall
in an age so lost to itself as to be unable to appreciate either.
And the opening century, whilst to some extent it shared
the king's character, was scarcely so lost as that.

I conclude: like many other things on which it has been
my lot all these years to give public statutory lectures, this
reign and this king, the more we study them, give the more
ground for questioning our own judgments, and the extent
and character of our knowledge: the Cheshire cat in
Alice's adventure faded away into a grin; we grow more
and more impatient of generalisations and idealisations, and
more and more intolerant of dogmatic assumptions, the longer
we study them. Perhaps this may be the whole lesson, and
if it is, it is a lesson that can never be too thoroughly learned
or too often repeated.

XVII.

A LAST STATUTORY PUBLIC LECTURE.

(May 8, 1884.)

A LAST statutory public lecture ought, I suppose, to combine the characteristics of an *Apologia* and a *Symposium*; or perhaps, in more modern fashion, as befits a Professor of Modern History, the qualities of an after-dinner speech, of the defence and confession of a penitent, of the last will and testament of one who has something to leave. I do not know that, in what I am going to say, I shall strike exactly on any one of such notes; but there are some things that I ought to say, some that I wish to say, and some that I can say to fill up the prescribed three-quarters of an hour. I will ask for your tolerance and sympathy for what I have to say, whether in jest or in earnest; for you will believe me when I say that even the last statutory public lecture is a matter which mingles pleasure with pain, in no slight measure of both.

Seventeen years ago, in the address which I delivered in this room by way of inaugural lecture, and eight years ago, when I was approaching the end of my first decade of office, I ventured to make the statutory public lecture an opportunity of stating what seemed to me to be points of interest touching the study of History, in relation to persons, subjects and methods of teaching. The inaugural lecture contained, as was very natural, some crude and carelessly treated material; I said some things which were misunderstood, and some which I had better not have said at all; probably both are forgotten by this time. But, as to the main object of the lecture, the stating of the proper part which the teaching of History has in mental education, I have not changed my mind, nor am I inclined to do so now. I still think that the aim of Historical teaching is the training of the judgment to be exercised in the moral, social and political work of life ; and that, as an instrument of education, such teaching will seek its fittest material in those portions of History which have enough of living interest to stimulate research, but have not enough of immediate practical importance to rouse political partisanship ; that accordingly we do best when we begin at the beginning of the history of the forces and materials out of which modern life has grown, and that, in so doing, we have a distinct advantage over those who start to work backward from the immediate interests of to-day. I do not now wish to enter on controversy about this ; I know that it is not uncontroverted ; I state it, however, as a principle on which I have taught, and have believed myself justified by results. As I stated it in my first, I stand by it in my last lecture.

The lectures of 1876 were given after several years of experience, during which I had learned my own weakness, and begun to find the way in which I trusted that I might be really helpful : years during which the study of History had greatly developed here, and in which we had tried to frame, and I think had succeeded in organising a method of combined teaching, which brought into play the ability of a considerable number of enthusiastic and laborious tutors, and which resulted not only in enlarged and improved schemes of reading, and enlarged and more highly valued distinctions in the way of class and prize, but also in very valuable and important work done for History in the way of research and in the production of books. At that time too, the University was engaged in taking stock of its means and requirements, in preparation for meeting the Commission which was understood to be impending, and which has since worked changes in our constitution, collegiate and academic, which are now only beginning to develope results. I attempted, in the two lectures which I delivered then, to take a comprehensive survey of the condition of Historical Study, so far as it affected our own material and method, both within and outside of our

own borders, and to express certain views which I hoped
might find favour in the expected reforms.

Without following the same plan, I propose now to take
up, and, in the desultory way which is almost necessary under
the circumstances, to remark upon some of the more important points which have varied our own history, as academic
and historic workers, since that time. If I speak too much of
myself, I will ask you to believe that it is not because I set
an especially high value on my own services, for none knows
or feels better than I do how much more I ought to have
done, or how little my share has been in what has been done ;
still less because I undervalue the labours of my fellow-
workers, who have had far more personal anxiety and more
direct and more measurable responsibilities than I have had ;
it is mainly because the retrospect of my own work is forced
upon me by the circumstances of my departure from Oxford ;
also because, not only as Professor, but in several other capa-
cities, as Delegate of the Press, Curator of the Bodleian,
a Member of Council, and as having a share too of the representation of our Oxford School of History before the outside
world, I have had work to do and a place to fill which it
would be very mock humility on my part to leave out of
sight now that I am parting from such a home as this.
You will pardon me, I hope and trust, because it is the
last time.

A word first on our losses and our gains : and our losses
and gains are so intimately bound together that I must take
them in the order in which they most naturally occur to me,
balancing one another by a law of compensation inseparable
from all progress : it is surely a matter of congratulation that
since 1876 we have so much enlarged the number of our
students that our class lists contain nearly double the tale of
names, and that, as a road to an honourable degree in arts, our
study is now followed by nearly, if not quite, as large a body
of pilgrims as any of the other honour schools. This is the
result of no lowering of the standard of the History Examination, but of the greater educational vivacity of the
University, of the increased interest felt in the country at

large in historical work, of the efforts of some of the Public
Schools to make a beginning of such work a part of elementary education, but chiefly I think to the zeal, and self-
denial, and labour, and personal sympathy of the History
tutors. The work is, so far as it is the bringing to bear of
historical influences, interests, and inducements on the individual students, entirely their work ; and their work also
mainly in the other bearings of our common design, in which
professorial teaching or other professorial working could be at
all utilised. I wish to say this distinctly, and shall say it
again before I close ; all the more distinctly, because I, for
my part, am well aware that, in many details of organisation
and division of labour, my opinions have differed from theirs,
and I would like them to remember that, where we have
differed, it has not been for want of sympathy on my part, or
for any wish to spare myself.

Since 1876 in the body of tutors we have had some few
losses ; our dear friend the Dean of Winchester has left us for
a place of more dignity, and more freedom for the working of
his unrivalled and peculiar gifts : we are sure that he will
never be idle, and whatever he does will be done well.
Mr. Jayne has left us, also for a place of honour and responsibility, where his presence will be to us the earnest of
sound work in our own as well as in the other departments
of clerical education, and where he has already enlisted the
help of one of the most successful and zealous of the younger
men who have followed our line here. Of our dear friend
Laing, whose absence we feel more and more every term,
what can I say, but that we trust and hope that one day
he may be restored to us and to the studies that he was so
wonderfully qualified to develope and adorn ? Well, with
these home losses we have counterbalancing gains in the
enlisting of new men. The continued vigour of our veterans
is hardly to be called a gain, but it is a matter of profound
congratulation : I rejoice to think that the Chichele Professor, Mr. Owen, and Mr. Boase are as young, and zealous,
and kind, and sympathetic as they ever were, and that is as
much as the best and kindest of men can be ; seventeen

years of a very trying Regius Professor have not worn out their goodwill.

Another point I will mention, though I need not tell too much of the secrets of the Seminar: there is a great gain to us in the spontaneous working of the little clubs of Historical debate which have sprung up within the last few years, collegiate and inter-collegiate. I will not talk of comparing great things with small, but I rejoice to see in these a continuity, with differentiation, of the old circles which I remember when I was an undergraduate and a bachelor: I was always proud of having been for a little time secretary of the Hermes, which Archdeacon Palmer, and, alas! how few besides, must recollect as a very small and earnest and affectionate literary brotherhood, well to be remembered as a seed-bed in the sowing time, not only of germinating ideas that spring and die with or without fruit-bearing, but of high sympathies and dear friendships that grow stronger and immortal by age. I would augur for our little History clubs as fair a future.

Another gain, which is still perhaps a matter for augury, is the formation of the Oxford Historical Society ; if the choice of subject, singularly and universally attractive, rich in materials and full of varied interest, if the zeal, ability and perseverance of the promoters, and the sympathy of all historical students, can secure success, the Society has a most happy future in prospect.

But the mention of it suggests irrepressibly the memory of the man whose genius inspired the idea, and of whom the Society is in this place the fittest possible monument. John Richard Green, the dear friend of many amongst us, has left behind him a name which cannot soon be forgotten. His books are by themselves the warrant of the fame which he so widely gained ; the extent of his reading, the power of his grasp, the clearness of his insight, the picturesque reality of his narration, are patent to all who are capable of judging. We, who knew him better than the world of his readers, know too of his unwearied industry, his zeal for truth, and the inspiring force of his conversation. For twenty years he and I were close friends ; with countless differences of opinion, we never quarreled ; with opposite views of the line of history and of the value of character, we never went into controversy ; his letters were a delight and honour to me ; I believe that my visits were a pleasure and in some way a comfort to him. In the joint dedication of his book I confess that I received a compliment which I place on a level with the highest honours I have ever received.

I am tempted to modify the excessive dryness, as the Edinburgh Reviewer puts it, of my discourse, by telling the story of our first introduction to one another, chiefly because it has been made the subject of a myth which has made us both a little, or not a little ridiculous. Some of you I dare say remember a paragraph that went the round of the September papers years ago ; and told how two persons, a stout and pompous professor and a bright ascetic young divine, met in a railway carriage ; how the burly professor aired his erudition by a little history lecture (an anticipation of the informal instruction of the Commissioners) on every object of interest that was passed on the road, and how each of his assumptions and assertions was capped by an answer from the ascetic divine which showed that he knew it all and knew it better. The professor at last, exasperated by the rejoinders, broke into a parody of the famous address of Erasmus, ' aut Morus aut diabolus,' substituting for Morus ' Johnny Green.' Could this be true ? It was in 1863 that we met ; I was not yet a professor, he had not begun to wear the air of an ascetic. We were invited to Wells, to a meeting of the Somerset Archæological Society, to stay with a common friend whom you will have no difficulty in identifying. I was told, ' if you leave the station at two you will meet Green, and possibly Dimock,' the biographer of S. Hugh whom I knew already. I knew by description the sort of man I was to meet ; I recognised him as he got into the Wells carriage, holding in his hand a volume of Renan. I said to myself, ' if I can hinder, he shall not read that book.' We sat opposite and fell immediately into conversation. I dare say that I aired my erudition so far as to tell him that

I was going to the Archæological meeting and to stay at Somerleaze. ' Oh then,' he said, ' you must be either Stubbs or Dimock.' I replied, ' I am not Dimock.' He came to me at Navestock afterwards, and that volume of Renan found its way uncut into my waste-paper basket. That is all ; a matter of confusion and inversion ; and so, they say, history is written. Well, perhaps a friendship between two historical workers may be called a historic friendship and, to be historical, should gather some of the mist of fable about its beginning : anyhow it was a friendship that lasted for his life, and the loss of which I shall never cease regretting.

Mr. Green's death is one of our greatest losses, but not the only one. In Sir Thomas Hardy the whole world of historical students lost a leader, a counsellor, and a friend ; whose services it is impossible to overrate. Practically the founder of the series of national Chroniclers to which I at all events, and our school here, owe so much ; a man full of carefully stored and readily imparted knowledge; full of business and as full of kindliness, to every Oxford student, of record or of chronicle, he was a most willing and ready helper. Soon after him we lost Mr. Brewer, who shared with him some of the most important sections of his work, and who added to his labours as a collector and arranger of record, those of an indefatigable writer and faithful, energetic, and stimulating teacher. Then we lost Dr. Pauli, the man who made English History a living study on the continent ; the most faithful and fair-minded of investigators, bound to me by peculiar bonds of friendship, and to Oxford by a number of ties ; an honourable recognition on our part, and a grateful affection on his. In Dr. Guest we have lost not indeed an Oxford man, but an Oxfordshire scholar, whose devotion to our studies, and whose only half completed labours, are well deserving to be had in remembrance. If I were able now to go beyond our immediate limits, I should say a word about Mr. Carlyle, but it would take me too far afield, and it is perhaps even a presumption in me to name him at all, or to claim for History a champion whose exploits are in all the regions of literary life.

But, although we grieve over personal and special losses, the work in which we are engaged goes on without flagging. The accumulation of historical literature since 1876, within and without our own particular range, has been remarkable for extent and interest. I cannot attempt to enumerate even the more conspicuous additions to our store, and it would be invidious to make a selection except in reference to our own share in the work. The Government publications, however, I may say, continue to maintain and even increase their value and interest: Mr. Gairdner, who has succeeded to Mr. Brewer's position, is giving us annual instalments of the history of Henry VIII, full of extraordinary revelations: before the year 1900 it may be possible that some one of us, gifted with strength, sight and perseverance, may write a complete history of the most critical of all reigns. Mr. Rawson Gardiner, a man who should be claimed and must be reclaimed for Oxford, is working, like a great constructive historian as he is, at the next most critical epoch. Mr. Creighton, even more entirely our own, has given us a splendid instalment of a great work which places him at once in the forefront of our phalanx. Mr. Freeman has completed his History of the Norman Conquest by the addition of the History of William Rufus. Mr. Fyffe has begun what will be a standard book on later history. I myself have finished my contributions, in a third volume, to Constitutional History; have edited six stout volumes of Chronicles in the Rolls series; and in the Appendices to the Report of the Ecclesiastical Courts Commission have put together a mass of matter, which, whether or no it is worth the paper on which it is printed, is both true history and the result of hard work: of other designs, the accomplishment of which my removal from Oxford will probably prevent, I can scarcely speak: but I hope that I may find time to complete two or three things on which I have made considerable progress, a fourth volume of Councils, an edition of William of Malmesbury, a second series of Select Charters, and possibly a sketch of the Constitutional History of the Reformation. I am, as I warned you, running off into my own concerns. Mr. Tozer's beautiful edition of

Finlay's Greece, Mr. Hodgkin's Italy and her Invaders, Professor Rogers' Extracts from Gascoigne, and two new volumes of the History of Agriculture, the collections and comments of Dr. Vigfusson and Mr. York Powell, Mr. Kitchin's third volume of French History, Mr. Sidney Owen's Selection of Wellesley and Wellington Dispatches, not to speak of the works in which History claims an equal share with Language or Law, testify to the zeal which the Delegates of the Press have encouraged in the same direction. Outside of our lines, time would fail me to tell of Mr. Skene's completed labours on Early Scotland, of the interesting and suggestive work of Mr. Seebohm, of Mr. Elton's searching and comprehensive examination into the history of Primitive Britain; or going further ahead, of the immensely valuable editions and republications of the Laws and Chronicles of Germany, now proceeding under the management of Dr. Waitz, and full of illustration of the history of the common institutions of the German races.

It is most gratifying to a student of the institutions of England to find that in the literature of more distant nations the study of our constitution is taking an important place. I cannot refrain from expressing the great pleasure which it gives me to receive, from time to time, heavy volumes and light pamphlets of dissertations on the subjects at which we have been at work here, from scholars in Germany, Russia, Denmark, France, Italy and America, who read and criticise and utilise our books. From Berlin we hear of Dr. Gneist, re-issuing and rewriting on his old subject; from Munich, of Dr. Liebermann re-editing the Anglo-Saxon Laws for the Bavarian Academy; from Vienna we have Dr. Budinger's lectures on the Englische Verfassungs-Geschichte; from Parma Signor Cardon's Svolgimento Storico; from Würzburg Dr. Schanz's Handelspolitik; Sickel doing the same work at Göttingen; Brunner at Berlin; Kovalefski and Vinogradoff in Russia; Steenstrup in Denmark; and in America, where our study has taken root with remarkable and most promising vigour, the clusters of searchers, such as the men of the Johns Hopkins University, and to specify particularly, Mr. Bigelow, the author of the work on *Anglo-Norman Procedure*, and the collector of the *Placita Anglo-Normannica*. Well, and let me confess—I hope that I have not been guilty of dishonestly receiving honours meant for other people—let me confess, that it has been exceedingly pleasant to me to receive from the Academies of Germany their recognition that the labours of the Oxford school have not been thrown away. I am very proud to be the recipient of diplomas signed by Döllinger and Giesebrecht, by Curtius, Pauli, Ritschl, and Dove, and to be numbered among the members of the American Academy.

But it is time that I should go on to another point. Since 1876 we have gone through the throes of a Commission and begun the struggles of a reorganisation. There is no reason why I should either speak or be silent about the general conduct of the Commission or the probable working of its results, except in relation to our own study and to the character of Professorial work as likely to be affected by the changes that are coming or come. I could have wished that the Commission had had more sympathy with literary and historical studies, that it had shown more appreciation of the true character of Professorial teaching, that it had seen, more distinctly than the new statutes seem to show that it did see, the imprudence of arranging the duties of Professors, the number and character of their lectures, not according to the nature of the subject but according to the amount of stipend forthcoming in the several cases. It surely was not necessary to treat the idle Professor as the typical Professor; it surely might have been enough to take the best means to secure a good Professor and have left him to work, not nominally but really, in the way in which he knew he could do the most good. Surely the idle professor, the *chimaera bombinans in vacuo comedens secundas intentiones*, should have been caught before he was tortured. No man has a greater capacity for idleness than I have, nor a greater desire of rest; sometimes I think the love of idleness is the greatest spur to exertion: anyhow I have been made to work, even without the Visitatorial Board. But what I want to say is this : it is possible in certain subjects to carry on research and elementary teaching together; it must be so in logic and grammar; in mathematics, possibly, although there it must be more difficult; in language, if the pupils are forward, it must be feasible: but in abstruse philosophy and in minute historical research it is not possible to do both things easily and at once. An arrangement of occasional epideictic lectures, ordinary elementary teaching in class, and informal instruction out of class, is symmetrical enough and useful enough where it can be applied, but it is not of universal application, or suited to Professors of all calibres. Restricting my remark to my own study, I will say, if an Oxford Professor of History is to be a man to be trusted to maintain the reputation of his University, to keep abreast with foreign scholars, and to conduct research on his own account, he ought to have been left with some discretion as to the management of his teaching. I have often felt, when I was busy with some matter that required concentration of thought and continuity of investigation, that I would rather have broken into my line of work by going and giving a lecture in Euclid or Algebra, than by coming down to an elementary discourse, in which, from the very affinity of the subjects, I should be constantly tempted to revert to the minute point on which my special labours in my study were fixed, to the confusion of the class and to the damage of the subject that I had to treat before them. It was in order to avoid this that for some years I wrote out my lectures before term began; a plan which has obvious drawbacks, chiefly in what is called losing touch with the class. Afterwards I lectured on texts rather more freely; latterly, as my classes regularly diminished, I took up more out-of-the-way subjects, and very nearly succeeded in getting rid of my classes altogether; in the end I have reverted to my first plan. Well, perhaps I never was fit for the place; anyhow, on the now stereotyped plan of the Professoriate, it is as well that I should go. I am told that the great historical works of the great foreign professors have been accomplished by men who have done much elementary lecturing and much informal instruction. That is true, but it is to be remembered that the great German professors have the power and the right to

direct the studies of their pupils, classes and individuals, to
the specialised and differentiated details of their own subject,
not merely to general class examinations in which all the candidates are expected to show the same sort of knowledge derived
from the same sort of books. What I wanted from the Commission was not less work but more liberty; what I succeeded
in getting was a little more elasticity of tether. But I will
not grumble any more: it is over; both the evidence, volu-
minous and appreciative, the formal audience, so redolent of
sympathy and profound attention on the part of the Commissioners, the lively meetings of council and committee, and the
truly charming debates of the professors and tutors : let them
have the light that never was on sea or land, in the sweetness
of memory,—a consecration, a professor's dream ; at all events
we have a system of faculties, informal instruction, and a
visitatorial board.

But let us go on to more serious things than these. I have
spent nearly eighteen very happy years in Oxford : holding
the office for a longer period than any of my predecessors
except Spence, who was professor for twenty-six years, Dr.
Nowell, who was professor for thirty years, and Dr. Nares, who
occupied the chair for twenty-eight years. The principal
event that touches the constitutional position of the Professorship during my occupation is its final and complete connexion
with Oriel College. Of the professors before me, three, Dr. Beeke,
who was in office during the early years of this century, and
two better known men, Dr. Arnold and Mr. Halford Vaughan,
had been fellows of Oriel. The Ordinance of 1857, passed
nearly at the end of Mr. Vaughan's tenure of office, allowed
Oriel College to undertake the payment of a considerable sum
in augmentation of the annual income provided by King
George II, which augmentation might be exchanged for a
fellowship of the College : and by a University Statute of
1859 a new body of regulations was provided for the conduct
of the professor. Under these Mr. Goldwin Smith and I have
held office ; he being, as fellow of University, ineligible for
the Oriel Fellowship, became by election after his resignation
an honorary fellow, and I was in 1868 elected to the fellowship

which I still hold: henceforth the Regius Professor will, under the Commissioners' Statutes, be a Professor Fellow. Whilst I look back with pride and gratitude on the honour which the College conferred on me so early in my career as professor, and with a lifelong pleasure on the friendships that my connexion with Oriel enabled me to form, I fear that I have been a very unprofitable member of governing body and educational staff: I console myself with the reflexion that there are some minds, which, in some situations, acquit themselves of their responsibilities most satisfactorily by never getting in the way. Non-obstructiveness is not the highest degree of efficiency, but there are worse faults. Anyhow my successor will have a chance in this line of work of approving his superiority to what has gone before.

The fact that two of my predecessors are alive and well is a matter of congratulation: Mr. Halford Vaughan and Mr. Goldwin Smith have both conferred on the Professorship an honour which I am glad to recognise. Both, eminent as scholars and political thinkers, lectured during the sixteen years of my absence from Oxford; there are some, however, left who remember Mr. Vaughan's lectures under the old system, the soundness and learning displayed in them and the stimulus which they supplied to the study of Modern History at the moment that it was taking its place among the recognised subjects of the Schools. It was whilst Mr. Vaughan was Professor that the School of Law and History was organised ; Mr. Goldwin Smith, as I said, lectured under the new arrangements of 1859 and was examiner in 1862. I rejoice to know that on neither of these gentlemen has the study of the subject, that I have lived and worked for, produced any exhausting or debilitating effects ; and, when I consider the case of my successor designate, 'the Regius Professor elect,' and think how many books he has written, and in how many fields he has shown his prowess, and how now, some few years my senior in standing, he is preparing to take my work on his shoulders, to go on writing, to give public statutory lectures, ordinary lectures, informal instruction, and to face the Board of Faculty and the Visitatorial Board, I flatter myself that the energy with which he will go to work will not be damped with the reflexion that his predecessors ever broke down. I am very glad to welcome him back to Oxford, to the home and the studies that he has loved so well, as the great champion and representative of that branch of historic literature on which I believe the success of the study here to depend. Not that he is eminent in this alone. But I am now flattering myself and not him.

And so I come to my parting words. I am going to leave Oxford, not for a' place of rest, but for a post of work. I frankly confess that I have always worked towards an ideal of rest ; my own anticipations have been, after a few years more here, during which I might see some of my boys started in the world, I might have retired, we will say to the Parks, and have given no more lectures. But I have always believed, in the case of other people, that the reward of good work is to have more work given you ; and I do trust that it may be so with myself. If the gifts that I have done my best to make useful here are such as can for a little time be made useful elsewhere, I am grateful and hopeful in the change, although it is so very different from anything that I thought I was working for.

I am going to leave with Oxford many, very many friends ; to leave but not I trust to lose them. I hope that I have made no enemies, I have more dread of making enemies than is at all consistent with a properly constituted moral courage. I hope that I have succeeded. At all events I have never re-viewed the books of ally or opponent, or any one else, I have never given pain or incurred hostility in that way. I have abstained from controversy, religious, political or historical, for I have tried to live up to my own ideal of a strong position, that it consists far more in proved confidence in your own cause, in the vigilant maintenance of your own defences, in the thorough realisation of your sources of strength and weakness, than in the most adroit use of weapons or the most energetic tactics of aggression. I have never scrupled to correct my own mistakes, and I have never made a captious use of the mistakes of other men. I trust that I have never plucked a candidate in the Schools without giving him every opportunity of setting himself right. I hope that I have never intrigued or bullied : I do not say this with any wish to imply that such things are ever done here ; although the popular idea of the professorial character might suggest the need of a disclaimer ; but, if there was temptation to do so, I claim to have resisted it. So much I trust that you will let me take credit for. I know that I have great faults ; I have a good deal of sympathy but too little zeal : sometimes I have feared that, in my lack of zeal, my fellow-workers have detected or suspected a lack of sympathy : somehow the adage 'melior est conditio prohibentis' does come to be confused with or to be interpreted into the policy of ' How not to do it ' : perhaps I have tried to work too much in my own way and too little in theirs. Then too, I have never been able to reconcile myself with smoking, late hours, dinner parties, Sunday breakfasts, or University sermons : nor is Joe Pullen's tree such a land-mark in my life as it might very well be to the benefit of my constitution. I will say no more about informal instruction ; I think that need not be remembered against me ; if I am not mistaken, I have read over many proof-sheets and my name appears as the name of a helper in many prefaces.

Well so much for my apologia and confession ! for want of zeal, for weakness of temper, for occasional absence of discretion, I do ask pardon of all whom I may have offended, or disappointed or misunderstood. I do not mind under the circumstances being called sentimental ; I feel sentimental. I confess that I do hope that you will remember me kindly ; and I wish to be judged, as I have tried to judge other historical personages, according as I have acted or have not acted up to my lights. I know that I have not been much of an organiser ; I dislike to organise for other people, I still more dislike other people to organise for me ; I have a great dislike of hard and fast rules, I would not so rule other people, I should still more dislike to have such rules made for me. If there is any virtue in this love of freedom, do not think that I am blind to the drawbacks which beset it. Only all men have not the same gifts, and happily all men are not set to the same tasks, even Professors under schedules. Please to think of me as of one who, very conscious of his own short-comings, and wanting, consciously wanting, in many of the instincts of the successful Academic administrator, still tried to do his duty ; tried to maintain for History its proper place among the studies of Oxford, and to maintain the reputation of Oxford as a nursery of historical study among the Academies of Europe ; tried and worked hard to do honour to the University, to Christ Church, and to the Colleges, to which he owes, humanly speaking, all that he has and is, and his capacity for doing better.

INDEX.

THE END.